MONET

and the Impressionists

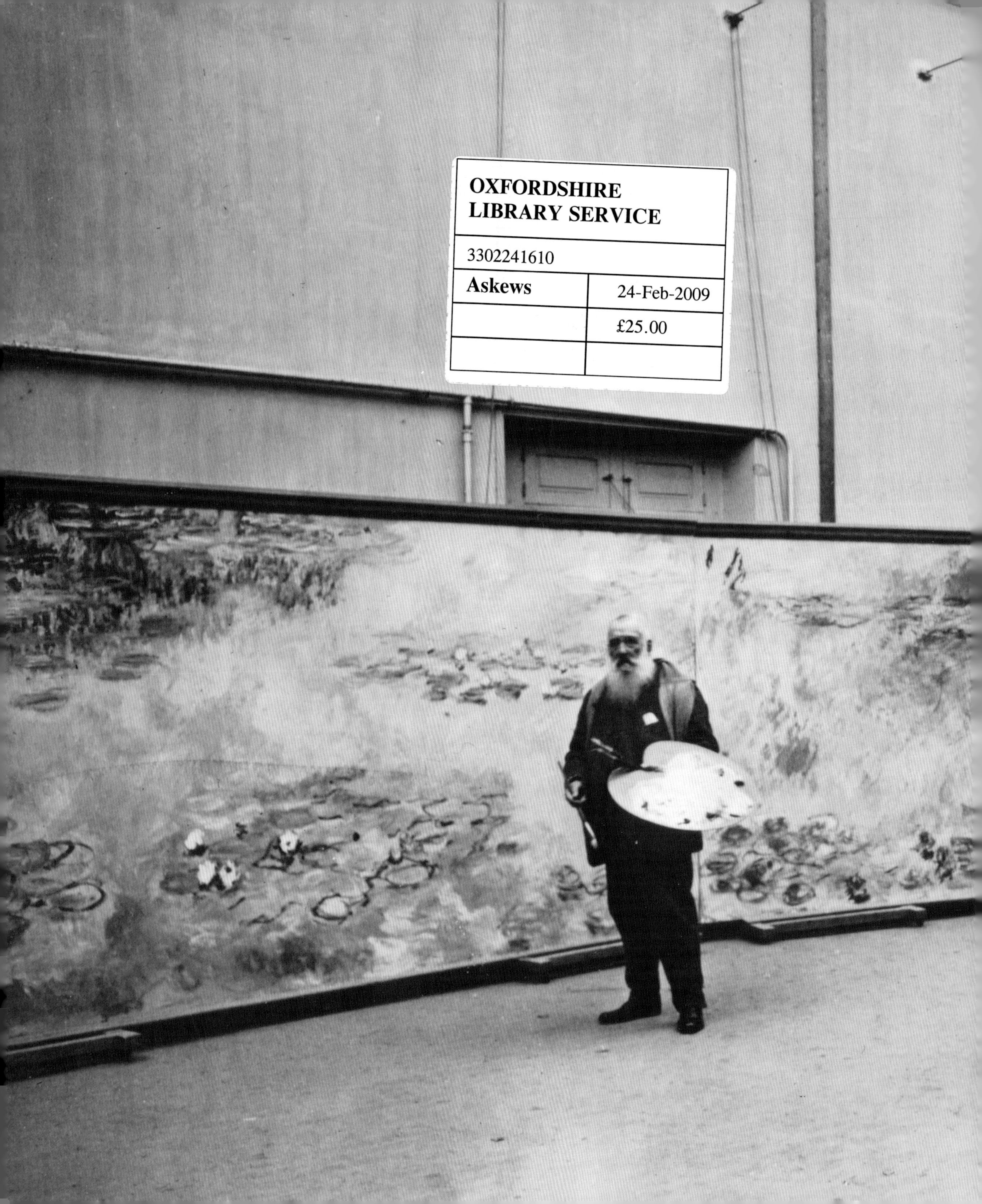

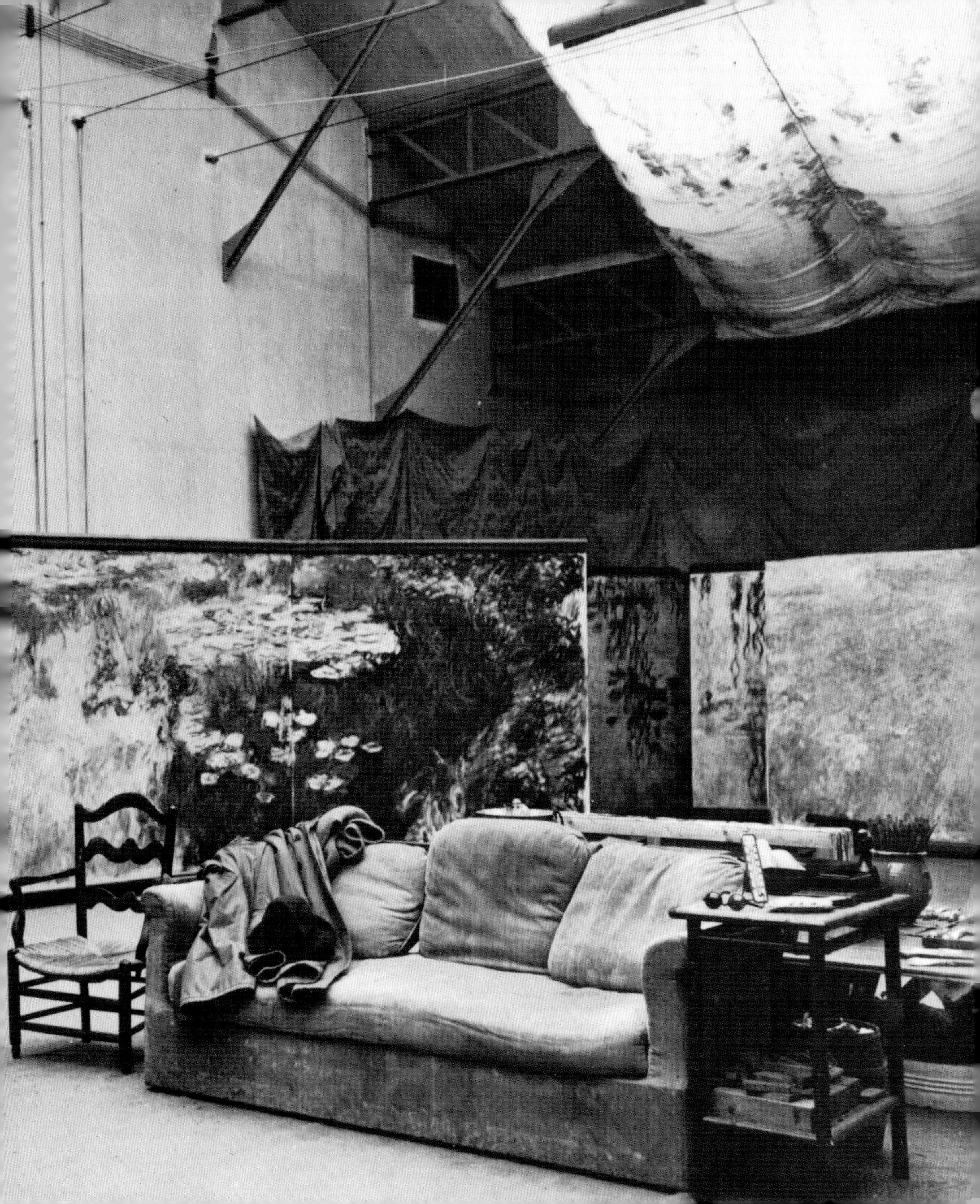

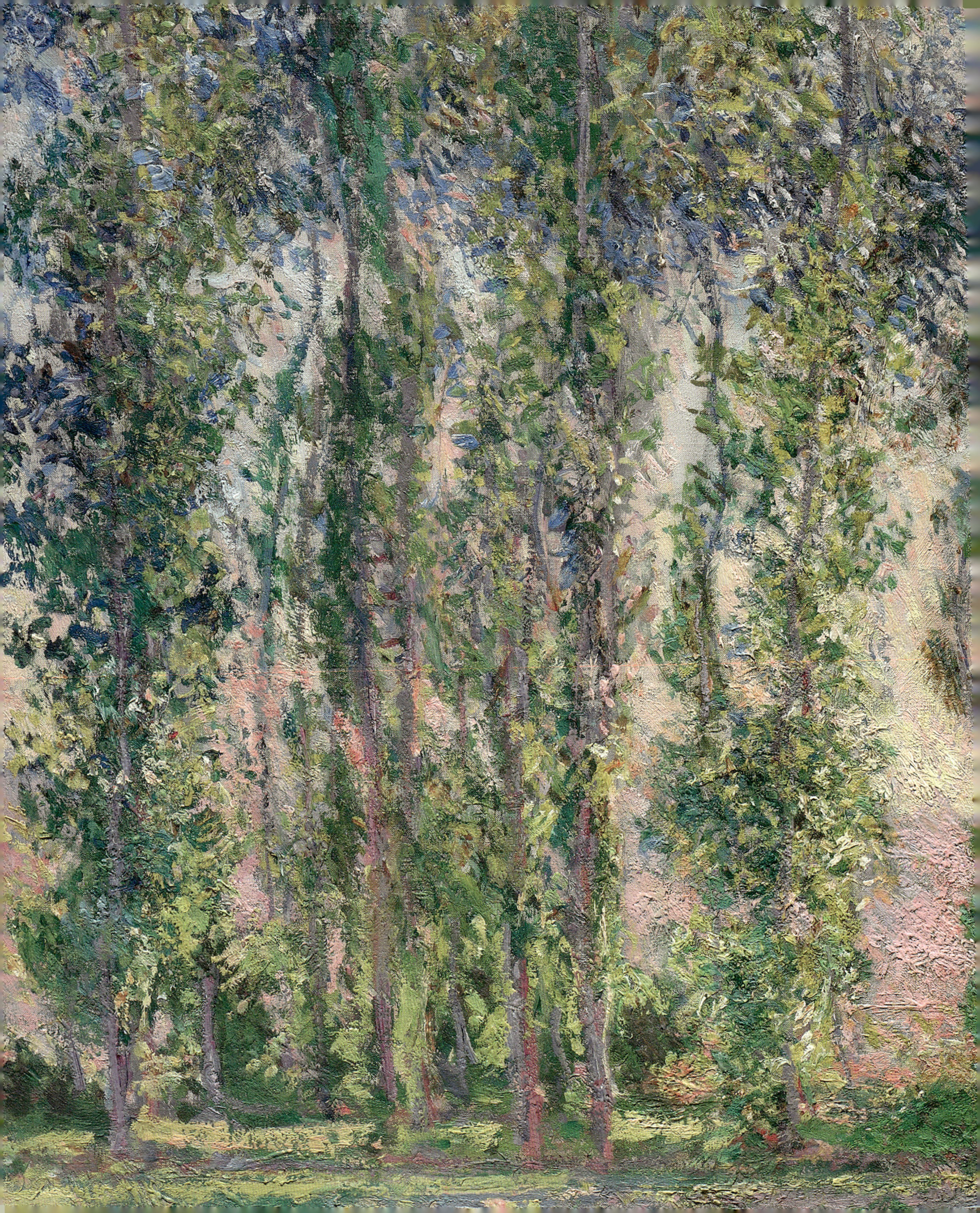

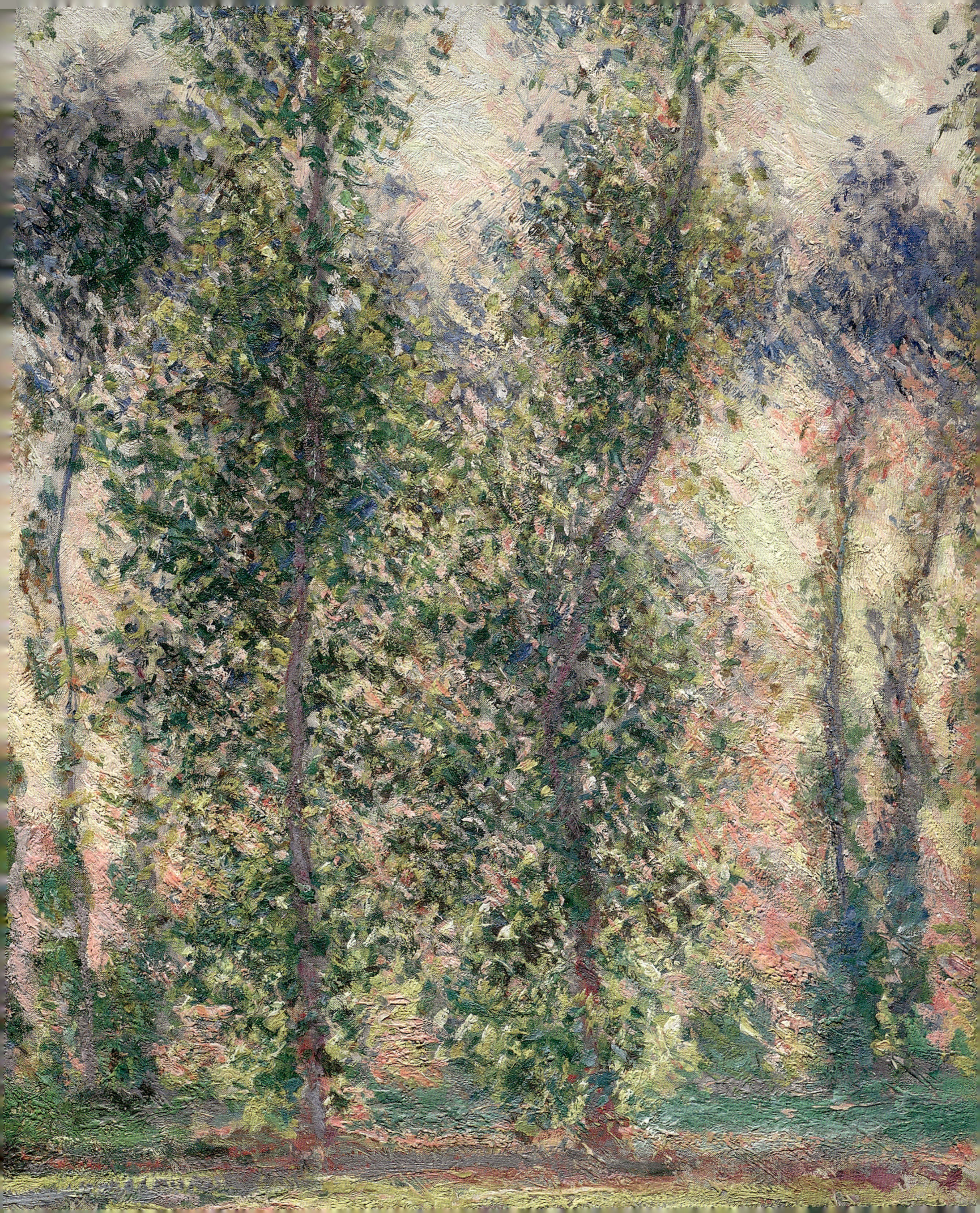

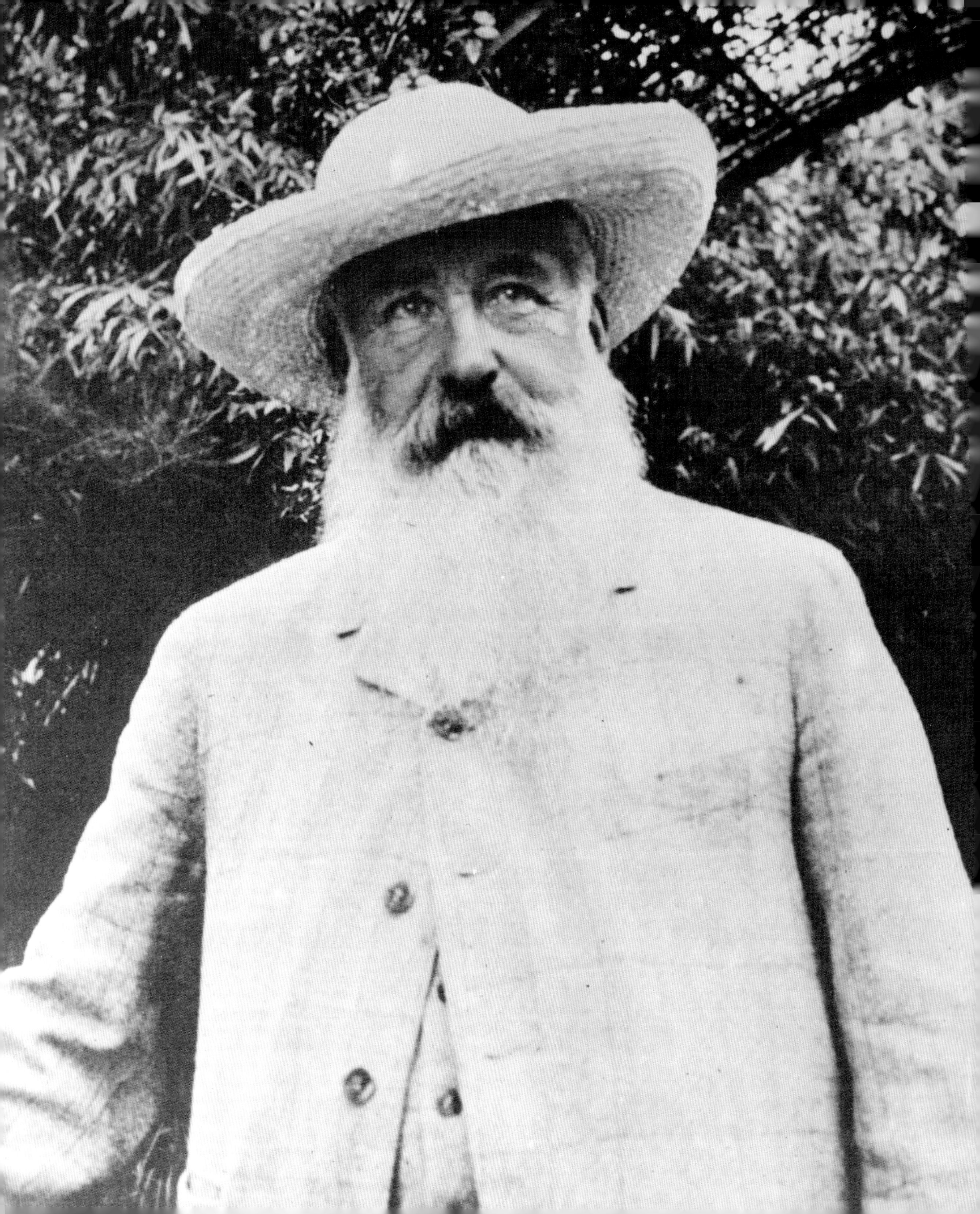

MONET AND THE IMPRESSIONISTS

George T M Shackelford

with contributions by Jonathan Mane-Wheoki,
Clare Durand-Ruel Snollaerts and Terence Maloon

ART GALLERY NSW

Claude Monet c1914 © Durand-Ruel Archives, Paris

ERNST & YOUNG
Quality In Everything We Do

Principal sponsor

At Ernst & Young we are passionate about helping the communities in which we live and work to achieve their potential. It's how we make a difference.

Our sponsorship of the arts is one way we contribute and enable communities to enjoy greater access to important works and exhibitions that may otherwise not be seen.

We are therefore delighted to support the Art Gallery of NSW in bringing *Monet and the Impressionists* to Australia.

The Art Gallery of NSW is the only Australian venue for this superb exhibition from the Museum of Fine Arts, Boston, which has one of the world's most extensive collections of Impressionist paintings.

We congratulate the Gallery on securing this exhibition and for providing our community with this unique opportunity to see not just Claude Monet's famous *Waterlilies*, but a range of his finest paintings alongside those of his contemporaries.

Art feeds the soul. It uplifts, inspires and enlightens us. And, in this fast-paced life, it offers us moments of stillness and reflection. We hope this is your experience of *Monet and the Impressionists* and that you enjoy it as much as we enjoy supporting the arts.

James M Millar
Area Managing Partner, Oceania
Chief Executive Officer,
Ernst & Young Australia

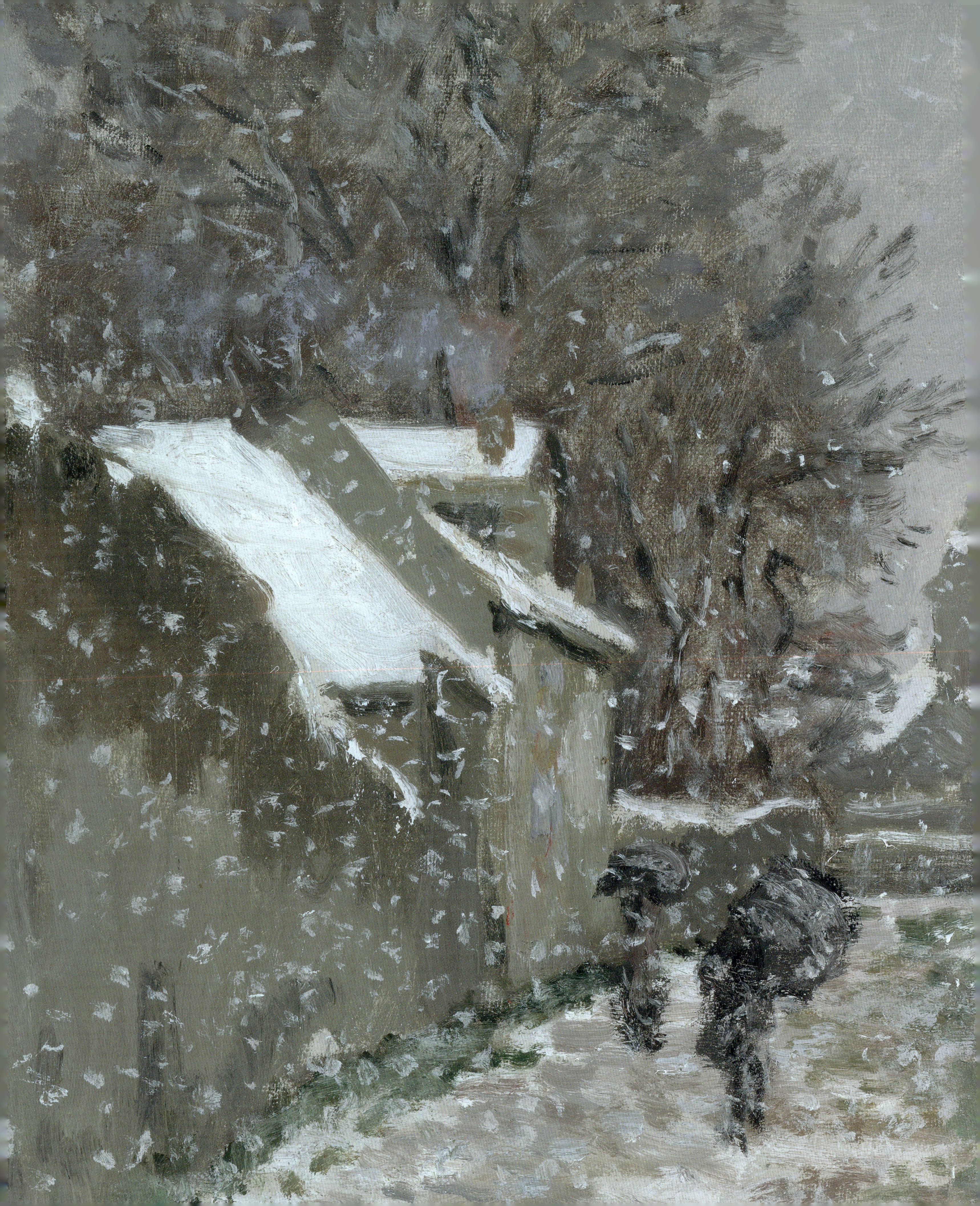

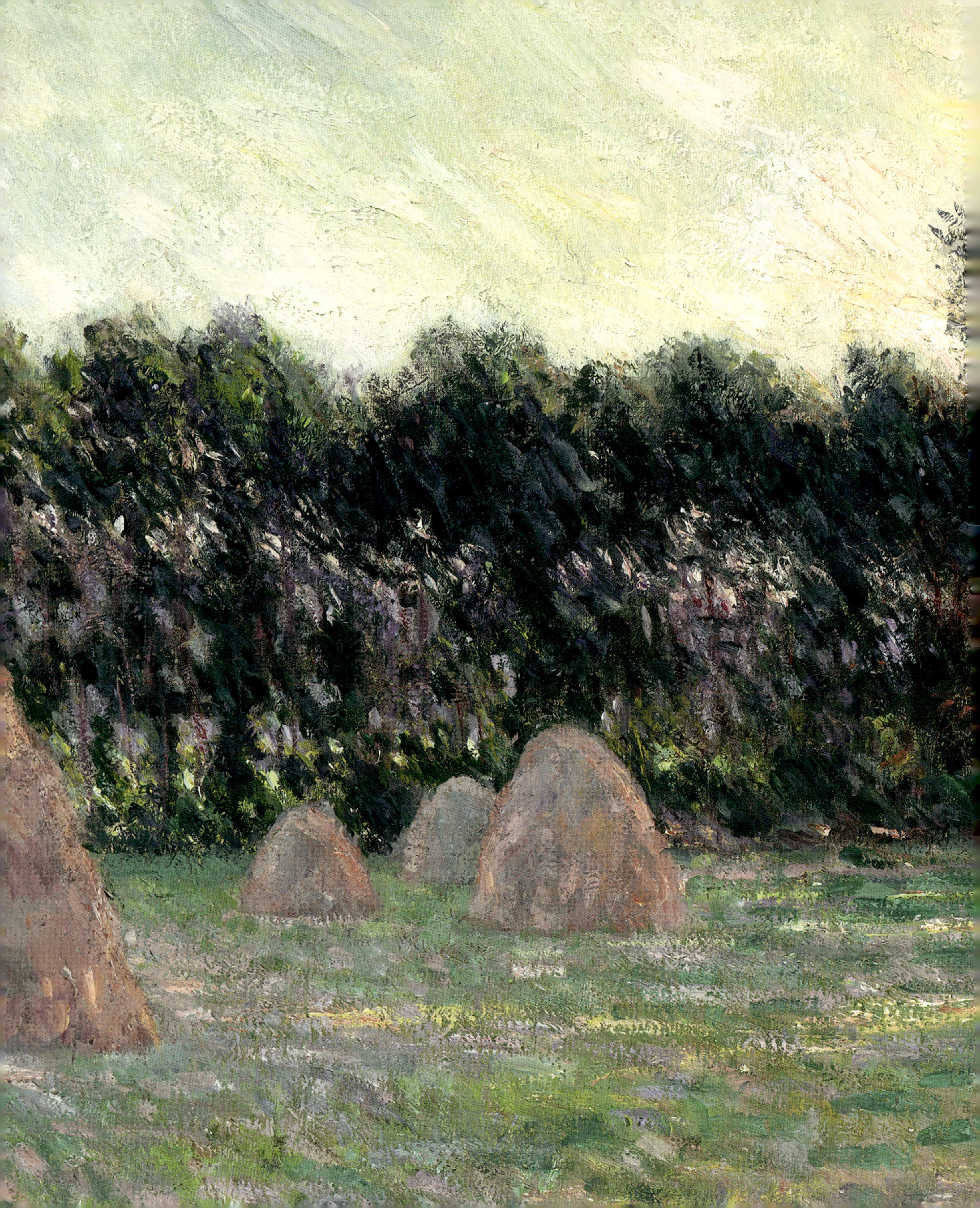

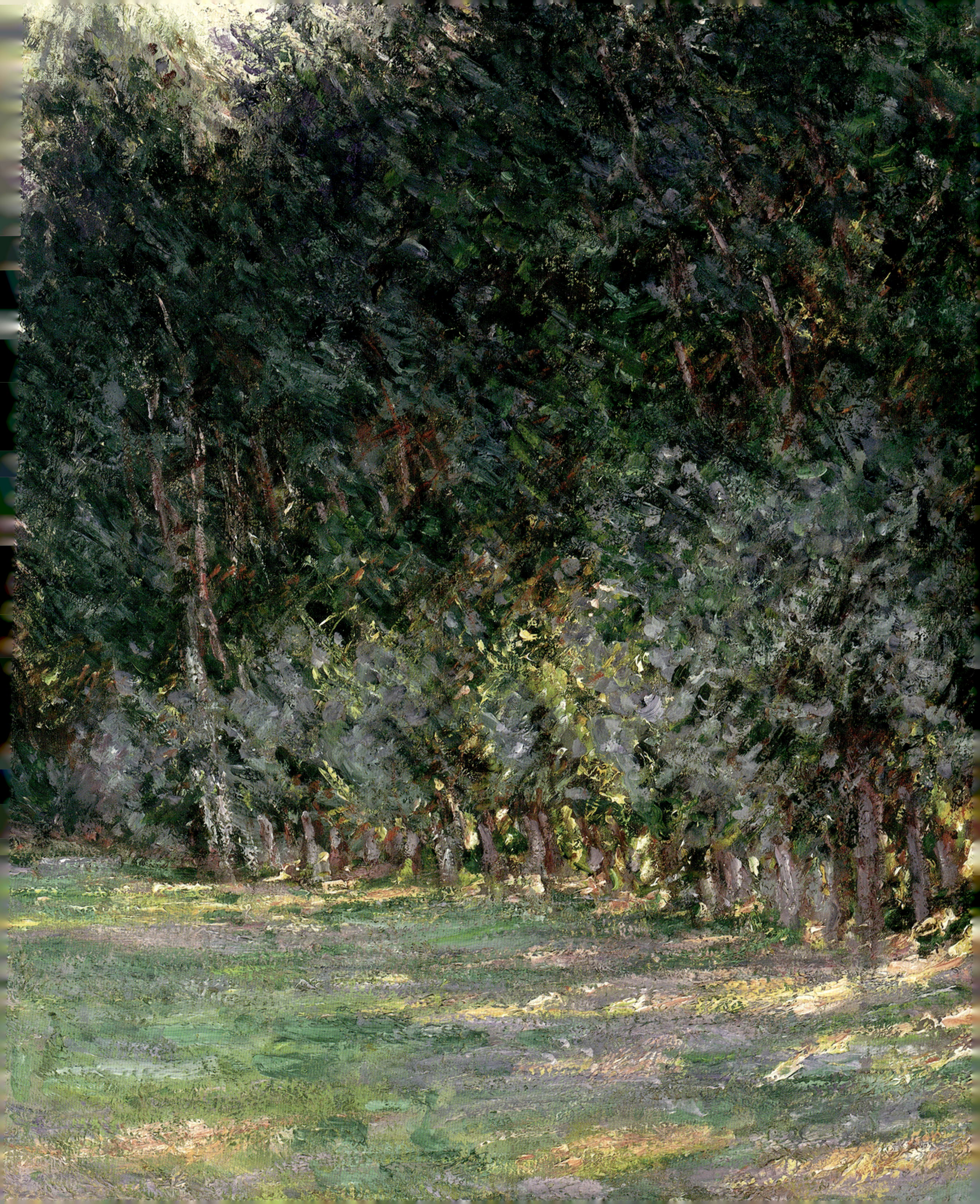

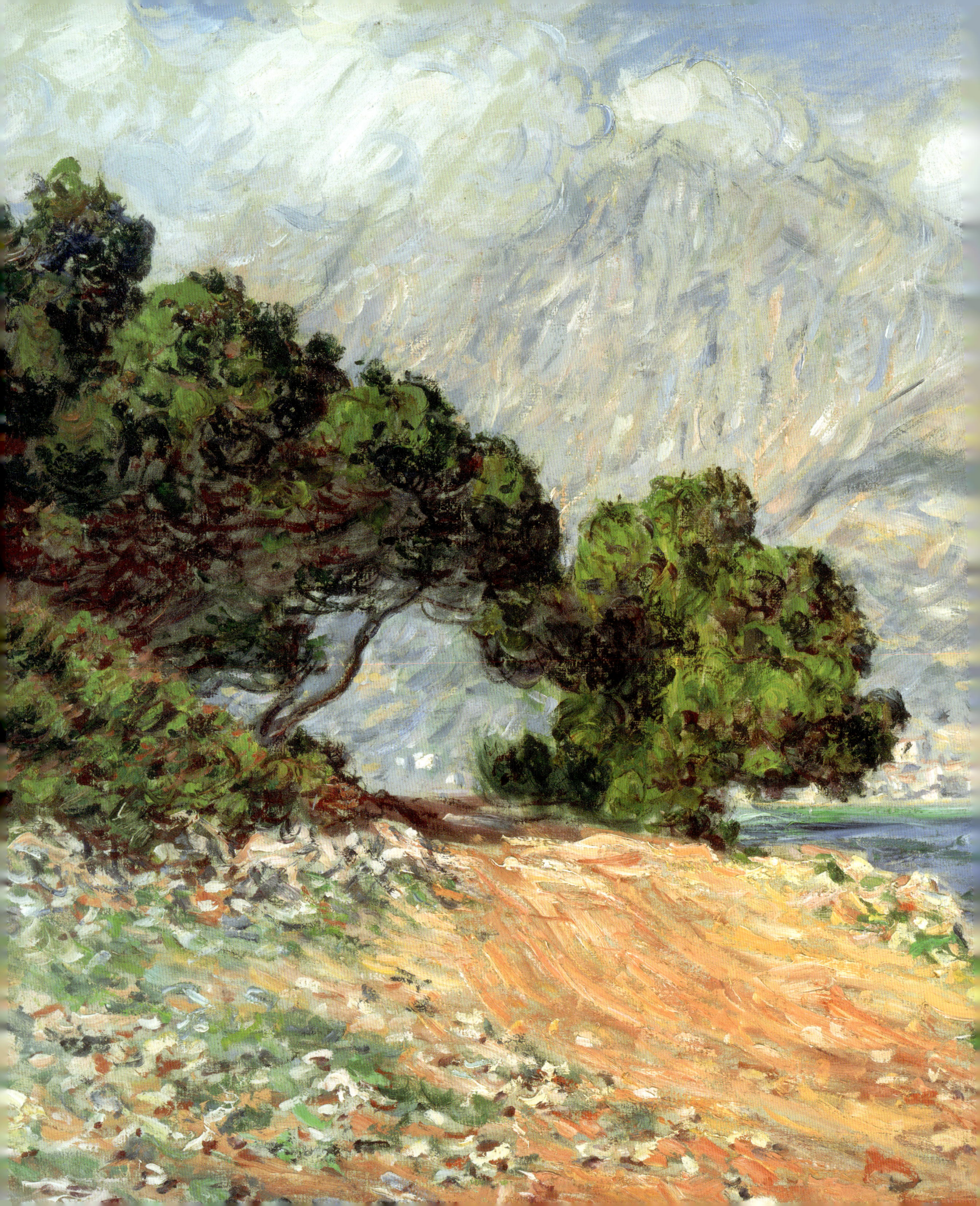

Foreword

We count ourselves extremely fortunate that this exhibition, *Monet and the Impressionists*, comes to us from one of the world's finest collections of French 19th-century painting, the Museum of Fine Arts in Boston (MFA). The opportunity to create an exhibition from a wealth of outstanding works concentrated in a single collection is rare indeed. In the late 1800s Boston became a centre for those interested in modern French painting, and Claude Monet in particular. American artists, collectors and museums were far more enthusiastic than their European counterparts in their response to Impressionist painting – much to the dismay of the Impressionists themselves. Monet complained to his art dealer, Paul Durand-Ruel in 1888: 'It breaks my heart to see all of my paintings leave for America'.

Durand-Ruel began to ship large consignments of French paintings to New York and Boston during the 1880s. His conquest of the American market was such a success that, today, the United States is home to more Impressionist paintings than any other country in the world. Some of the bequests that form the basis of the MFA's Impressionist collection derive from these early sales, and the museum has continued to expand its holdings ever since.

It is with great pride that we are presenting this exhibition in Sydney and Wellington. Our thanks go to Malcolm Rogers, the Ann and Graham Gund director of the MFA, for offering this exhibition to us. We also express our deep appreciation to the exhibition's curator George T M Shackelford (chair, the art of Europe and Arthur K Solomon curator of modern art at the MFA).

Over the past three years the MFA, the Art Gallery of NSW and Te Papa have worked closely together on the organisation and presentation of this exhibition. We acknowledge the professionalism and dedication of staff who have contributed to the project.

Terence Maloon, senior curator of special exhibitions at the Art Gallery of NSW, takes responsibility for the exhibition in Sydney, and Jonathan Mane-Wheoki, director of art and collection services at the Museum of New Zealand Te Papa Tongarewa, is overseeing it in Wellington. Claire Durand-Ruel Snollaerts was our Paris consultant for this project, and we thank her for many services, great and small.

To the authors of the catalogue we extend congratulations on their collective achievement of a beautiful and informative publication that makes new contributions to the knowledge and understanding of the work of Monet and his contemporaries.

For additional loans which have enriched this exhibition we thank Gerard Vaughan, director of the National Gallery of Victoria. The Art Gallery of NSW is grateful to Ron Radford, director of the National Gallery of Australia, and to Kerry Stokes for their contributions. Te Papa would like to thank the Art Gallery of NSW for loans to New Zealand.

The Art Gallery of NSW extends its thanks to the NSW Treasury Managed Fund for providing indemnity, and to its exhibition sponsors: principal sponsor Ernst & Young; major exhibitions program partner, the Gallery's President's Council chaired by Steven Lowy, president of the Board of Trustees; support sponsors Delta Electricity, Qantas and Sofitel Sydney Wentworth; and media partners City of Sydney, *The Sydney Morning Herald* and JCDecaux.

Te Papa would like to acknowledge the New Zealand Government Indemnity for Touring Exhibitions program, administered by the Ministry for Culture and Heritage. Te Papa also extends thanks to its ongoing supporters: the New Zealand Government, Wellington City Council, the Earthquake Commission (EQC), TelstraClear Ltd, Hewlett Packard (HP), GNS Science and Ricoh; and the New Zealand exhibition sponsors, listed in full in the New Zealand edition of this catalogue.

Edmund Capon
Director, Art Gallery of New South Wales

Seddon Bennington
Chief executive, Museum of New Zealand Te Papa Tongarewa

Claude Monet *Cap Martin, near Menton* 1884 (detail), cat 25

Monet's work is one of the great turning points of painting, a commotion, the primacy of light ... Sun-loving, he saw luminosity everywhere, even in shadow, and there was nothing black in the festival he brought along with him, not even coal.

André Masson 1952

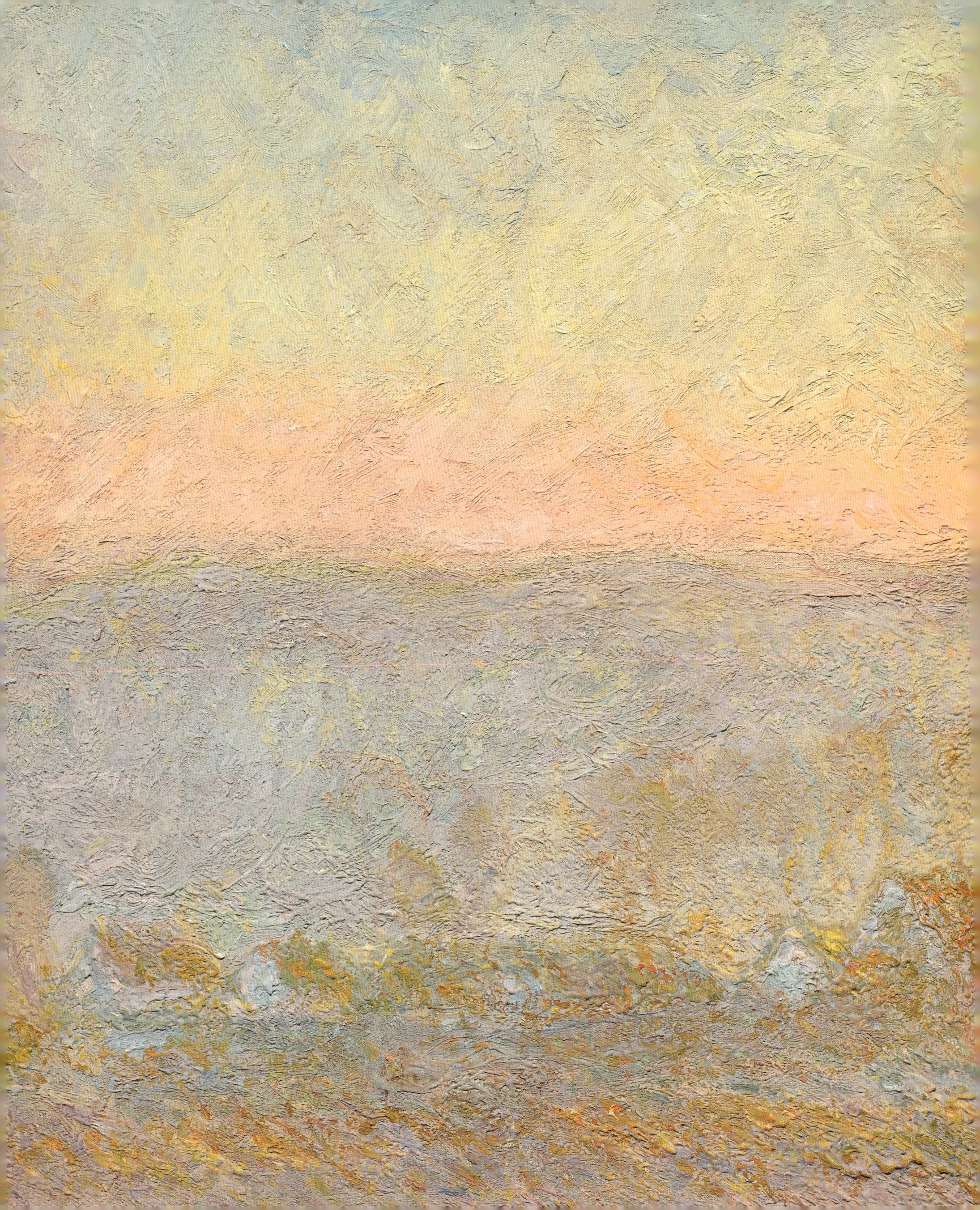

INTRODUCTION

George T M Shackelford

Monet and the Impressionists presents a selection of some 30 paintings by Claude Monet, as well as works by figures of the generation before him that he admired – not only French painters, but also the Japanese artist Utagawa Hiroshige – and by his contemporaries, the Impressionists, many of whom shared Monet's sources of inspiration. It begins with the roots of the Impressionist landscape in the art of Jean-Baptiste-Camille Corot and the Barbizon school and extends as far as the late landscapes of Monet himself. Drawn principally from the great collection of paintings and graphic arts at the Museum of Fine Arts, Boston, with selected loans from private collectors close to the institution and from Australian collections, this book showcases some of Boston's most famous works by Monet, and by others such as Jean-François Millet, Pierre-Auguste Renoir, Paul Cézanne and Edgar Degas.

The development of the French 19th-century landscape – Monet's world, so to speak – forms a complex tale, yet too often the narrative has been reduced to a simple and direct trajectory: from the plein-air cloud studies of the British painter John Constable, whose work exerted a profound influence across the English Channel, to the freely painted compositions of the Barbizon school; and on from there to Monet's *Impression: sunrise* (fig 2) and his last great works painted in his Giverny studio. This story recognises the fact that Monet and the Impressionists, encouraged by the example of their forebears at Barbizon, rejected the fussy, overly finished effects of paintings intended for exhibition at the official Salons. They opted instead to paint sketchlike compositions in the open air and to exhibit these 'impressions' as finished works, thus forging a modern landscape style, much to the consternation of the critics as well as the public. Their advances, in turn, were the background against which the artists of the end of the century elaborated their own vision of what landscape art should be.

It is a story that is undoubtedly true, but it describes only one of the many ways in which the art of landscape emerged across the century from the achievements of the Men of 1830, as Corot and his contemporaries were called; the French landscape's development from 1860 to 1910 – the years of Monet's ascendancy – was not a simple linear progression away from the preoccupations of an official style and toward a modernist idiom. This study of Monet in context attempts to trace some of the major paths of that development, through the collections of the Museum. Beginning with the French artists who brought landscape into a new light at the beginning of the century, it focuses on the painting of the Barbizon masters: Corot, Théodore Rousseau and Constant Troyon, as well as the Barbizon artist most closely identified with the Museum, Jean-François Millet. Boston's phenomenal holdings of Impressionist landscape painting – most significantly, the work of Monet, but also the achievements of his contemporaries – are treated in turn, from the late 1860s until the years just after 1900.

What of the artists who came before Monet? Corot, whose achievement in landscape dominates the first half of the 19th century, began his own artistic journey by going to terrain that was considered, in his day, the source of the great landscape traditions of art history: Italy. He followed in the footsteps of a generation of painters whose great contribution was in the stress that they placed on the experience of nature *en plein air*, advocating the use of the painted oil sketch made in the landscape. Their landscape sketches did not necessarily serve directly for the elaboration of 'composed' landscape paintings worthy of the Salon (the juried exhibitions sponsored by the Academy of Fine Arts); often, the studies were executed for their own sake, to perfect the artist's sensibility.

Corot made sketches not only in Italy but also in his native France. A sketch taken in the wild regions around Fontainebleau in the early 1830s served as the inspiration for the *Forest of Fontainebleau* (fig 1), the only picture of four he submitted to the Salon of 1846 that was accepted by the jury. The Salon exhibitions, usually held each year in Paris, were the prime venue for the public display of the new work of painters and sculptors. At the Salon, reputations were made, maintained or lost. There collectors, dealers and the

Claude Monet *Grainstack/Haystack (sunset)* 1891 (detail), cat 47

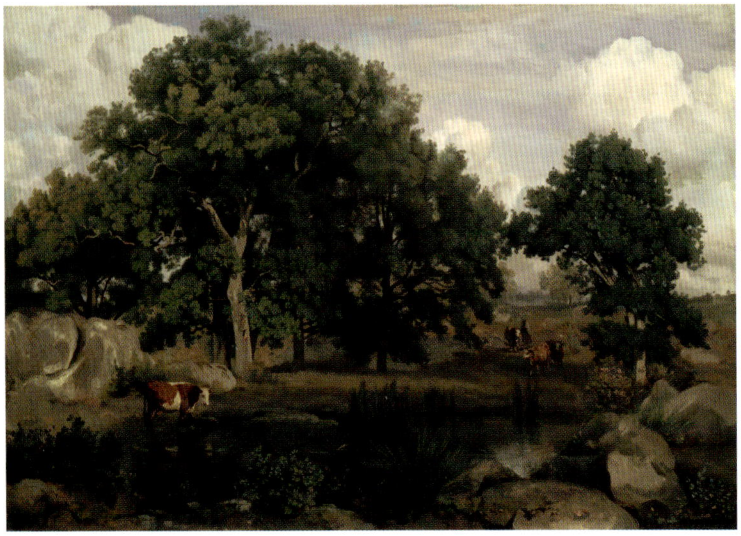

fig 1
Jean-Baptiste-Camille Corot
Forest of Fontainebleau 1846
oil on canvas, 90.2 x 128.8 cm
Museum of Fine Arts, Boston,
gift of Mrs Samuel Dennis Warren
90.199

interested public could encounter the works of newly emerging talents whose pictures had been selected for exhibition by the jury, and see the latest output of established figures who, by virtue of their previous success, were allowed to bypass the jury and exhibit the work of their own choosing. A staggering number and variety of paintings were placed on view. While figural compositions – history paintings, portraits or scenes from daily life – were in the majority in the early years of the century, landscape came increasingly to dominate Salon exhibitions by the middle decades of the 1800s. Corot's *Forest of Fontainebleau*, which a recent critic has called 'the greatest pure landscape of his middle years', was accepted for exhibition but was not well received.[1] Corot's contemporaries found it awkward and raw, one caustically remarking that 'Monsieur Corot, the famous landscape artist, paints everything with the dirt that falls from his boots as they're being cleaned'.[2]

The village of Barbizon, at the edge of the forest, became in the 1840s the centre of a new artistic community that celebrated the kind of landscape that could be depicted with the dirt of the painter's boots – the so-called Barbizon school. The most important painters of the landscape vanguard thus practised their craft in this region: not only Corot, but also Rousseau, Troyon, Narcisse Virgile Diaz de la Peña, Millet and Gustave Courbet. In the years before and after the Revolution of 1848, Courbet and Millet struggled to establish a new movement in art, Realism, which would react against the prevailing tendencies of both the Classical and Romantic schools. Rejecting both the ancient past and fanciful exoticism, they gave precedence to scenes drawn from the experience of the meek and lowly and sent to the Salon paintings of peasants, stonebreakers and winnowers of grain.

The rise of Realism in French painting gave forth not only the heroic figural compositions of Courbet and Millet but also a new notion of how landscape should be interpreted. Painters such as Corot and Rousseau sought to depict commonplace settings – ordinary meadows, fields or woodlands – and to invest these simple landscapes with a sense both of poetry and of the quiet dignity of the earth itself. The mood of Corot's paintings could indeed be humble, painted with the earth. But by the later 1840s he was also capable of painting works of profoundly lyrical sensitivity, as he demonstrated in the elegiac *Twilight* (cat 4). Throughout the 1840s and 1850s, he was generally regarded as the chief landscape painter in France – 'the greatest landscape painter of our time', wrote Philippe de Chennevières in 1851.[3]

By the 1860s, the pioneers of the Barbizon school were artists in their 50s (or in Corot's case, 60s) and a younger generation of artists was beginning to make its mark on the art of French landscape. A group of them – Monet, of course, but also Renoir, Camille Pissarro, Cézanne, Alfred Sisley and Degas, all born since 1830 – would later be known as the Impressionists. Although each of them played an important role in the story of the Impressionist landscape, that story is especially linked to the career of Monet, its most famous, most steadfast and arguably most innovative practitioner.

Monet's career began at the moment that Barbizon painting had achieved its great success in France, but it had its start not in the Ile-de-France or in Paris, where he was born, but in Normandy, where the young artist was raised. In 1857, when he was 16, Monet met in Le Havre the marine painter Eugène Boudin (see cats 10 and 11), who took an interest in the youth and invited him along to paint in the open air. Later, Monet said that the experience was a revelatory one for him: 'Boudin, with untiring kindness, undertook my education. My eyes were finally opened and I really understood nature; I learned at the same time to love it.'[4]

In May 1859 Monet went to Paris to see the Salon exhibition and to try his hand at learning more about painting landscape. During that year, writing to Boudin from the capital, the younger man singled out for praise the landscapes he saw at the Salon by the Barbizon masters Charles-François Daubigny, Troyon, Rousseau and Corot. Troyon's paintings were particularly attractive to Monet, who greatly admired the older artist's ability to capture the fleeting effects of clouds, sunlight and atmosphere. 'A magnificent sky,' he wrote, 'a stormy sky. There is a lot of movement, of wind in these clouds.'[5] Earlier, Monet had visited Troyon in his studio, and he immediately recognised Troyon's skill. 'I could not begin to describe all the lovely things I saw there', he wrote to Boudin. Looking at Monet's canvases, Troyon advised the young man to learn how to draw by studying the human figure, at that time the foundation of every artist's education. 'Don't neglect painting,' he nevertheless told Monet, 'go to the country from time to time and make studies, and above all develop them'.[6] Monet might have seen in Troyon's studio sketches made in the open air, like *Field outside Paris* (cat 7), which Troyon would develop and refine into paintings for the Paris art market and which also lay behind the large-scale pictures he painted for the official Salon exhibitions.

In the Salon, still controlled by the Academy, as well as in the more informal market of picture dealers, landscape had taken the place of history painting in the public imagination and in the minds and hearts of critics. Monet, recognising the ascendancy of landscape painting, was determined to follow the path on which he had set out under Boudin. Still, taking Troyon's advice, he embarked in 1860 on a course of study to learn to draw the human figure, entering an informal art school, the Académie Suisse. In 1862 he entered the studio of Charles Gleyre, a history painter, where he met Renoir, the American James McNeill Whistler and Frédéric Bazille, each of whom practised not only figure painting but also landscape, and Sisley, who was to devote himself to pure landscape.

Aware of the historical associations of the Fontainebleau forest and the plains that abutted it, Monet often painted there, producing such works as *Woodgatherers at the edge of the forest* (cat 2), the subject of which was derived from those of artists of the Realist generation. At this period in his development, most of Monet's subjects and compositions reflected his awareness of the art of these masters, as well as the continuing importance of Boudin and of Johan Barthold Jongkind (see cat 12), a Dutch marine painter whom Monet had met on the Normandy coast in 1862.

Boudin's influence on Monet, however strong, was by no means exclusive, even in the early 1860s. The simplified landscape of *Woodgatherers at the edge of the forest*, for example, with choppy, broad strokes of warm browns and greens set against the blue of the sky, recalls the boldly painted landscapes of Gustave Courbet. Courbet's earthy palette and his preference for dense, boldly painted volumes may have inspired Monet again when, about 1864, he took his easel into the streets of Honfleur, near Le Havre, to paint on site a view of the Rue de la Bavole (cat 13). Perhaps following Troyon's advice to 'develop' his studies, Monet used this plein-air canvas as the basis for a later version, in which the effects he studied before the motif were further refined.

Monet's experience had its parallels in that of his future Impressionist colleagues Renoir, Pissarro and Sisley, each of whom felt the strong pull of Barbizon style in the mid 1860s. Renoir painted both sober portraits inspired by Realist genre scenes and large-scale nudes; both echoed Courbet's style and his subject matter – his bathers as well as his scenes of daily life. At the Salons of 1864, 1865 and 1866, Pissarro exhibited riverbank landscapes in the tradition of Daubigny, who made a specialty of such themes. In 1866 Sisley exhibited *A street at Marlotte: environs of Fontainebleau*, a painting that recalls Corot in its massing of farm buildings and both Daubigny and Courbet in its sober palette. Degas, not yet allied with the landscape painters, exhibited at the same Salon a large-scale scene of a steeplechase. An amalgam of Realist landscape and figure painting, Degas's ambitious composition nodded to Courbet's dramatic scenes of the hunt, as well as to the images of figures in the landscape painted by the mentor he shared with Monet: Edouard Manet.[7] At about the same time, Monet was at work on his largest ever painting – *Luncheon on the grass*, depicting a group of men and women at life size, picnicking in the Fontainebleau forest (the painting was later cut into fragments); one of the models for this painting, and for his *Camille in a green dress* (Kunsthalle, Bremen) and *Women in the garden* (Musée d'Orsay) was Camille Doncieux, whom he met in Paris in 1866 and would marry a little more than four years later, shortly before the outbreak of the Franco-Prussian War, with Courbet acting as a witness.[8]

By the end of the 1860s, however, the young artists of the nascent Impressionist movement were advancing in uncharted directions, beyond the idiom of Barbizon painting. In 1869, working side by side at the fashionable boating place of La Grenouillère, Monet and Renoir began to paint works in which the optical experience of sunlight falling on rippling water was recorded on canvas with a new vocabulary of brushstrokes. They were inspired by Courbet and Manet, but their aim was the invention of an altogether new pictorial language.

These paintings marked a turning point in the history of the French landscape, but they flow from the experiments that Monet had conducted in the middle years of the decade. His careful, deliberate technique, particularly evident in the handling of the alternating lights and shadows in his views of the river, recalls the thick brushstrokes he used to paint the Rue de la Bavole. It seems, moreover, that Monet again intended to use these riverside paintings – which were executed on the scale of canvases intended for the marketplace, if not for the Salon – to develop other compositions in the studio. In late September 1869 he wrote to Bazille from a village near the Seine: 'I do have a dream, of a picture, the bathing place at La Grenouillère, for which I have made a few bad sketches, but it's only a dream. Renoir, who has just passed two months here, would also like to paint this picture.'[9]

A conventionally ambitious, larger-scale Salon composition that derived from these studies never materialised – like theorists before him, Monet found the making of the sketch its own reward. It seems likely, however, that Monet sent a more developed version of one of the *pochades*, as he called them, to the Salon of 1870, along with an interior. The jury rejected both works.[10] Renoir shrewdly ignored his new landscapes and exhibited at the same Salon two magnificent but less innovative figure paintings. In the wake of Monet's exclusion from the Salon, both Daubigny (long a defender of the young painter) and Corot resigned from the jury in protest. But despite his absence in the exhibition, much was made of Monet's being at the vanguard of painting. The critic Arsène Houssaye wrote: 'The two real masters of this school which, instead of saying art for art's sake, says nature for nature's sake, are Messieurs Monet (not to be confused with Manet) and Renoir, two real masters, like Courbet of Ornans, through the brutal frankness of their brush.'[11]

Although his first attempt at exhibiting one of his 'bad sketches' of La Grenouillère was rebuffed, Monet was to exhibit another work of this type in the second Impressionist exhibition, in 1876. By that time, he had already presented to the public the now-famous *Impression: sunrise* (1872, fig 2), the sketchy, lightly worked view of the port at Le Havre that gave the Impressionist movement its name. That picture was initially shown at the first exhibition of the newly founded Société Anonyme Coopérative d'Artistes-peintres, Sculpteurs, Graveurs, etc (the artists who would become known as the Impressionists), held in the former studio of the photographer Félix Nadar on a busy commercial street in Paris. The show opened on 15 April 1874. Writing ten days later, the satirist Louis Leroy presented the comments of two fictional visitors to the exhibition:

> [...] What does that painting represent? Look in the catalogue.
>
> *Impression: sunrise.*
>
> Impression, I was sure of it. I said to myself, too, because I am impressed, there must be some impression in it. [...] And what freedom, what ease in the execution! An embryonic wallpaper is still more finished than that seascape there![12]

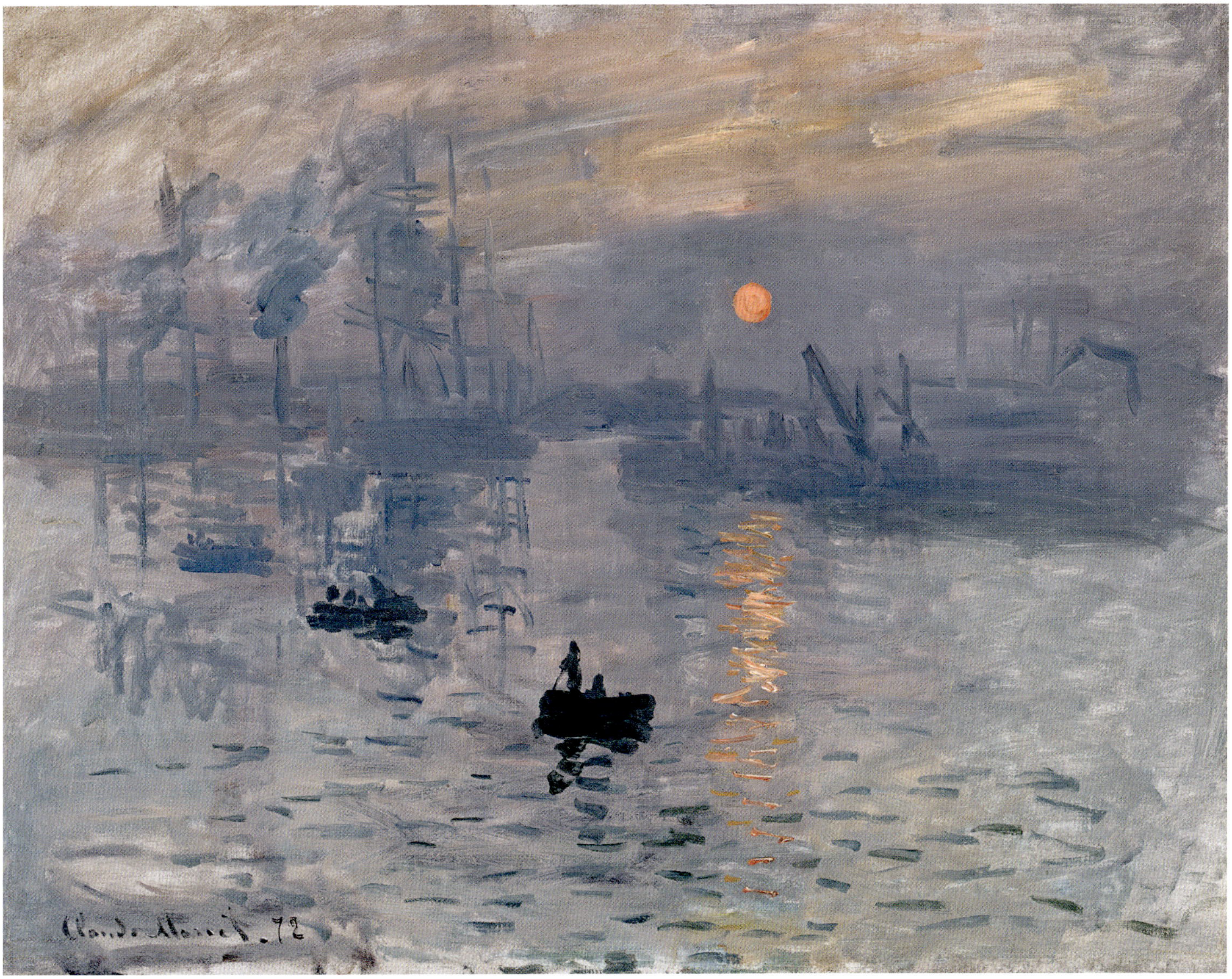

fig 2
Claude Monet
Impression: sunrise 1872
oil on canvas, 48 x 63 cm
Musée Marmottan, Paris
Photograph: Giraudon/The Bridgeman Art Library

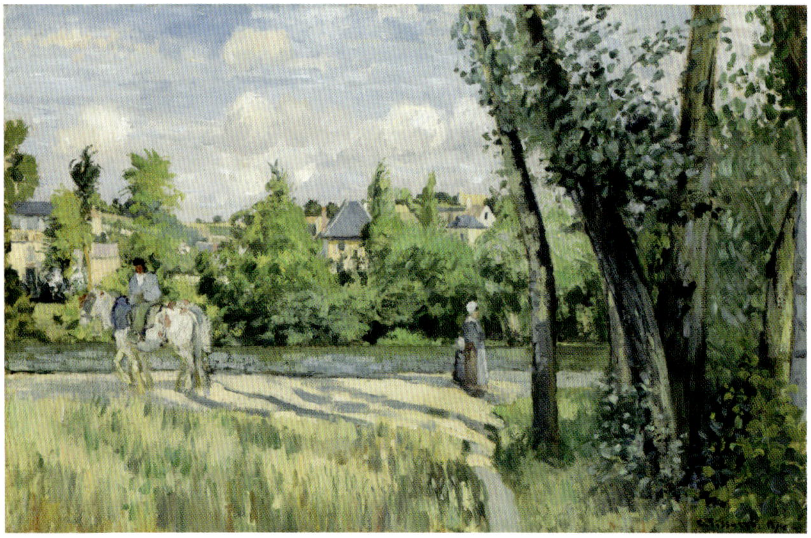

fig 3
Camille Pissarro
Sunlight on the road, Pontoise 1874
oil on canvas, 52.4 x 81.6 cm
Museum of Fine Arts, Boston,
Juliana Cheney Edwards Collection
25.114

Leroy's humorous exchange aside, the critics' response to the newly named Impressionists was generally favourable, and on the whole they praised the Impressionists' desire to exhibit free from the strictures of the Salon system – to institutionalise, as it were, the notion of a salon des refusés, an exhibition of artists working outside Academic taste and tradition. Recognising that the group assembled artists from a wide variety of backgrounds, critics such as Armand Silvestre made an attempt to understand the landscape painters' common motivations and to help their readers distinguish one participant from another:

> At their head are three artists whom I have spoken of several times and who have, at least, the merit of being immutable in their goals. This immutability even touches on an aspect common to all three, which gives priority above all to the processes of their painting. At first glance, one is hard pressed to distinguish what differentiates the paintings of Monsieur Monet from those of Monsieur Sisley and the manner of the latter from that of Monsieur Pissarro. A bit of study will soon teach you that Monsieur Monet is the most able and the most daring, Monsieur Sisley is the most harmonious and timid, Monsieur Pissarro is, in the end, the inventor of this painting, the most real and the most naive [...] What is sure is that the vision of things that these three landscape painters affect does not resemble in the least that of any earlier master; that it has its plausible side; and that it affirms itself with a character of conviction that does not admit the possibility of disdain.[13]

By the mid-1870s, in spite of the critics' recognition of close affinities between them, each artist had evolved a mature vision of how landscape might be painted. Both Renoir and Monet had formulated a wholly individual manner of painting in the open air. Renoir's *Woman with a parasol and small child on a sunlit hillside* (cat 19), painted about 1874–76, shows his distinctive feathered brushstroke, with which he suggests both the sheer white fabric of the reclining woman's dress and the soft tufts of grass on which she lies. Monet's 1875 depiction of his wife, Camille, sewing in a garden while a child is playing at her feet (cat 20) employs a characteristic flickering pattern of small daubed or curved brushstrokes. This has the result of conveying the action of the light on the bed of flowers and the grassy verge that make up the background of the picture, while the figures are set off from the vegetation by their blue and white clothing.

The overall effect of these treatments of the figure set in a landscape is a sense of freedom and improvisation, contrasting sharply with the more classically refined surfaces of such works as Degas's *Racehorses at Longchamp* (cat 17). Degas, who in the 1850s had painted pure landscapes in Italy and had used landscape backgrounds in his early history paintings, in the 1860s specialised in painting people in everyday scenes, mostly indoors – at home, in a café, or at the opera. Although he is known to have painted pastels *en plein air*, he did not take his easel and canvas into the countryside (at least until much later in life).

A middle ground between the sense of improvisation that Monet and Renoir cherished and the calculated strategies of Degas can be found in the paintings of Pissarro and Cézanne. Working together in the environs of Pontoise and nearby Auvers in the 1870s, these friends evolved a more geometrically structured response to the landscape. Pissarro, who in these years turned to themes taken from the lives of the agricultural workers in his district, often chose to order his paintings by introducing straight lines or geometrical shapes, as in *Sunlight on the road, Pontoise*, of 1874 (fig 3). Likewise, Cézanne employed the rhythmic architectural forms of walls and houses both to animate and to anchor his composition. In the middle years of the decade, both artists, along with Sisley, adopted a lightened palette in which the deeper shades of green and brown were softened by the admixture of whites and greys. And all three artists, particularly Cézanne, employed opaque, layered paint structures that together

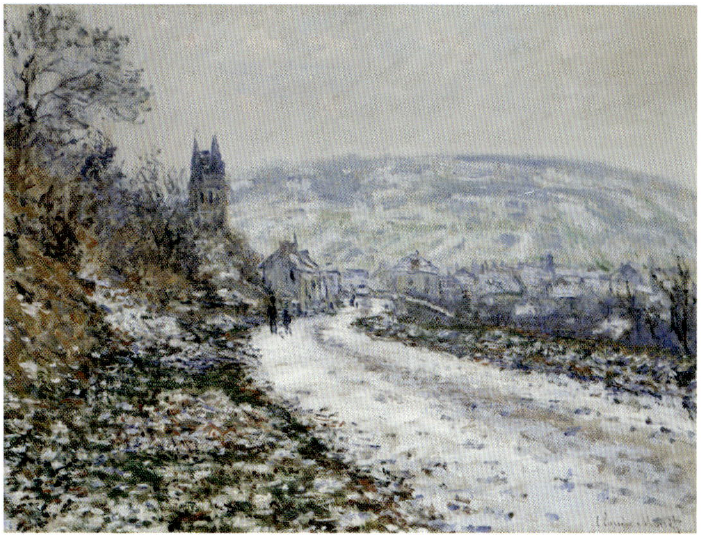

fig 4
Claude Monet
Entrance to the village of Vétheuil in winter 1879
oil on canvas, 60.6 x 81 cm
Museum of Fine Arts, Boston, gift of Julia C Prendergast in memory of her brother, James Maurice Prendergast
21.7

with their carefully shaped compositions confirm the studied processes by which these ordinary views were elaborated.

As the loosely affiliated artists explored different manners of depicting the landscape, each member of the group chose his sites and themes according to his particular temperament. On the whole, however, they shared a preference for motifs that veered away from the conspicuously picturesque, avoiding the hackneyed compositional formats that they scorned in the work of Salon painters. Thus, Monet painted an uneventful section of the road outside Vétheuil (fig 4), Pissarro painted an equally uninspiring street in Pontoise on a dingy, snowy day (cat 21), and Sisley, who might have chosen to paint a fountain in the park at Versailles, preferred to paint the pumping station at the Marly reservoir (cat 22). By choosing subjects and points of view that seemed to contemporary audiences not only unimportant but somehow undignified, the Impressionists emphasised the distinction between their landscapes and those of the Barbizon school and its latter-day adherents at the Salon.

During the 1870s, the Impressionists concentrated on depicting places close to Paris, along the Seine or its tributaries downstream from the capital, in such towns as Argenteuil, Bougival and Pontoise. Monet left Argenteuil and settled briefly in Paris, before moving to the slightly more distant village of Vétheuil, where he cultivated a garden that provided motifs for his riverside paintings (see cat 30). The house was shared by the Monet family and the family of Ernest Hoschedé, a merchant and collector of Impressionist art. After Camille Monet's death in 1878 – and the failure of Hoschedé's business – Monet and Madame Hoschedé formed a liaison that would endure until her death.

Though they continued to live in villages along the Seine, Monet abandoned the riverside places frequented by Parisians in favour of sites – some equally touristic, others more remote in character – on the coasts of France. Monet typically avoided the views that Boudin had painted at the height of the Second Empire in such works as *Fashionable figures on the beach* (cat 10), which exploited the relationship between sea and sky; instead he turned to painting the sea in juxtaposition with the land.

Monet's works of the early 1880s attest to his love for the rough Normandy coasts, where Delacroix, Courbet and Millet had painted in the previous generation. There, at Pourville, Fécamp and Etretat, Monet explored motifs that he had first treated in the late 1860s and early 1870s. Monet, like Millet, felt a profound connection to the Normandy landscape: 'The countryside is very beautiful and I am very sorry I did not come here earlier', he wrote to Alice Hoschedé from Pourville in February 1882.[14]

As we shall see, a group of these Normandy landscapes by Monet was presented at the Impressionist exhibition of 1882, where just under a third of Monet's paintings showed such cliffside views, sometimes stormy, sometimes sunny – among them, *Seacoast at Trouville* (cat 38) and probably *Cliffs of the Petites Dalles* (fig 5). The 1882 exhibition was heralded by critics as a great moment for the Impressionist landscape painters, who one by one had dropped out of the most recent group shows. Monet had 'defected' in 1880 to exhibit at the Salon; and in 1881 Degas's band of figural artists had dominated the planning of the exhibition, causing Renoir and Sisley to withdraw as well. But in 1882, the landscape painters had returned to the fold – and the figure painters had decamped.[15] However, not all the landscape Impressionists shared Monet's passion for coastal scenery. At the same exhibition, Sisley presented *Overcast day at Saint-Mammès* (fig 16), a view of the village on the Seine near Moret-sur-Loing, the town in which he had settled in 1880. Unlike Monet, he rarely travelled outside the Ile-de-France; Renoir, on the other hand, was represented in 1882 by a varied group of paintings that included not only a large group of figure compositions but also views taken along the Seine, among them *The Seine at Chatou* (cat 28) and his new views of Venice (fig 17).

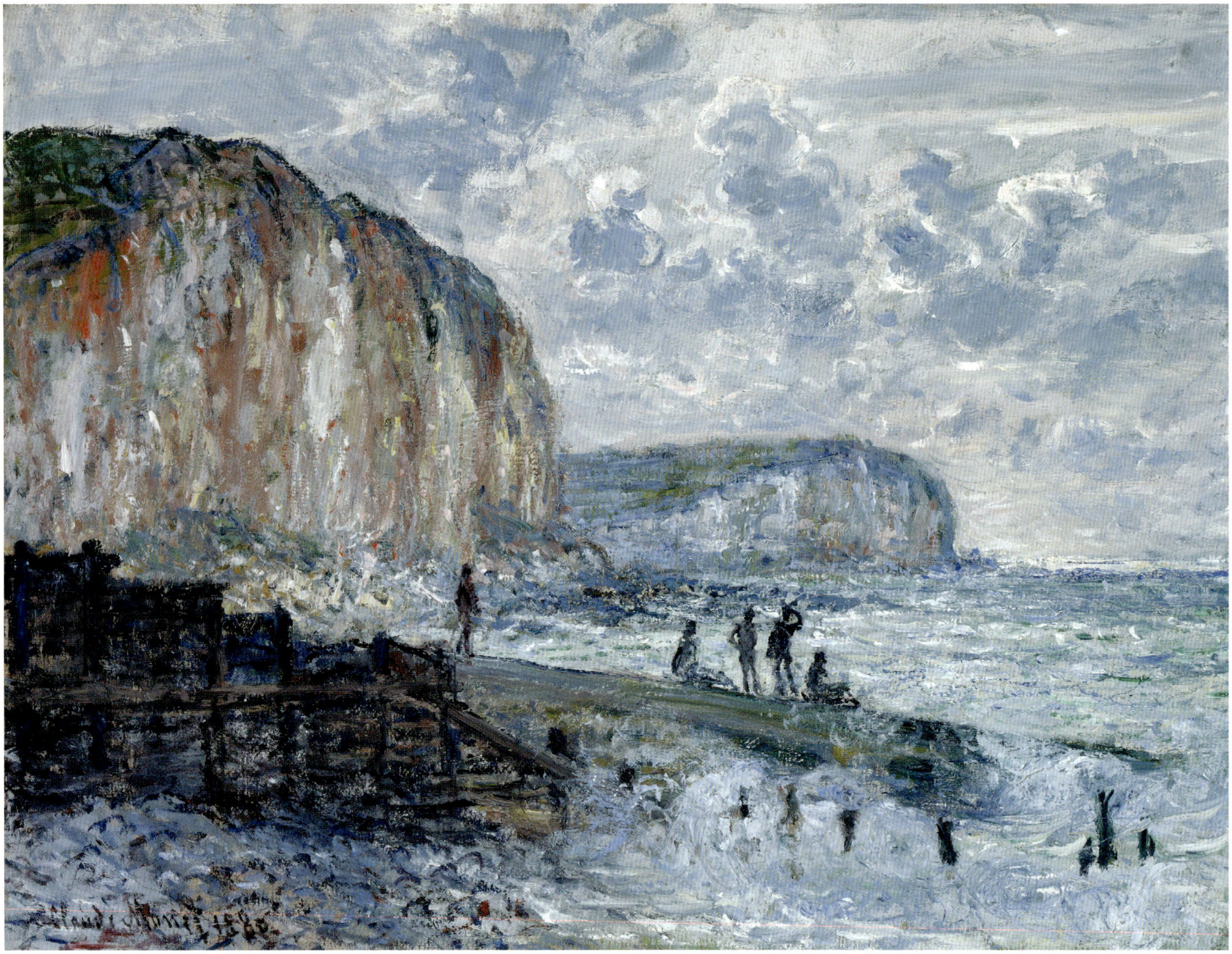

fig 5
Claude Monet
Cliffs of the Petites Dalles 1880
oil on canvas, 60.6 x 80.3 cm
Museum of Fine Arts, Boston,
Denman Waldo Ross collection
06.116

fig 6
Claude Monet
Road at La Cavée, Pourville 1882
oil on canvas, 60.3 x 81.6 cm
Museum of Fine Arts, Boston,
bequest of Mrs Susan Mason Loring
24.1755

fig 7
Vincent van Gogh
Ravine 1889
oil on canvas, 73 x 91.7 cm
Museum of Fine Arts, Boston,
bequest of Keith McLeod
52.1524

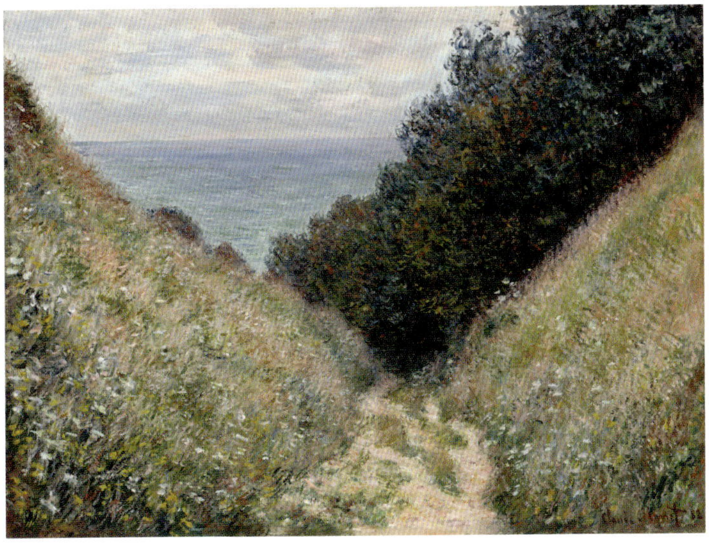

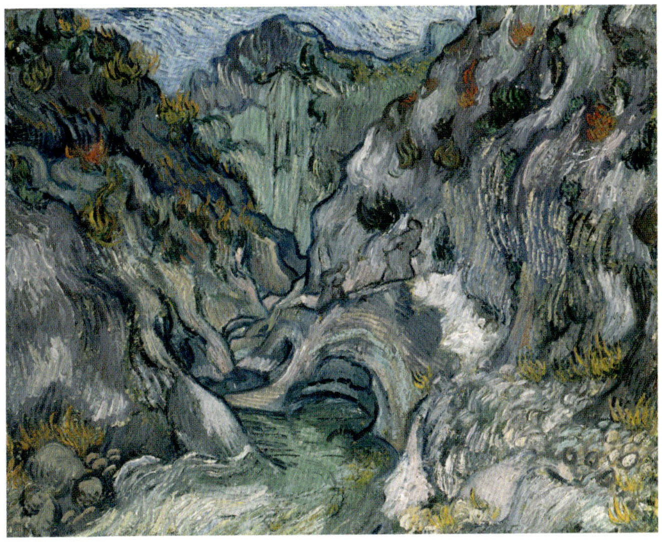

Many of Monet's recent views of Normandy were then featured in the first of his solo exhibitions at the Galerie Durand-Ruel (including, perhaps, *Road at La Cavée, Pourville*, fig 6), held in the spring of 1883. In the autumn of that year, Durand-Ruel dispatched to the new world – to the American Exhibition of Foreign Products, Arts & Manufactures held at the Mechanics' Building in Boston – a group of paintings by artists he represented: the Impressionists, but also more conservative painters. 'A shipment has been made of some of our paintings for the exhibition in Boston', Pissarro wrote to Monet in June. 'The information from Americans that I know, is that it is a mediocre exhibition which will have no influence. I have spoken of this to Durand-Ruel; he replied to me that this is a test, that he will profit from the occasion by showing us.'[16] The exhibition was, indeed, a trial run toward the larger exhibition of Impressionists that Durand-Ruel would send to New York three years later. Along with paintings by Manet, Pissarro, Renoir and Sisley, there were three paintings by Monet in the Boston show: an early view of his Argenteuil home, *The artist's house at Argenteuil*, and two Normandy views, *The customs house at Dieppe* and *Low tide at Varengeville*.[17]

At home, contrary to the opinion of critics in Boston, Monet's works only increased in popularity – in part because the painter continued to pursue new avenues of exploration. In the 1880s, for example, Monet's contact with the Mediterranean – a contact established through his friend Renoir – was to have lasting consequences for his art as well as for the history of Impressionist landscape painting. In Italy and the south of France, Monet found the warm golden light that had attracted artists there for centuries, a light that had clearly marked the work of a previous generation. The landscape inspired some of his most daring paintings to date: his view of the Menton coastline (cat 25), a riot of colour and brushstroke, prefigures the most audacious southern landscapes of Vincent van Gogh (fig 7).

It was several years later, on a return visit to the Mediterranean coast – this time to Antibes – that Monet was to refine his practice of painting a fixed motif under changing conditions of light at different times of day, a practice that he was to develop almost into a system over the next decade. Monet had often painted multiple views of a particularly interesting motif, and he had already presented to the public groups of paintings of related subjects. In 1876 he had painted 12 views in and around the Gare Saint-Lazare.[18] In his last exhibition with the Impressionists, in 1882, closely related views of the Normandy coast had constituted a kind of series within the group of paintings that Durand-Ruel selected to represent. As the decade drew to a close, in the early spring of 1889 Monet painted a group of landscapes in the valley of the river Creuse in a remote region of central France. Setting up his easel high above the spot where two small rivers converged, he painted the valley in vivid sunlight (cat 46) and in the gloom of twilight, as well as views of a smaller tributary under differing conditions of light and atmosphere (cats 44 and 45). These, following the paintings of Antibes, were steps in the process toward Monet's fully developed serial method, which he would explore more deeply in the 1890s with such series as his 1890–91 *Grainstack* paintings (see cats 47 and 48), his 1894 *Rouen Cathedral* images (see cat 49), and his 1897 *Mornings on the Seine* series (see cat 50), and in the first decade of the 20th century with his triumphant 1903–08 series *Waterlilies*, which were exhibited as a group in 1909 (see cat 53).

The paintings of the Creuse Valley were shown as a group at the Galerie Georges Petit at an exhibition timed to coincide with the 1889 Exposition Universelle. The venue was perhaps the most luxurious in Paris. Monet's works – more than 140 paintings – were paired with sculpture by his friend Auguste Rodin. The exhibition was a resounding critical success. 'Nature has never been revealed with more intensity and truth', wrote the critic Octave Maus.[19] At the same moment, however, a challenge was

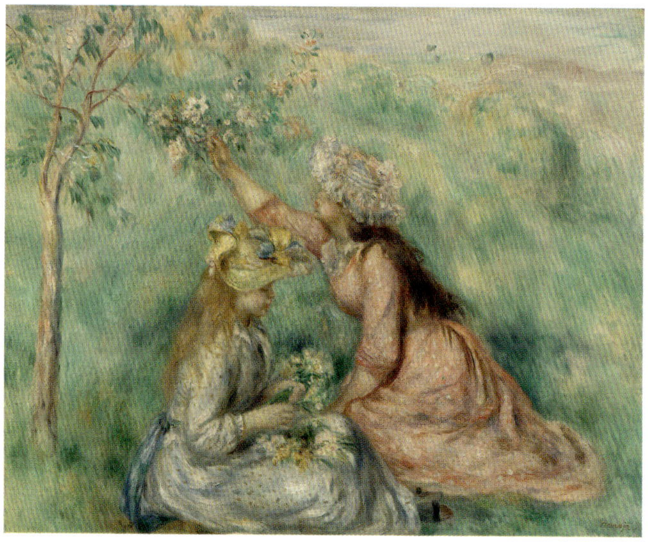

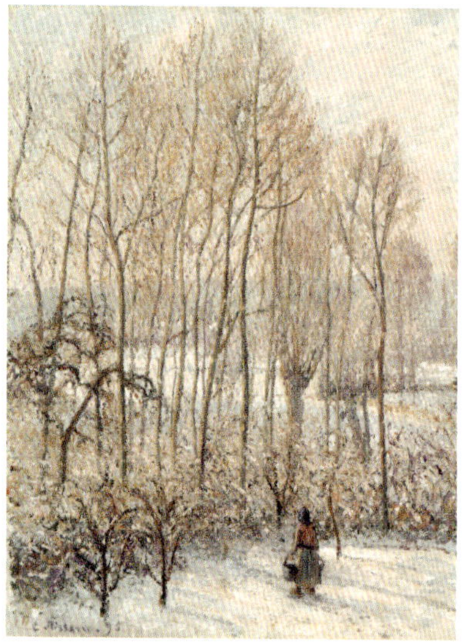

fig 8
Pierre-Auguste Renoir
Girls picking flowers in a meadow c1890
oil on canvas, 65.1 x 81 cm
Museum of Fine Arts, Boston,
Juliana Cheney Edwards collection
39.675

fig 9
Camille Pissarro
Morning sunlight on the snow, Eragny-sur-Epte 1895
oil on canvas, 82.3 x 61.6 cm
Museum of Fine Arts, Boston,
the John Pickering Lyman Collection,
gift of Miss Theodora Lyman
19.1321

being mounted to Impressionism, and perhaps most specifically to Monet's vision of nature. At a café near the site of the Exposition, the painter Paul Gauguin and some of his friends had exhibited some of their recent work in a new style, which sought to unite colour and form with deeply-charged emotion and to leave behind the Impressionists' slavish imitation of optical reality. They dubbed their new style Synthetist – though they were not above capitalising on the public recognition of the Impressionists by calling themselves the Groupe Impressioniste et Synthétiste.

In the last half of the 1880s, Gauguin, Odilon Redon, Georges Seurat and Paul Signac – all of whom had exhibited with the Impressionists in 1886, in Monet's absence – and Vincent van Gogh, whose brother Theo had displayed Monet's *Antibes* paintings, rejected the Impressionists' methods as overly dependent on optical effects and searched for some new stylistic means. Gauguin gradually abandoned the broken Impressionist brushstrokes that he had used in the early 1880s in favour of stylised forms and large masses of colour. Redon, who had always been at odds with the prevailing landscape tendencies of the movement, continued to pursue his unique vision of a fantastic dream universe, thereby making an important contribution to the development of Symbolism across Europe. Seurat and Signac, likewise, left the feathered brushstroke of Impressionism behind to evolve a method of painting with small dots of colour, a technique that they thought more scientific and rational than the subjective optics of Monet and Renoir. A critic would later label their work with the term 'Neo-Impressionism'. Van Gogh ended up rejecting the Impressionists' delicately nuanced palette in favour of an emphatically drawn, boldly coloured painting style, which he believed expressed his deepest emotions.

Partly because of these challenges, Monet, Renoir and Pissarro themselves altered their landscape styles in the final decade of the century. Monet evolved his series as a way of expressing his continuing belief in the power of visual sensation and in the validity of representing these sensations as a means of artistic expression (see cats 47–53). Renoir, who in the late 1880s had expressed his dissatisfaction with the modes of traditional Impressionism, in the 1890s approached a manner that associated his art with the great traditions of French painting, deliberately referencing such painters of the 18th century as Jean-Antoine Watteau and Jean-Honoré Fragonard. Thus, many of his late landscapes peopled by beautiful young women, such as *Girls picking flowers in a meadow* (fig 8) seem like fictions, as he reduced 'the setting to little more than a freely brushed coloured backdrop, with only the merest hints of natural features'.[20] Pissarro, who in the mid 1880s had briefly adopted the Neo-Impressionist style advocated by Seurat and his disciple Signac, returned to his structured compositions of the 1870s in such paintings as *Morning sunlight on the snow, Eragny-sur-Epte* (fig 9). At the end of the decade he embarked on a series of Parisian street scenes that seemed to bring his art back to the views of urban life that Monet, Renoir and even Gustave Caillebotte had pioneered in the late 1860s and early 1870s. And, most remarkably, the figure painter Degas, who had once commented, 'if I were the government I would have a special brigade of gendarmes to keep an eye on artists who paint landscapes from nature', took up landscape once again in the 1890s, even holding a solo exhibition of his landscape pastels in 1892.[21]

By the first years of the 20th century, the artists of the Impressionist vanguard were internationally renowned. Their paintings were shown in exhibitions and collected enthusiastically throughout Europe and North America, and a growing appreciation of their achievements was felt in Japan. In the 1890s, Monet's series exhibitions had regularly shaped public understanding of the evolution of his style, and in the early 20th century the exhibitions of his London views, his *Waterlilies*, and his views of Venice (fig 10) had garnered him lavish praise. The work of Cézanne, by contrast, had received little public recognition during the artist's

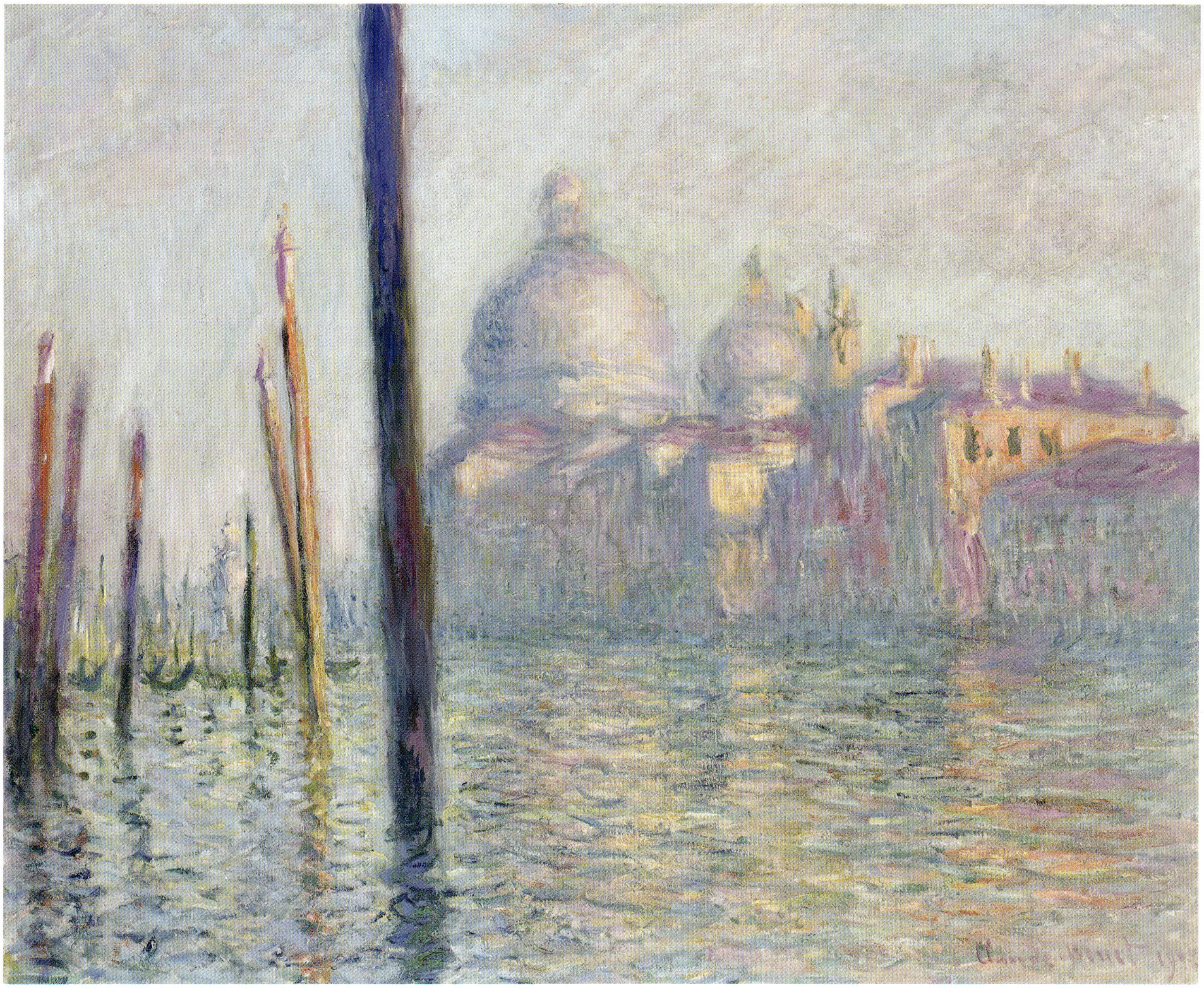

fig 10
Claude Monet
Grand Canal, Venice 1908
oil on canvas, 73.7 x 92.4 cm
Museum of Fine Arts, Boston,
bequest of Alexander Cochrane
19.171

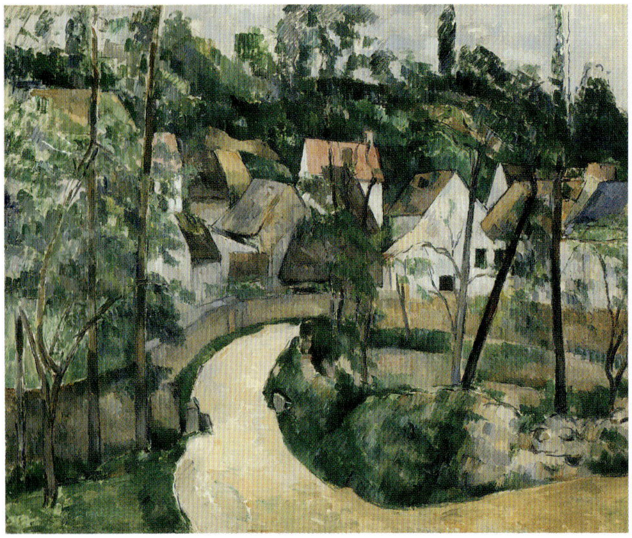

fig 11
Paul Cézanne
Turn in the road c1881
oil on canvas, 60.6 x 73.3 cm
Museum of Fine Arts, Boston,
bequest of John T Spaulding
48.525

lifetime, except perhaps from a handful of critics and from other painters: it is interesting to note that Cézanne's *The pond* (cat 18) was owned by the painter Gustave Caillebotte, while his *Turn in the road* (fig 11) passed from the collection of the critic Théodore Duret to the painter Paul-César Helleu and eventually to Cézanne's friend Monet. After the turn of the century, however, a young generation of painters – in which were counted Henri Matisse, Pierre Bonnard, Pablo Picasso and Georges Braque – found in the works of Cézanne, as well as in the works of Gauguin and Van Gogh, the inspiration for their vivid experiments with colour and the radical distortion of form.

But Monet continued to work well into the 20th century, longer than any of his Impressionist colleagues – and his art continued to evolve in ways that were as radical as the late works of Cézanne, if less overtly identified with the Modernist revolution of the years around 1910. Following the exhibition of Monet's Venetian views in 1911 – and following Alice Hoschedé Monet's death – for a time he ceased to paint. But around 1915 he returned in force to studying the pond in his Giverny garden, enlarging and expanding on the efforts that he had begun at the turn of the century (see cats 43, 53, and fig 28). Painting on a larger scale (his canvases were often 2 x 2 metres), he created extraordinarily modern, often roughly finished or unfinished, studies of waterlilies on the surface of the pond, as well as of grasses, flowers and willows growing on its banks. At the time of the Armistice that ended the First World War, Monet offered to his friend the French premier Georges Clémenceau 'a bouquet of flowers for France'. His initial proposal to donate several of his large-scale finished murals of the water garden eventually grew to encompass the vast cycle of decorations that now adorns the Musée de l'Orangerie in Paris.[22] These works, the creations of a master in his 80s, are the artist's last great contribution to the history of painting, an extraordinary culmination to a career that spanned more than 60 years. Although by the time of Monet's death in 1926 modern painting had evolved in directions that Monet would never follow, his own path – from the *Woodgatherers at the edge of the forest* of about 1863 to the *Waterlilies* of 1905 and beyond – was a radical evolution of its own kind. *Monet and the Impressionists*, by showing that evolution in context, gives us a sense of the importance of Monet's vital contribution to the history of art – not only of painting, but of perception, of sight itself.

Parts of this introduction and subsequent essays by George Shackelford were previously published in George T M Shackelford, Fronia E Wissman et al, *Impressions of light: the French landscape from Corot to Monet*, MFA Publications, Boston 2002

The Wildenstein catalogue numbers cited in the endnotes (eg W 284) refer to Daniel Wildenstein, *Monet: catalogue raisonné*, 4 vols, Taschen, Cologne 1996

1 Michael Pantazzi, 'Le plus grand paysagiste de notre temps' in Gary Tinterow, Pantazzi and Vincent Pomarède, *Corot*, exh cat, Metropolitan Museum of Art, New York 1996, pp 195–207

2 Anonymous critic quoted in Tinterow, Pantazzi and Pomarède 1996, p 268, no 91; this author's translation from the French

3 Philippe de Chennevières, quoted in Tinterow, Pantazzi and Pomarède 1996, p 195 and note 9; this author's translation from the French

4 Monet to the journalist Thiébault-Sisson, 1900, quoted in John Rewald, *The history of Impressionism*, 4th rev ed, Museum of Modern Art, New York 1973, p 38

5 Monet to Boudin, 3 Jun 1859, quoted in Daniel Wildenstein, *Claude Monet: biographie et catalogue raisonné*, 5 vols, La Bibliothèque des arts, Lausanne 1974–91, vol 1 p 419; this author's translation from the French. Troyon's paintings were *Return to the farm* and *View taken from the heights of Suresnes* (Musée d'Orsay and Musée du Louvre, Paris)

6 Recorded by Monet in a letter to Boudin, 19 May 1859, quoted in Richard Kendall ed, *Monet by himself: paintings, drawings, pastels, letters*, trans Bridget Strevens Romer, Macdonald Orbis, London 1989, p 18

7 Renoir's *Cabaret* (1866) is at the National Museum, Stockholm; *Diana* (1867) is at the National Gallery of Art, Washington DC; Pissarro's riverbank views may be found at the Glasgow Art Gallery and Museum, Kelvingrove, the National Gallery of Scotland, Edinburgh and the Art Institute of Chicago; Sisley's *Marlotte* (1866) is at the Albright-Knox Art Gallery, Buffalo, New York; and Degas's *Steeplechase* is at the National Gallery of Art, Washington DC

8 See Charles F Stuckey, *Claude Monet, 1840–1926*, exh cat, Thames and Hudson, New York and Art Institute of Chicago, Chicago 1995, p 194

9 Monet to Bazille, Sept 1869, quoted in Wildenstein 1974–91, vol 1, p 427; this author's translation from the French

10 See Henri Loyrette and Gary Tinterow, *Impressionnisme: les origines, 1859–1869*, exh cat, Réunion des musées nationaux, Paris 1994, pp 436–38, and Stuckey 1995, p 194. According to Wildenstein 1974–91, vol 1 no 136, the rejected view of La Grenouillère was probably the work formerly in the Arnhold Collection, Berlin, presumed destroyed

11 Arsène Houssaye to Karl Bertrand in 'Salon de 1870', *L'Artiste*, 1870, p 319, quoted in Loyrette and Tinterow 1994, p 438; this author's translation from the French

12 Louis Leroy, 'L'exposition des impressionnistes', *Le Charivari*, 25 Apr 1874, pp 79–80, quoted in Ruth Berson ed, *The new painting: Impressionism, 1874–1886, documentation*, 2 vols, The Fine Arts Museums of San Francisco, San Francisco 1996, vol 1, p 26; this author's translation from the French

13 Armand Silvestre, 'Chronique des beaux-arts: Physiologie du refusé – l'exposition des révoltés', *L'Opinion nationale*, 22 Apr 1874, pp 2–3, quoted in Berson 1996, vol 1, p 39; this author's translation from the French

14 Monet to Hoschedé, 15 Feb 1882, quoted in Kendall 1989, p 100

15 For an extended discussion of the seventh Impressionist exhibition (1882), see Joel Isaacson, 'The painters called Impressionists' in Charles S Moffett et al, *The new painting: Impressionism 1874–1886*, exh cat, The Fine Arts Museums of San Francisco, San Francisco 1986, pp 373–93

16 Pissarro to Monet, 12 Jun 1883, in Camille Pissarro, *Correspondance de Camille Pissarro*, ed Janine Bailly-Herzberg, 5 vols, Presses Universitaires de France, Paris 1980–91, vol 1, pp 216–17, quoted in Eric Zafran, 'Monet in America' in Joseph Baillio et al, *Claude Monet (1840–1926): a tribute to Daniel Wildenstein and Katia Granoff*, exh cat, Wildenstein and Company, New York 2007, p 85

17 *The artist's house* is at the Art Institute of Chicago (W 284); *The customs house* is at the Metropolitan Museum of Art, New York; and *Low tide* is at the Thyssen-Bornemisza Collection, Madrid

18 For a discussion of Monet's paintings of the train station in the context of Manet's work, see Juliet Wilson Bareau, *Manet, Monet, and the Gare Saint-Lazare*, exh cat, National Gallery of Art, Washington DC and Yale University Press, New Haven, Connecticut 1998

19 Octave Maus in *L'Art moderne*, 1889, quoted in Paul Hayes Tucker, *Monet in the '90s: the series paintings*, exh cat, Museum of Fine Arts, Boston in association with Yale University Press, Boston 1989, p 55. See Tucker's chapter 3, pp 41–67, for a discussion of the *Creuse* series and the exhibition of 1889

20 John House, in Michael Raeburn ed, *Renoir*, exh cat, Hayward Gallery, Arts Council of Great Britain, London 1985, p 257

21 Degas quoted in Ambroise Vollard, *Degas: an intimate portrait*, trans Randolph Weaver, George Allen and Unwin, London 1928, p 91, quoted in Richard Kendall ed, *Degas by himself: drawings, prints, paintings, writings*, Macdonald Orbis, London 1987

22 For the most comprehensive study of Monet's work after 1900, see Paul Hayes Tucker et al, *Monet in the twentieth century*, exh cat, Museum of Fine Arts, Boston and Royal Academy of Arts, London 1998

MONET AND THE IMPRESSIONISTS

George T M Shackelford

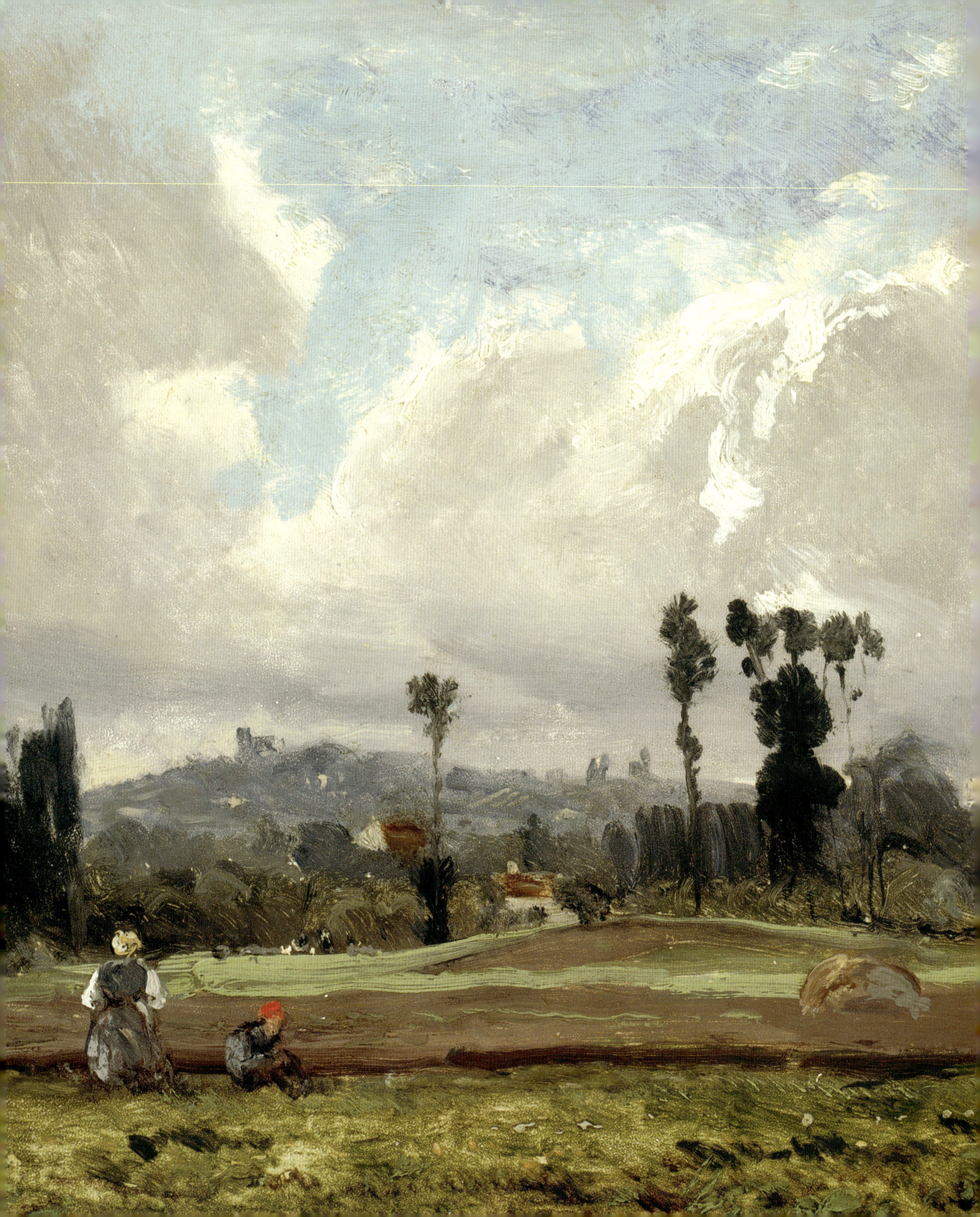

MONET'S EARLY YEARS: SOURCES OF INSPIRATION

In *Woodgatherers at the edge of the forest* (cat 2), Monet shows two women carrying bundles of kindling wood that they have picked up from the forest floor. The painting is the earliest work by Monet in the MFA's collection; its inspiration was certainly the forest of Fontainebleau, to the south of Paris, where painters had worked for a generation or more before Monet made a trip there – to the village of Chailly, on the edge of the woods – in 1863, in the company of his friend Frédéric Bazille. They arrived in early April, but Monet stayed on until late May and returned there a year later. The forest was to provide motifs for his art throughout the middle years of the 1860s, including views of famous trees, well-known roadways cut through the forest, and picnicking friends beneath its trees.

Woodgatherers at the edge of the forest is Monet's modern response to the previous generation's subject matter and style, one that is typical of the painter in his early years. The subject is a classic one in the art of the Barbizon school. Théodore Rousseau, for instance, in his *Gathering wood in the forest of Fontainebleau* (cat 1), shows a similar pair of women, one laden with a bundle of fallen branches, the other riding a donkey that carries the branches she has culled from the forest floor. As Monet after him explored the intersection of open space with woods, Rousseau contrasts the forest with the plain – almost certainly the plain of Chailly – but with his meticulous touch he takes care to delineate fine effects that Monet would ignore. In *Gathering wood*, for example, tiny flickering strokes of golden orange paint seem to depict individual leaves on the trees in the middle distance, while the dying sun, obscured by the silhouetted trunk of a tall tree almost exactly at the painting's centre, casts rays that lighten, with subtle pinks, the undersides of mauve clouds floating against the blue sky. The path that the women follow is rutted, and Rousseau carefully shows the reflection of the sunset in a puddle of water in the foreground.

By contrast, Monet's painting is marked by abbreviation, simplification and swiftness of execution. His women walk along a path that is rendered as a broad stroke of paint. In this, Monet has more in common with Corot. In Corot's *Morning near Beauvais* (cat 3) of about ten years earlier, as in Monet's *Woodgatherers* the forms of trees and foliage are suggested rather than depicted, both literally and figuratively painted with a broader brush than Rousseau's. Like Corot, Monet applies daubs of paint to convey the feeling of wind-blown leaves in the trees at left in his painting; as in Corot's painting, the leaves cling to branches that have dimension and volume at ground level, but evolve into long, thin, gestural strokes of paint as they rise against the sky. Monet, like both Corot and Rousseau, condenses his figures into a handful of brushstrokes, but places them in a landscape where every element has been simplified.

How did Monet reach this point in his evolution as a painter? Comparison of *Woodgatherers* with landscape sketches by Constant Troyon would suggest that the younger artist had heeded his precursor's advice, at their meeting in 1859, to make studies directly from nature. Troyon's *Field outside Paris* (cat 7), for example, is painted with the same brevity as Monet's later panel. The difference, of course, is that Monet's painting is roughly four times as large as Troyon's – so that Troyon's strokes have been amplified and broadened (as Corot's have) to a level of simplification not found in traditional landscape painting before Monet's time.

Surely Monet took little from the time he spent with Auguste Toulmouche, whose *Reading lesson* of about 1865 (cat 9) typifies his scenes of elegant Parisian women in domestic interiors. Toulmouche, about a decade older than the young Monet – who began to work with him at the end of 1862 – was married to a cousin of Monet's aunt. It was Toulmouche who connected the younger painter to the studio of Charles Gleyre, whose history paintings were equally antithetical to the direction Monet's art was taking, but who was also teaching a number of young painters – Renoir, Bazille and Sisley – who were to become Monet's close friends and artistic allies.[1] And if Toulmouche's own subjects were unlike the ones that Monet was to produce in later years, it should be noted that genre

Constant Troyon *Field outside Paris* 1845–51 (detail), cat 7

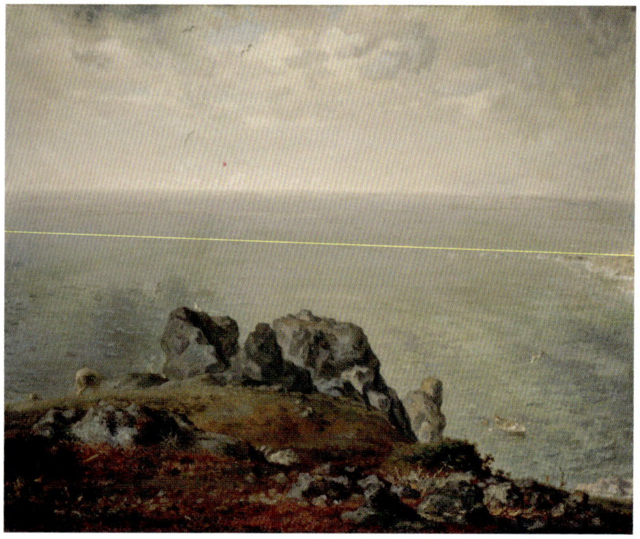

fig 12
Jean-François Millet
Cliffs at Gruchy 1870–71
oil on canvas, 60 x 74 cm
Museum of Fine Arts, Boston,
gift of Quincy Adams Shaw through
Quincy Adams Shaw Jr and
Mrs Marian Shaw Haughton
17.1529

painting held a place – decidedly second to landscape, but still present – in Monet's art in the 1870s. His *Camille Monet and a child in the artist's garden in Argenteuil* (see cat 20) is radically different in visual effect from Toulmouche's polished, well-mannered image of a mother and child, but it is pervaded by a similar tender sentiment meant to appeal to an audience, and by a sense of quiet intimacy that reflects the painter's fond feeling for his subjects.

From the artists of a previous generation, Monet would also learn lessons about light and emotion. In later years, he would focus on creating visual effects that convey an even stronger sense of mood. His paintings of the 1880s and especially the 1890s are often marked by visual effects that translate to the viewer as joyful or pensive or sometimes melancholy. Often these effects are associated with natural phenomena or with time of day. His paintings of Rouen Cathedral (see cat 49) and his series of daybreak views of the river (see cat 50) – not to mention the many sunset or twilight views of grainstacks (see cat 47), or later, waterlilies (see cats 43, 53 and fig 28) or Venetian palaces (see fig 10) – stress the poignancy of changing light. So had his predecessors, in such works as Corot's *Twilight* (cat 4) or Jean-François Millet's *Washerwomen* (cat 5), used the fading light to engender a mood of quiet contemplation a generation earlier. Both earlier painters employ figures to give narrative to their scenes. Corot shows a pair of women, one of whom is gathering branches – traditionally identified as laurels – from a tree whose leaves are silhouetted against a twilight sky, as later Monet would paint the trees along the Seine riverbank. Millet's washerwomen similarly stand out against the twilight sky; in a device that Monet would later use often, Millet uses a watery middle ground to reflect that sky and the horizon. Monet would never employ such a direct reference to the world of working people (except in one remarkable 1875 painting of men unloading coal barges, *The coal workers*). But as many scholars have noted, Monet's paintings of fields of wheat and stacks of hay and grain imply the labours of the seasons and celebrate France's agricultural economy, themes that Millet explored more explicitly in his peasant paintings of the 1850s and 1860s.[2]

Echoes of Corot, Millet and other Barbizon artists are to be perceived again and again in the post-1870 work of Monet. It is doubtful that Monet could ever have seen Millet's *Priory at Vauville, Normandy* (cat 6), commissioned by a Boston collector in 1871. But Millet's image of a priory-turned-farmhouse on the coast of the English Channel – one of many views of the Normandy coast in Millet's oeuvre – reminds students of Monet's art of the younger painter's many views of cliff-side buildings, such as the customs watch station-turned-dwelling in *Fisherman's cottage on the cliffs at Varengeville*, painted some ten years later (see cat 24). Millet's *Cliffs at Gruchy* of 1870–71 (fig 12), likewise presages Monet's views of the sea painted in the early 1880s from the high Normandy cliffs, and was, interestingly enough, included in an 1871 London show organised by Durand-Ruel, the 2nd Annual Exhibition of the Society of French Artists, in which a work by Monet, a view of the beach at Trouville, was also on display.[3] (Whether Monet saw this Millet painting is not known.)

By the early 1870s, however, Monet already had become an acknowledged member of the vanguard. The Normandy beach scenes that he showed with Durand-Ruel in London in 1870 and 1871 were greatly influenced by the work of two older artists who had become his mentors outside the academic system: Eugène Boudin and Johan Barthold Jongkind. Monet had met Boudin, the painter of the Normandy seaside, in Le Havre around 1856–57, and he would later recall their encounter as the beginning of his conviction that he could become a painter. Jongkind he was to meet several years later, in 1862, at which time he introduced the Dutch painter to Boudin. Boudin and Jongkind, 16 and 21 years Monet's senior, had tutored Monet in the methods of plein-air landscape and had instilled in him an admiration of vividly observed and seemingly quickly rendered natural effects. Such characteristic works as Boudin's *Fashionable figures on the beach* (cat 10) of about 1865, his earlier panel *The beach* (cat 11), or Jongkind's *Harbour scene in Holland* (cat 12) of a few years later, represent the kind of finished paintings, meant for gallery exhibition and sale, that these artists were producing in the middle years of the decade – paintings that extol the virtues of the rapidly brushed effect of the open-air sketch.

By the time that he painted *Rue de la Bavole, Honfleur* (cat 13), around 1864, Monet had well absorbed the influences of Boudin and Jongkind and was already moving beyond them. The harsh contrasts of light and shadow in Monet's depiction of the street, its buildings and its inhabitants suggest a new manner of painting that would transcend the more tonal effects still practised by his elders. Here, shadow is rendered with geometric precision but also with a sense of acutely observed reality, a reality that erases all thoughts of the touristic or picturesque potential of the motif.

In this image of a city street in Normandy, Monet achieves again, but with greater mastery, a visual language of abbreviation that distinguishes his work from the Normandy views of Boudin or Jongkind and more closely approaches the kind of stylistic simplification that Edouard Manet was practising at the time. Although Manet had not yet encountered the younger artist when he painted his *Basket of fruit* (cat 14) around 1864, he was to learn of Monet as early as 1865, since their names were sometimes confused.[4] By the time they met in 1866, it was clear that Monet's art was evolving on lines that paralleled Manet's in the summary depiction of forms, the reduction of visual sensation to a minimum of marks on the painted surface. As he worked in concert with his young friends Renoir, Bazille and Sisley, however, Monet was to evolve painting methods that would advance beyond Manet's, and his example would eventually inspire Manet and others to a new manner of free and light painting based on Impressionist methods. By the 1870s, the young Monet had come of age.

1 See Stuckey 1995, pp 188–89
2 For the image of workmen unloading coal, now in the Musée d'Orsay, see W 364. For a discussion of Monet and agriculture, see Tucker 1989, pp 65–105
3 W 158a, present location unknown
4 See Stuckey 1995, pp 190–91

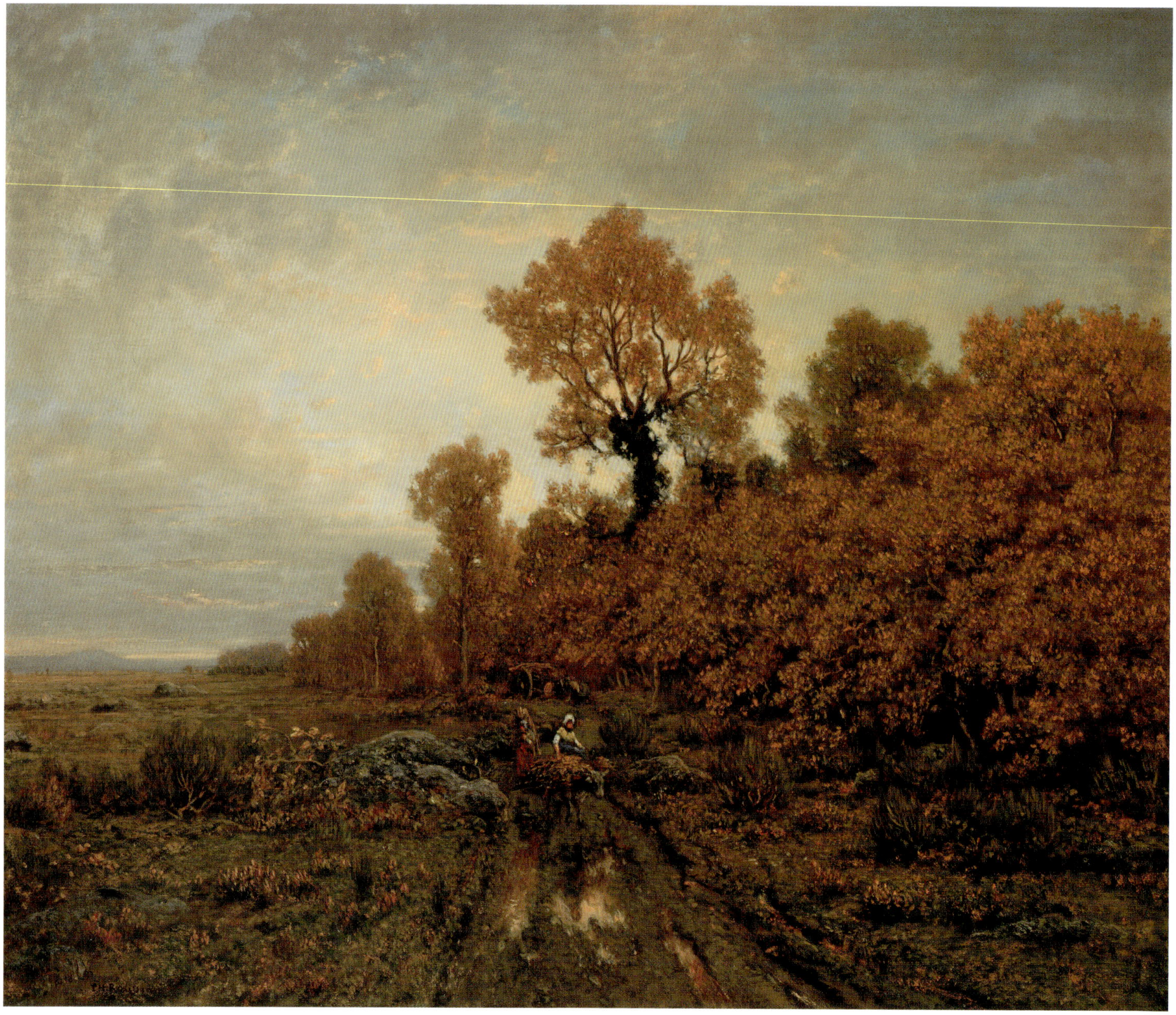

1
Théodore Rousseau
Gathering wood in the forest of Fontainebleau c1850–60
oil on canvas, 54.6 x 65.4 cm
Museum of Fine Arts, Boston,
bequest of Mrs David P Kimball
23.99

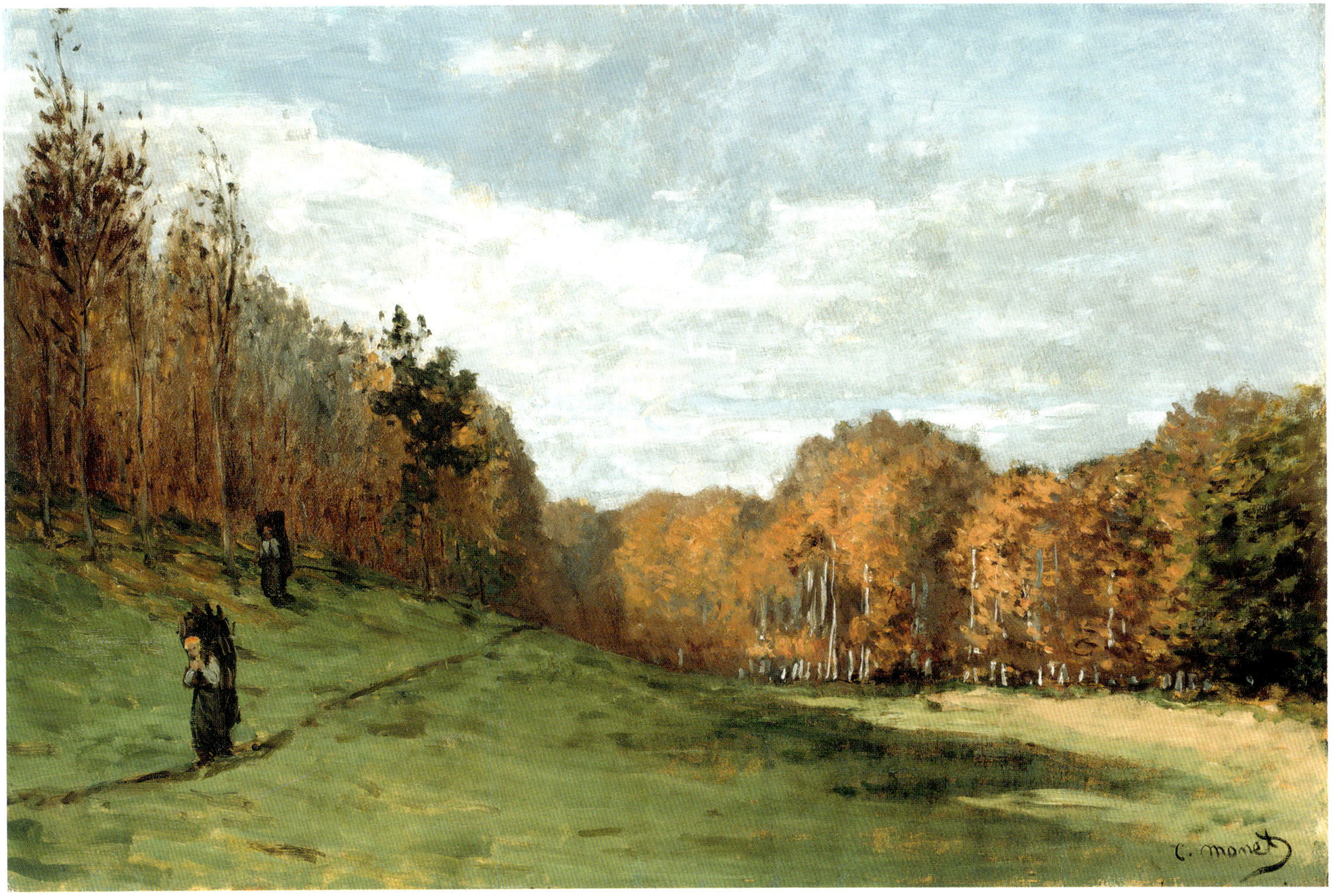

2

Claude Monet

Woodgatherers at the edge of the forest c1863

oil on panel, 59.7 x 90.2 cm
Museum of Fine Arts, Boston,
bequest of Mrs David P Kimball
1974.325

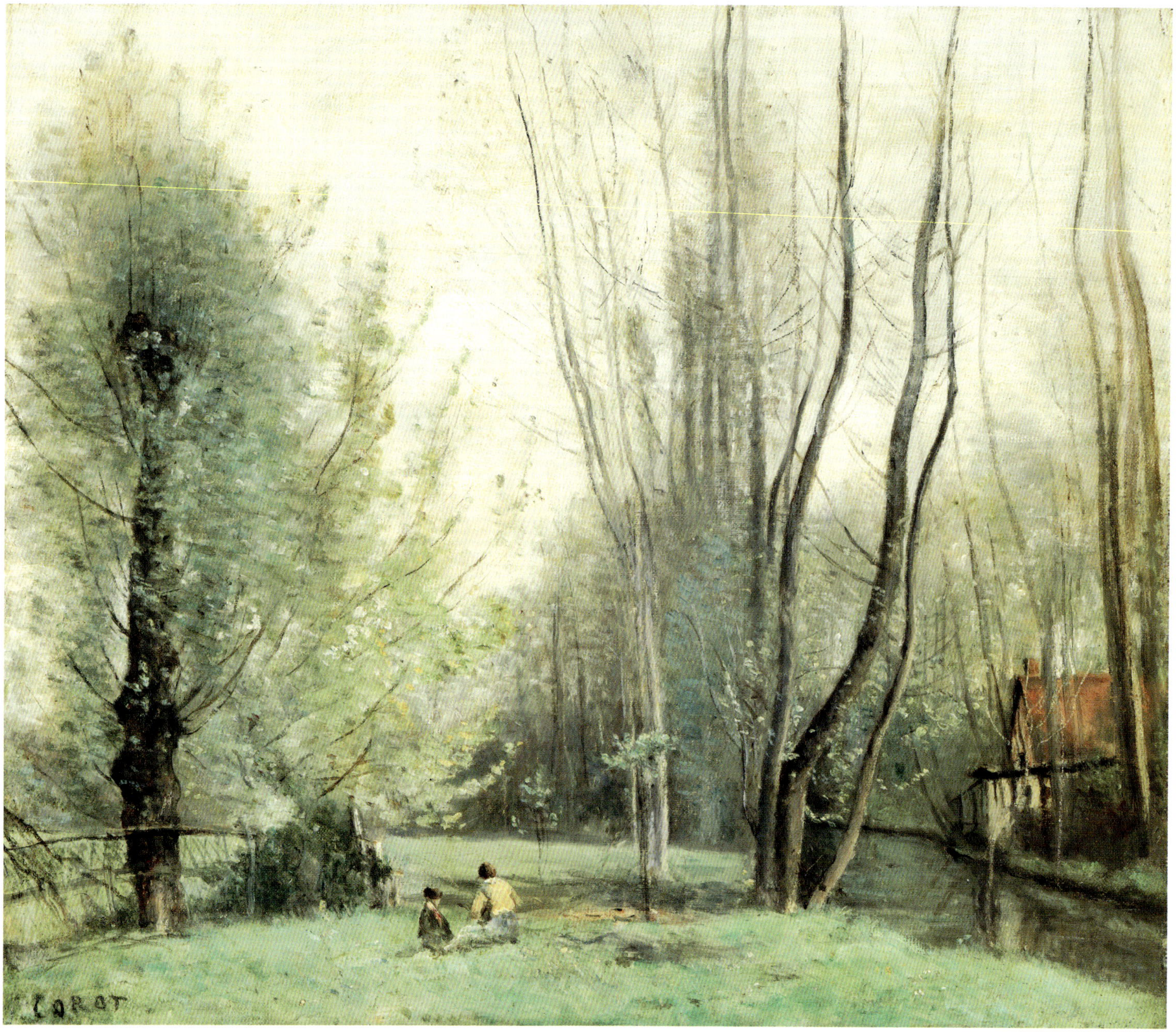

3

Jean-Baptiste-Camille Corot
Morning near Beauvais c1855–65

oil on canvas, 35.9 x 41.6 cm
Museum of Fine Arts, Boston,
Julia Cheney Edwards Collection
39.668

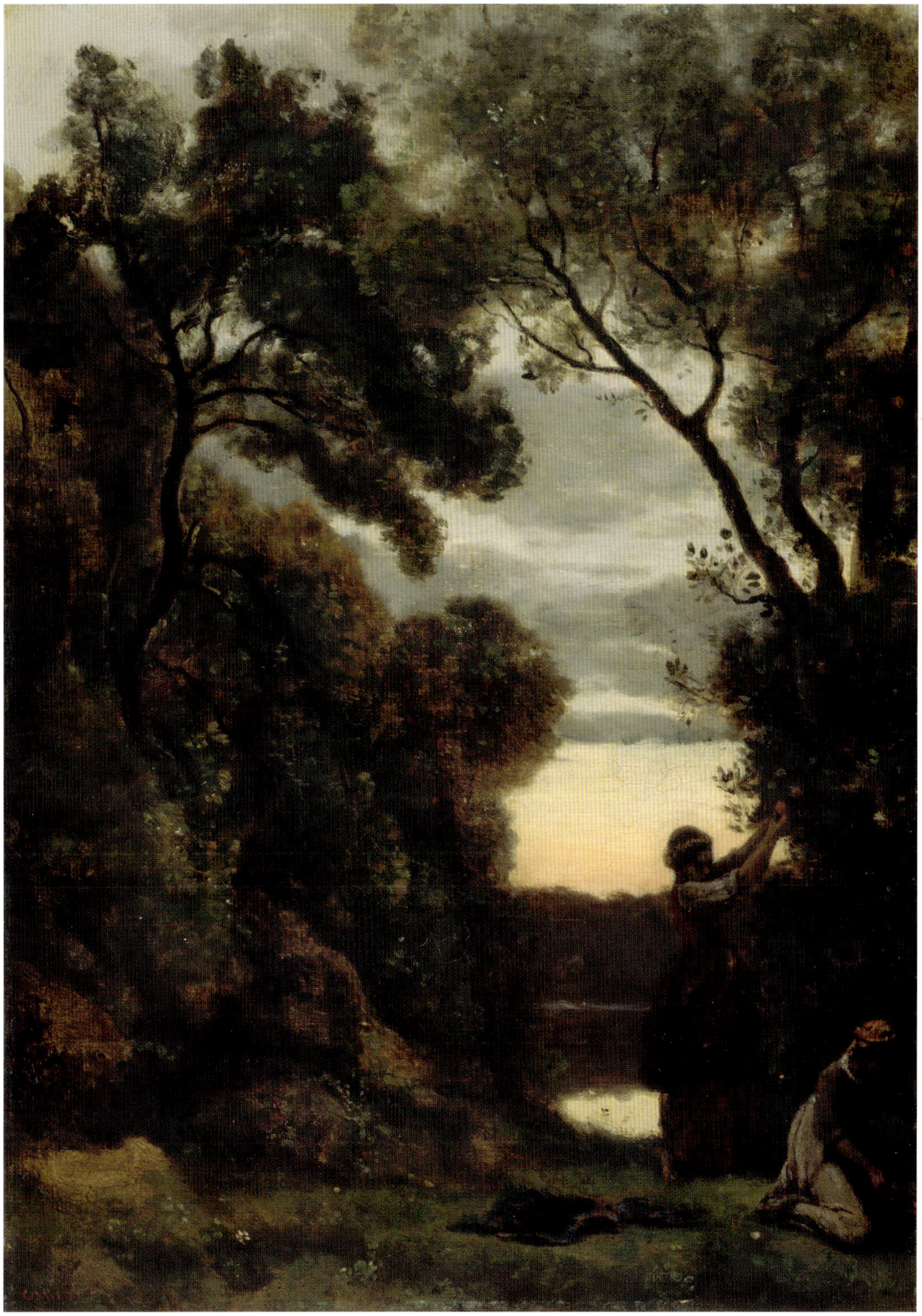

4

Jean-Baptiste-Camille Corot
Twilight 1845–60
oil on canvas, 50.2 x 37.1 cm
Museum of Fine Arts, Boston,
bequest of Mrs Henry Lee Higginson
35.1163

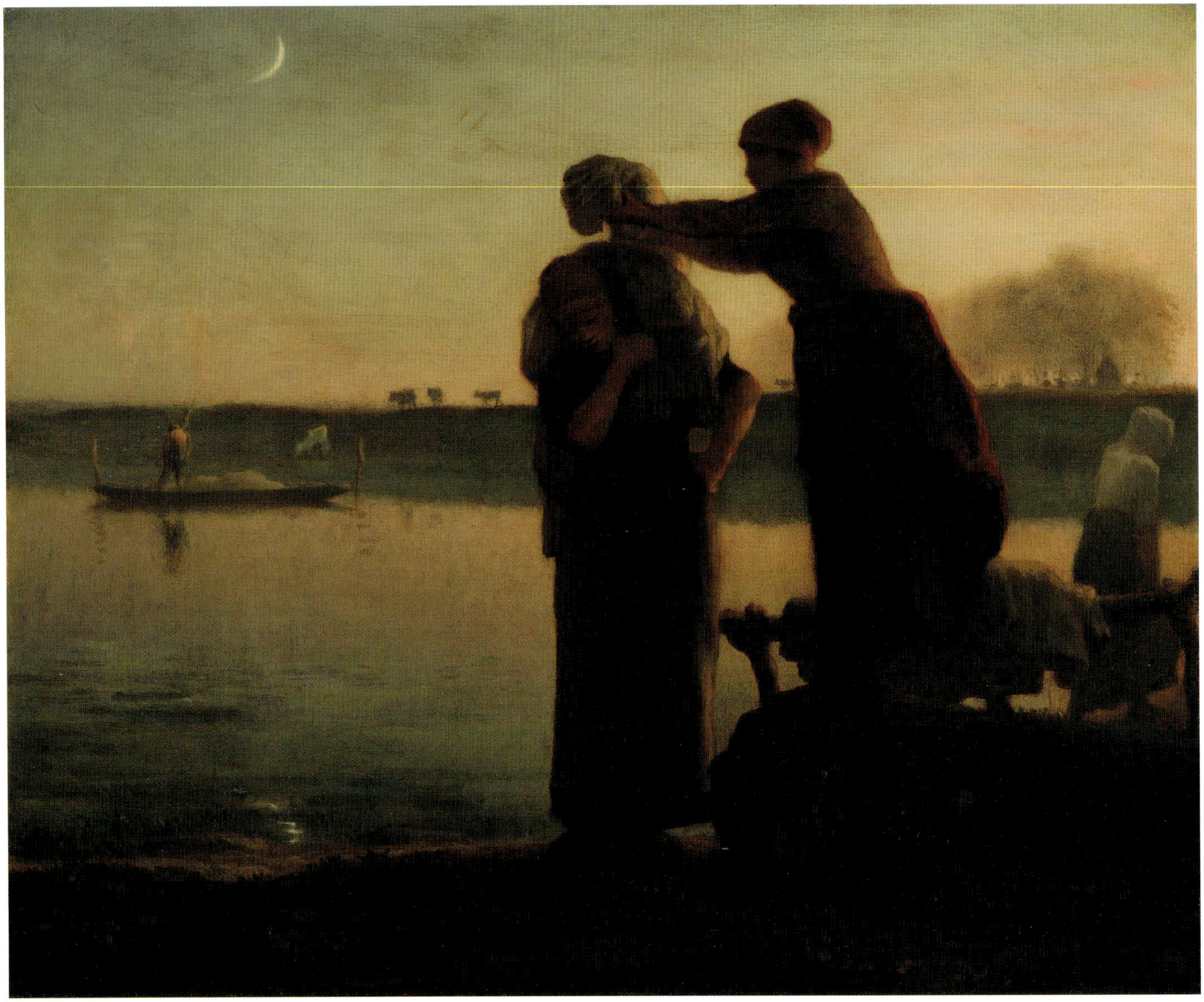

5
Jean-François Millet
Washerwomen c1855
oil on canvas, 43.5 x 53.7 cm
Museum of Fine Arts, Boston,
gift of Mrs Martin Brimmer
06.2422

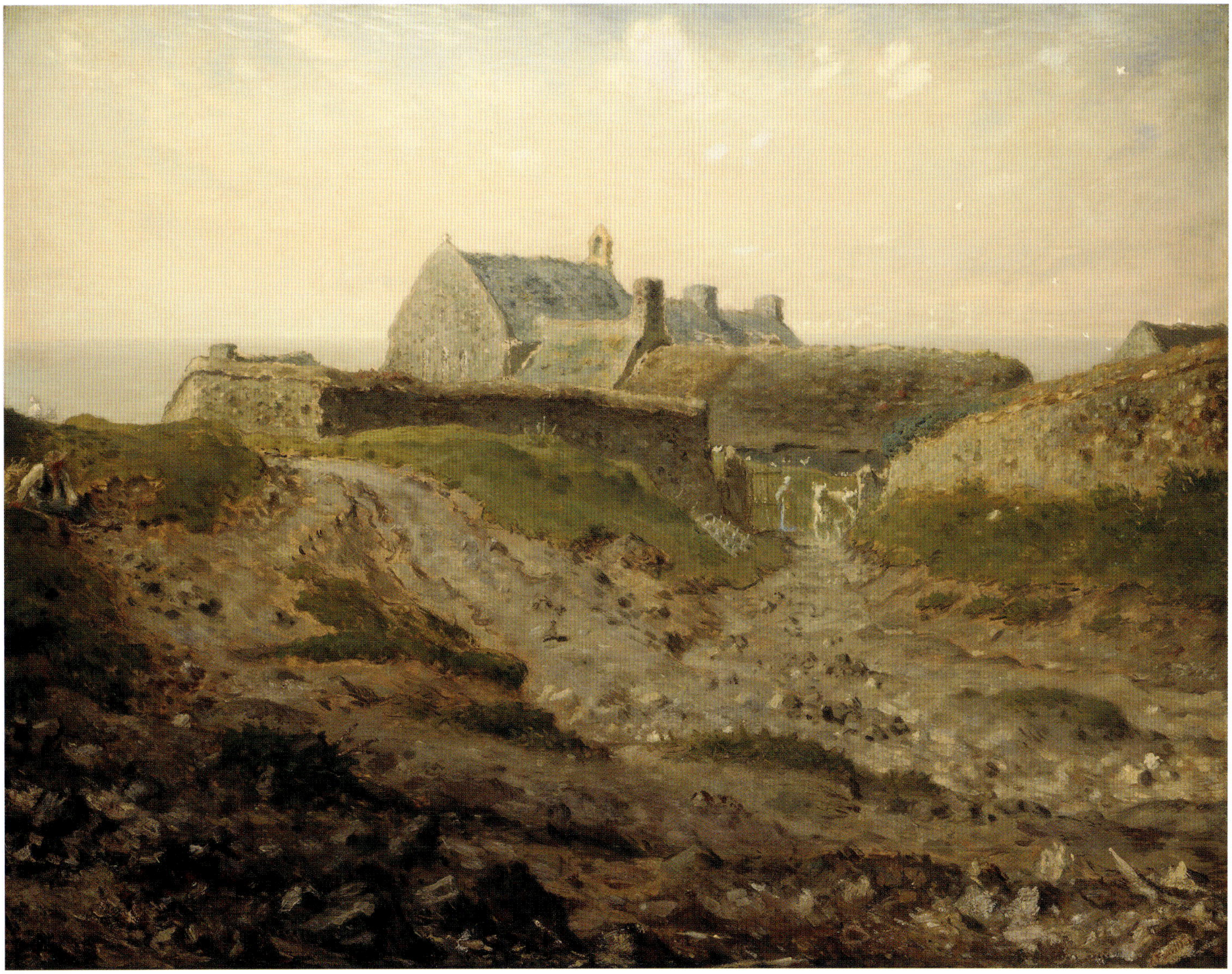

6

Jean-François Millet
Priory at Vauville, Normandy 1872–74

oil on canvas, 89.9 x 116.8 cm
Museum of Fine Arts, Boston, gift of Quincy Adams Shaw through Quincy Adams Shaw Jr and Mrs Marian Shaw Haughton
17.1532

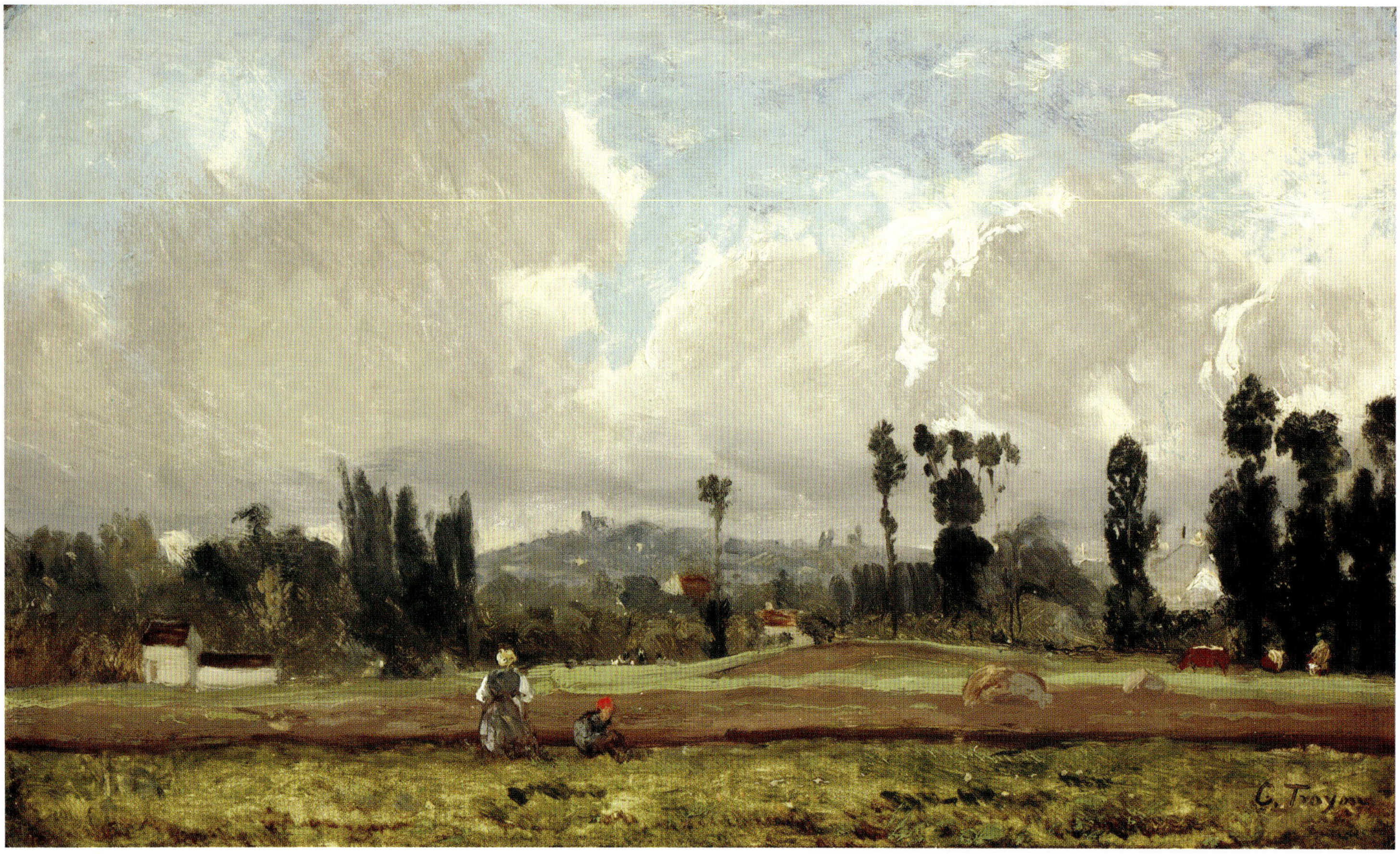

7

Constant Troyon
Field outside Paris 1845–51

oil on paperboard, 27 x 45.5 cm
Museum of Fine Arts, Boston,
Henry C and Martha B Angell Collection
19.117

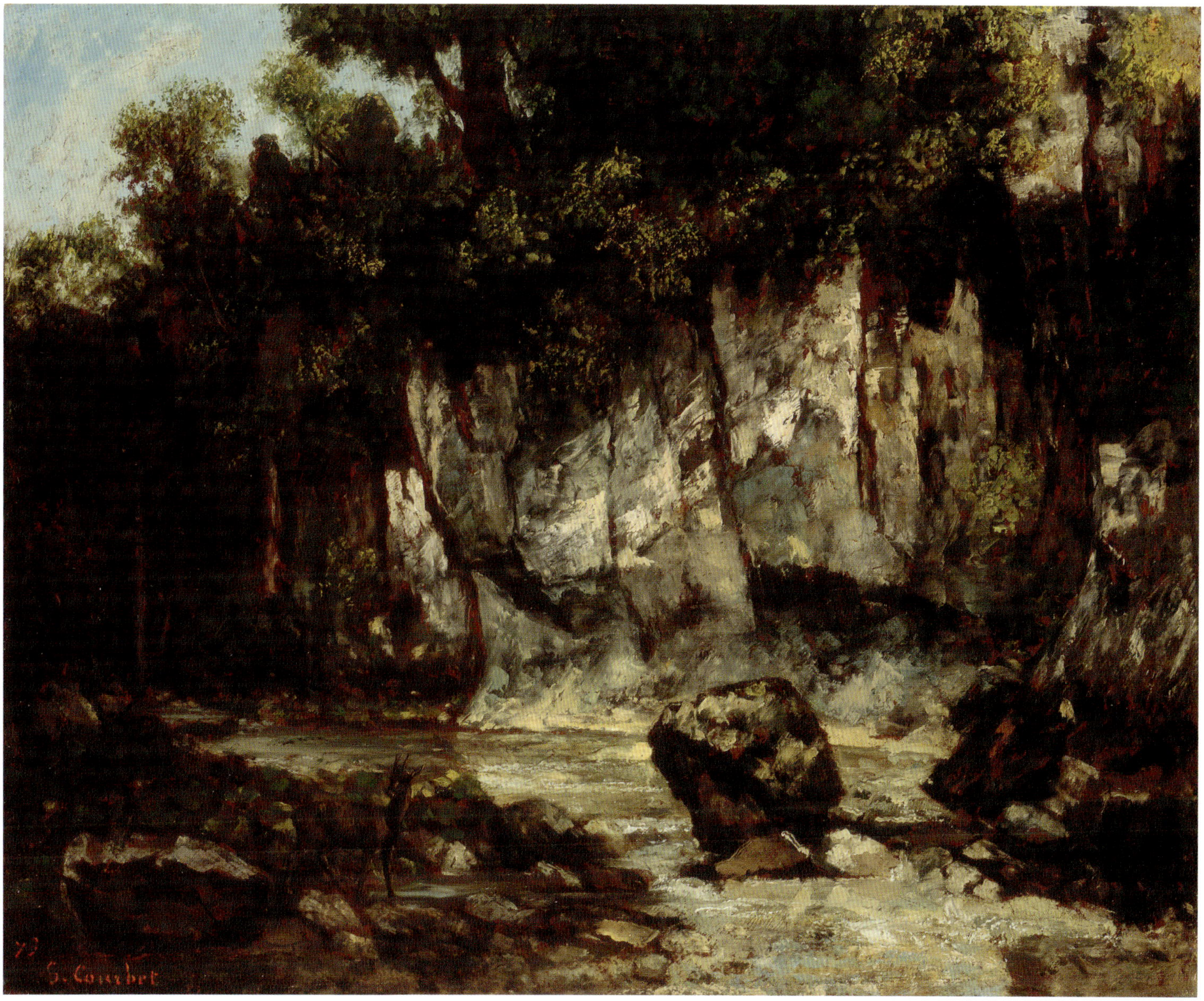

8

Gustave Courbet
Landscape with stag 1873

oil on canvas, 65.5 x 81.6 cm
Art Gallery of New South Wales,
purchased 1997

194.1997

9

Auguste Toulmouche
Reading lesson 1865

oil on canvas, 36.5 x 27.6 cm
Museum of Fine Arts, Boston,
gift of Francis A Foster
24.1

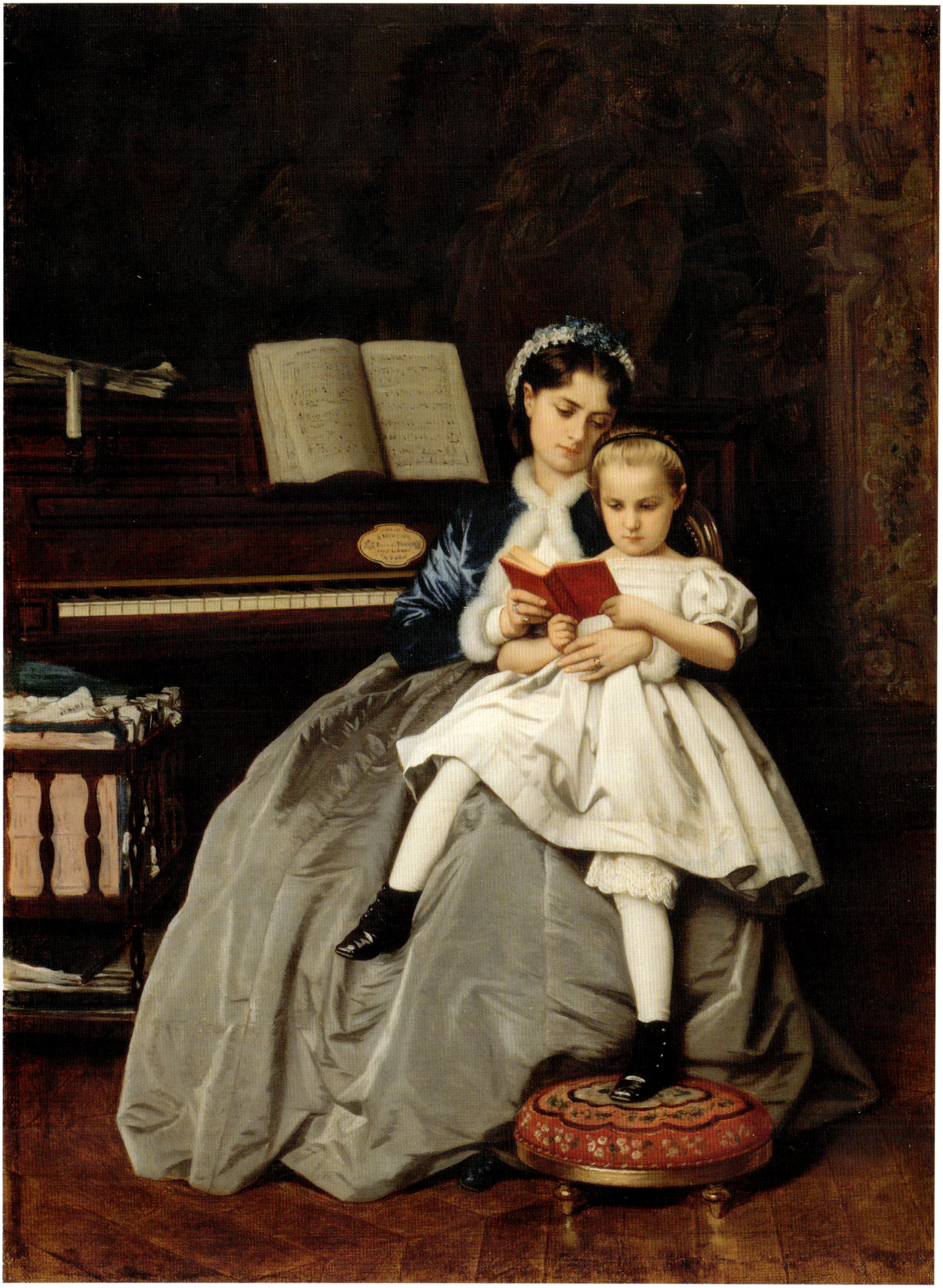

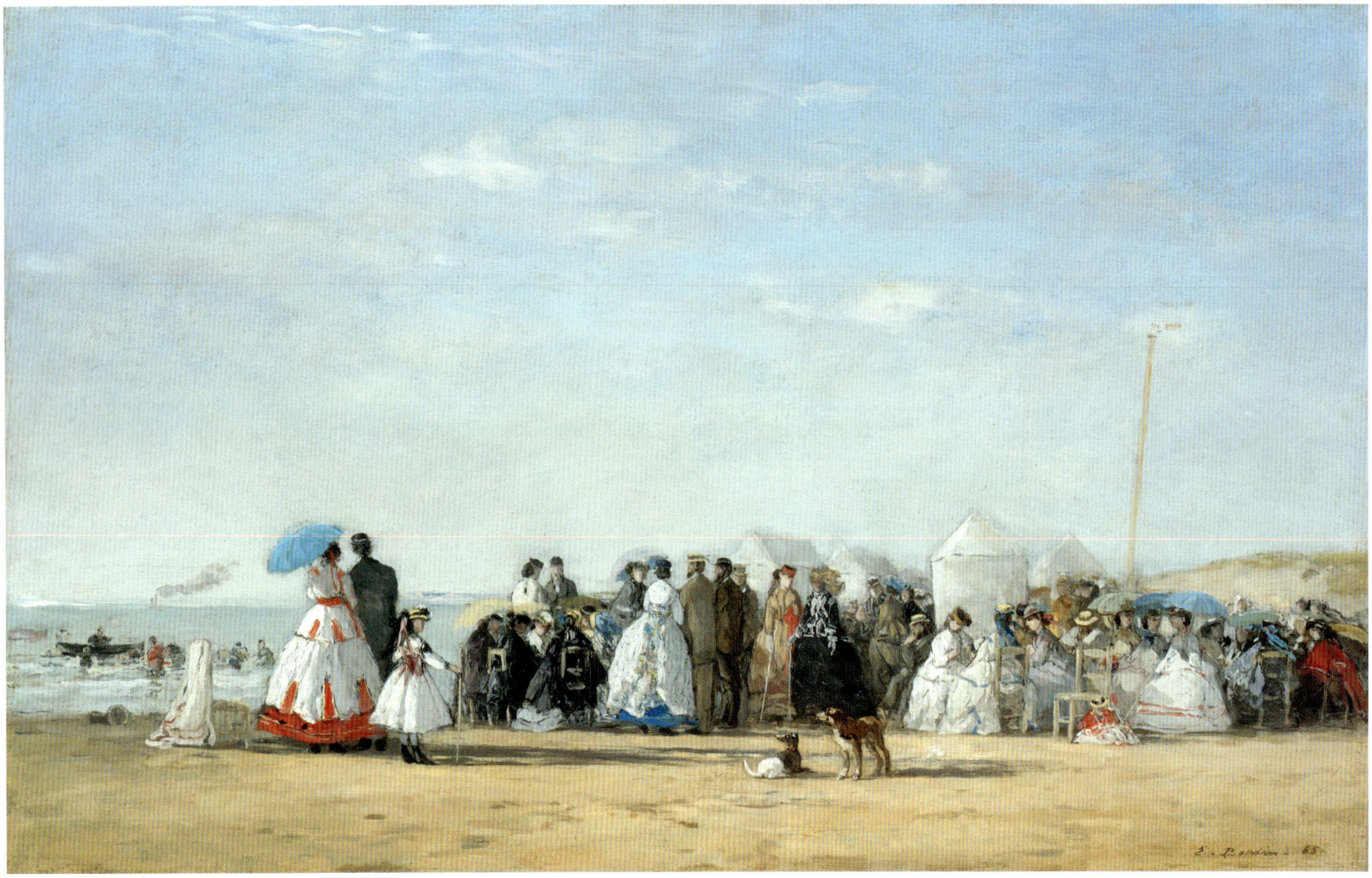

10

Eugène Louis Boudin

Fashionable figures on the beach 1865

oil on panel, 35.5 x 57.5 cm
Museum of Fine Arts, Boston,
gift of Mr and Mrs John A Wilson
1974.565

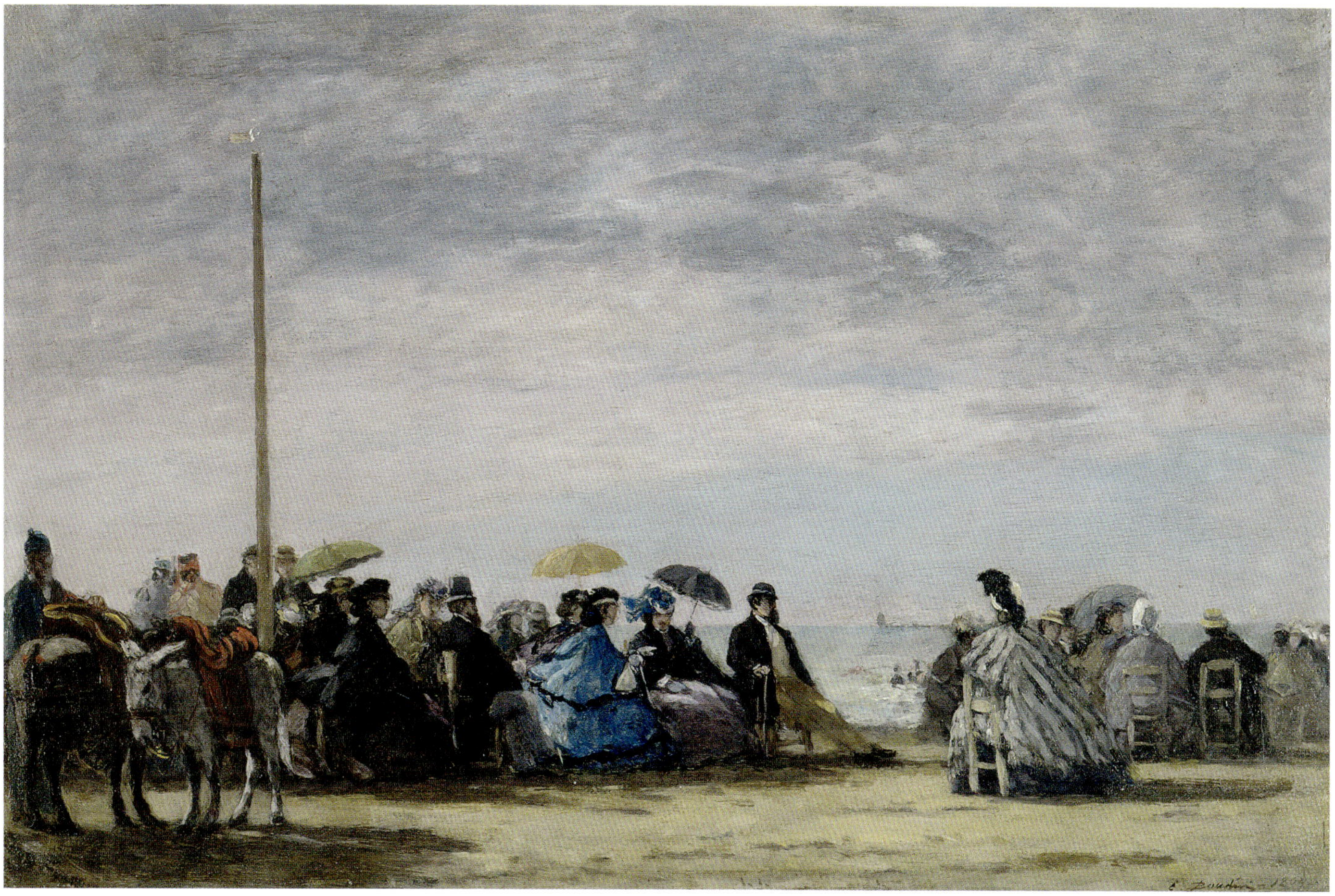

11

Eugène Louis Boudin
The beach 1864

oil on panel, 30.9 x 47.1 cm
Art Gallery of New South Wales,
purchased 1926
1123

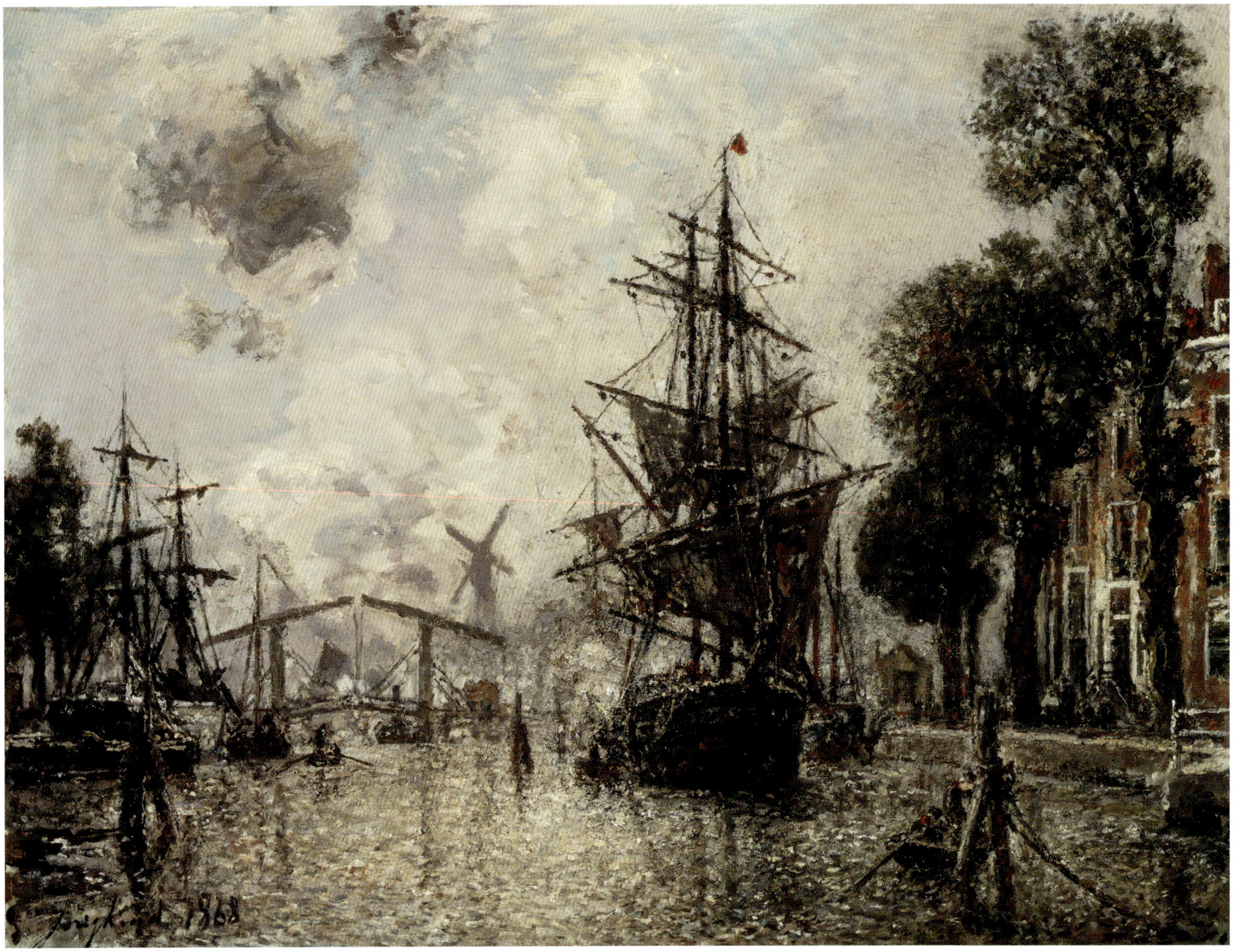

12
Johan Barthold Jongkind
Harbour scene in Holland 1868
oil on canvas, 41.9 x 55.9 cm
Museum of Fine Arts, Boston,
gift of Count Cecil Pecci-Blunt
61.1242

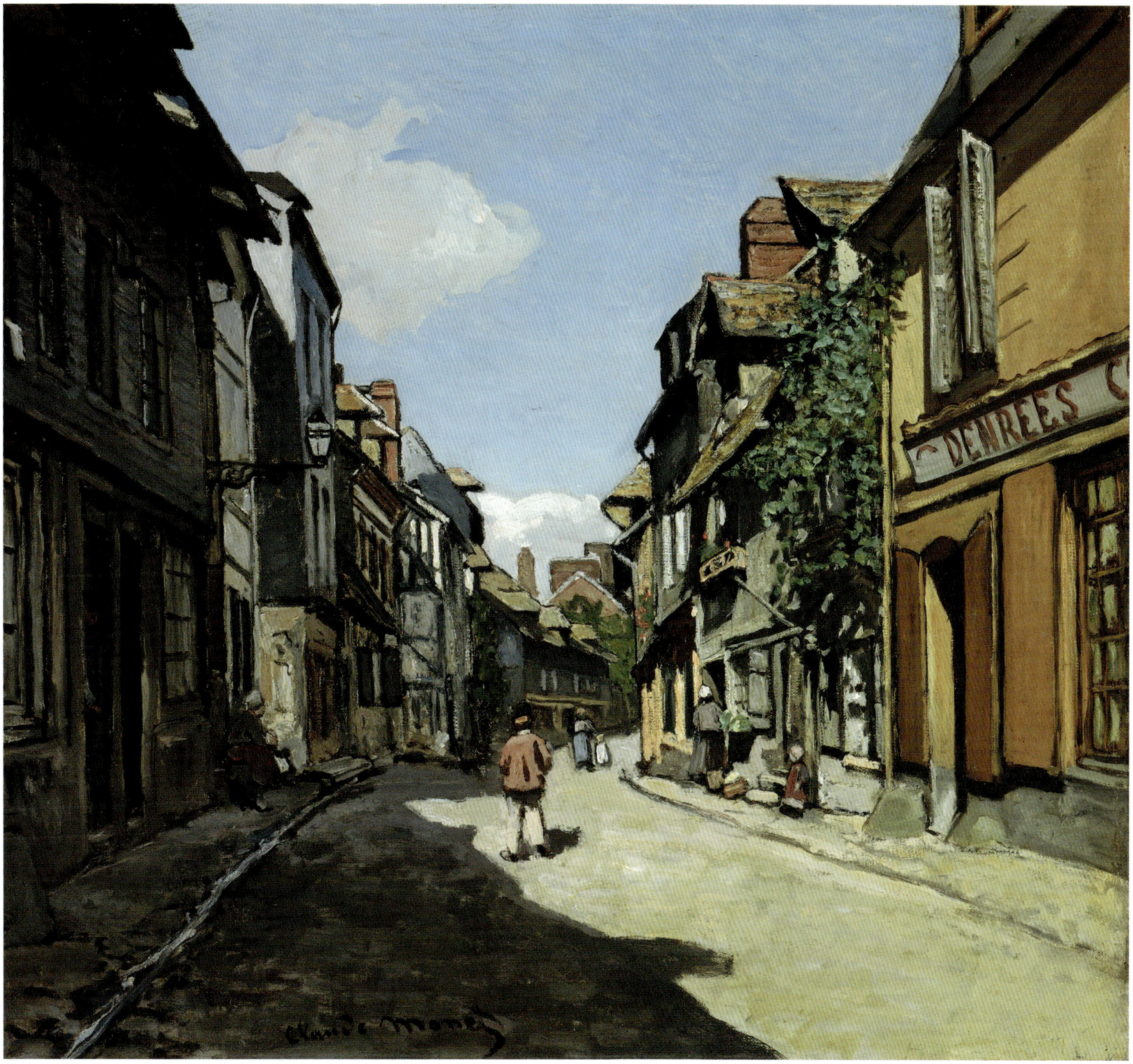

13

Claude Monet

Rue de la Bavole, Honfleur c1864

oil on canvas, 55.9 x 61 cm
Museum of Fine Arts, Boston,
bequest of John T Spaulding
48.580

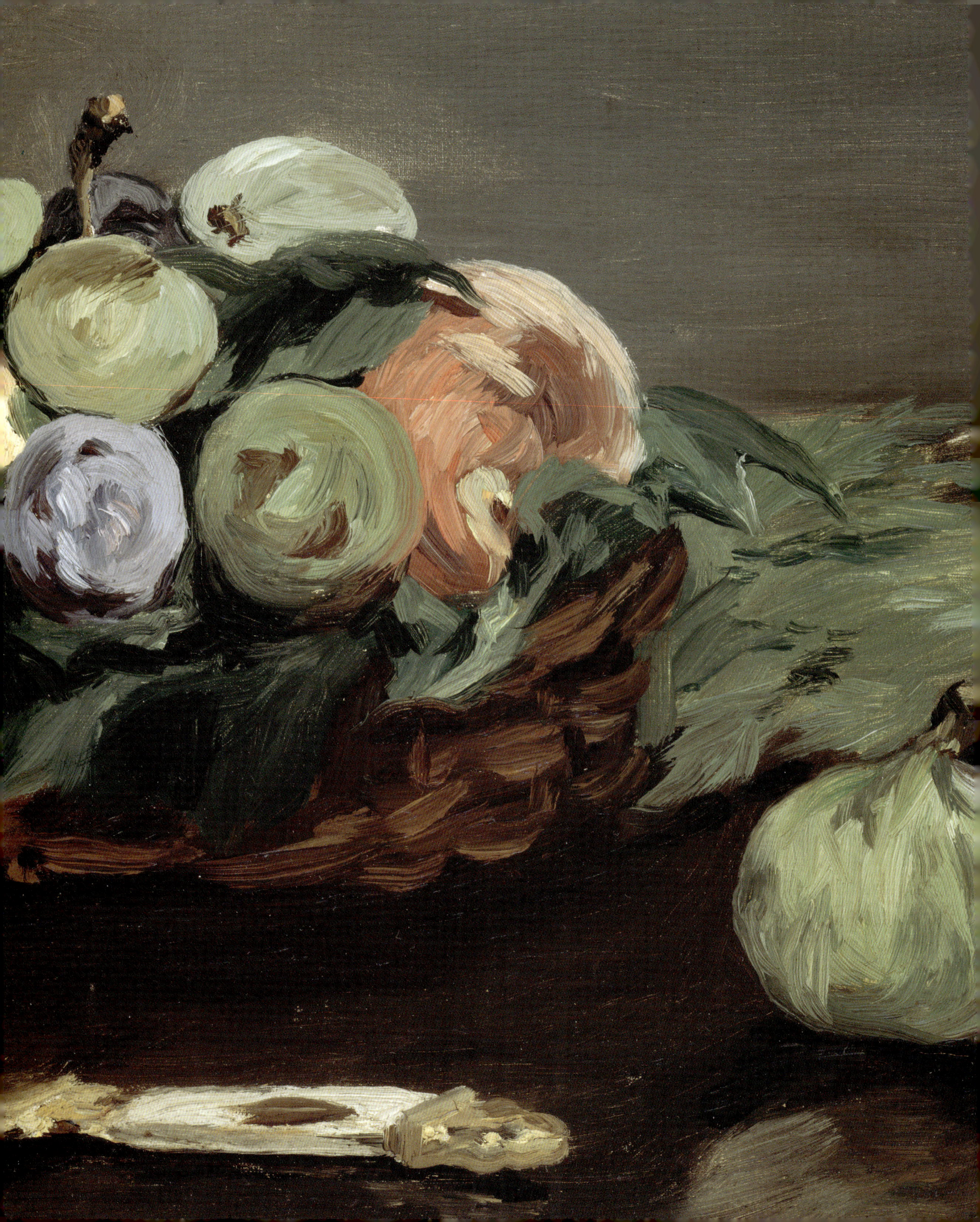

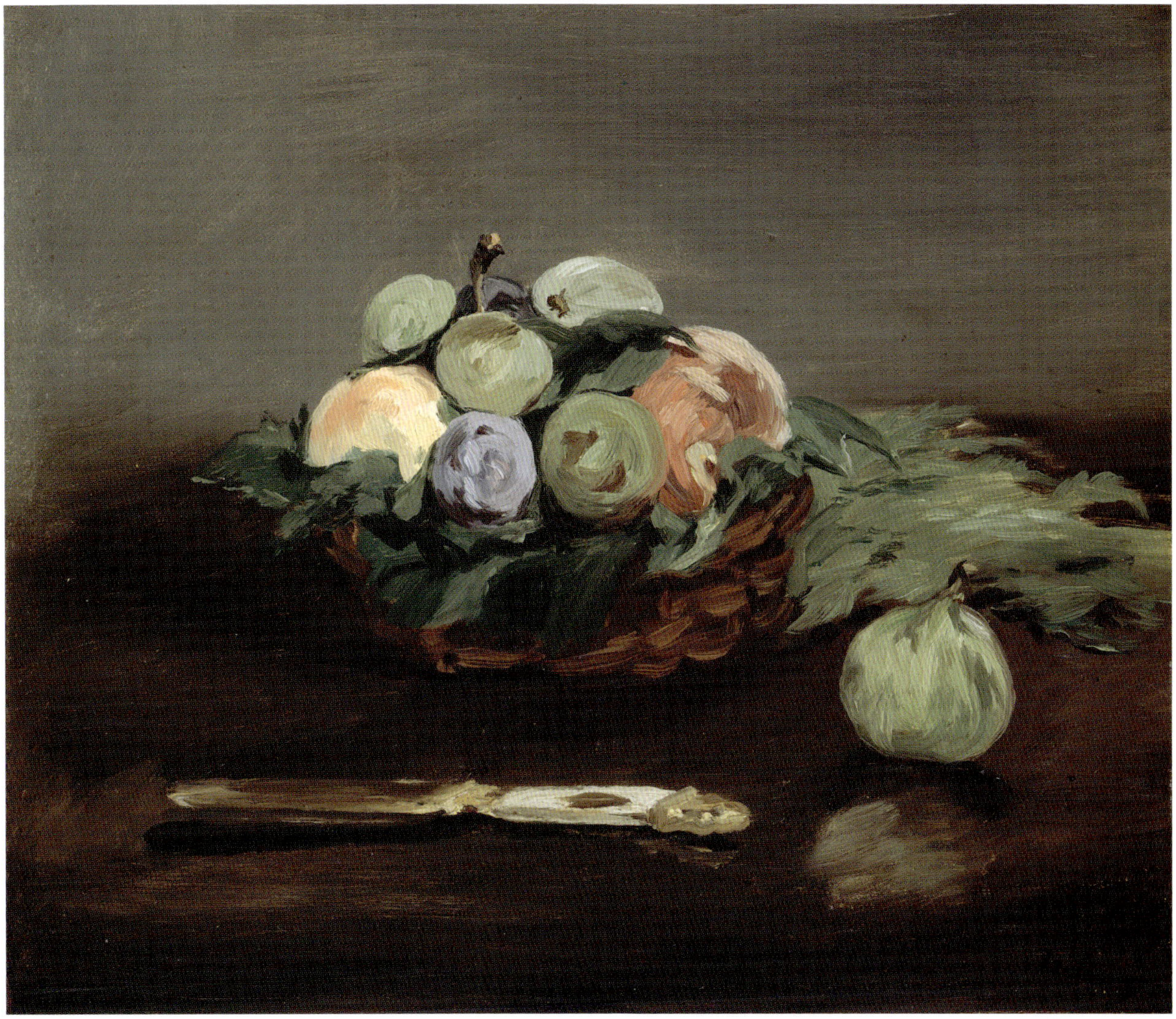

14

Edouard Manet

Basket of fruit c1864

oil on canvas, 37.8 x 44.4 cm
Museum of Fine Arts, Boston,
bequest of John T Spaulding
48.576

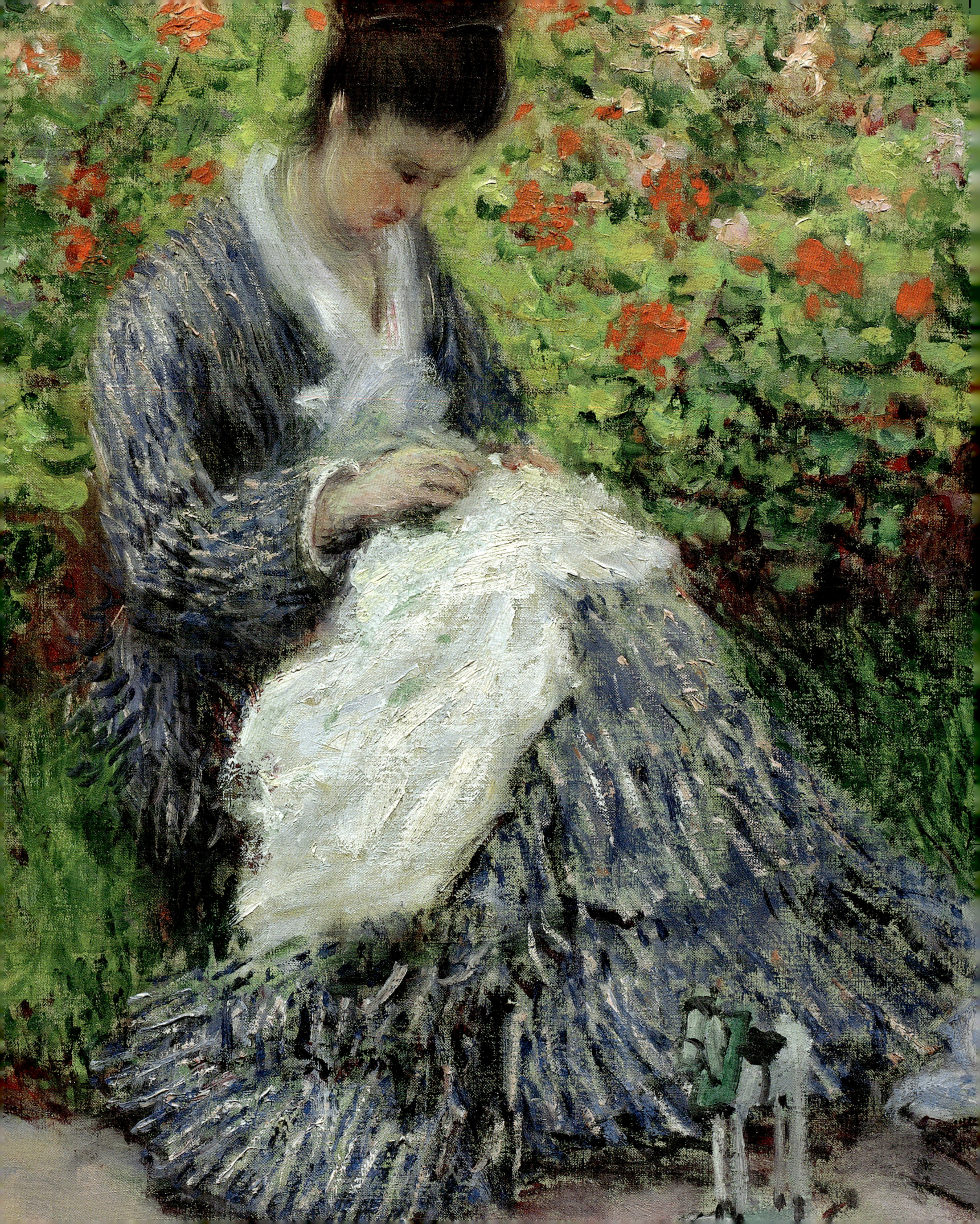

MONET AND EARLY IMPRESSIONISM

Subsequent to their plein-air experiments on the banks of the Seine in 1869, Monet and Renoir pursued tracks that intersected at times; for instance, they painted again side by side, at a farm in Argenteuil in 1873, and in the following year at a riverside dock in the same town during preparations for a regatta.[1] Although they were frequently in each other's company and working in tandem, their methods of painting had remained distinct. Monet had, for instance, evolved a fluid sketch style that he would use, in 1872, to paint the study with the famous title *Impression: sunrise* (fig 2). His *Ships in a harbour* (fig 13), thought to date from a year later, employs the same thin, liquid application of paint and sinuous treatment of the reflections of forms on water, although without the amorphous treatment of the boats, steeped in the surrounding atmosphere, which made *Impression: sunrise* a *succès de scandale* at the first Impressionist exhibition in 1874.

By the time of that first exhibition, Monet was fully committed to an art of observation, recording his impressions of natural effects under varying conditions of light, as occasioned by season, weather and time of day. Over the winter of 1874–75, for instance, he painted a series of views of the town of Argenteuil in the snow. Among them were *Snow at Argenteuil* (cat 15) and *Boulevard Saint-Denis, Argenteuil, in winter* (see cat 36). Braving the elements, Monet seems to have set up his easel to lay in the initial stages of the compositions, at the very least. His goal was to capture the hue and the tonality of the landscape covered with snow – what artists called an *effet de neige* or 'snow effect' – which was so different from the light of spring, summer or autumn. In *Snow at Argenteuil*, Monet was intent on capturing the almost grisaille colouration of the landscape; the sky, trees, buildings and people are rendered in varying tones of white, grey or near black, relieved only by a few subtle strokes of green to suggest grass peeking through the fallen snow at lower right. Another painting was made from the same vantage point – perhaps on the following day, as the snow had ceased to fall and the landscape was lit by brilliant sun.[2] In *Snow at Argenteuil*, however, the landscape is covered with cloud. Could it be that Monet actually painted the canvas while snowflakes fell? If so, he probably worked under some sort of cover. The tiny flickering strokes of pure white that are selectively positioned over parts of the canvas to suggest how falling snow is perceived by the eye must surely have been applied later in the studio.

Probably the next summer, Monet positioned himself in a field near Argenteuil to paint *Meadow with poplars* (cat 16), an archetypal image of a sunlit landscape in rural France. At the horizon, a band of blue hills rises; against this deep background, mounds and stacks of hay have been constructed, indicating that the harvest of grasses has begun. But in the foreground, a sweeping swathe of field is still in flower. Monet indicates the tones of the flowers with tiny strokes of white, lavender blue and the red of corn poppies. He places in the middle of this foliage the form of a young boy, clad in a white shirt and a bright straw hat, who gives a sense of scale to the field and gazes back at the painter. Two rows of poplar trees rise at left, their outlines growing ever more indistinct as they recede into the distance. The sky is painted with Monet's most brilliant blue, and billowing clouds are indicated by broad strokes of pure white paint against the blue ground. Like *Snow at Argenteuil*, this view of a meadow is apparently a straightforward record of the artist's impression of a particular landscape at a given time. And in truth, both images may have resulted from real confrontations of the landscape on the painter's part.

Similar pictorial strategies of immediacy were called into play in such works as Renoir's *Woman with a parasol and small child on a sunlit hillside* (cat 19, about 1874–76) and Monet's *Camille Monet and a child in the artist's garden in Argenteuil* (cat 20, dated 1875). It has been suggested that not only Monet's canvas but also Renoir's painting may represent Camille Doncieux, Monet's wife; whether a golden-haired child shown in both paintings might be the same person is not clear (the child does not correspond in age to either of the couple's children).[3] Renoir seems to be intent on suggesting through the application of his paint the immediacy of his impression

Claude Monet *Camille Monet and a child in the artist's garden in Argenteuil* 1875 (detail), cat 20

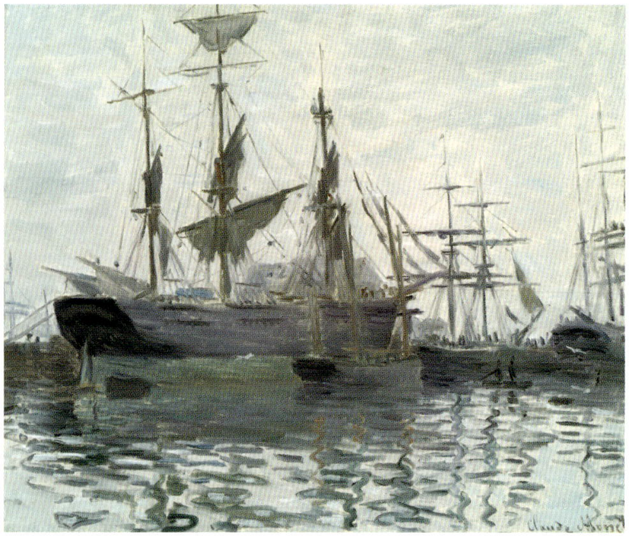

fig 13
Claude Monet
Ships in a harbour 1873
oil on canvas, 49.8 x 61 cm
Museum of Fine Arts, Boston,
Denman Waldo Ross Collection
06.117

of the scene, painting wet into wet, blending colours not only on the palette but on the canvas. The woman's white dress is shot through with passages of grey, black and pink, the latter harmonising with the lining of her parasol and with the clothing of the child walking away from her in the middle ground. Subtly blending these strokes – as he blends the tones of deep green, yellow and pink in the surrounding grasses – Renoir convinces the viewer of the truth of his observation. The evident speed of execution of the painting reinforces the sense of a fleeting moment.

Where Renoir uses feathery strokes of paint blended into one another to suggest the play of reflected light, Monet, in his image of his wife with a child, employs a careful juxtaposition of discrete patches of colour. In depicting the floral background, for instance – a close-up view of the bed of roses or geraniums that formed one of the central features in the artist's Argenteuil garden – Monet placed tiny strokes of colour side by side, occasionally overlapping or layering on top of other strokes, but rarely blending together in Renoir's manner. While painstaking in its execution, the effect of the massing of small independent marks is as visually exciting as Renoir's; the flowers behind Camille seem to flutter, in contrast to the quiet concentration of her pose and that of the child beside her, who has put aside a toy horse to take up a book.

Like Monet and Renoir, Alfred Sisley and Camille Pissarro were determined, in the middle years of the 1870s, to advance the cause of 'the New Painting', as Edmond Duranty described the nascent Impressionist movement in 1876.[4] Pissarro's *Pontoise, the road to Gisors in winter*, from 1873 (cat 21), shows the distance that early Impressionism had travelled from the tight and crisp manner of Monet's *Rue de la Bavole, Honfleur* a decade earlier. Softening the contours of the buildings that line the falling road, Pissarro does not mix his paint in Renoir's manner, nor juxtapose small strokes of paint as Monet does. Instead, he uses a square brush to drag strokes of paint over and against one another, creating staccato rhythms of shorthand brushstrokes that convey the cold, wet atmosphere of a winter morning. Horizontal strokes suggest the pattern of cobblestones on the street and sidewalk, or melting snow on a shingled roof; vertical strokes describe windows, shutters and chimneys; broader patches of paint represent unswept snow or the façade of a building. The citizens of the town are indicated with the minimum of precision – each stick-like figure is composed of only a few strokes of paint. Using a palette of greys, browns and whites every bit as restrained as Monet's in *Snow at Argenteuil*, Pissarro chooses to enliven the composition with small accents of colour, which go almost unnoticed: little strokes of blue indicate an exposed stone on the corner of a building, but equally the blue shirt of a man who drags a cart uphill at the centre of the canvas. A patch of green, at left, depicts the covering of another cart.

Pissarro, who made a specialty of painting unprepossessing rural or village landscapes, showed a number of snow scenes at the Impressionist exhibitions that began in 1874. His colleague Sisley chose to exhibit that year a view of the pumping station on the Seine at the town of Marly, built in the 1850s to replace an earlier waterworks constructed there in the time of Louis XIV. The site – filled with royal associations but conspicuously unpicturesque – evidently held a strong appeal for Sisley, for he painted seven views of it within a few years.[5] *Waterworks at Marly* (cat 22) is thought to have been painted in 1876 – apparently in autumn, given the colour of the foliage in the background, and thus probably after the Impressionist exhibition of that year, where a winter view of the basin was exhibited.[6] Sisley showed in the 1870s a marked preference for views that incorporated water, in the form of rivers, pools or even flooded streets, as seen in his series recording the inundation at Port-Marly in 1876.[7] Like Monet and Renoir in their paintings of the bathing place at La Grenouillère in 1869, Sisley uses an expanse of water in the foreground of *Waterworks at Marly* to showcase his ability to render the effect of light on a moving surface. Reflecting the building, the screen of trees at centre and the sky above, the surface of the water – punctuated, at right, by a geometric structure

fig 14
Edgar Degas
At the races in the countryside 1869
oil on canvas, 36.5 x 56 cm
Museum of Fine Arts, Boston,
1931 Purchase Fund
26.790

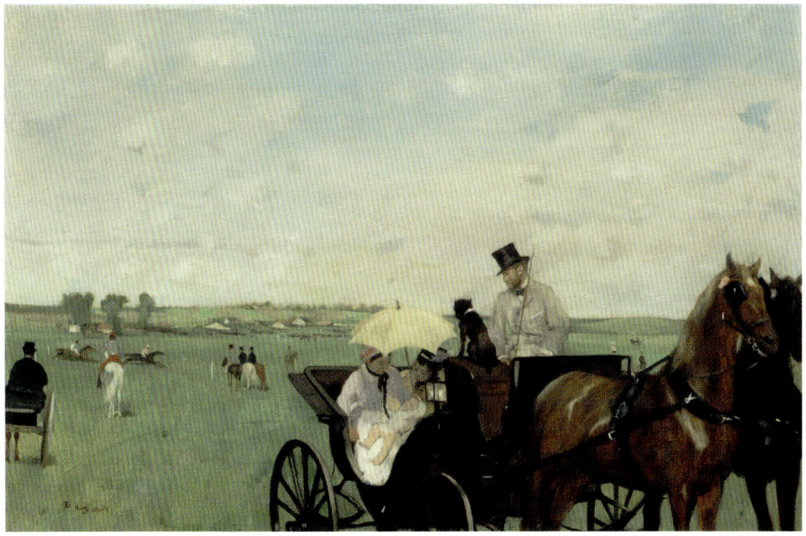

built of dark wood – becomes a changing mirror. Sisley wants the viewer to appreciate his ability to capture that sense of transience in paint on canvas.

Monet, Renoir, Pissarro and Sisley were joined in the early Impressionist exhibitions by a number of other artists. Some of them, like Berthe Morisot, Manet's sister-in-law, contributed broadly brushed studies of landscape that were sometimes more radical than the inventions of Monet or Renoir.[8] Paul Cézanne participated in the first exhibition, in 1874, notably with a group of landscapes painted in Auvers-sur-Oise, where he worked in the company of Pissarro from 1872 to 1874. He did not reappear in 1876 in the second exhibition, but in 1877 he submitted still lifes and a group of landscapes described in the catalogue of the show as *études d'après nature* – studies from nature. Also present in 1877, though not listed in the catalogue, was a scene of boaters, fishermen and tourists along a riverbank, which is, roughly, the subject of Cézanne's *The pond* (cat 18).[9] Far from being a study from nature, *The pond* is evidently the product of the artist's imagination, derived from his observation of nature, certainly, but composed from memory in the studio. Scholars have pointed to the enigmatic narrative, which parallels the disjointed or distorted perspective of the scene. As one has commented, the 'unsatisfactory attempt to read a story into the painting demonstrates how beside the point such a narrative is'; the author goes on to note that the point of the painting may truly be the way in which 'Cézanne's brushstrokes here have moved beyond description or careful delineation of form to become almost independent marks'.[10]

And what of Degas, who was so different from Monet – the artist seen by Duranty as the other side of the Impressionist coin, concerned with seizing gesture, pose and arresting movement rather than conveying a sense of windblown landscape? Degas would become known for his scenes of Parisian life – laundresses, dancers and bathers, for instance. He sent to the first Impressionist show a landscape painted around 1869 inspired by visits to an informal racecourse near the Normandy home of his friends the Valpinçons – who occupy the carriage in the foreground (fig 14). Here, as in his *Racehorses at Longchamp* (cat 17) painted a few years later, Degas masterfully records the effect of landscape, effortlessly employing patches or swathes of colour to depict the scattered clouds of Normandy near the sea, or the overcast sky of the Parisian suburbs, using short vertical strokes of green to suggest the texture of turf. But within these naturalistic surroundings Degas is careful to pose his figures exactly, and to model them with great precision. X-rays of *Racehorses at Longchamp* reveal that Degas moved whole segments of the composition in the course of his work.

By the end of the 1870s, Monet had become the leader of the landscape camp of Impressionism, as Degas had become the leader of the figure painters. As the decade turned, a schism would evolve between the two groups, leading to Monet's eventual defection from the Impressionist exhibitions in 1880 and, in turn, to Degas's refusal to exhibit in the 1882 show. In 1882, Monet, Renoir and Sisley rejoined Pissarro and Morisot, who had continued to exhibit. Their return to the fold was seen as a triumph for the Impressionist landscape.

1 See Colin B Bailey et al, *Renoir landscapes, 1865–1883*, exh cat, National Gallery, London and Yale University Press, New Haven, Connecticut 2007, cats 20, 21 and 23
2 This painting, W 349, is in the collection of Marion and Henry Bloch of Kansas City, Missouri
3 See John Zarobell in Bailey et al 2007, pp 152–53
4 See Moffett et al 1986 for a translation of Duranty's text and for articles on each of the eight Impressionist exhibitions
5 See Fronia E Wissman in George T M Shackelford, Fronia E Wissman et al, *Impressions of light: the French landscape from Corot to Monet*, exh cat, MFA Publications, Boston 2002, p 156
6 Another view of the pumping station was shown in 1874. See Berson 1996, pp 29, 64
7 See Richard Shone, *Sisley*, Phaidon, London and Harry N Abrams, New York 1992, pp 103–07
8 See Berson 1996, pp 39–41
9 For Cézanne's submissions in 1874 and 1877, see Berson 1996, pp 21–22, 86–89
10 See Wissman in Shackelford, Wissman et al 2002, p 174

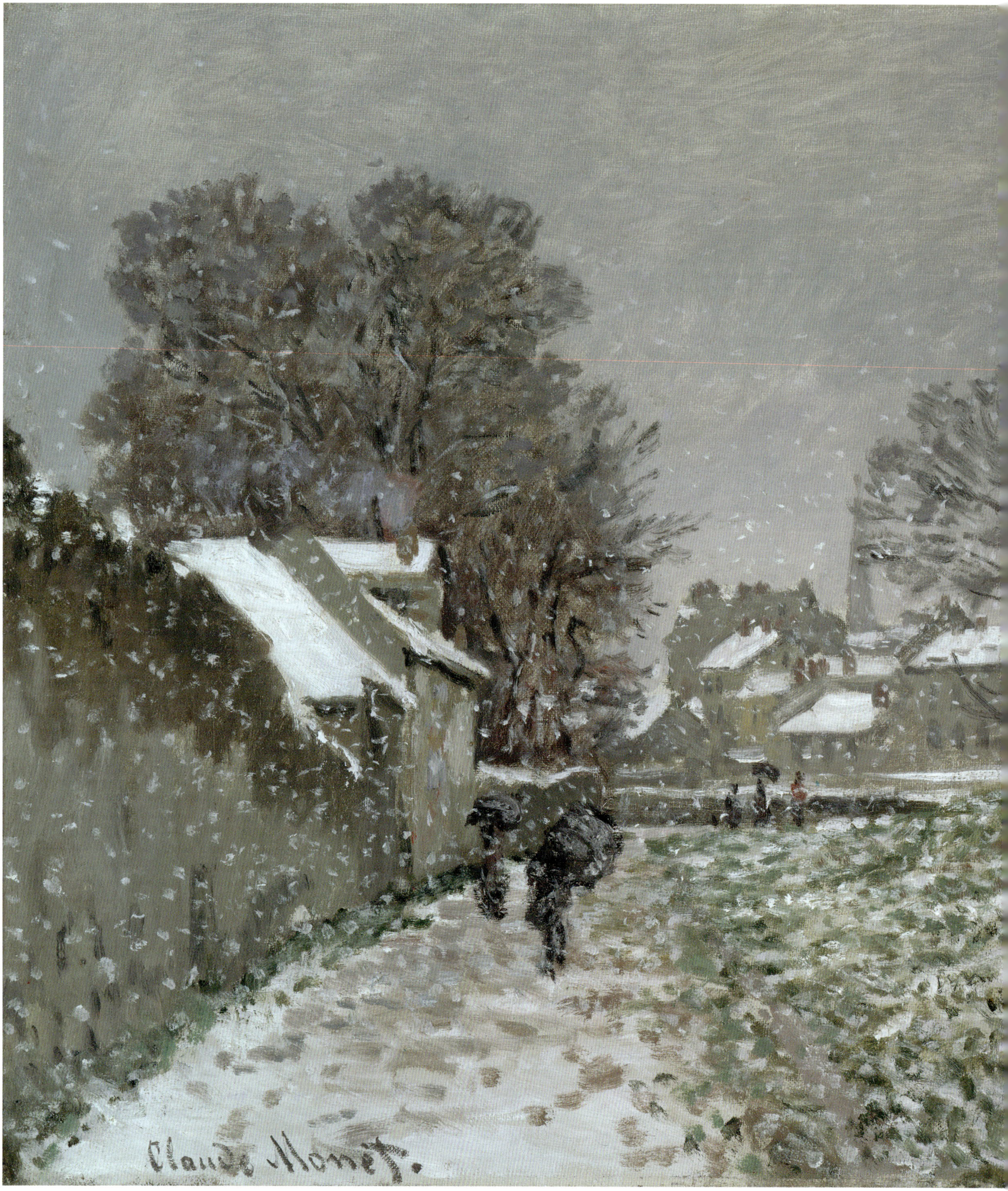
Claude Monet.

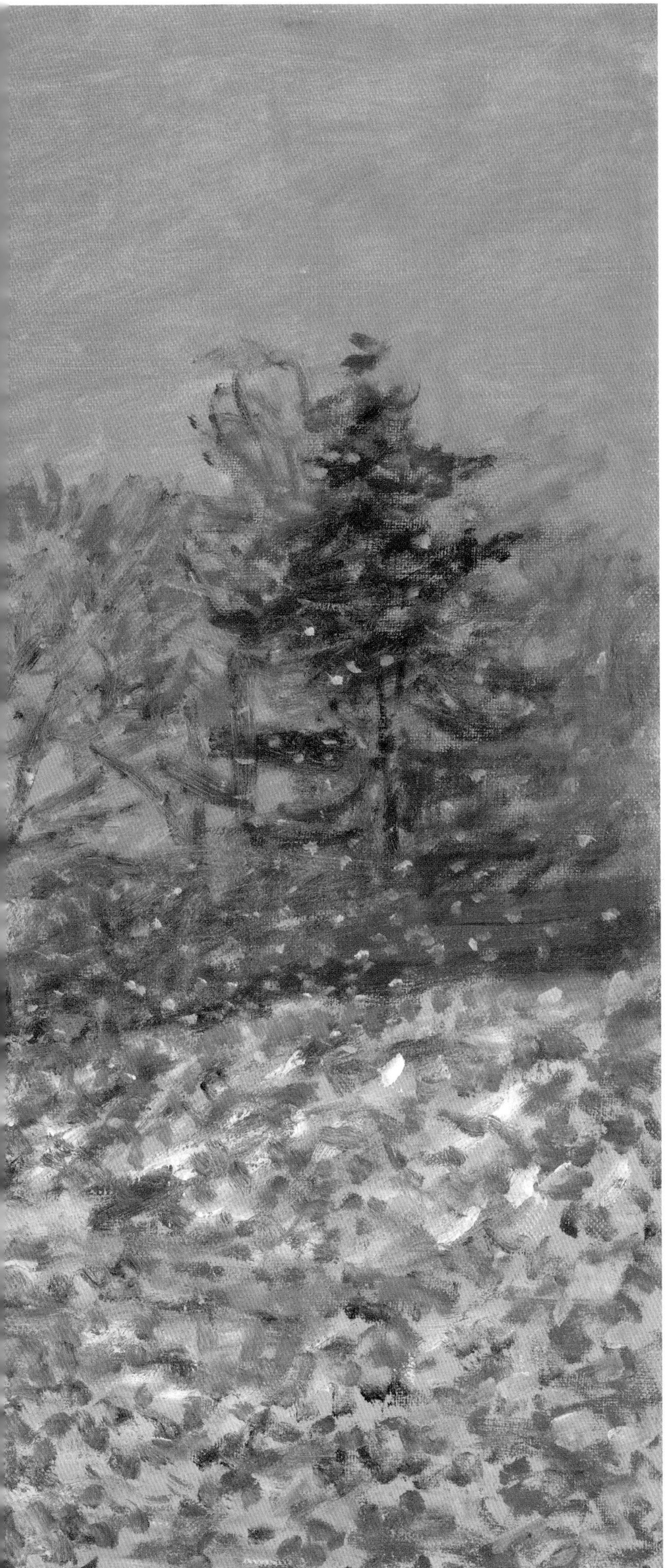

15

Claude Monet
Snow at Argenteuil c1874
oil on canvas, 54.6 x 73.7 cm
Museum of Fine Arts, Boston,
bequest of Anna Perkins Rogers
21.1329

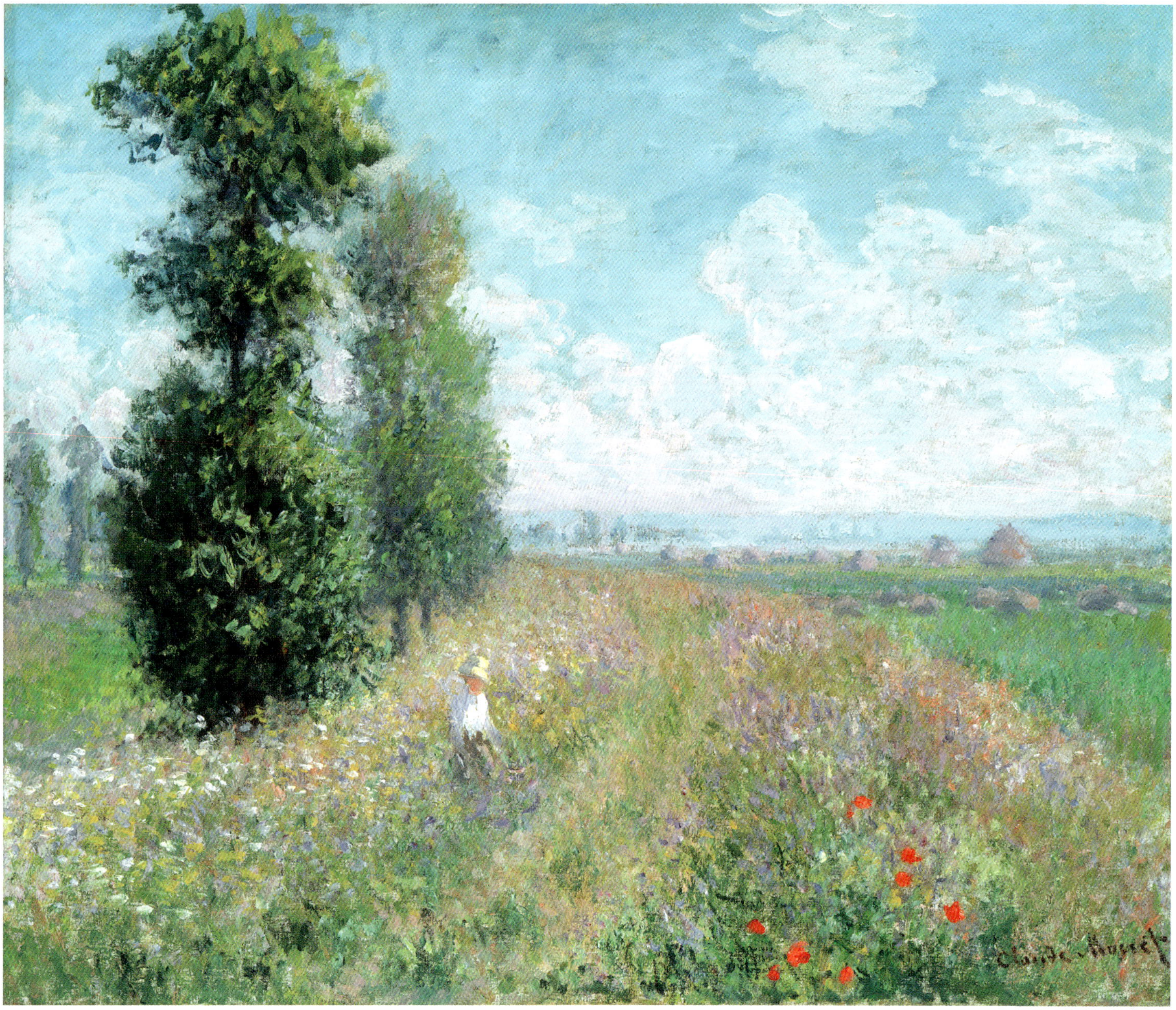

16

Claude Monet
Meadow with poplars c1875

oil on canvas, 54.6 x 65.4 cm
Museum of Fine Arts, Boston,
bequest of David P Kimball in memory
of his wife Clara Bertram Kimball
23.505

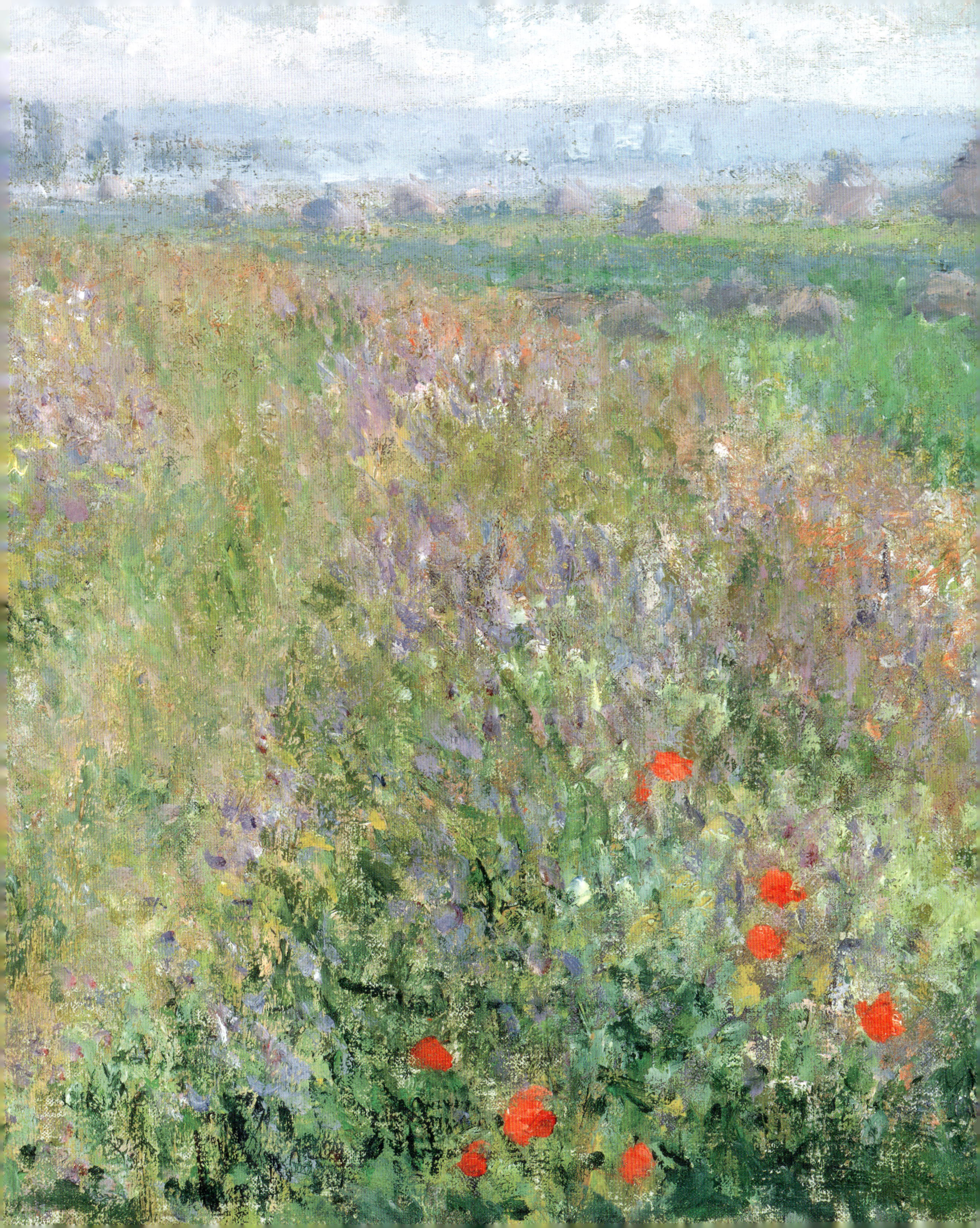

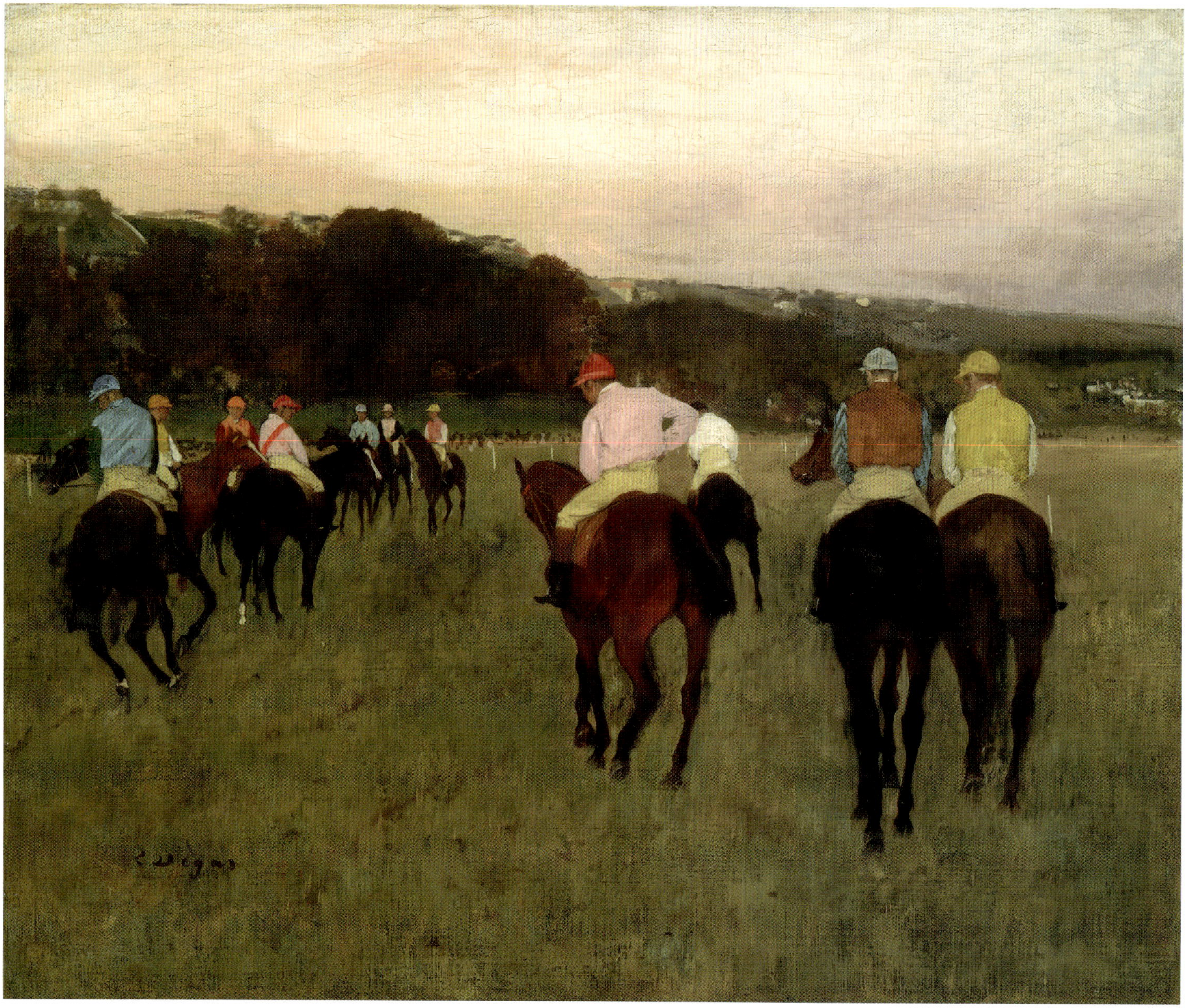

17

Edgar Degas
Racehorses at Longchamp 1871
(possibly reworked in 1874)

oil on canvas, 34 x 41.9 cm
Museum of Fine Arts, Boston,
S A Denio Collection – Sylvanus Adams
Denio Fund and general income
03.1034

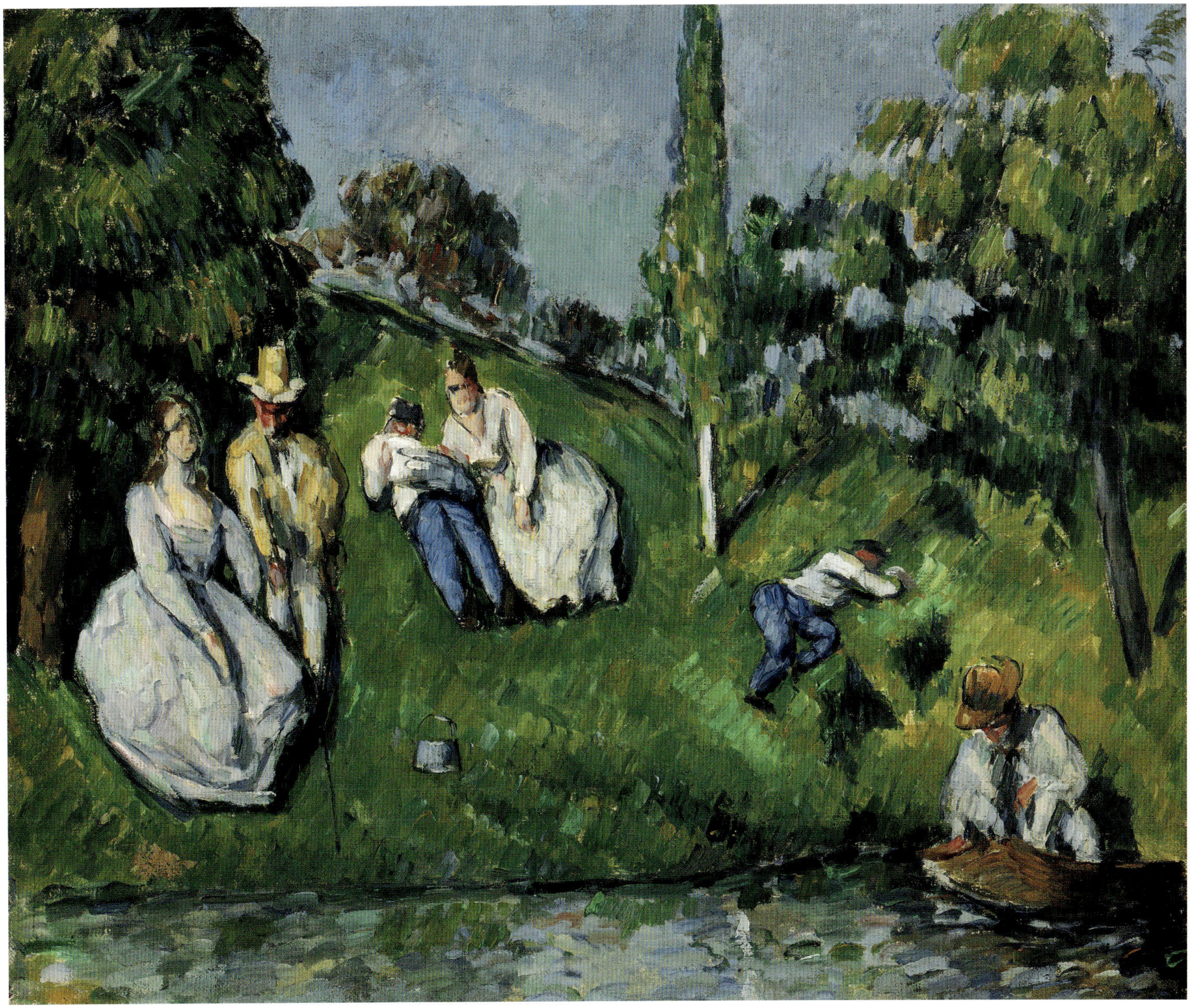

18

Paul Cézanne

The pond c1877–79

oil on canvas, 47 x 56.2 cm
Museum of Fine Arts, Boston,
Tompkins Collection –
Arthur Gordon Tompkins Fund
48.244

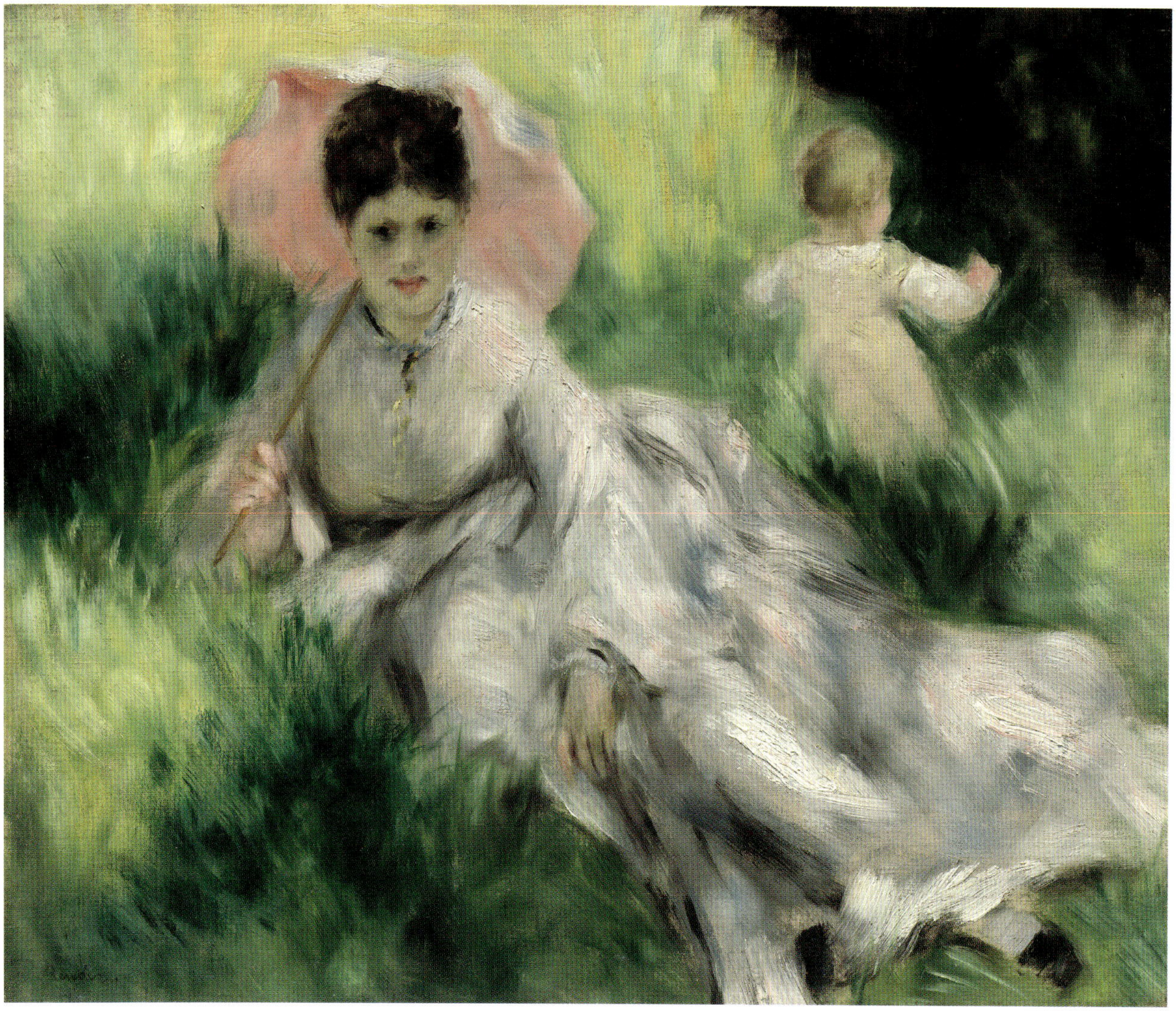

19

Pierre-Auguste Renoir
Woman with a parasol and small child on a sunlit hillside c1874–76

oil on canvas, 47 x 56.2 cm
Museum of Fine Arts, Boston,
bequest of John T Spaulding
48.593

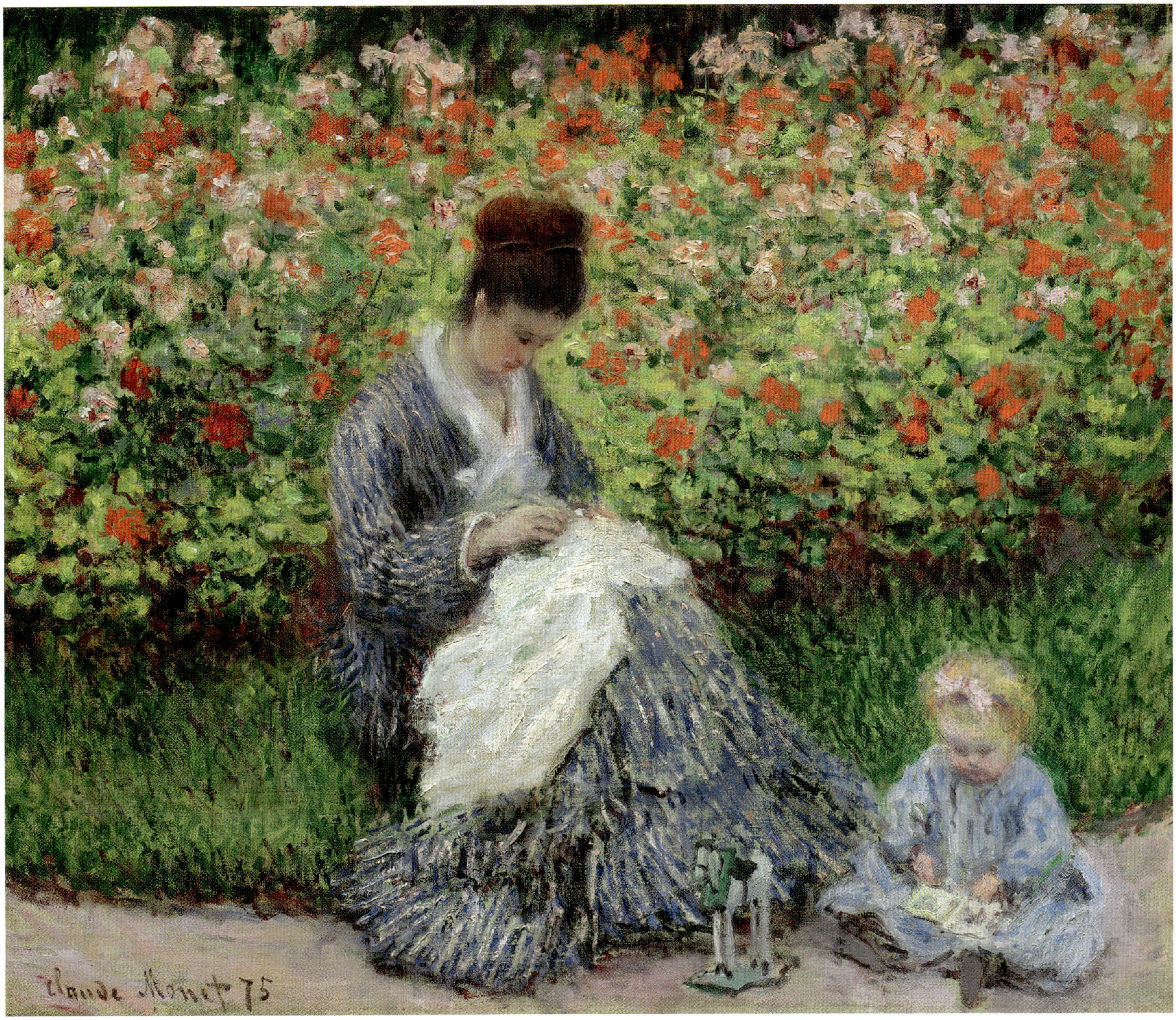

20
Claude Monet
Camille Monet and a child
in the artist's garden in Argenteuil 1875
oil on canvas, 55.3 x 64.7 cm
Museum of Fine Arts, Boston, anonymous gift
in memory of Mr and Mrs Edwin S Webster
1976.833

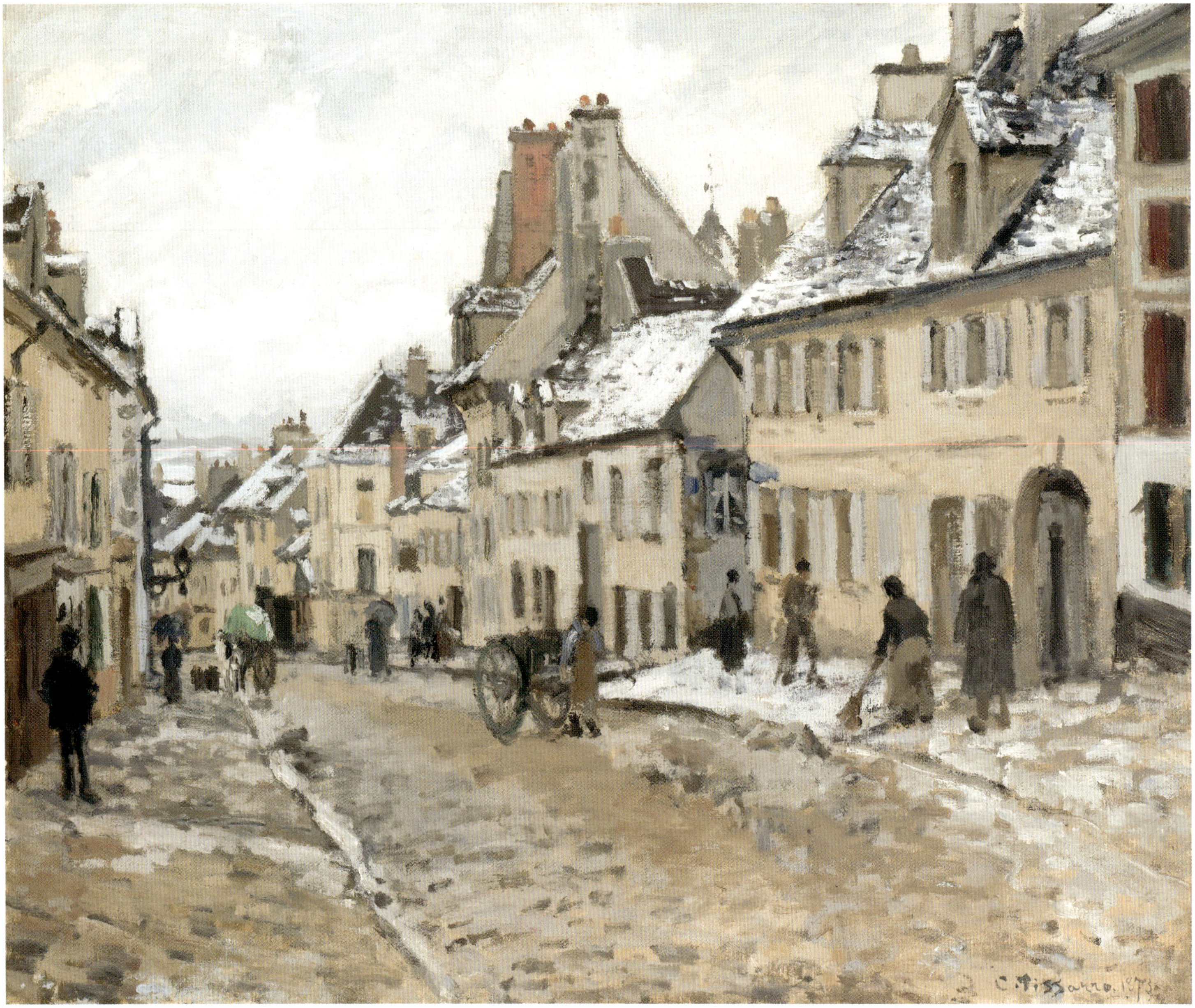

21

Camille Pissarro

Pontoise, the road to Gisors in winter 1873

oil on canvas, 59.7 x 73.7 cm
Museum of Fine Arts, Boston,
bequest of John T Spaulding
48.587

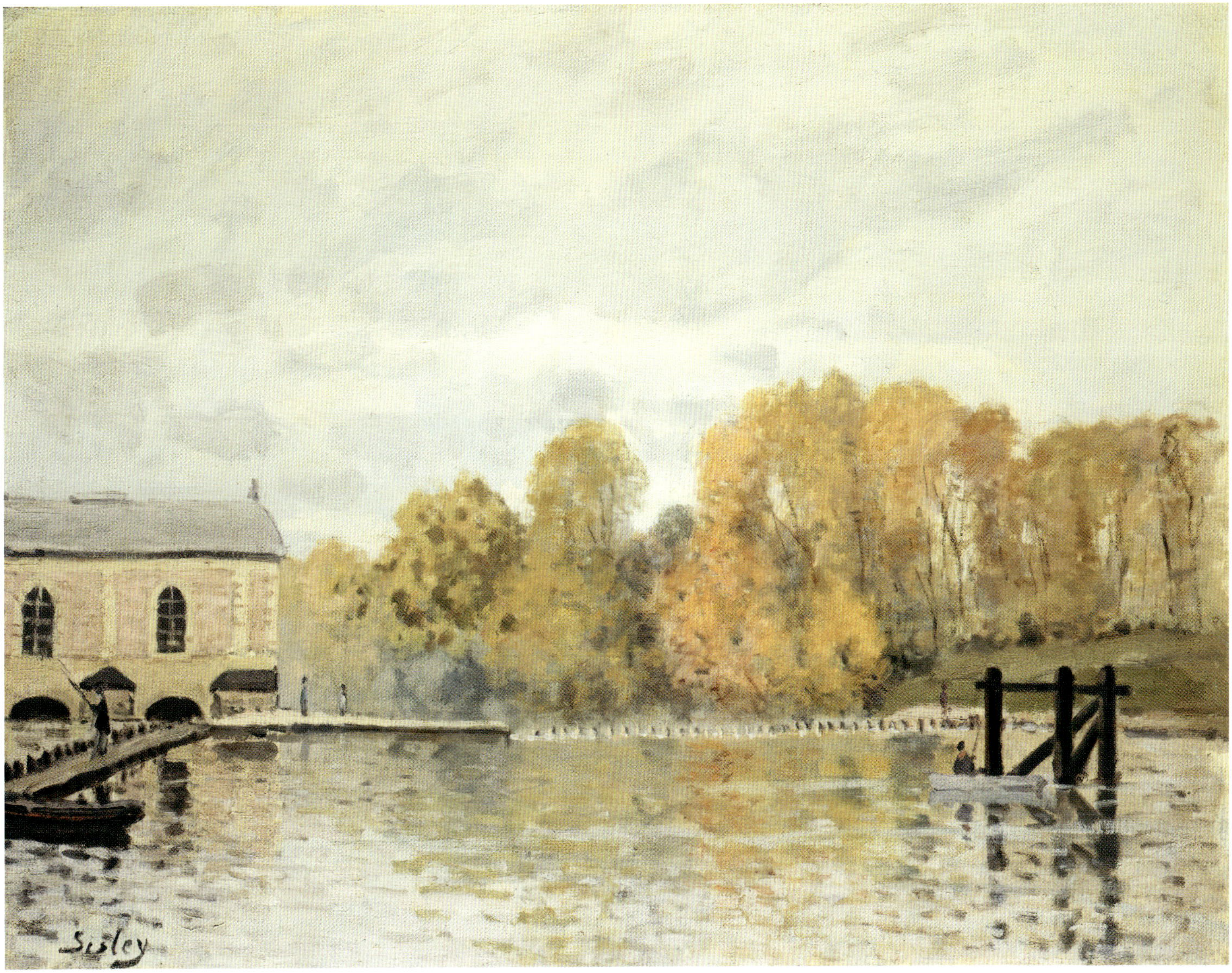

22

Alfred Sisley

Waterworks at Marly c1876

oil on canvas, 46.5 x 61.8 cm
Museum of Fine Arts, Boston,
gift of Miss Olive Simes
45.662

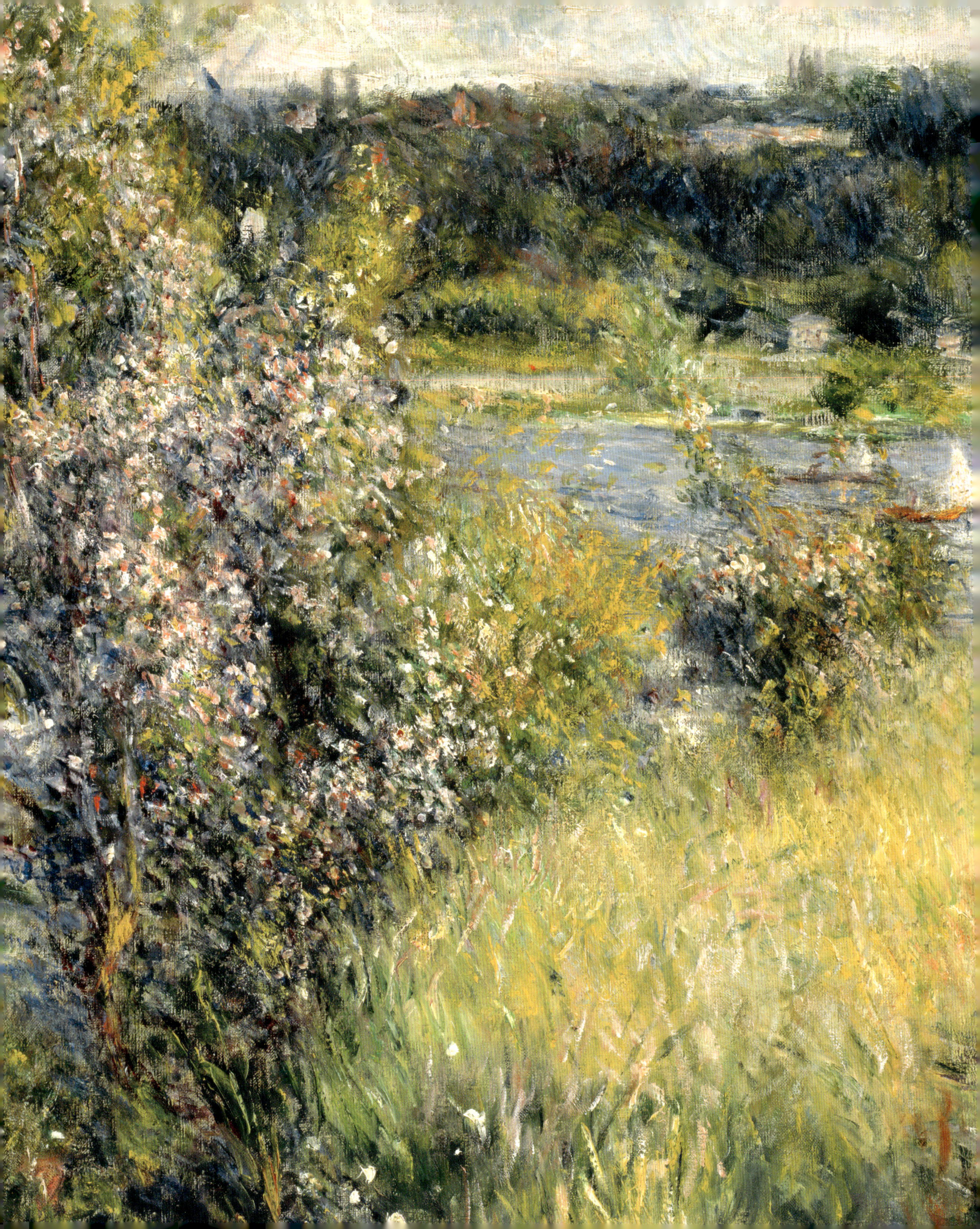

MONET AND THE TRIUMPH OF IMPRESSIONISM: THE 1880s

At the end of the summer of 1878, Monet and his family moved from Paris, where they had briefly resettled after leaving Argenteuil, to the village of Vétheuil, down the Seine and near the border of Normandy. There they set up housekeeping with members of the family of Ernest Hoschedé, a friend of Monet's and a collector of his works. The two families remained together thereafter; following Camille Monet's death in 1879, Alice Hoschedé, her husband absent in Paris, became Monet's companion.

Vétheuil became the locus of or the vantage point for most of Monet's paintings (such as *Vétheuil*, cat 30) in the years 1878–80. His *Seine at Lavacourt* (fig 15), showing the village of Lavacourt on the bank of the river opposite Vétheuil, with the river in the foreground and a willow-covered island midstream, was painted in 1878. It is probably the first of some seven views taken from this location in 1878 and 1879, which culminate in an eighth version of the subject, a large painting that Monet submitted to the Salon in 1880.[1] The painter was preoccupied with images of the river that flowed just below his garden, painting it at all hours of the day, from both banks, and in varying conditions of weather – including in a series of paintings of the frozen river breaking up, begun in early 1880.

It was in September 1880 that Monet returned to Normandy to visit his brother Léon, who took him to the seaside town of Petites Dalles, where the painter embarked on a series of cliff views, such as *Rough weather at Etretat* (cat 23), that announced one of his major themes for the coming decade. *Cliffs of the Petites Dalles* (fig 5) may be the first of these to be completed. Seen from the beach, the cliffs undulate in the distance, red and white in the middle ground, growing bluer as they recede towards the horizon; in the foreground, a fence-like breakwater protects the beach, on which several tourists stand and sit as if to give scale to the immense cliffs beyond them.

Monet returned to the Normandy coast in 1881 and 1882, embarking on such works as *Seacoast at Trouville* (cat 38) of 1881 and the next year's *Road at La Cavée, Pourville* (fig 6) and *Fisherman's cottage on the cliffs at Varengeville* (cat 24). Monet had painted in this part of Normandy in the 1860s and 1870s (see cat 13). His family had a home in Saint-Adresse, near Le Havre and Honfleur, where he had worked on paintings of seaside leisure and labour; in 1870, before fleeing to England at the outbreak of the Franco-Prussian War, he had depicted the fashionable boardwalk of Trouville (a seaside resort just to the west of Honfleur, near the mouth of the Seine) lined with hotels, as well as scenes of Camille and companions on the beach. A decade later, however, he avoided the summer crowds, painting at the less hospitable Fécamp (to the northeast of the mouth of the river) in the early spring and returning to Trouville only in late August or early September of 1881. *Seacoast at Trouville* is one of four paintings executed during that short trip. While it does not show the human presence of seaside life, it does, in fact, have a protagonist: the wind-blown tree, its trunk deformed by the power of the elements, may stand in, as some critics have suggested, for the artist himself, who had been battered by the wind and rain during his Trouville campaign. 'The continuing bad weather having prevented me from doing any kind of work, I have been forced to come back and I return empty-handed', he wrote to Durand-Ruel in mid-September 1881.[2]

By February 1882, Monet had returned to the coast, settling first in Dieppe, to the northeast, and then moving on to the village of Pourville, to the west, which was to become the centre of his spring campaign. From there he wrote to his companion Alice: 'One could not be any closer to the sea than I am, on the shingle itself, and the waves beat at the foot of the house.'[3] Exploring the cliff walks at Pourville and at neighbouring Varengeville, Monet discovered a motif that was to be one of his favourites: a customs agent's watch station built during the reign of Napoleon I at the edge of the cliff as a lookout for smugglers over the English Channel. This is the central motif of *Fisherman's cottage on the cliffs at*

Pierre-Auguste Renoir *The Seine at Chatou* 1881 (detail), cat 28

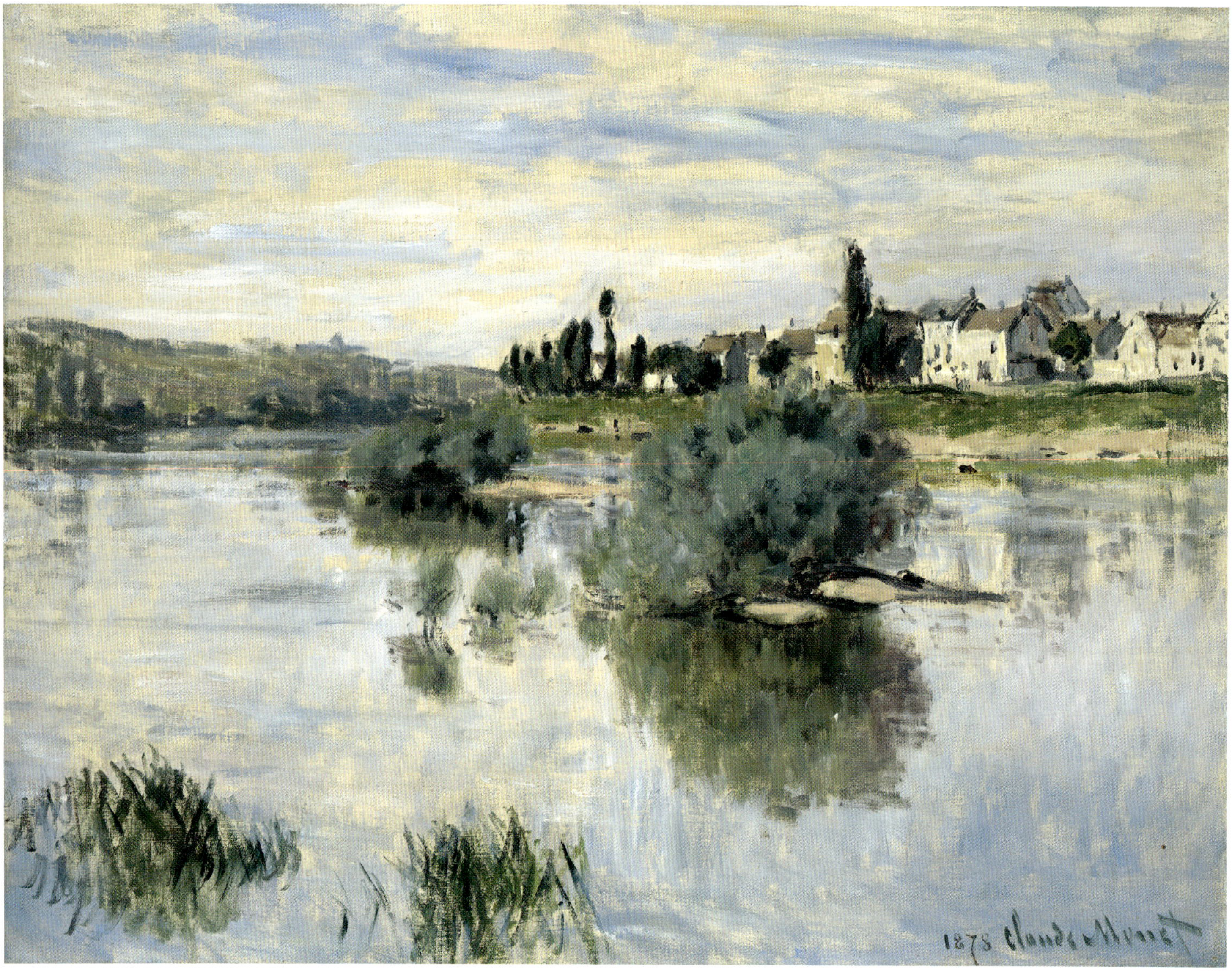
1878 Claude Monet

fig 15
Claude Monet
The Seine at Lavacourt 1878
oil on canvas, 56 x 73.7 cm
Scott M Black Collection

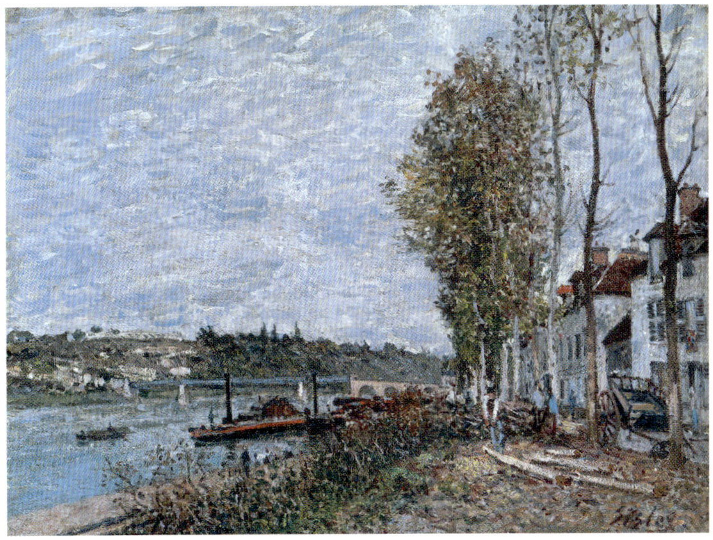

fig 16
Alfred Sisley
Overcast day at Saint-Mammès c1880
oil on canvas, 54.9 x 74 cm
Museum of Fine Arts, Boston,
Juliana Cheney Edwards Collection
39.679

Varengeville; Daniel Wildenstein notes that Monet used the titles *Cabane des douaniers* (customs agents' hut) and *Maison du pêcheur* (fisherman's house) interchangeably for this picture; in fact, a fisherman did live in the cottage, which could be reached by a path through the cliff vegetation like the one recorded in *Road at La Cavée, Pourville*.

Of the 14 paintings that Monet devoted to this motif in 1882, this one gives the cabin unusual prominence. First of all, the cottage is far larger, in comparison to the size of the composition, than in any other work in the series. In each of the other works, moreover, the cabin is always seen against the sea or the land – the horizon line is placed above its tallest point, relegating the building to a corner or an edge of the picture space. In the MFA's *Fisherman's cottage*, however, the house stands high against the horizon and seems to dominate or survey the sea below it, which acts, with the surrounding vegetation, as a foil of blue and green against the glowing reds, oranges and pinks of the structure's masonry and its tile roof.

While Monet was at work on the Normandy coast in 1882, the seventh exhibition of independent artists – the Impressionists – was being organised in Paris. Initially reluctant to participate, Monet finally assented, but due to his absence it was Durand-Ruel who selected some 35 works from his stock to represent the painter. Among the works on view were several from the Normandy campaigns of 1880 and 1881, perhaps including *Cliffs of the Petites Dalles* and *Seacoast at Trouville*.[4] Renoir also was indisposed, suffering from pneumonia, and so Durand-Ruel chose works for him, too, including not only his magnificent *Luncheon of the boating party* (Phillips Collection, Washington) but also, most probably, *The Seine at Chatou* (cat 28).[5]

Perhaps the most radical of any of the paintings Durand-Ruel chose to represent Renoir at the exhibition, *The Seine at Chatou* was painted in April or May of 1881 at a small town on the river near Bougival, where the artist had often painted before. Its audacity – some might have said effrontery – lies in its lack of any central motif. Compared to Monet's *Seacoast at Trouville*, for instance, which was painted later in the same year, there is no identifiable subject; the subject is, in fact, light falling on an undistinguished area of riverbank, with scrubby grasses and a tangle of bushes and trees. There is a human presence in the form of a young person at right who has gathered flowers; and the flowering tree, at left, holds a claim to be the dominant element in the compositional framework. But as one scholar has noted, *The Seine at Chatou* is fundamentally 'an exercise in painterly improvisation in which we see the artist striving to find, as quickly as possible ... an equivalency between an object in nature and the response it evokes in his mind and eye as his hand moves across the canvas'.[6]

Sisley, too, had returned to the exhibition, showing more than 20 canvases, all of them landscapes. Among them was the recent *Overcast day at Saint-Mammès* (fig 16), showing the bank of the Seine in the little town near the confluence of the Seine and the Loing, on the southeastern edge of the forest of Fontainebleau. Sisley had settled in the region in 1880, leaving Sèvres, between Paris and Versailles, from which location he had ventured out to paint *Waterworks at Marly* (cat 22). Over the next several years, Sisley proceeded to explore the surrounding riverbanks of the Seine and the Loing for motifs, repeatedly painting in the towns of Moret, on the Loing, and Saint-Mammès, situated between the two rivers. In 1884, for instance, he painted *La Croix-Blanche at Saint-Mammès* (cat 29), an image that is notably more colourful than the grey and overcast atmosphere of his earlier painting of the same village (fig 16). The two views do not represent the same buildings, but they conform to the same compositional structure, with the Seine seen at left and the perspective of trees and buildings receding from the right margin of the space towards the horizon at centre. In both paintings, the commerce of the

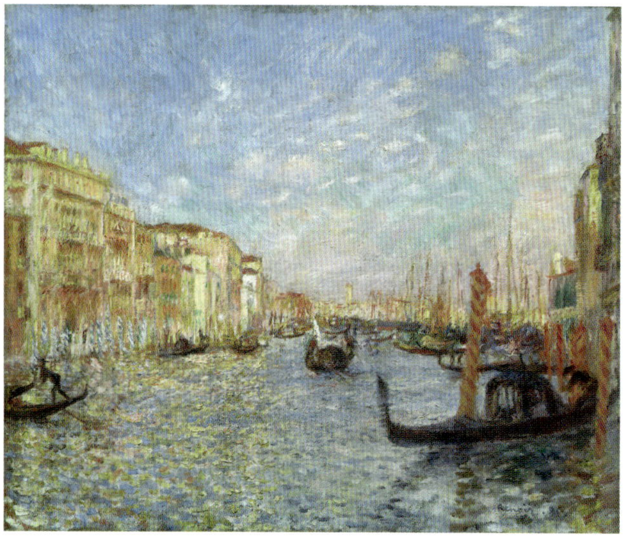

fig 17
Pierre-Auguste Renoir
Grand Canal, Venice 1881
oil on canvas, 54 x 65.1 cm
Museum of Fine Arts, Boston,
bequest of Alexander Cochrane
19.173

river – one of Sisley's preoccupations in images of the region – is suggested, with steamboats and rowboats under way on the river or at anchor along its banks.

Renoir's exploration of the boating-places along the Seine, like Sisley's exploration of the more prosaic quarters of Moret and Saint-Mammès, were extensions of the Impressionist enterprise of the 1870s, depicting the landscapes along the great river that linked the countryside near Fontainebleau to the capital in Paris and flowed from there out to the sea on the Normandy coast. Renoir, however, was to venture farther afield. Just before he painted *The Seine at Chatou* in the spring of 1881, he had made a journey to Algiers, and he would return there a year later; in the fall of 1881 he was to make an extended trip to Italy, where he painted both in Venice (fig 17) and in Naples, returning via Marseilles, where he painted with Cézanne at L'Estaque in late winter, 1882 (fig 18). By the last weeks of December 1883, having spent time that year in the Channel Islands, he was ready to depart again, returning to Italy, this time in the company of Monet.

In April of 1883, Monet, Alice Hoschedé and their children had relocated to Giverny, a tiny village on the Seine to the northwest of Paris, and into the house that was to be their final permanent residence. The house at Giverny was to become the springboard for Monet's painting campaigns in the 1880s – largely in France, but also in Italy – and in the 1890s, when he often selected his motifs from subjects close to hand. Following his visit to Italy and the south of France with Renoir in late 1883, Monet returned almost immediately to the Riviera, this time without Renoir and without telling his friend that he was making the voyage. Leaving in mid January 1884, Monet would first sojourn on the Italian Riviera at Bordighera, making forays to nearby Menton in February. His return to Giverny in April involved a nine-day stay at Menton, during which time he painted *Cap Martin, near Menton* (cat 25). Among the most freely painted images of all of Monet's Mediterranean canvases, with slashing strokes of red, green and blue defining a road, pine trees and the distant Maritime Alps, this work has rightly been compared to the paintings of Edvard Munch and the German Expressionists.[7]

Monet was to return to the Côte d'Azur in 1888, remaining in Antibes from mid January until early May. In late January he wrote to Alice, describing the motif that he was working on in a group of paintings that included *The fort of Antibes* (cat 27). It was, he wrote, 'a small fortified town, baked to a golden crust by the sun, standing forth from beautiful blue and pink mountains and the eternally snow-capped chain of the Alps'. About ten days later, he went on to complain that the light on the motif was 'so bright, so pure with this pink and blue, that the slightest touch of paint that is not right looks like a stain of dirt'.[8] Monet painted some six views from this same vantage point, taken at different times of day and under different conditions of light and atmosphere, anticipating his serial production of the 1890s. At the same time, he explored other views of the Baie des Anges, facing Antibes, and its topography. In *Cap d'Antibes, mistral* (cat 26), for example, he shifted his position so that he looked up the coast to the northeast, to the right of the town he had represented earlier. The pale blue sky, the blue and white mass of Maritime Alps and the deep blue sea still form the ground for his image, which in this case centres on a stubby, spherical bush blown by the mistral that came from the sea.

The effect of wind – on the leaves of a tree, on grasses or even on the waves of the sea – is a theme that Monet had explored intermittently for some 20 years before painting *Cap d'Antibes, Mistral* in 1888. One of the most extraordinary paintings devoted to this idea is his *Poplars at Giverny* of 1887 (cat 34). Like his scenes of meadows painted in 1885 and 1886 (cats 32 and 33), this painting represents a landscape from the environs of Monet's house. Two rows of poplar trees – seven in the foreground and

fig 18
Pierre-Auguste Renoir
Rocky crags at L'Estaque 1882
oil on canvas, 66.4 x 81 cm
Museum of Fine Arts, Boston,
Juliana Cheney Edwards Collection
39.678

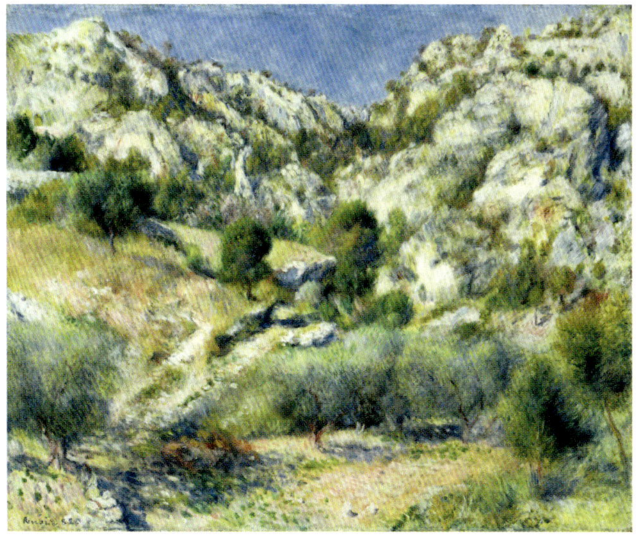

more in the distance, partially screened – line the flat banks of a small river, the Epte, which runs through the plain of Les Ajoux to the south of Monet's house and garden, before it joins the Seine just south of town.[9] This painting is among a group of experimental works executed in 1887 along the banks of the Epte, featuring the thin and sinuous trunks of poplar trees, often cropped, as here, by the frame of the picture space. Deliberately ambiguous in terms of the depiction of depth, *Poplars at Giverny* comes from an investigation of the decorative, abstract qualities of composition, using nature and its rhythms (here, in fact, a rhythm imposed by the spacing of the trees when they were planted) as the source of inspiration. Painted with a kind of delicate frenzy, the leaves and even the trunks of the trees take shape and then seem to dissolve in the light of the setting sun, which fills the background and casts long shadows across the foreground. This remarkable painting, among the most sensuous and optically exciting of Monet's works of the 1880s, culminates the series of poplar views he had begun earlier in the year and prefigures the more structured series of poplars on the banks of the Epte (fig 23) that Monet would begin some four years later.

1 See W 475–76, pp 538–41
2 Monet to Durand-Ruel, 13 Sept 1881, quoted in Kendall 1989, p 33
3 Monet to Alice Hoschedé, 15 Feb 1882, quoted in Kendall 1989, p 100
4 See Berson 1996, pp 205–06
5 See Berson 1996, p 211
6 Christopher Riopelle in Bailey et al 2007, p 230
7 See Joachim Pissarro, *Monet and the Mediterranean*, exh cat, Rizzoli, New York in association with Kimbell Art Museum, Fort Worth, Texas 1997, p 108
8 Monet to Alice Hoschedé, 1 Feb 1888, quoted in Pissarro 1997, p 120
9 See the notice for W 1155

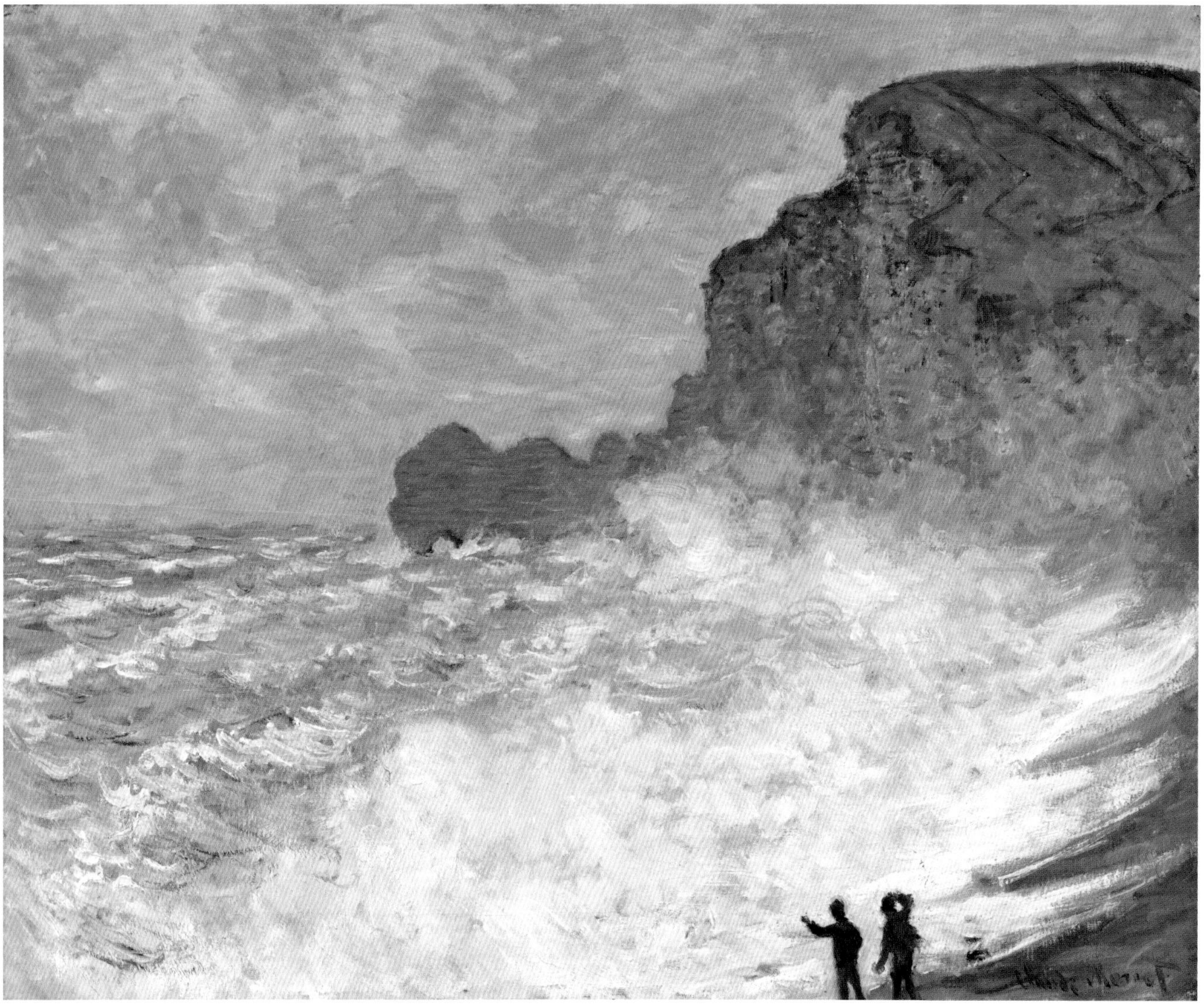

23

Claude Monet

Rough weather at Etretat 1883

oil on canvas, 65 x 81 cm
National Gallery of Victoria, Felton Bequest 1913
582-2

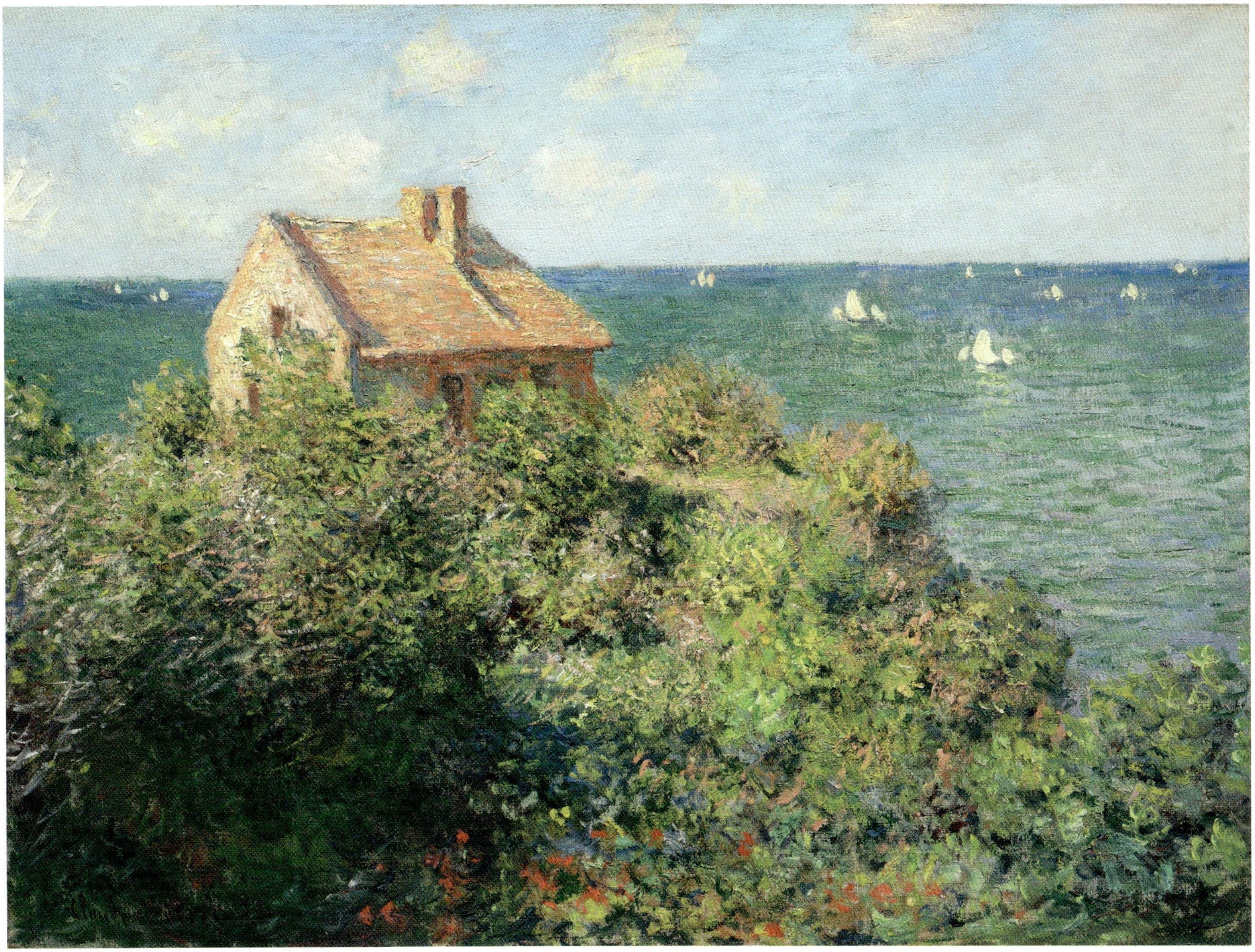

24

Claude Monet

Fisherman's cottage on the cliffs at Varengeville 1882

oil on canvas, 60.6 x 81.6 cm
Museum of Fine Arts, Boston,
bequest of Anna Perkins Rogers
21.1331

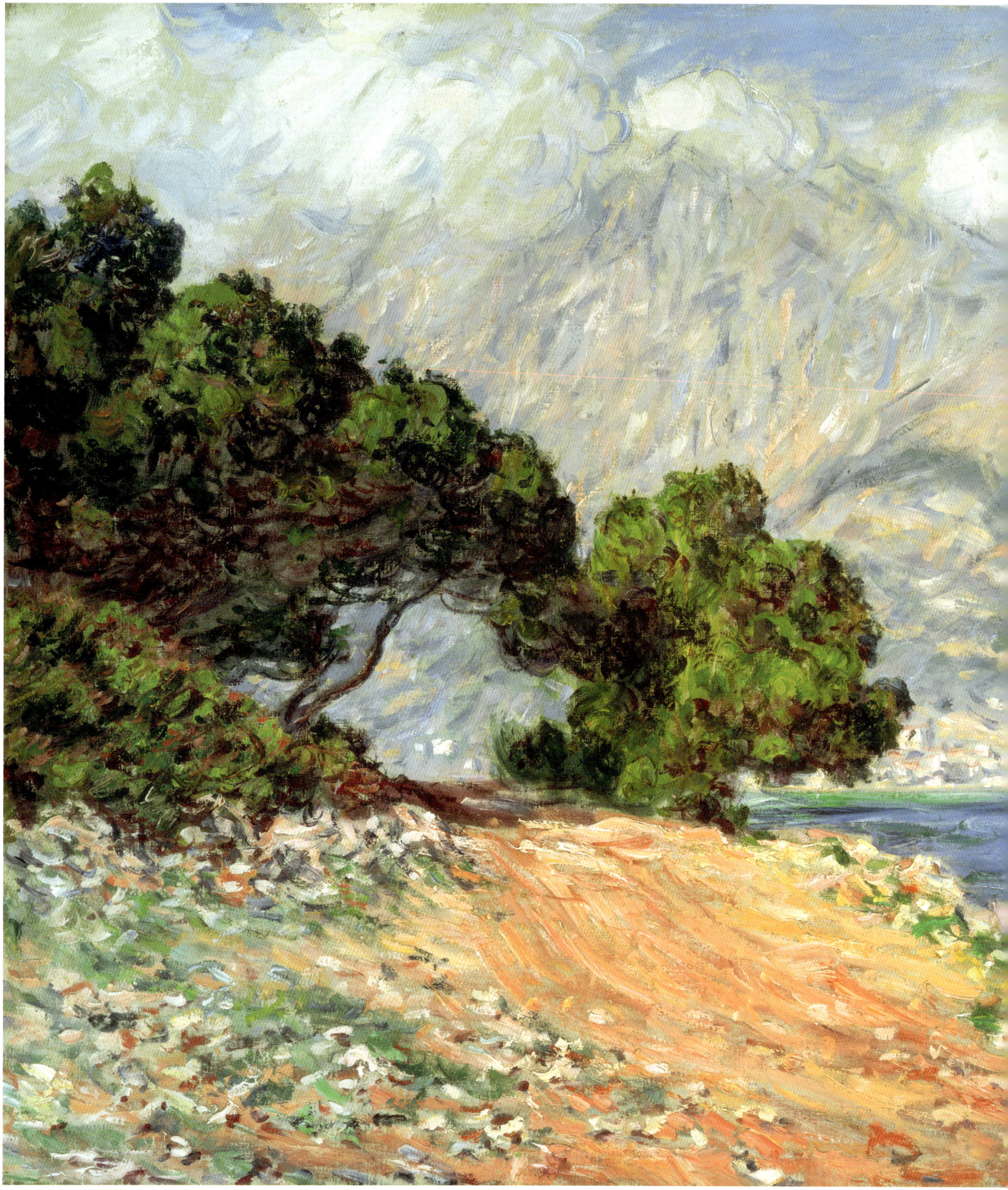

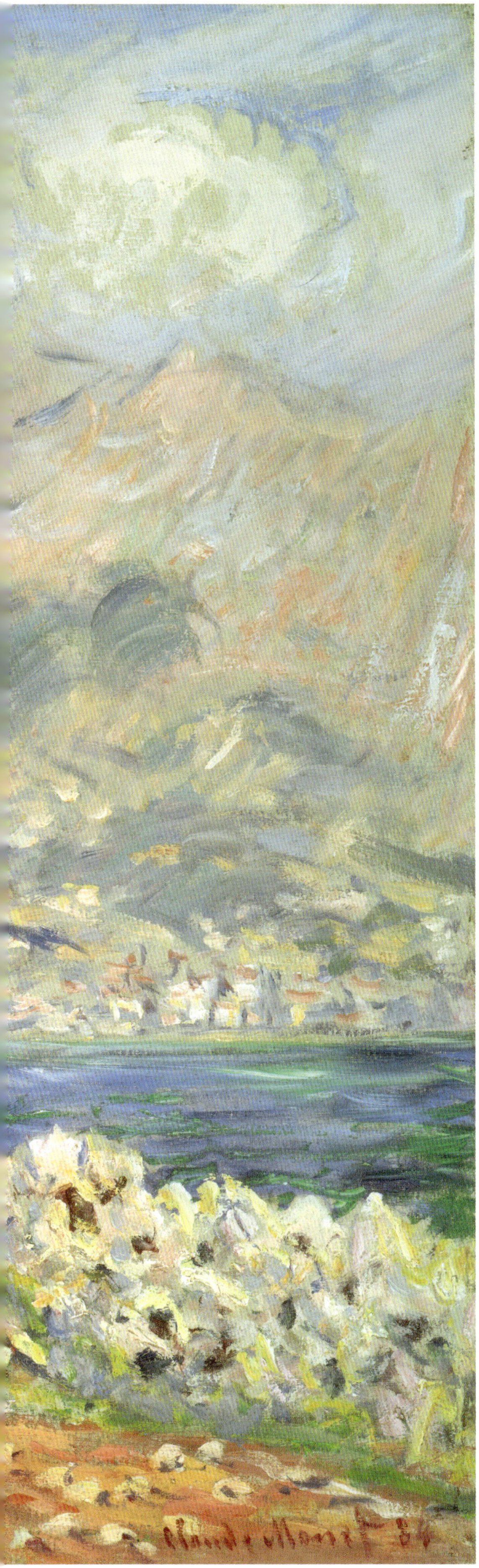

25

Claude Monet
Cap Martin, near Menton 1884
oil on canvas, 67.2 x 81.6 cm
Museum of Fine Arts, Boston,
Juliana Cheney Edwards Collection
25.128

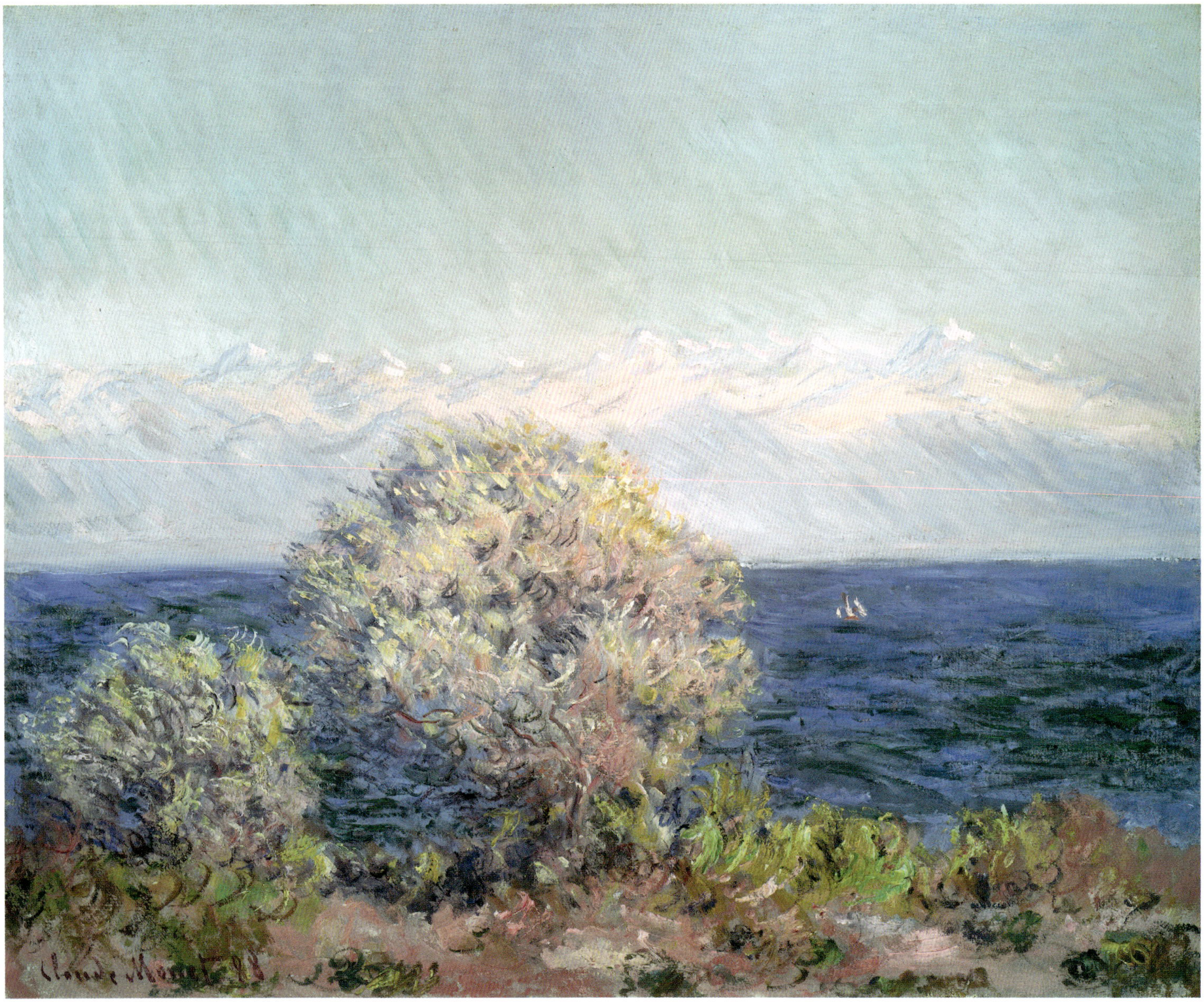

26

Claude Monet
Cap d'Antibes, mistral 1888
oil on canvas, 66 x 81.3 cm
Museum of Fine Arts, Boston,
bequest of Dr Arthur Tracy Cabot
42.542

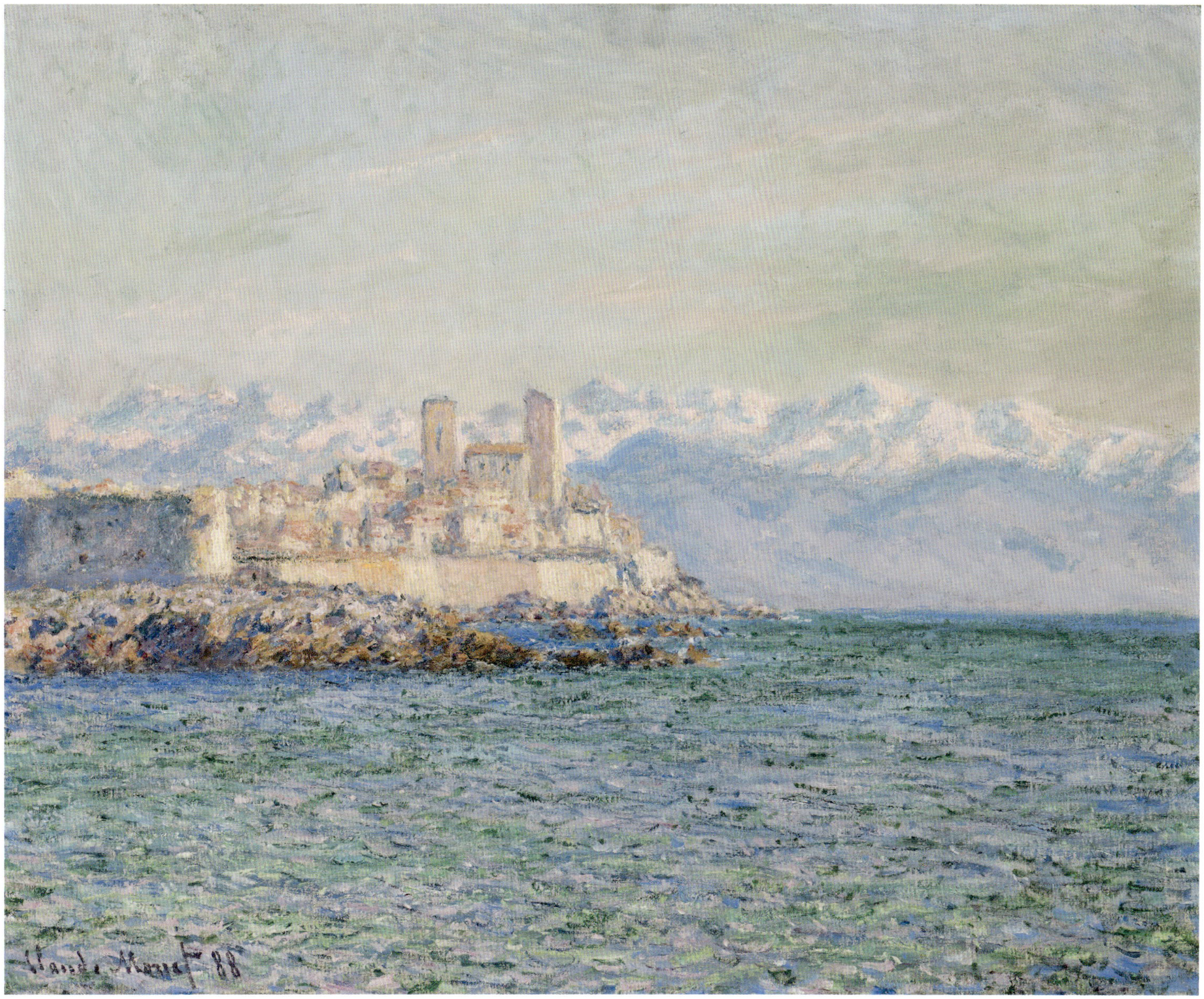

27

Claude Monet

The fort of Antibes 1888

oil on canvas, 65.4 x 81 cm
Museum of Fine Arts, Boston,
anonymous gift
1978.634

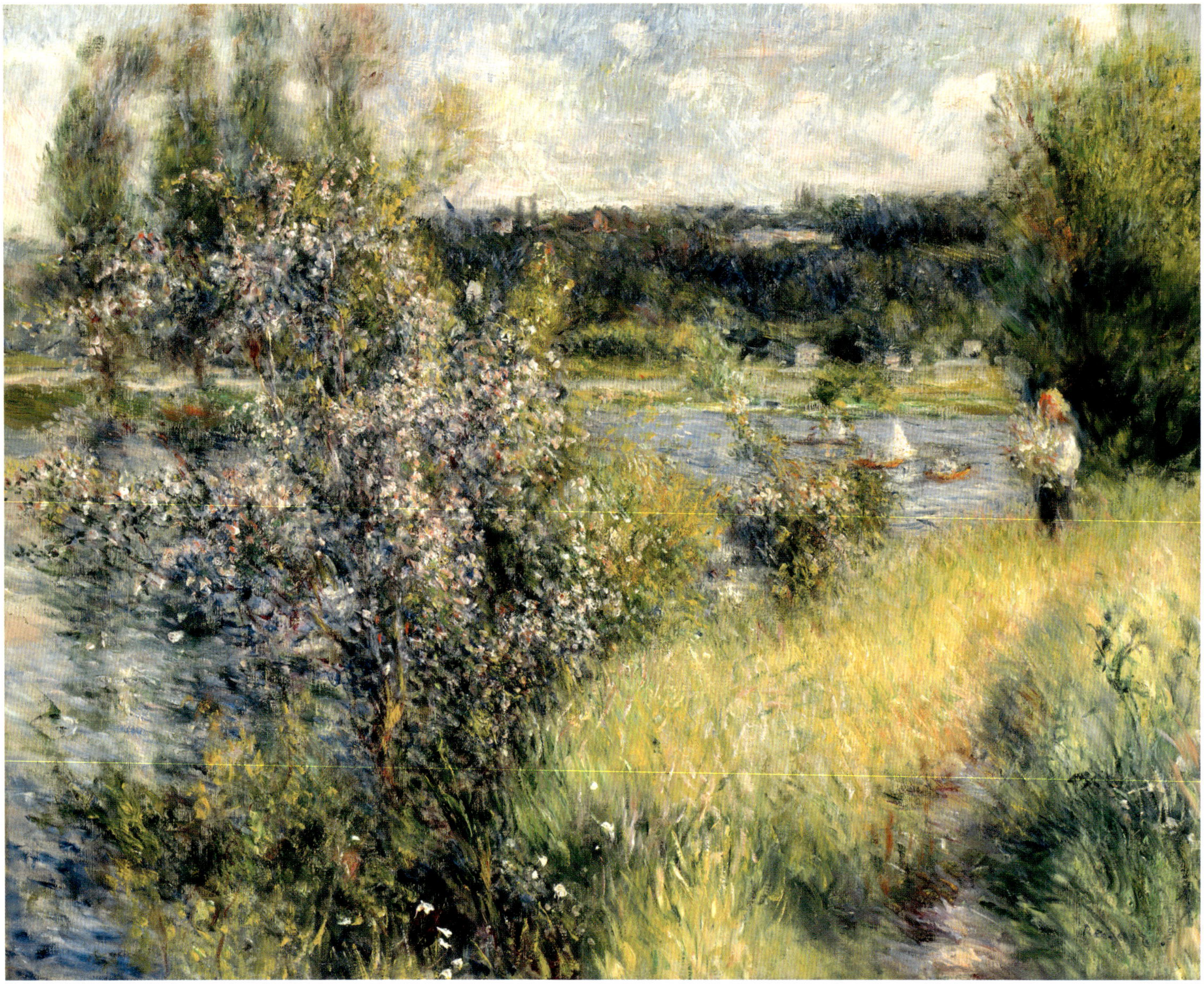

28

Pierre-Auguste Renoir
The Seine at Chatou 1881

oil on canvas, 73.3 x 92.4 cm
Museum of Fine Arts, Boston,
gift of Arthur Brewster Emmons
19.771

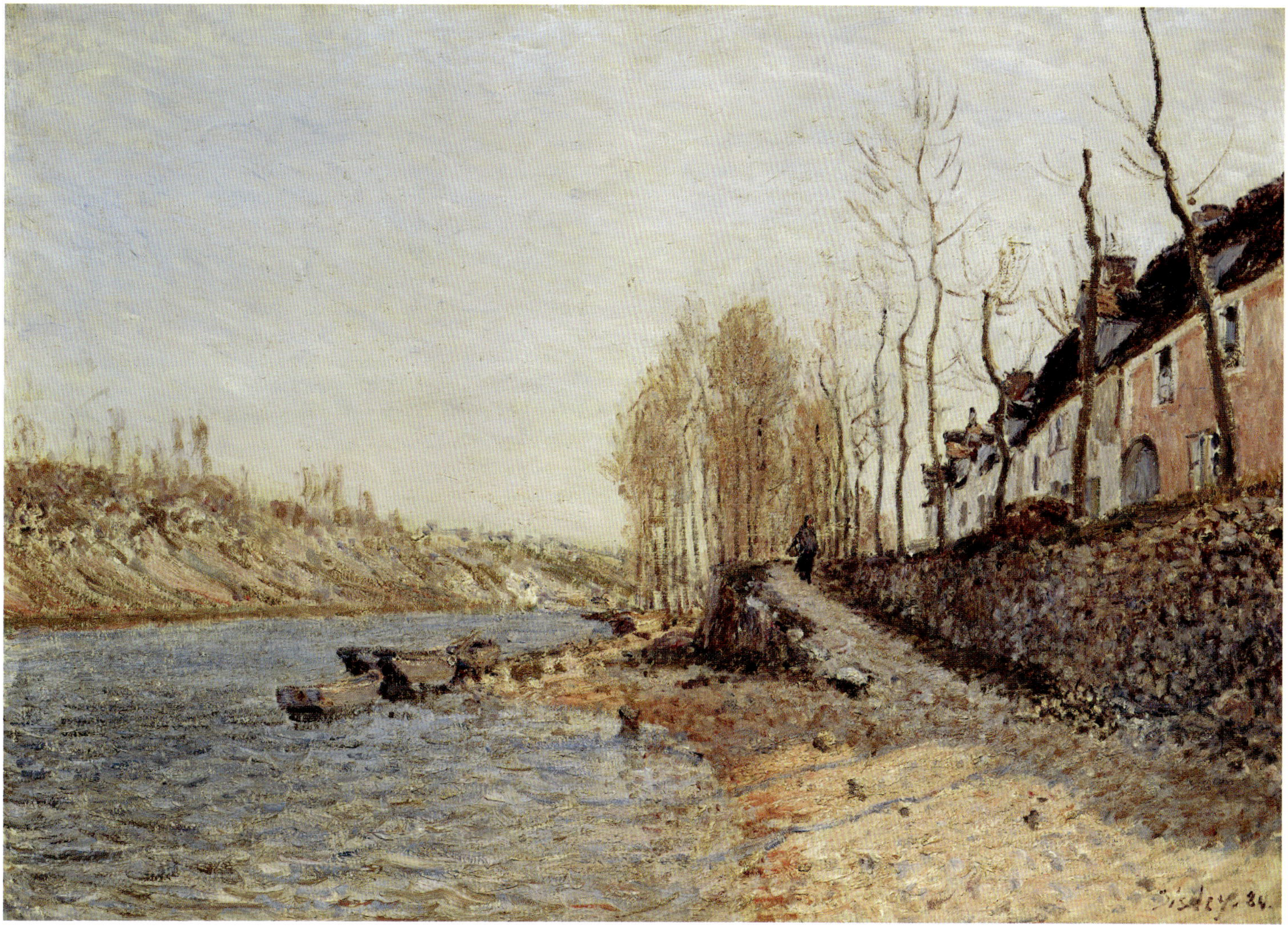

29

Alfred Sisley

La Croix-Blanche at Saint-Mammès 1884

oil on canvas, 65.4 x 92.4 cm
Museum of Fine Arts, Boston,
Juliana Cheney Edwards Collection
39.680

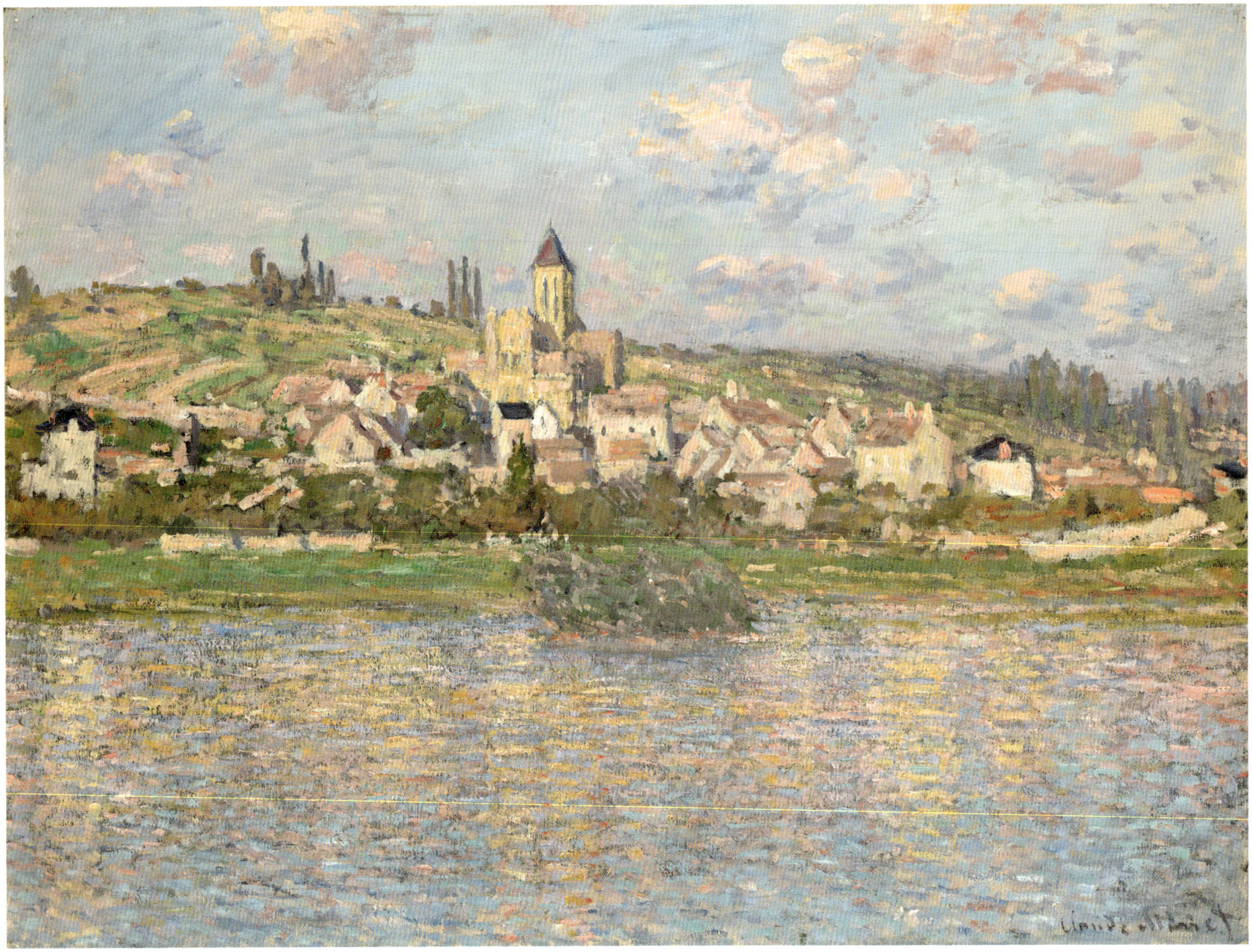

30

Claude Monet
Vétheuil 1878

oil on canvas, 60 x 81 cm
National Gallery of Victoria,
Felton Bequest 1937
406-4

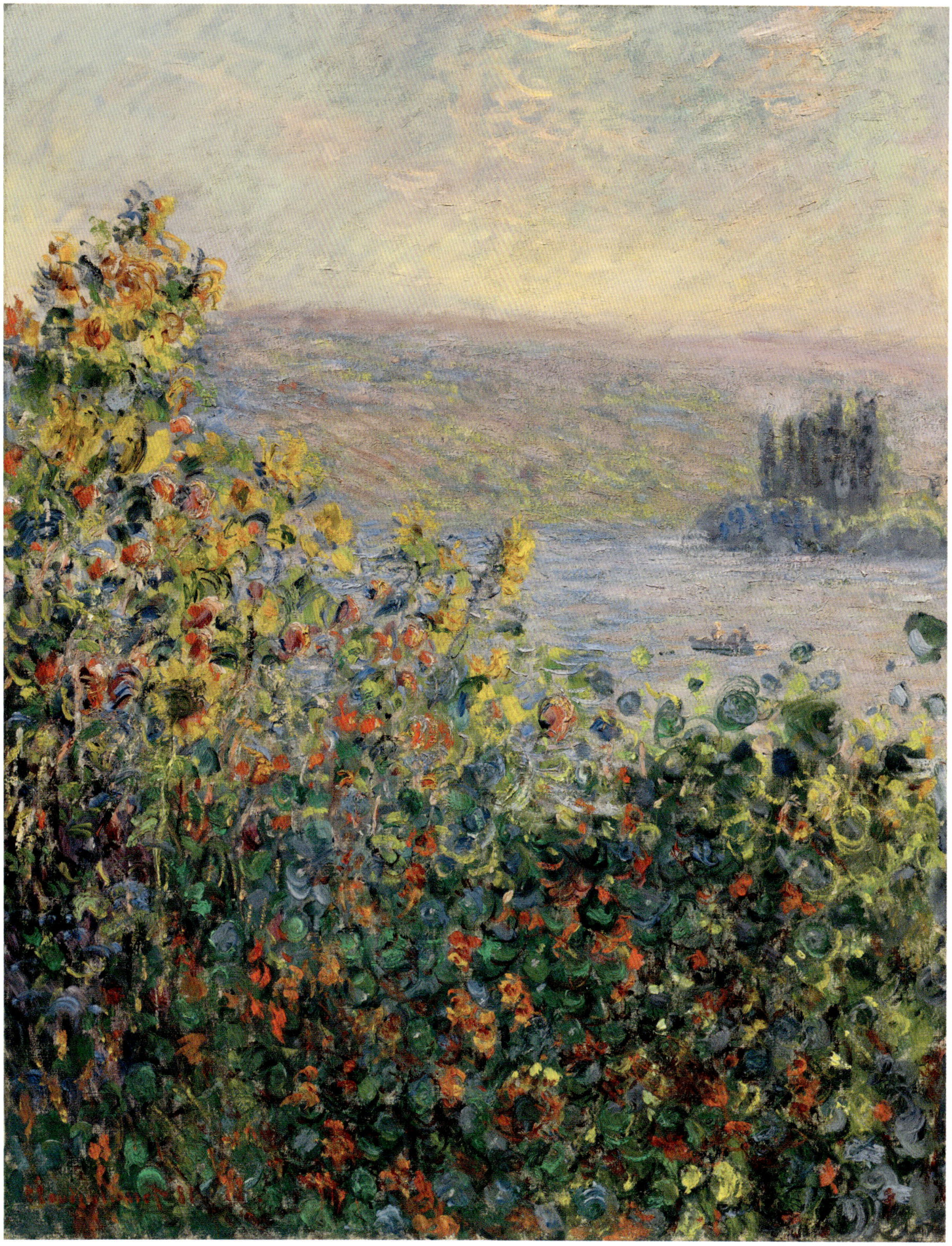

31

Claude Monet
Flower beds at Vétheuil 1881

oil on canvas, 92.1 x 73.3 cm
Museum of Fine Arts, Boston,
John Pickering Lyman Collection,
gift of Miss Theodora Lyman
19.1313

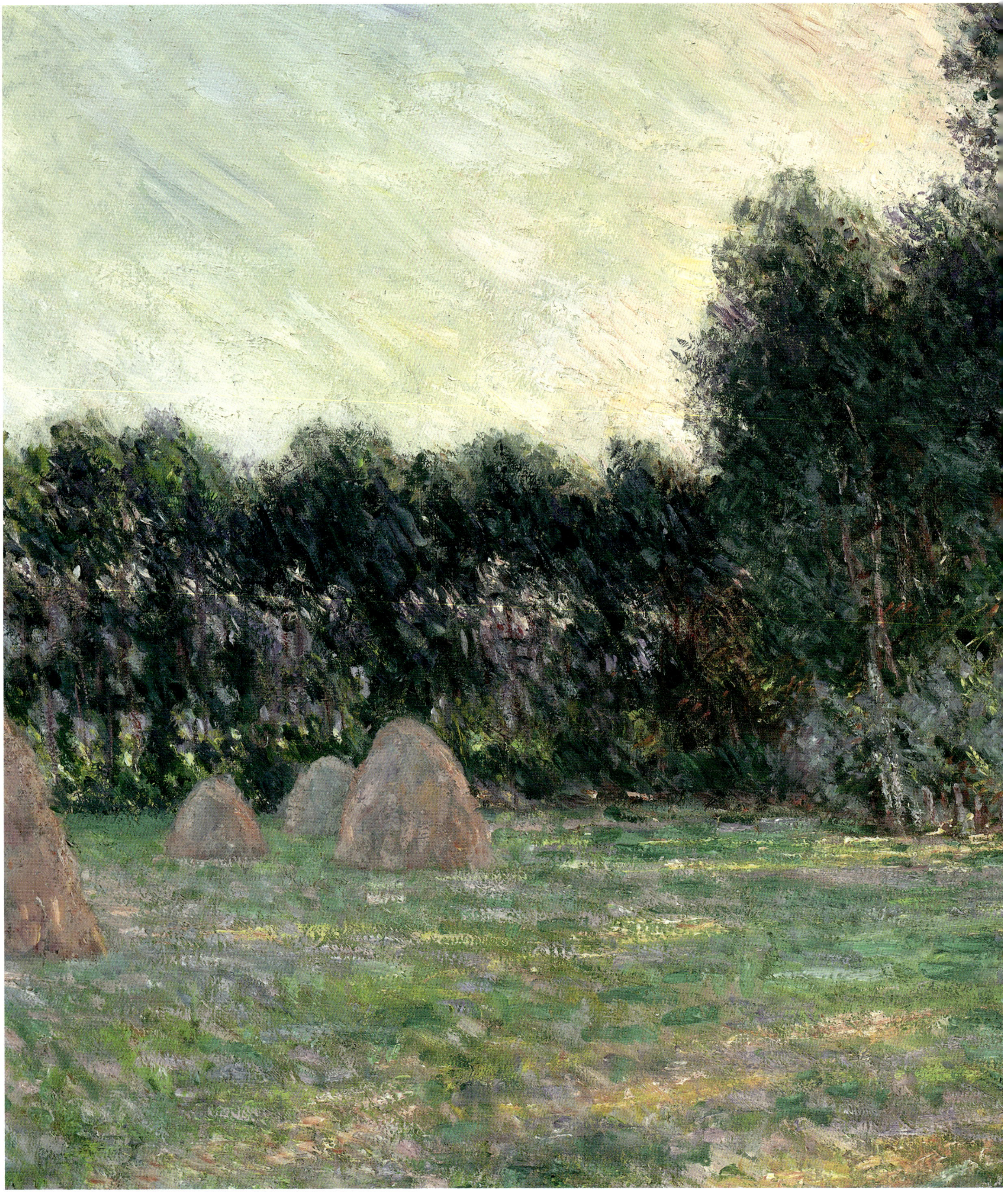

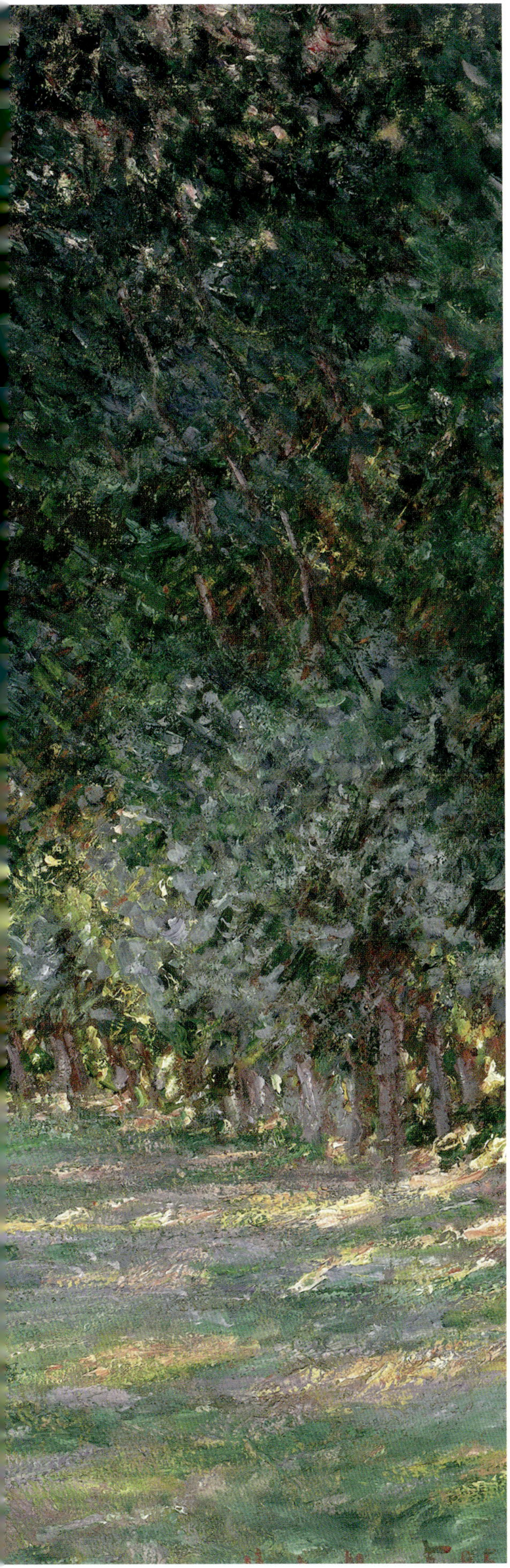

32

Claude Monet

Meadow with haystacks near Giverny 1885

oil on canvas, 74 x 93.5 cm
Museum of Fine Arts, Boston,
bequest of Dr Arthur Tracy Cabot
42.541

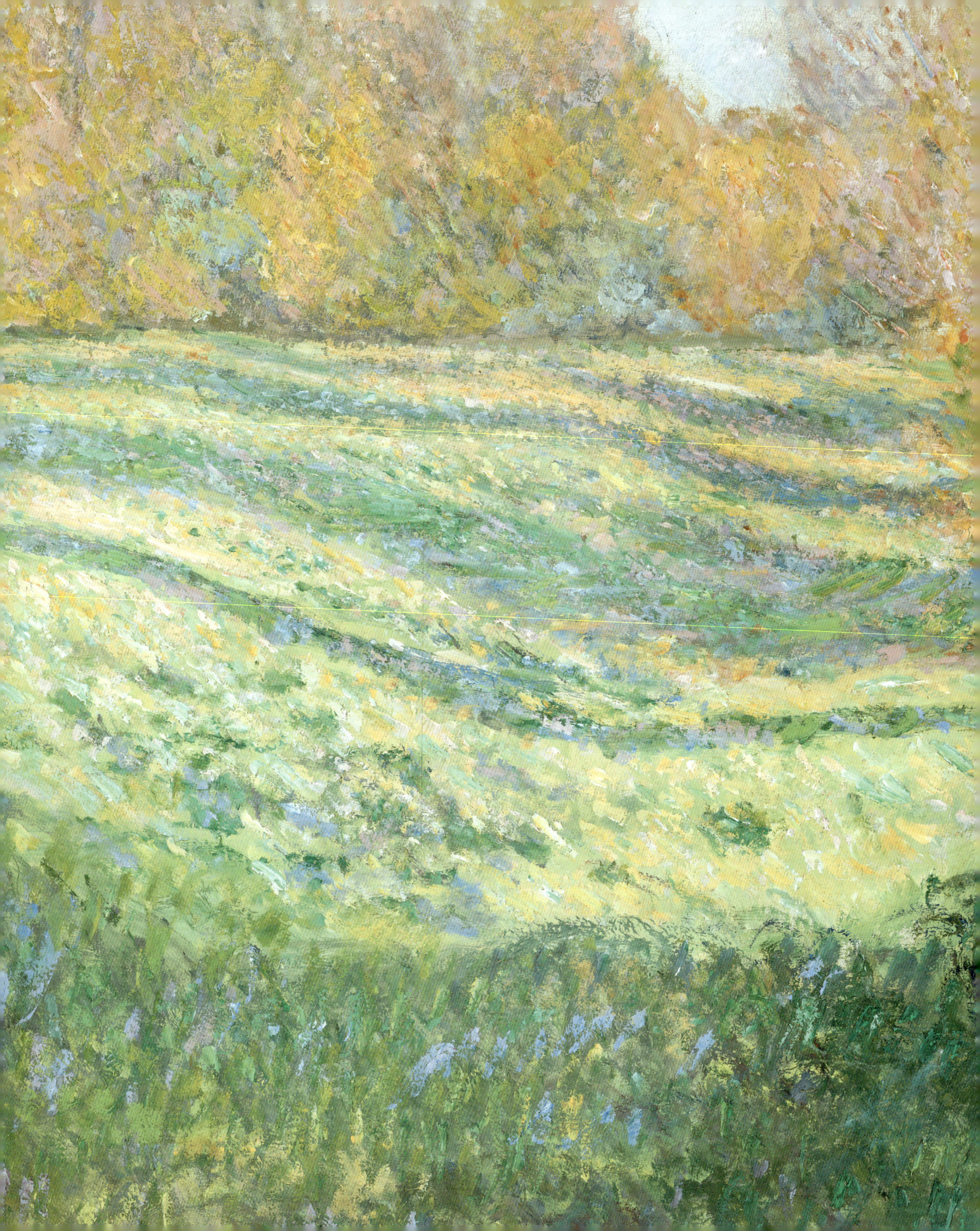

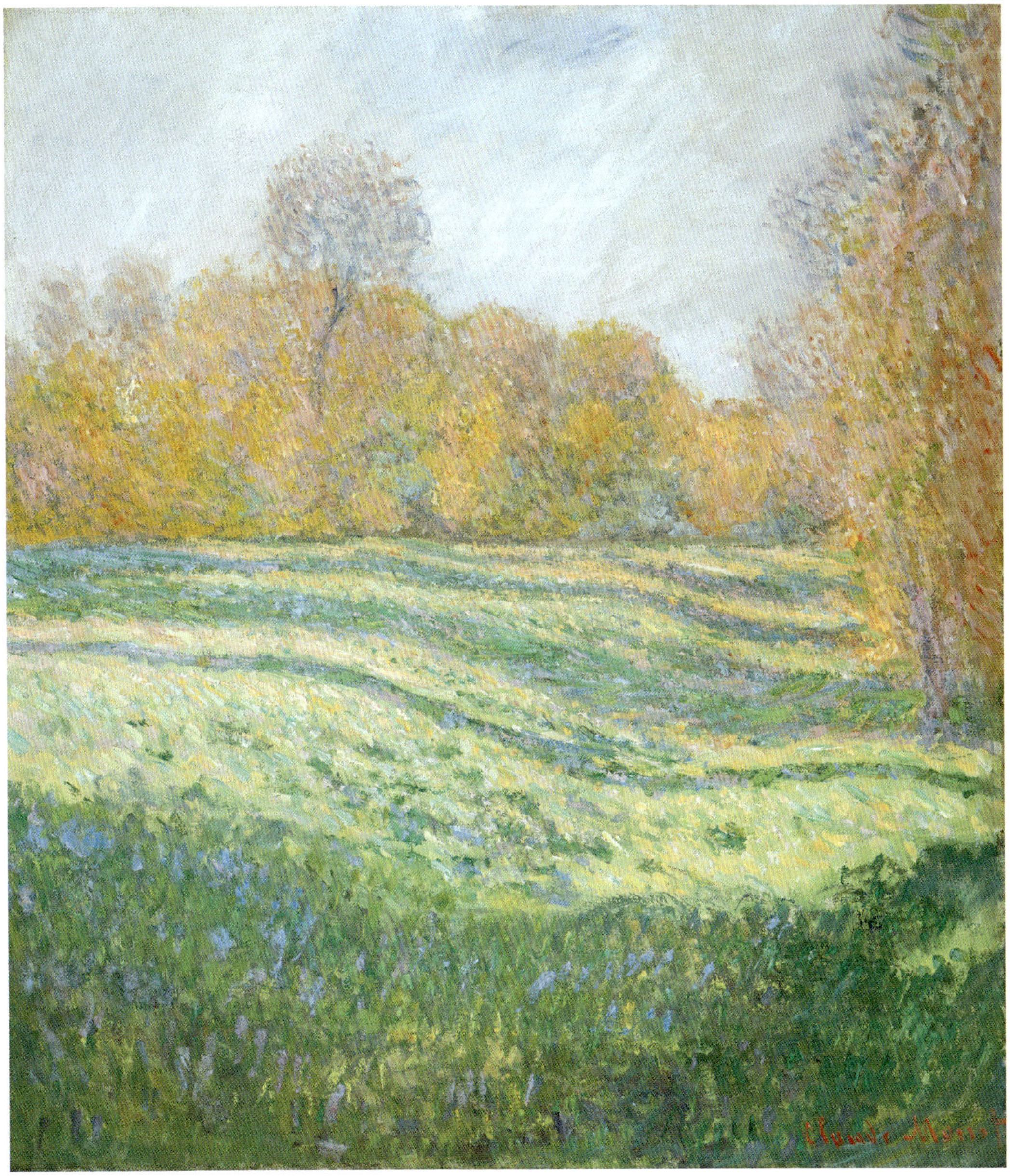

33

Claude Monet
Meadow at Giverny 1886

oil on canvas, 92.1 x 81.6 cm
Museum of Fine Arts, Boston,
Julia Cheney Edwards Collection
39.670

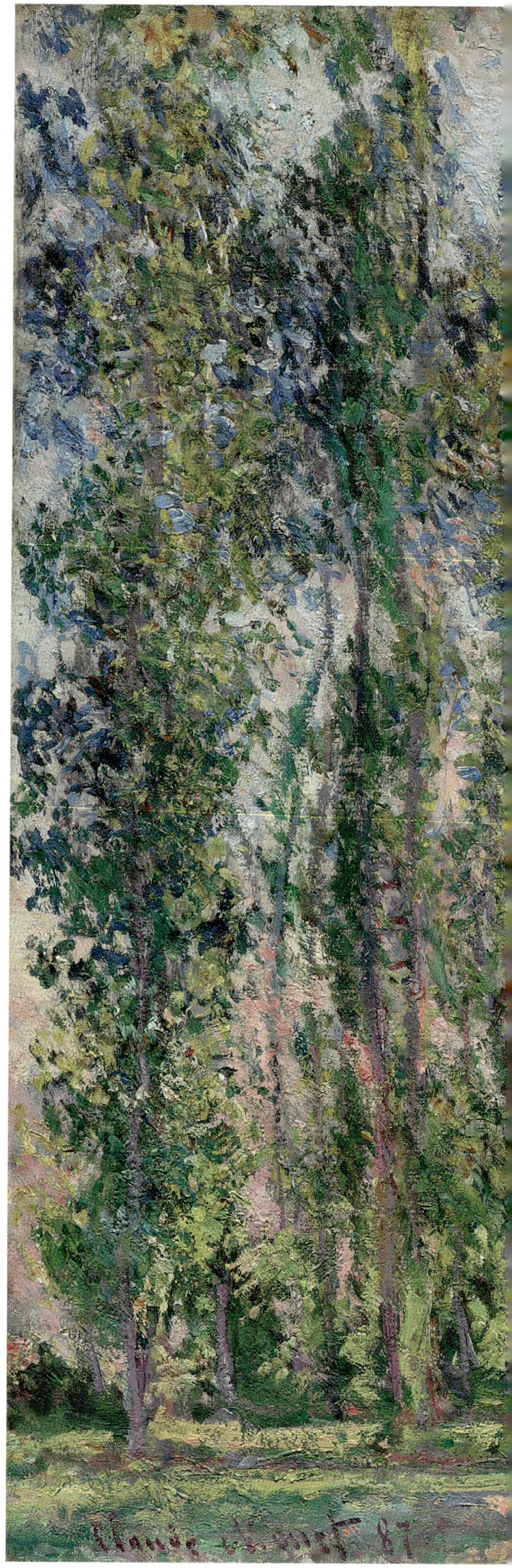

34
Claude Monet
Poplars at Giverny 1887
oil on canvas, 74.3 x 91.4 cm
Private collection, courtesy
Museum of Fine Arts, Boston

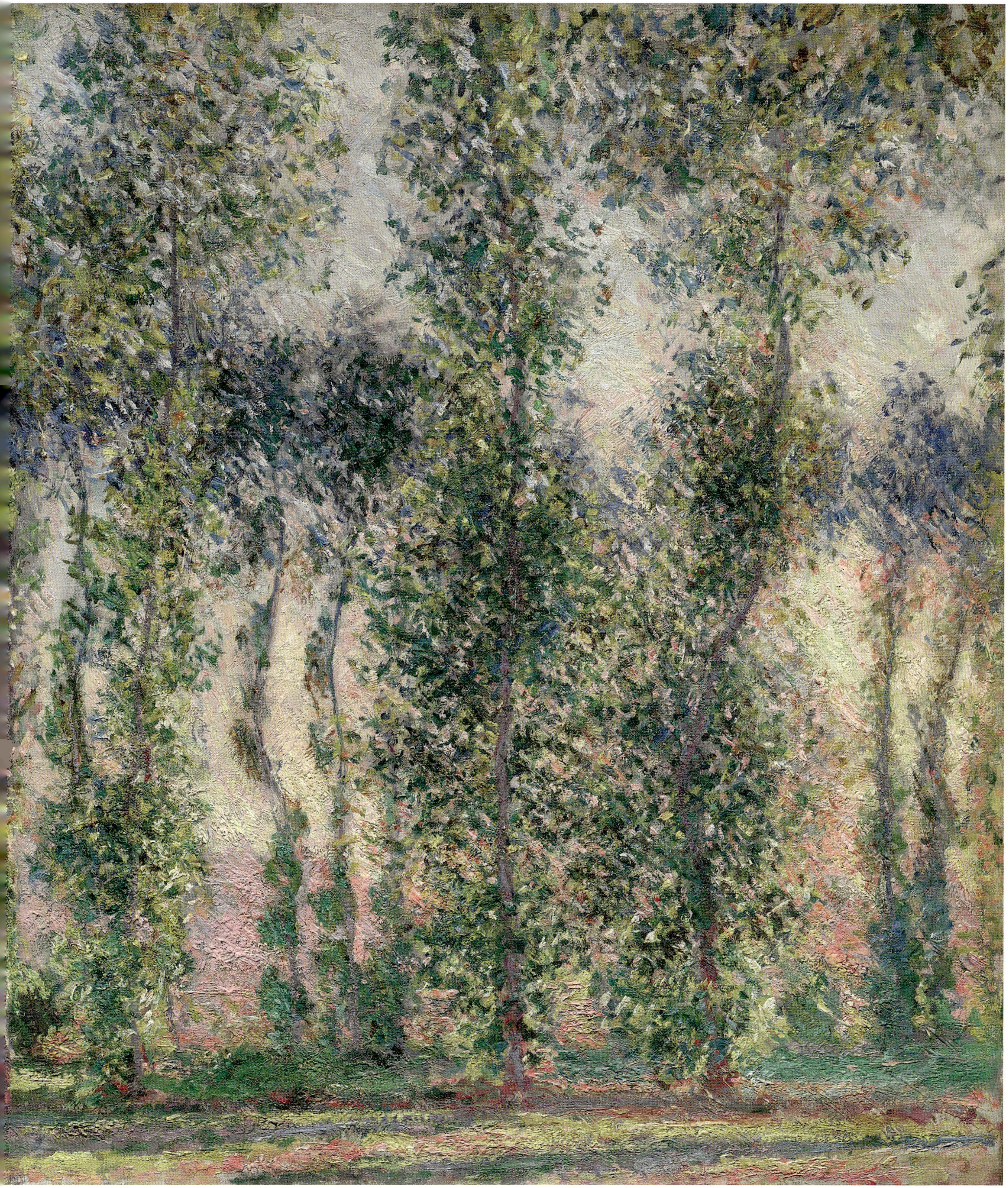

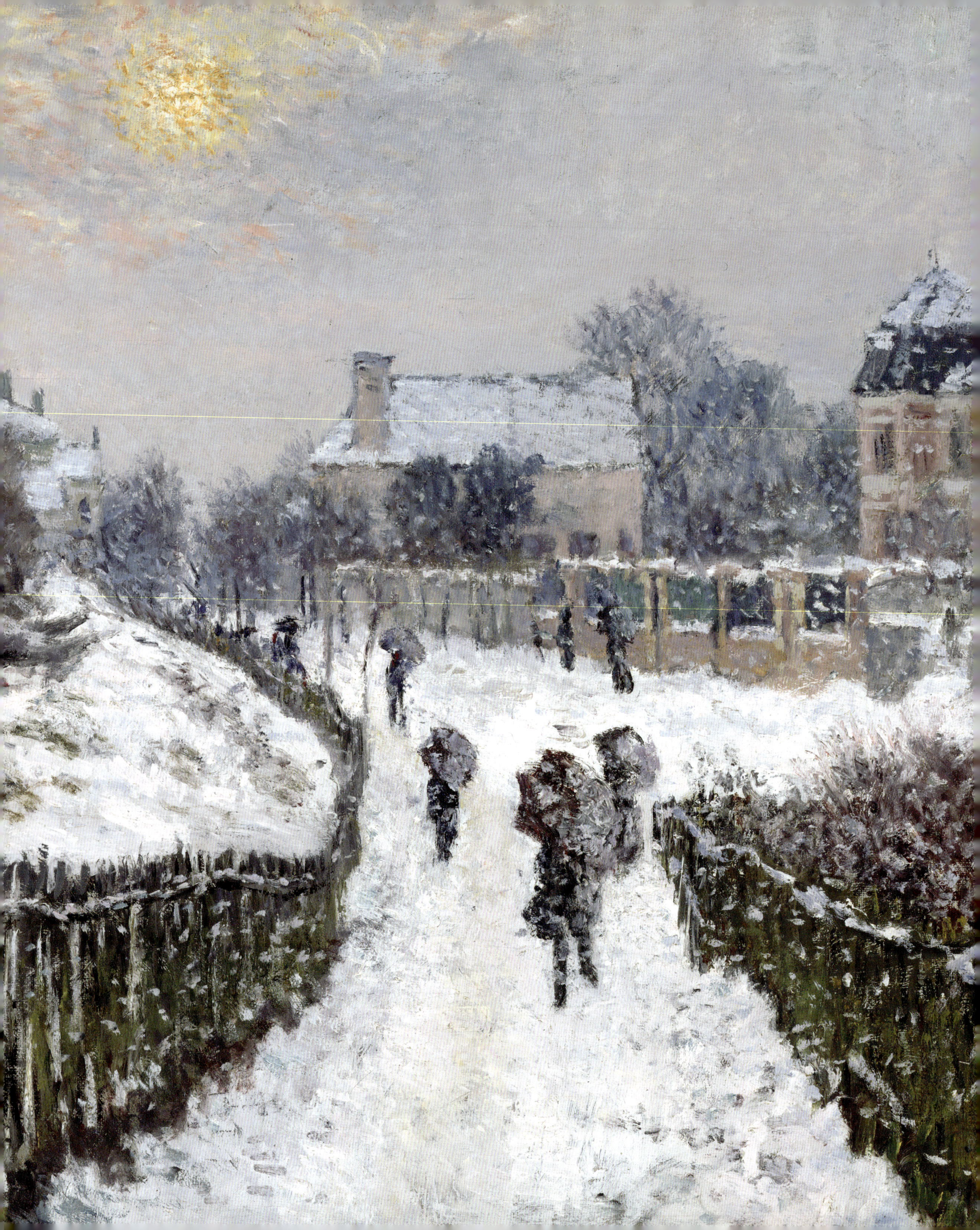

MONET AND JAPANESE ART

In 1920 the Duc de Trévise, an aristocratic collector, paid a visit to Monet's house at Giverny. He recorded his impressions and published them as a homage to the painter in the year after Monet's death. The duke was shown through the garden, which 'along with the Japanese prints [was] one of the only luxuries indulged in at Giverny', and noted the Japanese bridge – '[Monet's] idea, he later finished it with an arbour in the Japanese style' – that spans a narrow section of the waterlily pond (see cat 43).

Later he was taken to Monet's studios, and finally into the house itself. Having visited Monet's collection of his fellow Impressionists' paintings in the artist's bedroom, 'on the ground floor', wrote Trévise, 'I did not want to miss the dining room, for here the rarest of Japanese prints, simply framed, placed at carefully studied intervals, with their delightful curves and their half-mourning tonalities, are a collector's delight'. Monet proceeded to explain and discuss his collection of ukiyo-e prints, in his only direct statement about them – made just six years before his death:

> Look closely at this flower with its petals turned by the wind: is it not Truth itself? [...] And here, near this Hokusai woman, look at *The bath*; look at these bodies whose consistency you can feel; they are made of flesh, and yet only their contours convey this. What we Westerners have particularly valued is the bold manner in which subjects are outlined. These people have taught us a different way of composing, no doubt about it.

'And thus', wrote Trévise, 'two memorable chapters are begun just as our visit comes to a close. It would be interesting to report what Monet thinks of his contemporaries and of the few faithful ones he welcomes with a fatherly kindness and also to hear him speak about Japan and the discoveries he made during a memorable period!'

'These people have taught us a different way of composing', said Monet.[1] This statement, made near the end of his life, is a tantalising primary clue to understanding how Monet valued the lessons of Japanese art, which for him largely meant ukiyo-e prints of the kind that he collected, versions of which are exhibited in *Monet and the Impressionists*. But as many scholars have noted, Monet's response to the art of Japan must largely be inferred from internal references and from what we know of the society he kept from the 1860s – the great beginning of French awareness of Japanese art – to the end of his career, when he befriended Japanese collectors and dealers and sold works directly to them, most notably to the Baron Matsukata, who was among the first to acquire paintings from Monet's last great period of work in preparation for the *grandes décorations* now in the Orangerie Museum in Paris.

It has been suggested that the flattened, unshaded surfaces of many of Monet's paintings from the 1860s – of which *Rue de la Bavole, Honfleur* (cat 13) is a good example – may be attributed to Monet's first awareness of Japanese prints, which such artists from his circle as Whistler and Manet were actively collecting.[2] *Rue de la Bavole*, in itself a seemingly straightforward view of a street in a Normandy seaside town, bears strong comparison with such ukiyo-e images as Utagawa Hiroshige's *Night view of Saruwaka-machi* (fig 20), from the series *One hundred famous views of Edo*. The plunging perspective of the street in Hiroshige's print – of which Monet owned an example, perhaps acquired later – creates a composition divided by two diagonals and, therefore, four triangular shapes, as in Monet's painting. Both artists then animate these triangles: at left and right, with openings into the buildings on either side of the street; below, with people seen from behind walking toward the vanishing point; at top, with a glowing moon or floating clouds.[3]

Glancing references to Japanese art abound in the conversation and works of Monet's circle and in discussions of his art in the 1860s. For instance, he referred to his famous painting of the seaside terrace garden of his Aunt Lecadre's villa in Sainte-Adresse as 'my Chinese painting with flags', conflating the notions of Chinese and Japanese art as so many Europeans did in the 1860s.[4] The composition is

Claude Monet *Boulevard Saint-Denis, Argenteuil, in winter* 1875 (detail), cat 36

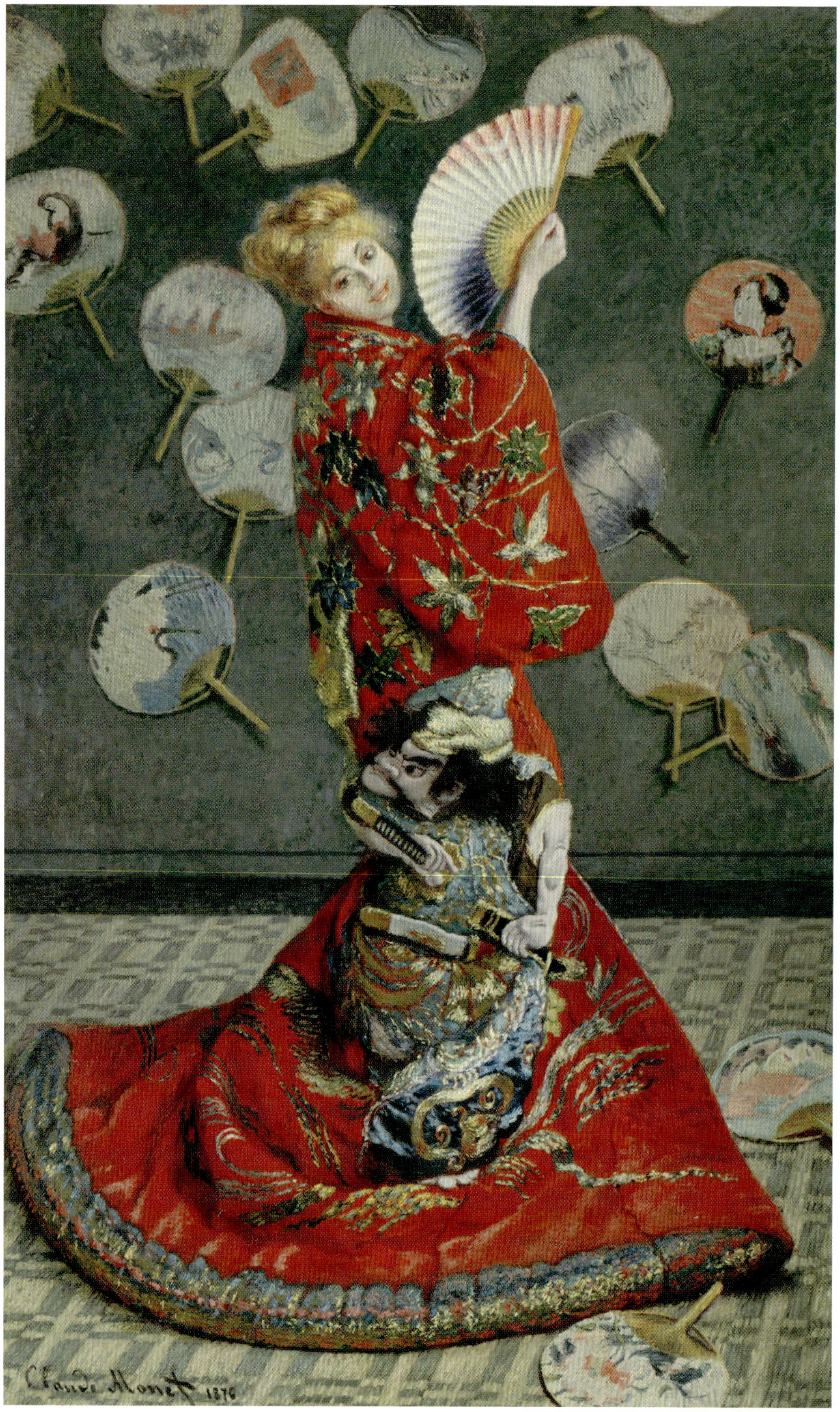
Claude Monet 1876

fig 19
Claude Monet
La Japonaise (Camille Monet in Japanese costume) 1876
oil on canvas, 231.8 x 142.3 cm
Museum of Fine Arts, Boston,
1951 Purchase Fund
56.147

fig 20
Utagawa Hiroshige I
Night view of Saruwaka-machi 1856
from the series *One hundred famous views of Edo*
woodblock print; ink and colour on paper,
approx 35 x 24.5 cm
Museum of Fine Arts, Boston,
William Sturgis Bigelow Collection
11.35840

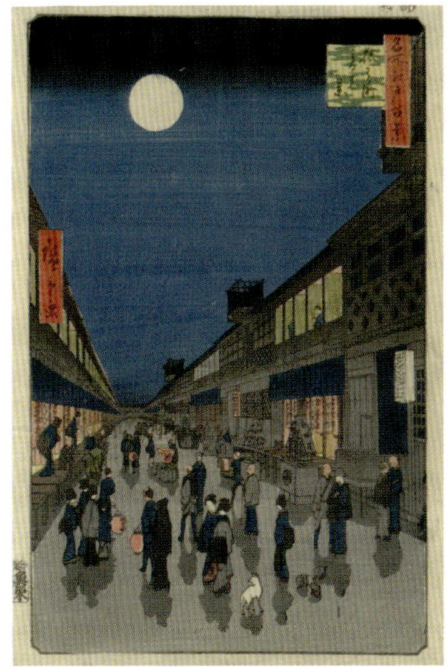

generally thought to be loosely based on a print from Katsushika Hokusai's series *Thirty-six views of Mount Fuji*. Monet, as we shall see, incorporated many such compositional devices from the art of Japan, but as John House notes, 'in painting [his landscape ...] subjects Monet was scrupulously following the natural forms in front of him, rather than manipulating nature to fit a preconceived pattern. Japanese art helped him to see the pictorial possibilities of such forms and suggested ways of framing them on the canvas, but the final structure of each picture is the result of his direct confrontation with the motif.'[5]

Thus, in painting his *Snow at Argenteuil* (cat 15) in about 1874 or the remarkable *Boulevard Saint-Denis, Argenteuil, in winter* (cat 36) a year later, Monet might have been inspired by such works as Hiroshige's *Kanbara: night snow* (cat 35), from the series *Fifty-three stations of the Tōkaidō road*, also known as the *First Tōkaidō* or *Great Tōkaidō*.[6] Hiroshige's composition would have interested Monet through its strong crossing diagonals but nonetheless flattened perspective, its jumble of rooftops beneath the snow, and its population of weary walkers sheltering under umbrellas. But Monet's painting of the Boulevard Saint-Denis – with a remarkable vision of the golden sun setting through the falling snow – is luminously coloured whereas Hiroshige's print is deliberately monochrome, and the canvas is painted with verve and brio, in passionate response to a visual sensation, whereas Hiroshige's print is calculated, controlled and elegant.

In the next year, Monet painted his most celebrated image dealing with the art of Japan. The life-size portrait of his wife in Japanese costume (fig 19) is quite possibly Monet's least sophisticated, or most voguish, response to the culture of Japan. Although now generally called *La Japonaise* ('the Japanese woman'), when it was exhibited at the Impressionist exhibition of 1876 the work was given the title *Japonnerie* (meaning either 'in the Japanese manner' or 'Japanese stuff'), a reference to the vogue for all things Japanese among Europeans by the mid 1870s. Monet had his wife, whose hair was brown (see cat 20), don a blonde wig to emphasise that she was a European surrounded by Japanese goods – clothed in a robe elaborately embroidered with a legendary swordsman who scowls as much as she smiles, standing on woven straw mats, against the background of cascading printed fans tacked to a wall, and carrying in her hand a fan bearing the blue, white and red of the flag of France.

While painting the picture – particularly the robe – Monet had said that it was 'superb to do'. But critics were divided in their opinion of the painting. One called it a 'huge scarlet machine'; another remarked that it 'explodes, blazes, whirls like a firework'.[7] The painting stands apart from Monet's work above all in its intentions: he created it to declare to the public his ability to paint the figure as well as landscape; to astonish his viewers with his mastery of colour; and to proclaim his modish modernity in a highly deliberate, even shocking way. He was never again to paint such a picture.

In his landscapes of the following decade, Monet often incorporated compositional devices borrowed from ukiyo-e prints, as he had in the 1870s. The windblown tree in *Seacoast at Trouville* (cat 38), one of his cliff-side views painted in Normandy in the early 1880s, might have been inspired by the eccentric tree in Hiroshige's *Yokkaichi: Mie River* (*Yokkaichi, Miegawa*) (cat 37), from the series *Fifty-three stations of the Tōkaidō road*. And when, at the end of the decade, he went to the coastal town of Belle-Ile (cat 41) or to the centre of France to paint the gorges of the Creuse River (see fig 30 and cat 46) or the *Ravine of the Petite Creuse* (cat 44), he might well have been thinking of Hiroshige's views of rivers, mountains and cliffs. A closely related example, for instance, is *Kai Province: Monkey Bridge* (cat 39), from the series *Famous places in the sixty odd provinces [of Japan]*, with its striated rocks and eddying waters; another might be *Hakone: view of the lake*

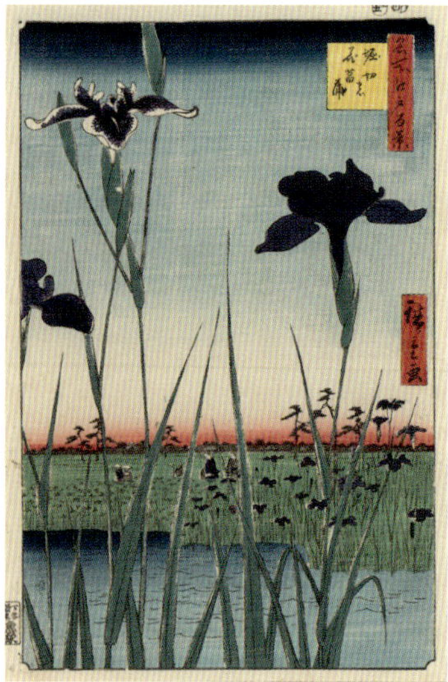

fig 21
Utagawa Hiroshige I
Horikiri iris garden
from the series *One hundred famous views of Edo*
woodblock print; ink and colour on paper, approx 35 x 24.5 cm
Museum of Fine Arts, Boston, William Sturgis Bigelow Collection
11.36876

right: cat 35
Utagawa Hiroshige I
Kanbara: night snow (detail)
Japan, Edo period, c1833–34

(cat 40), from the series *Fifty-three stations of the Tōkaidō road*.[8] These compositionally similar examples are only two among many that might be proposed. Again, it must be remembered that Monet's visual impression was paramount – so much so that while painting in the Creuse Valley, he was constantly obliged to modify his canvases in response to the changing seasons, even going so far as to hire men to cut sprouting leaves from a tree that had changed its appearance as the spring progressed.[9]

By the 1890s, Monet had thoroughly assimilated the art of the Japanese print. Painting a mountain in snowy Norway, he wrote, 'I have a delicious motif there of little islets almost level with the water, and a mountain in the background. One would say it was Japan, which is a common experience in this country. I am at work on a view [...] which looks like a Japanese village, and I'm also doing a mountain which one can see from anywhere here and which makes me think of Fujiyama.'[10] It has been proposed that Monet's *Grainstacks* of a few years earlier are related to Hokusai's Fujiyama series, and contemporary critics, including Edmond de Goncourt, related the two series.[11]

Thus, when he began to work seriously on building and then painting his water garden at Giverny, Monet was already completely infused with the spirit of Japanese art and its recurrent motifs. He created there a waterlily pond that would supply him with a virtually endless series of views to paint over the next 30 years. Among the first features of the man-made garden was the so-called Japanese bridge, erected in 1893; although he first painted the structure in the mid 1890s, he devoted an important series of canvases to it in 1899 and 1900, including *The waterlily pond* (cat 43). Here, the graceful horizontal arc of the bridge is juxtaposed with the verticals of the leaves of willows behind, much as an arched bridge and staked wisteria blossoms are juxtaposed in Hiroshige's *Inside Kameido Tenjin shrine* (cat 42), from the series *One hundred famous views of Edo*. Monet, inspired by such prints as *Horikiri iris garden* (fig 21), would plant the banks of the pond with clumps of iris and agapanthus and would later, in fact, erect a superstructure for the bridge, on which he grew the wisteria vines that became one of his favoured late motifs.

If Japan had been a fresh source of compositional inspiration for Monet in the 1860s and a means of asserting his modernity and stylishness in the mid 1870s, by the 1880s and 1890s its art had become second nature to him. When he transformed his garden, he created for himself at Giverny a Japan that was to become his paradise.

1 The Duc de Trévise, recording a 1920 conversation with Monet, in an article written in 1927; quoted in Charles F Stuckey ed, *Monet: a retrospective*, H L Levin, New York 1985, pp 320, 340

2 Throughout this essay the author is indebted to the research of Virginia Spate and David Bromfield, whose essay, 'A new and savage beauty: Monet and Japanese art' appears in *Monet and Japan*, exh cat, National Gallery of Australia, Canberra and University of Washington Press, Seattle 2001, hereafter cited as Spate, Hickey and Bromfield 2001. For their comments on flattened colour and perspective in Monet's paintings of the 1860s, see pp 12–13

3 For a complete catalogue of Monet's collection of Japanese prints, see Geneviève Aitken and Marianne Delafond, *La collection d'estampes japonaises de Claude Monet à Giverny*, Bibliothèque des arts, Lausanne 2003

4 The painting, now in the Metropolitan Museum of Art, is W 95; Renoir referred to it at the same time as 'Monet's painting, the Japanese one with little flags'. See Spate, Hickey and Bromfield 2001, p 201

5 John House, *Nature into art*, Yale University Press, New Haven, Connecticut 1986, pp 57–58

6 Monet seems not to have owned an impression of this print, but he owned other snow scenes by Hiroshige; see Aitken and Delafond 2003, cats 132, 147, and 149

7 Monet, Charles Bigot and Marius Chaumelin, quoted in Spate, Hickey and Bromfield 2001, pp 201–02

8 Monet owned an impression of the *Monkey Bridge*. See Aitken and Delafond 2003, cat 142

9 See Stuckey 1995, p 218

10 Monet writing in 1895, quoted in House 1986, p 58

11 See Spate, Hickey and Bromfield 2001, pp 40–41

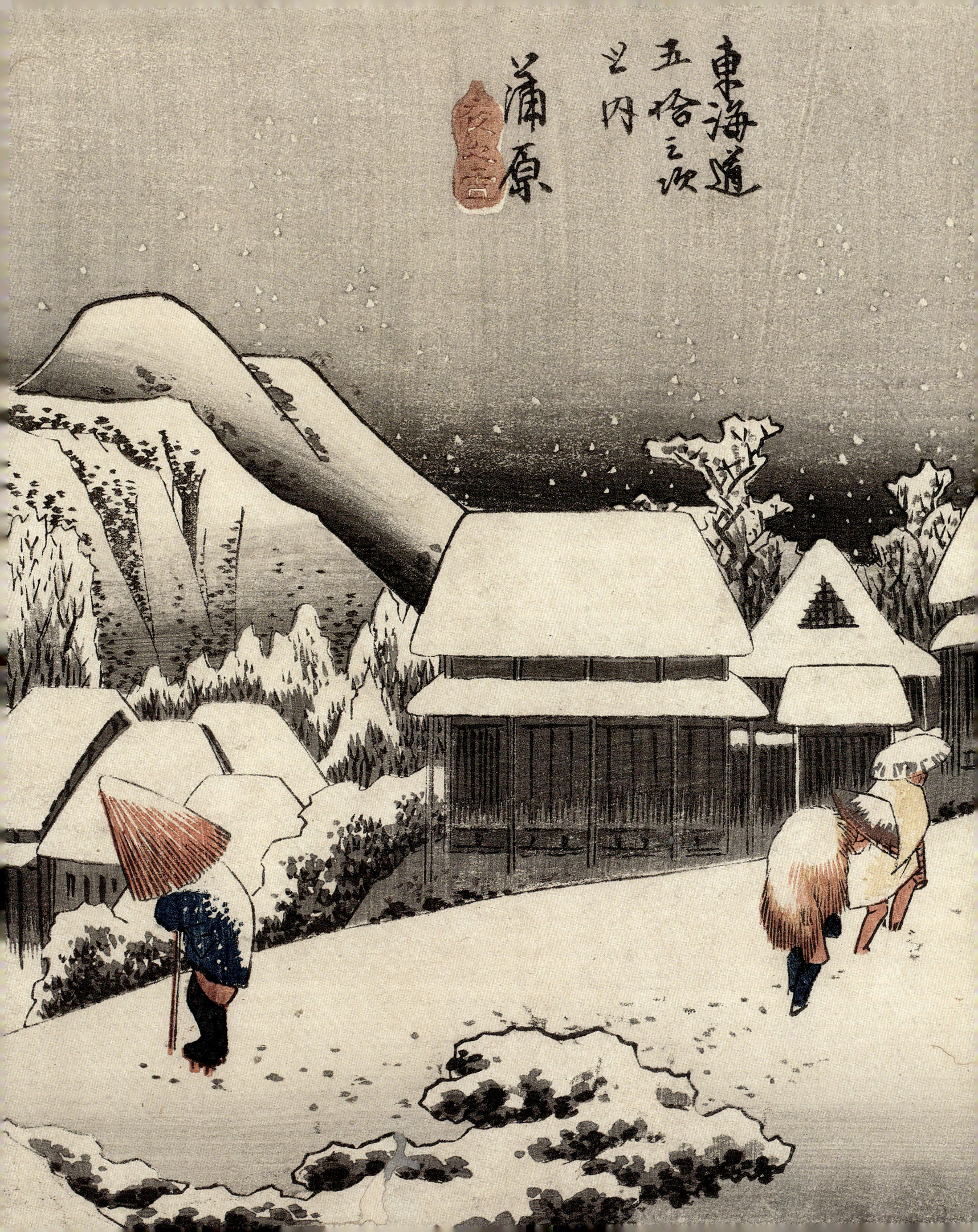
東海道
五拾三次
之内
蒲原
夜之雪

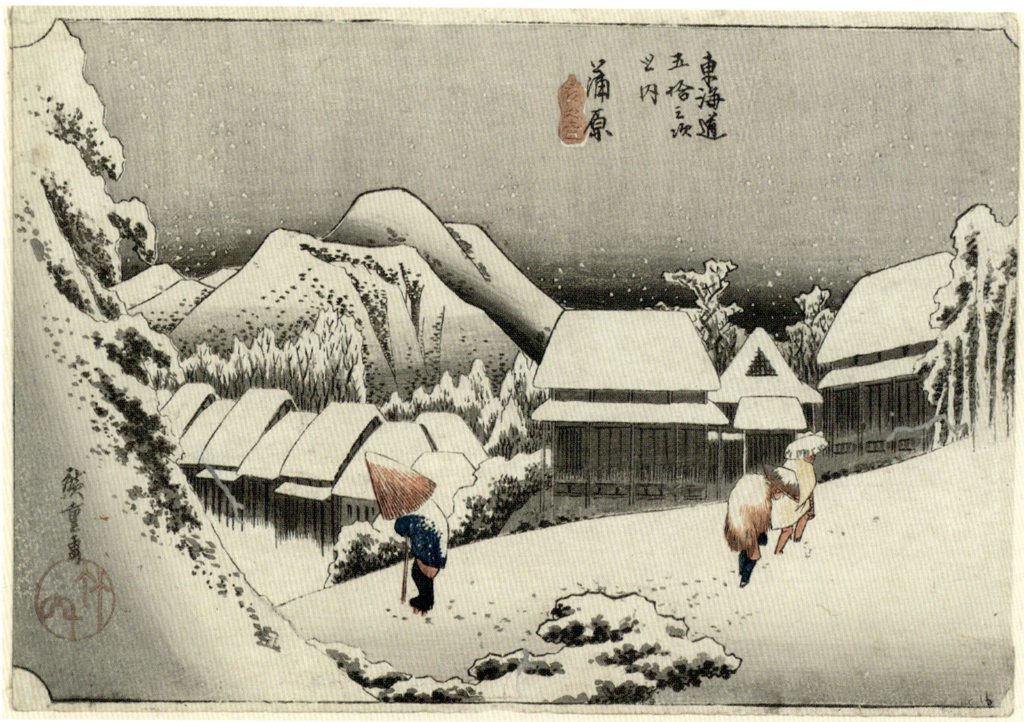

35

Utagawa Hiroshige I

Kanbara: night snow

Japan, Edo period, c1833–34

woodblock print; ink and colour on paper,
approx 24.5 x 35 cm
Museum of Fine Arts, Boston,
William Sturgis Bigelow Collection
11.17295

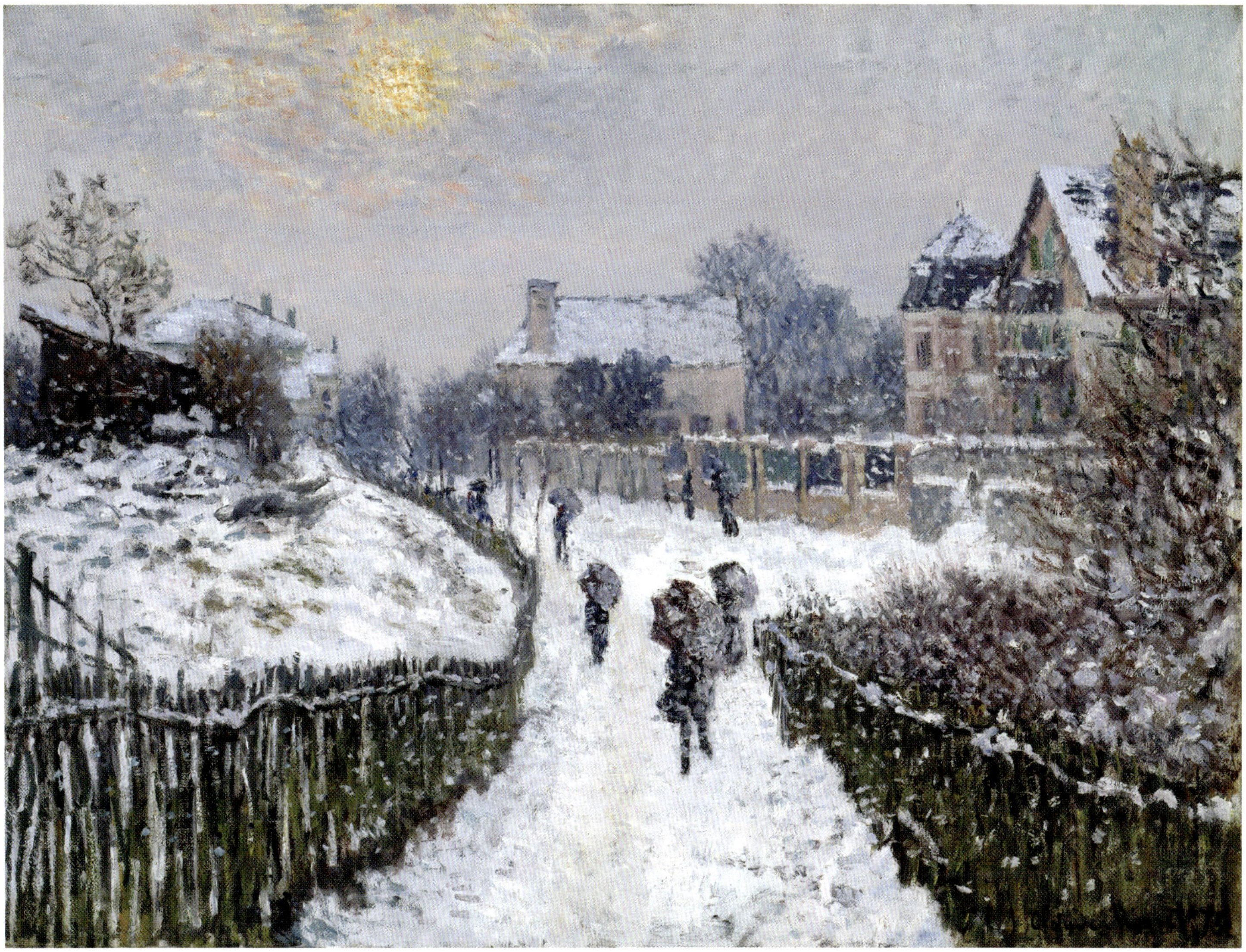

36
Claude Monet
Boulevard Saint-Denis, Argenteuil, in winter 1875
oil on canvas, 60.9 x 81.6 cm
Museum of Fine Arts, Boston,
gift of Richard Saltonstall
1978.633

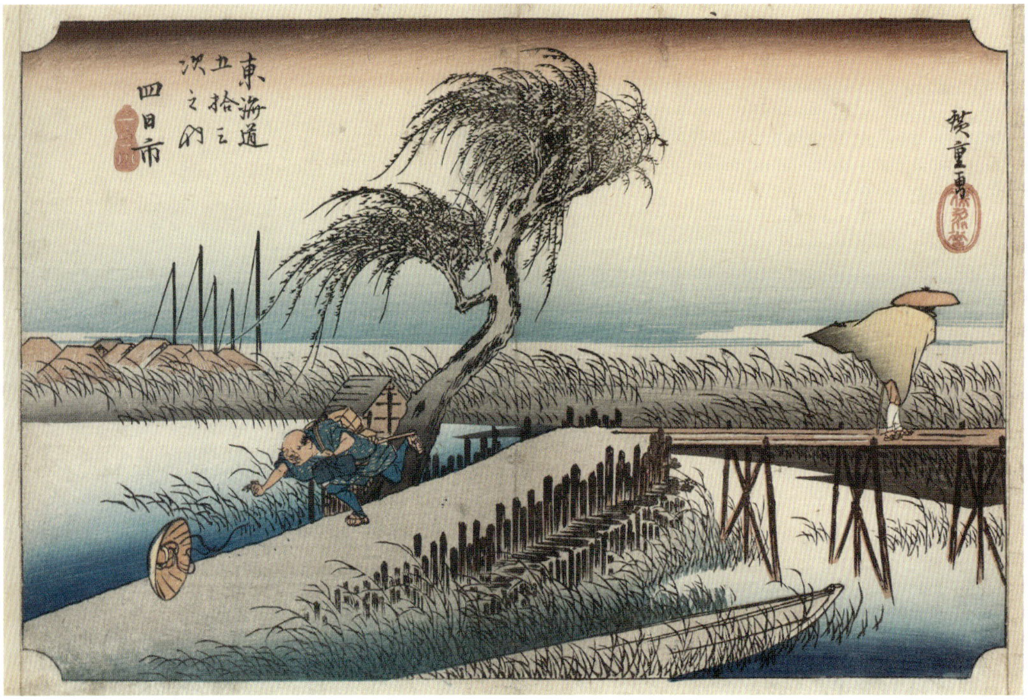

37

Utagawa Hiroshige I

Yokkaichi: Mie River

Japan, Edo period, c1833–34

woodblock print; ink and colour on paper,
24.5 x 35 cm
Museum of Fine Arts, Boston,
William Sturgis Bigelow Collection
11.30167

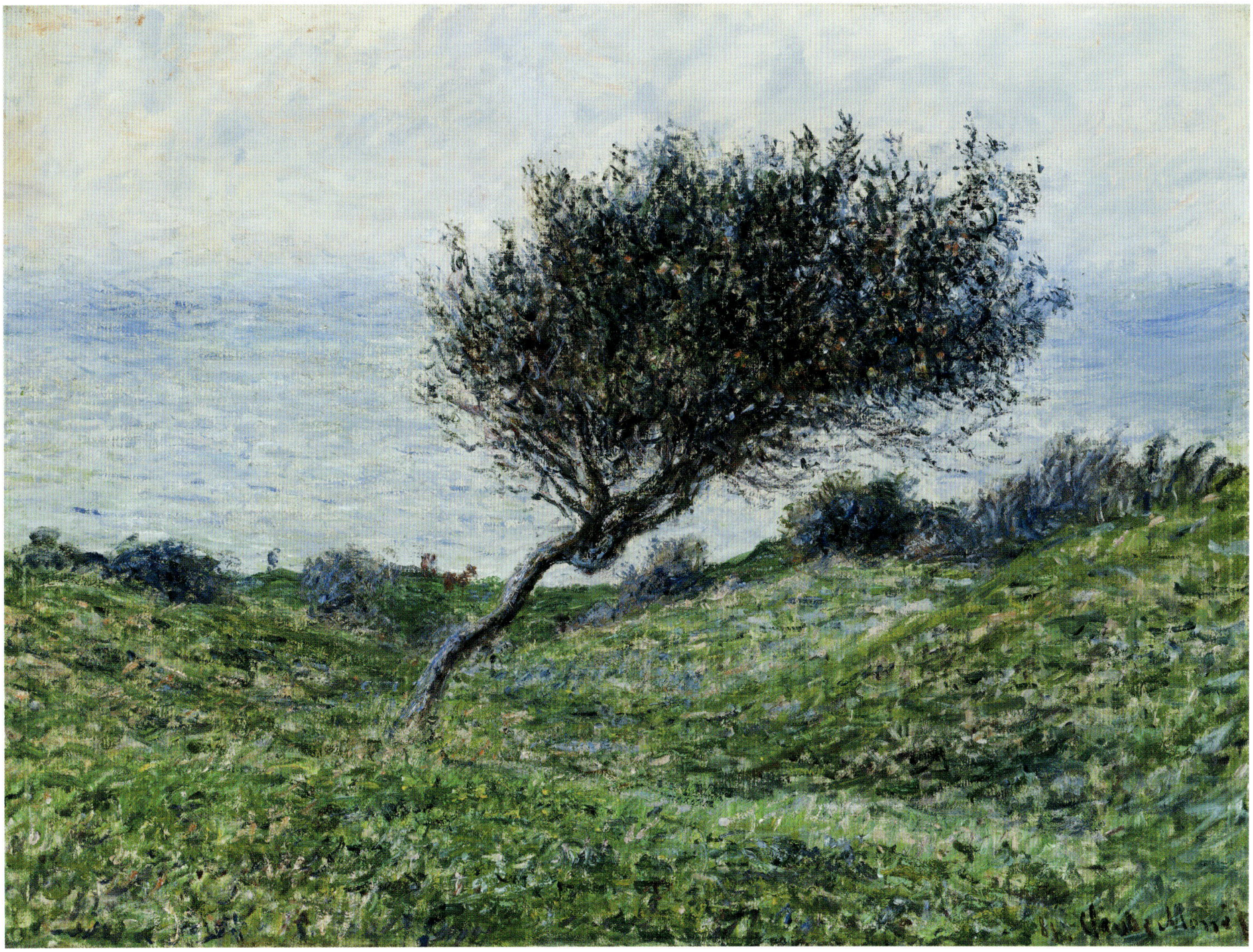

38

Claude Monet
Seacoast at Trouville 1881

oil on canvas, 60.7 x 81.3 cm
Museum of Fine Arts, Boston,
John Pickering Lyman Collection,
gift of Miss Theodora Lyman
19.1314

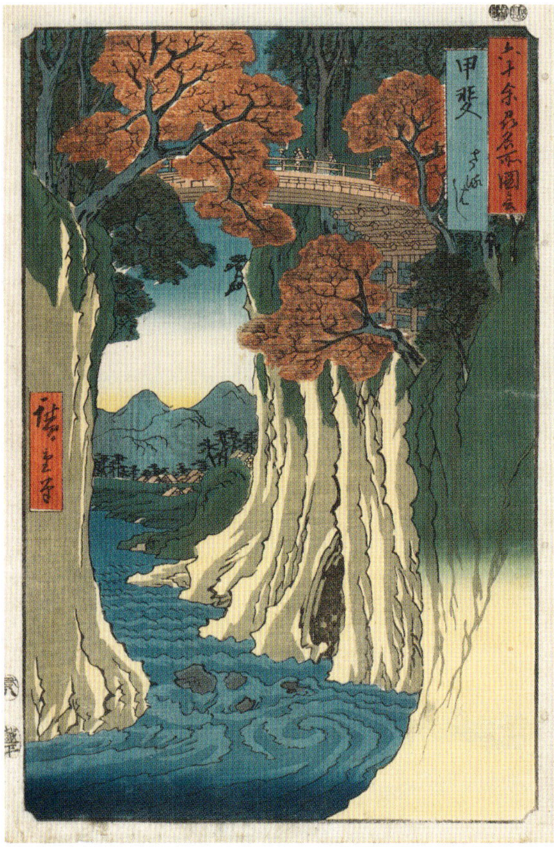

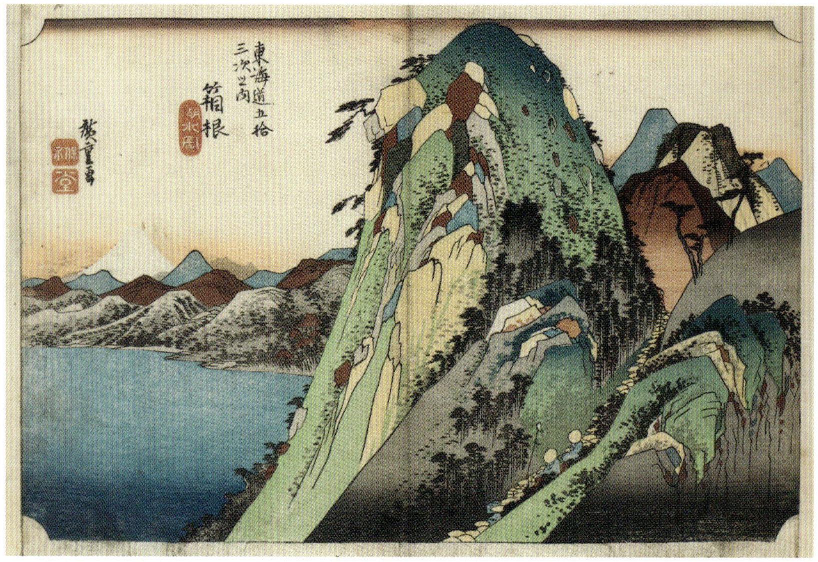

39
Utagawa Hiroshige I
Kai Province: Monkey Bridge
Japan, Edo period, 1853
woodblock print, ink and colour on paper,
37 x 25.4 cm
Museum of Fine Arts, Boston,
William Sturgis Bigelow Collection
11.26224

40
Utagawa Hiroshige I
Hakone: view of the lake
Japan, Edo period, c1833–34
woodblock print, ink and colour on paper,
24.7 x 34.8 cm
Museum of Fine Arts, Boston,
William Sturgis Bigelow Collection
11.26106

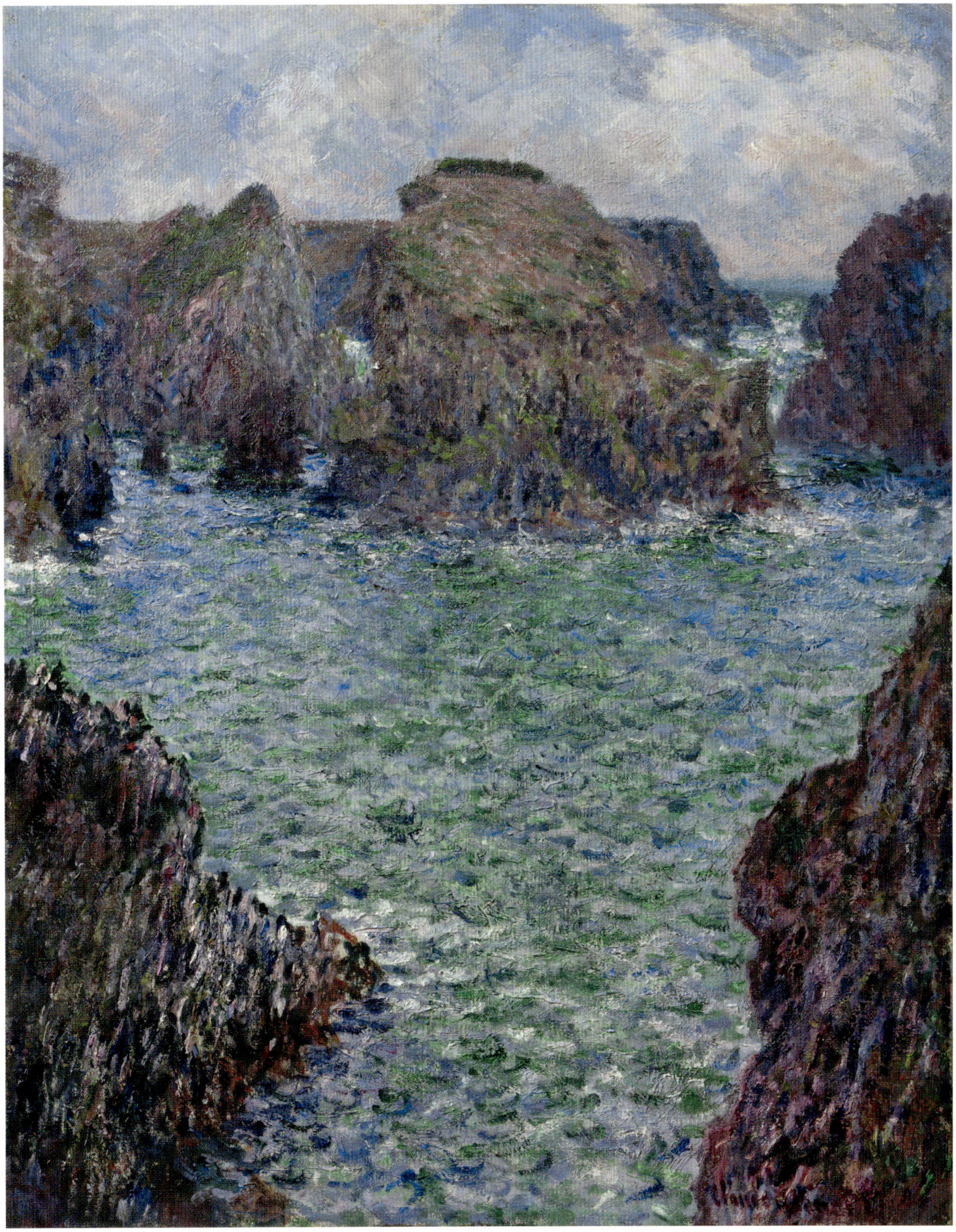

41

Claude Monet

Port-Goulphar, Belle-Ile 1887

oil on canvas, 81 x 65 cm
Art Gallery of New South Wales,
purchased 1949
8356

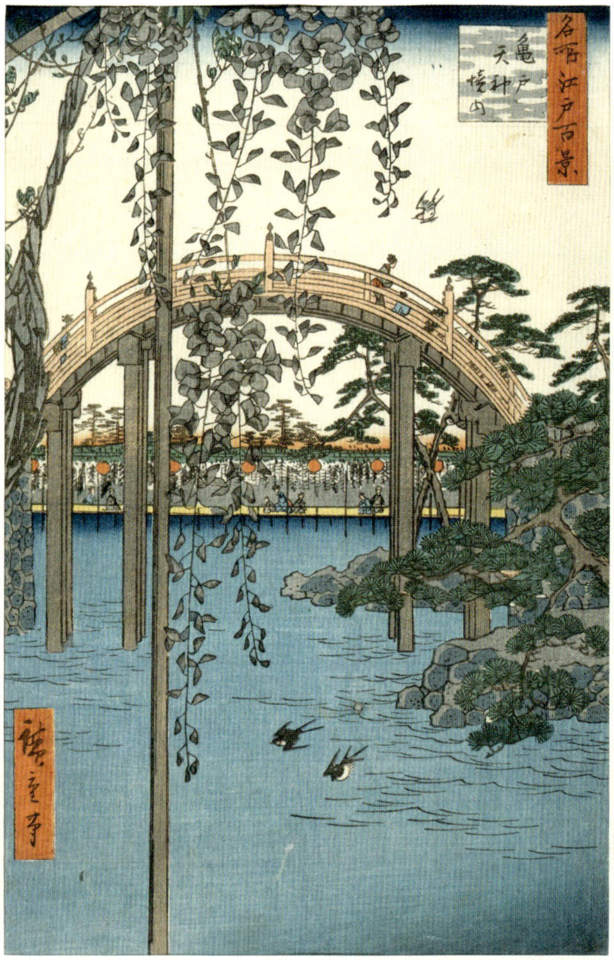

42

Utagawa Hiroshige I

Inside Kameido Tenjin shrine

Japan, Edo period, 1856

woodblock print; ink and colour on paper,
35.6 x 24.2 cm
Museum of Fine Arts, Boston,
gift of Dr G S Amsden
52.1423

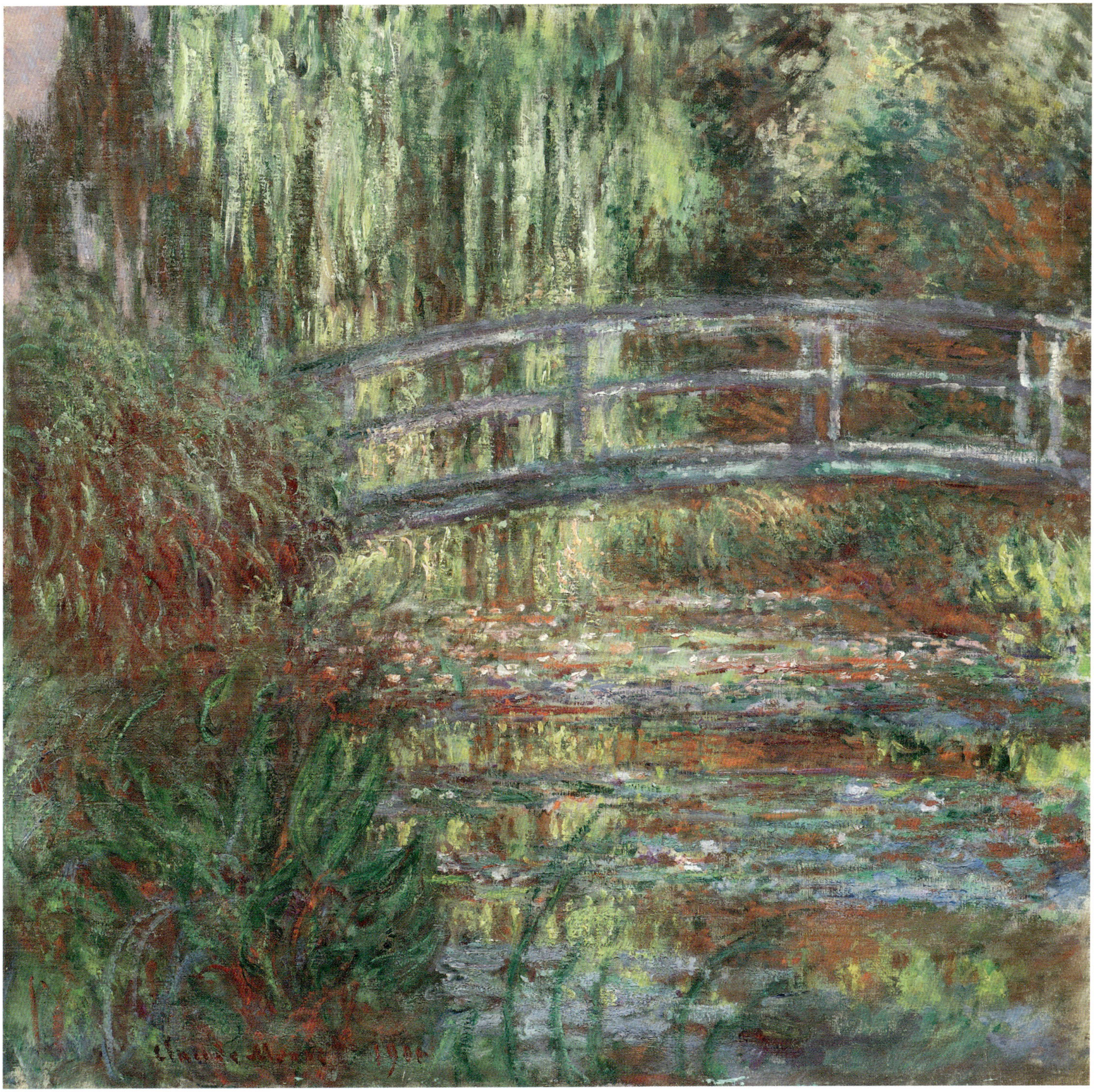

43
Claude Monet
The waterlily pond 1900
oil on canvas, 90.2 x 92.7 cm
Museum of Fine Arts, Boston,
given in memory of Governor Alvan T Fuller
by the Fuller Foundation
61.959

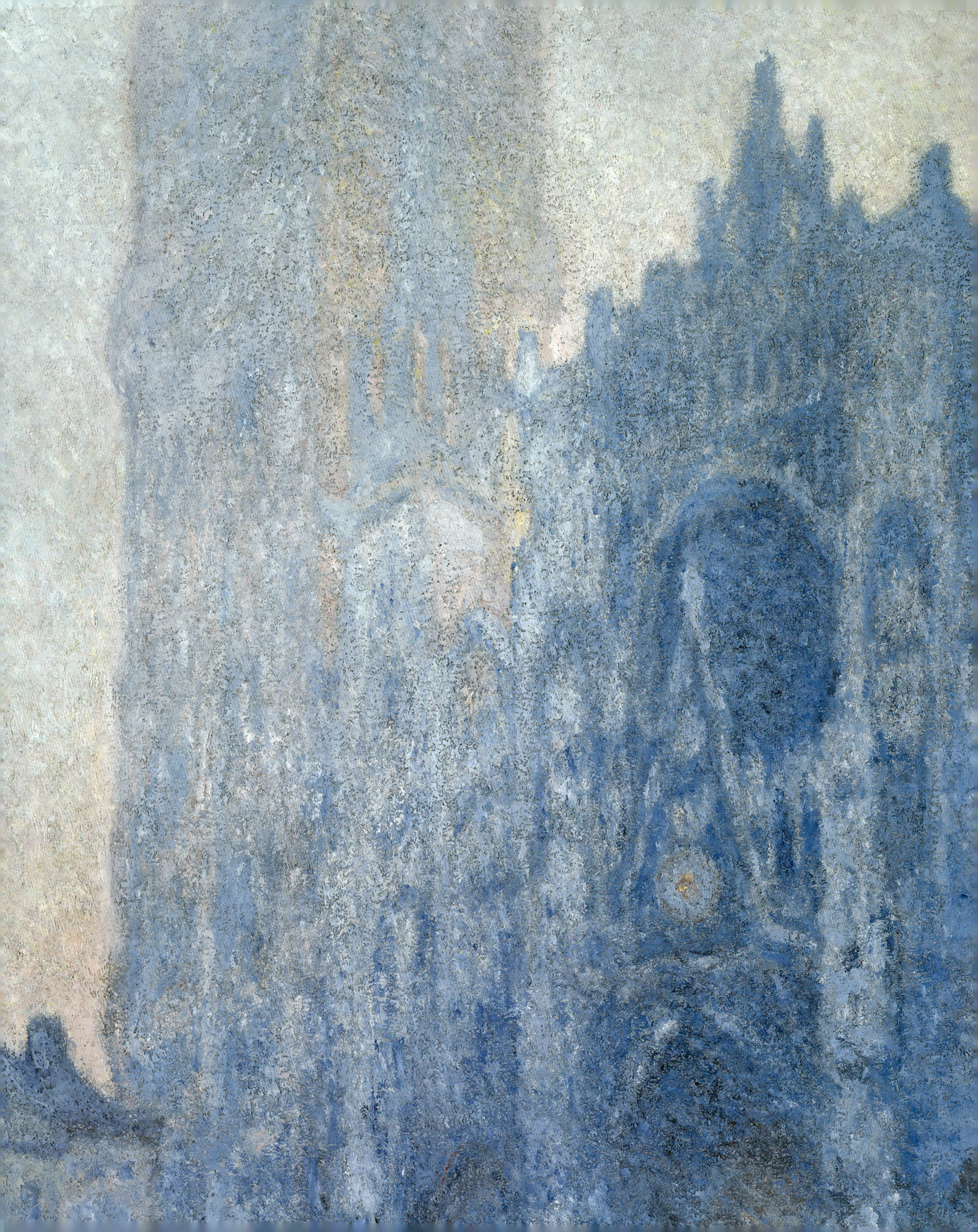

MONET'S SERIES

Monet's series paintings are generally regarded as a product of the 1890s. It is important to remember, however, that since the mid 1870s the artist had been at work on groups of works painted in a single locale: various bridges over the Seine at Argenteuil, for instance, which he depicted in 1874; the train shed and tracks of the Gare Saint-Lazare in Paris, where he painted nearly a dozen canvases in 1876; the cliffs of Normandy at Pourville, Varengeville, Trouville and Etretat, where he painted in the early to mid 1880s (see cats 23 and 24 and figs 5 and 6); or sites on the Mediterranean, such as Antibes, where he made concentrated groups of related works in 1888 (see cats 26 and 27). Some of these had been exhibited together shortly after their completion. Several views of the Gare Saint-Lazare were shown at the Impressionist exhibition of 1877; a number of Normandy coastal scenes were among the many canvases chosen by Durand-Ruel to represent Monet at the 1882 exhibition; and in 1888 Theo van Gogh had shown Monet's recent views of Antibes at the Boussod & Valadon gallery. These latest paintings, imbued with the jewelled light of the Mediterranean, were ironically regarded by Monet's friends Pissarro and Renoir, as well as his rival Degas, with equal distaste – because they were variously 'made to sell', 'vulgar' or 'retrograde'.[1]

While Monet had found the challenge of capturing the brilliant light of the south of France almost unbearable, he decided in the next year to set himself a more difficult problem. Rather than venturing to the seaside, he would go in midwinter to one of the most remote regions of France, the Massif Central, and to Fresselines above the Creuse Valley, where in the course of three months he was to embark on some two dozen canvases. Fourteen of these new works were shown as a group within an exhibition of more than 140 canvases by Monet, accompanied by sculptures by his friend Auguste Rodin at the Galerie Georges Petit between 21 June and 21 September 1889. (Although many of the *Creuse* paintings shown are not precisely identifiable, it has been proposed that cats 44 and 46 and fig 29, p 142 were among the group chosen by Monet for display.[2]) Critics praised the paintings for their 'incomparable majesty', or 'extraordinary mastery'.[3]

In spite of the success of his exhibition, Monet ceased to paint for a considerable period, consumed with the project to purchase his late friend Manet's 1863 masterpiece *Olympia* for the state by a subscription. When he returned to his paints and canvases in 1890, it was in the fields surrounding Giverny – some literally in his backyard – that he concentrated his efforts. Views of wheat pastures filled with poppies became a favoured subject – a remarkable example is *Field of poppies near Giverny* (fig 22). It is a particularly simple but still sophisticated composition, with bands of green and red leaves and flowers in the foreground and brilliant blue sky with white clouds above, the sky punctuated by the trees rising from the horizon, rising and falling and mounting to a crescendo in the form of one tall, straight poplar to the right of centre, coming to a conclusion in the mass of a hill that merges with a block of trees at right.

By the end of the year Monet was fully engaged in painting the stacks of wheat that the farmers of Giverny massed in careful constructions, protected by thatch, in the fields on the high ground behind his house. As Paul Tucker has noted, the house-like grainstacks that dominate these images are almost always juxtaposed with actual farm buildings and houses. In *Grainstack/Haystack (sunset)* (cat 47), for instance, the roofs and gables of houses clustered beneath the hill almost dissolve in the light of the setting sun at left, while in *Grainstack/Haystack (snow effect)* (fig 23) they cluster at the right of the space defined by the canvas, as if huddling in the cold of a bright but snowy day.

When, in May of 1891, Monet exhibited a number of works at Durand-Ruel, including 15 of the grainstack paintings (one of which was *Haystacks, midday*, cat 48), he asked his friend Gustave Geffroy to write a preface to the catalogue. 'The grouping together of 15 canvases of grainstacks,' Geffroy wrote, 'each representing the same subject, with a rendition of the same landscape, is an extraordinarily victorious artistic demonstration. For his part, Claude Monet has been able to substantiate the continuous appearance in new aspects,

Claude Monet *Rouen Cathedral façade and Tour d'Albane (morning effect)* 1894 (detail), cat 49

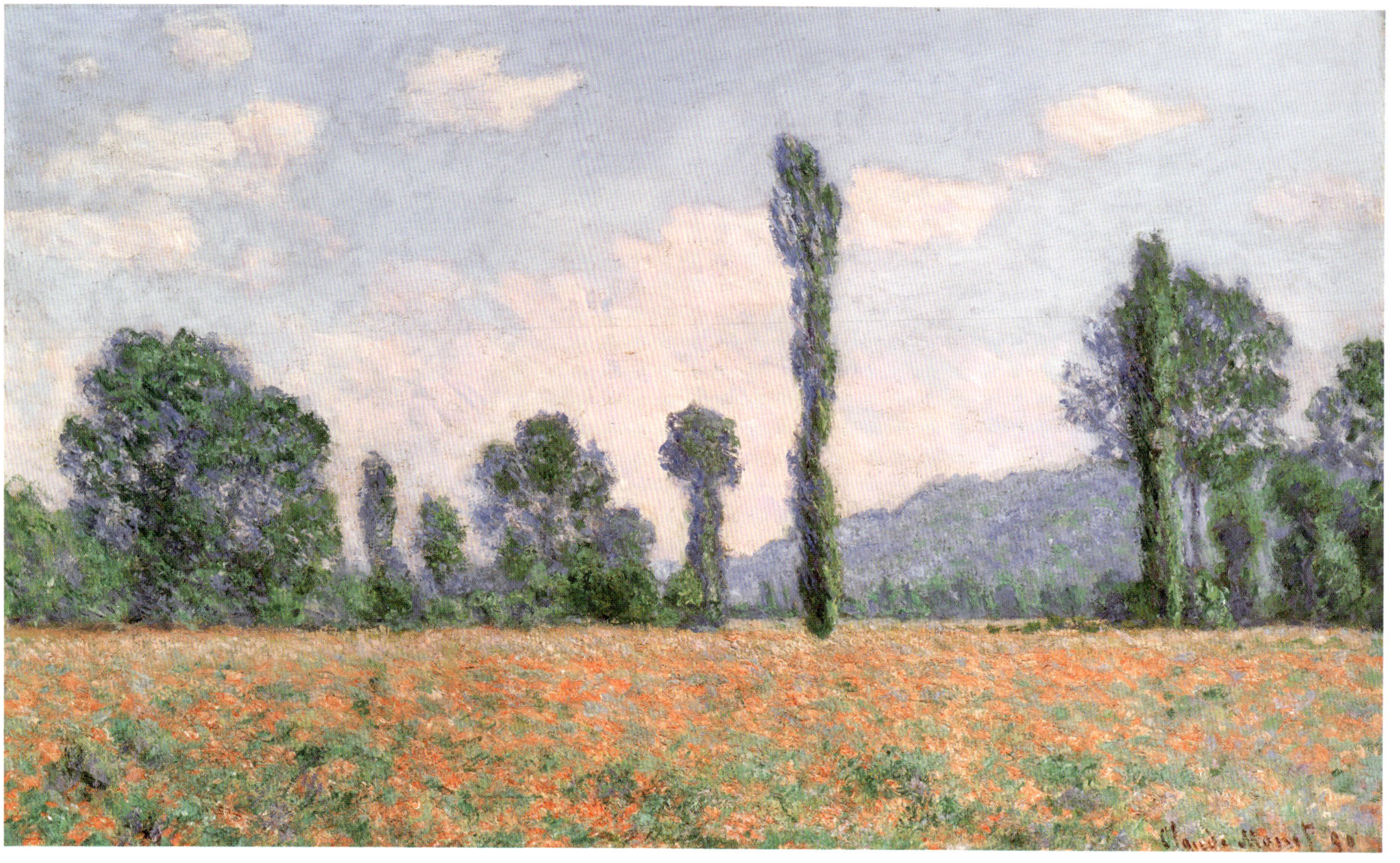

fig 22
Claude Monet
Field of poppies near Giverny 1890
oil on canvas, 60.8 x 101 cm
Museum of Fine Arts, Boston,
deposited by the Trustees of the
White Fund, Lawrence, Massachusetts

fig 23
Claude Monet
Grainstack/Haystack (snow effect) 1891
oil on canvas, 65.4 x 92.4 cm
Museum of Fine Arts, Boston, gift of Miss Aimée and Miss Rosamond Lamb in memory of Mr and Mrs Horatio Appleton Lamb
1970.253

fig 24
Claude Monet
Poplars on the bank of the Epte river 1891
oil on canvas, 100.3 x 65.2 cm
Philadelphia Museum of Art, Pennsylvania, bequest of Anne Thomson in memory of her father, Frank Thomson, and her mother, Mary Elizabeth Clarke Thomson, 1954
1954-66-8 Photograph: The Philadelphia Museum of Art / Art Resource, NY

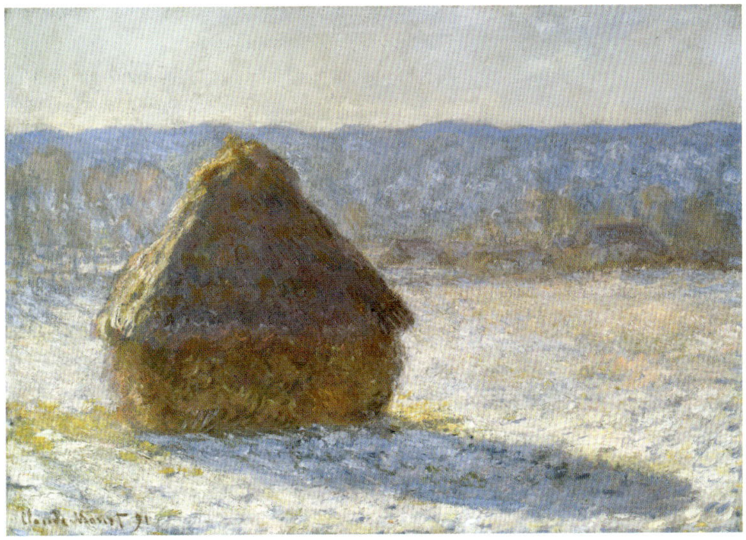

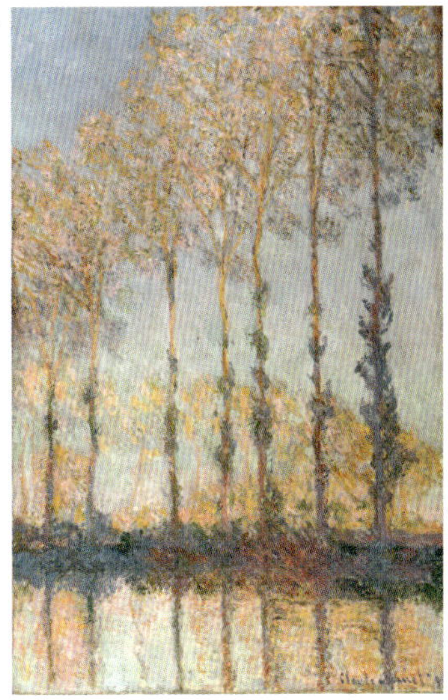

of immutable objects, the uninterrupted flood of changing and inter-related sensations, apparent in the face of a changeless spectacle. He substantiates the possibility of summing up the poetry of the universe within a circumscribed space'.[4]

'The possibility of summing up the poetry of the universe within a circumscribed space' was to become Monet's greatest desire in the next decade, as again and again he chose a quite limited subject and subjected it to the power of his vision. By the spring of 1891, while the *Grainstacks* exhibition was still on view, he had already turned to the idea of painting the rows of poplars that flanked the Epte river near his home (fig 24) – refining and abstracting still further the theme that he had announced in such paintings as *Poplars at Giverny* in 1887 (see cat 34). With their strict geometries of vertical trees, horizontal bands of water and receding diagonal lines of foliage and tree trunks into the distance, the *Poplar* paintings were enormously varied within their range of scale and layout, but each was rigidly controlled compositionally. Monet's friend the critic Octave Mirbeau saw them in early February of 1892 and, in admiring these formal qualities, declared that the painter had 'attained the absolute beauty of great decoration'.[5]

Even before the exhibition of his *Poplars* at Durand-Ruel's gallery – which opened on 29 February 1892, and closed less than two weeks later – Monet was at work seeking out other subjects for similar campaigns of painting and resulting exhibitions. His next target was decidedly uncharacteristic for the man widely considered the greatest living landscape painter: he decided to go to the city of Rouen, the spiritual heart of Normandy, to paint the great Gothic cathedral constructed between the 13th and 16th centuries, the façade of which – Monet's primary motif – is a masterpiece of the flamboyant style. Geffroy, as early as 1891, predicted that Monet would seek out such new motifs, 'as lofty and beautiful as the rocks on promontories'.[6] After an exploratory trip in February 1892, when he made small sketches in a pocket notebook, Monet returned in earnest to Rouen in March, beginning the series of canvases that would, in all, number more than 30 views. In late March, he wrote to Madame Alice Monet – whom he had married after the death of Ernest Hoschedé – that he had worked on '14 paintings today, it's unprecedented. If I lived in Rouen, it's now that I'd be starting to understand my subject.'[7]

The vast majority of Monet's paintings focus on the facade of the church, generally rising from the bottom of the canvas to the top, as in *Rouen Cathedral, façade* (1894, fig 25), where the face of the cathedral is bathed in red gold light, contrasting with the clear blue sky above. Sometimes, however, Monet would take a different point of view, as in *Rouen Cathedral façade and Tour d'Albane (morning effect)* (cat 49), dated 1894 but conceivably begun much earlier, where the tower disengages from the left margin of the picture space, allowing the lower houses of the town to be seen in dramatic contrast to the height and majesty of the cathedral, and calling attention to the early light engulfing the upper regions of the canvas. As Tucker explains, 'Monet emphasised the building's irregularities more than its symmetries', so that 'the whole façade appears to be moving [...] a collection of individual parts that are related intrinsically, not according to some structural rationale'.[8]

The sense of contained movement perceived in the *Cathedrals* is calmed and restructured in Monet's next great series, a group of views of the Seine seen in early morning, undertaken after he had returned to the coastal cliffs of Dieppe and Pourville in 1896. The Seine – the locus of some of Monet's most important paintings of the 1860s, 1870s and 1880s – had not been far from his imagination in the early 1890s; he had painted the breakup of its frozen water in 1893 and a group of views of Vernon seen from Giverny in 1894 – all in the midst of completing the *Rouen Cathedral* series. But following the success of the Rouen paintings at exhibition in 1895, Monet opted for an altogether new scheme: he would go out to the Seine every morning just after dawn and try to depict the river changing from moment to moment as the sky brightened behind the trees on either bank. The paintings all partake of the same composition: the river typically reaches a vanishing point roughly halfway up the

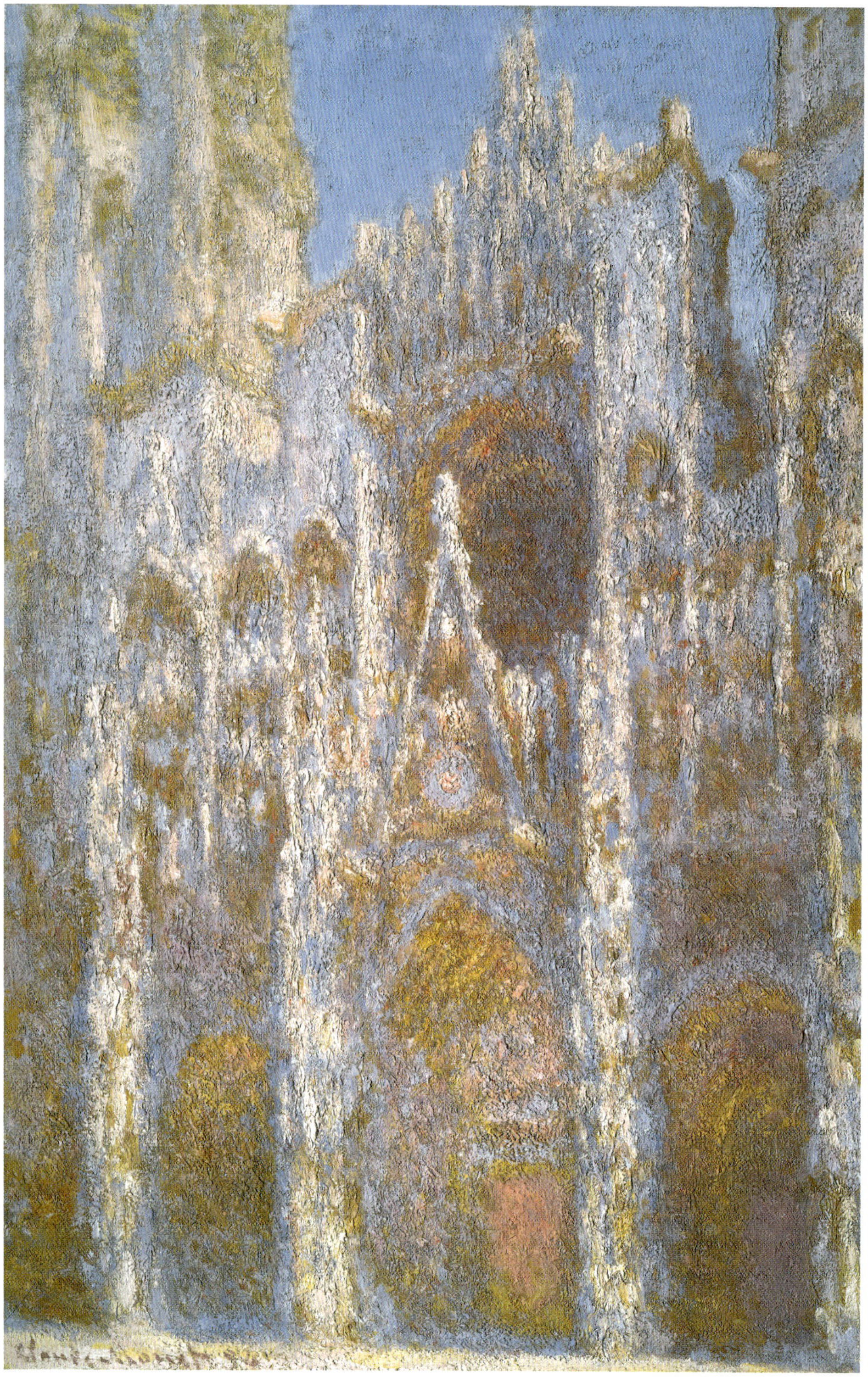

fig 25
Claude Monet
Rouen Cathedral, façade 1894
oil on canvas, 100.6 x 66 cm
Museum of Fine Arts, Boston,
Juliana Cheney Edwards collection
39.671

fig 26
Claude Monet
Morning on the Seine, near Giverny 1896
oil on canvas, 73.7 x 93 cm
Museum of Fine Arts, Boston,
Juliana Cheney Edwards collection,
bequest of Grace M Edwards in memory
of her mother
39.655

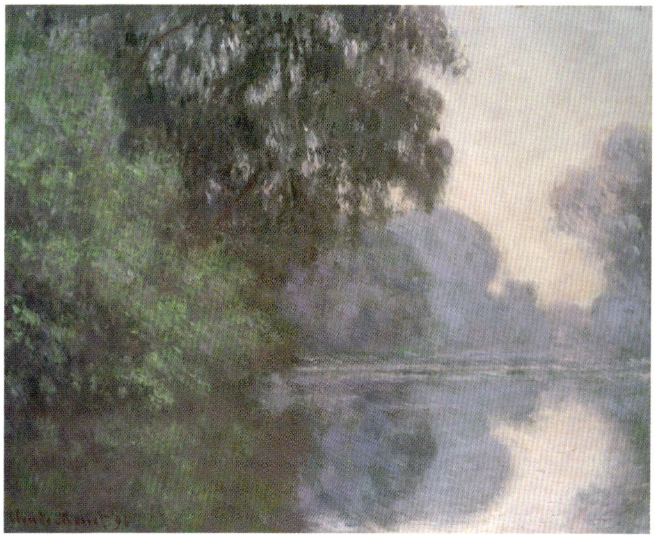

canvas. On either side are stands of trees overhanging the water, which are reflected in the surface, creating a nearly perfect symmetry (clearest if the painting is rotated 90 degrees in either direction). The vagaries of the river itself make clear what is seen only in reflection, but often Monet overlays the reflection with additional foliage that is near to him in his painting boat, the locus for this series of exquisite studies. In *Morning on the Seine, near Giverny* (1897, cat 50), for example, the symmetrical patterns of reflection are distinct at right, but at left a filmy cloud of pale green stands out from the dark branches of the pattern of the trees – almost certainly meant to represent a willow bush on the bank nearest Monet's boat.

And symmetry was not always Monet's goal: in another *Morning on the Seine* (fig 26), perhaps completed as early as 1896, Monet disturbs the balance of the composition by lowering the vanishing point, giving the whole composition a greater sense of spatial depth and, ultimately, reducing the decorative qualities that he had prized in *Poplars* of 1892. Within the series, Monet used an enormous range of atmospheric effects, but a remarkably uniform palette – greens, mostly cool and dark but sometimes sharper and pale, combined with grey-blues, mauves, soft purples and pinks: the colours of morning. Many critics, both Monet's contemporaries and some in modern times, have recognised that the *Mornings* are recollections or elegies to the art of Monet's great predecessor Camille Corot.[10]

Monet's last great series paintings of the 1890s deal with bridges of very different sorts. On the one hand, there is the group of paintings of the Japanese bridge in the water garden at Giverny that had its tentative start shortly after the bridge's construction in 1893 but took firm hold in 1899, with a series of beautiful images begun in July that were resumed in 1900 (see cat 43). These works announce the great pond-surface paintings that would dominate the first decade of Monet's work in the 20th century, with their tension between direct observation and reflection – beautifully prefigured in the *Mornings* of 1896–97. But a most remarkable development took place in Monet's art in 1899.[11]

He decided to travel with Madame Monet to London to paint the Thames, which he had not depicted since his exile there in 1870–71. He arrived in London in September 1899 and stayed just over a month, painting views of the Thames from his riverside hotel room; among the works that he may have begun – or at least planned – on that first trip are *Waterloo Bridge* (cat 51) and *Charing Cross Bridge (overcast day)* (cat 52). The latter canvas was almost certainly finished only in 1900 – concurrent with *The waterlily pond* (cat 43). Monet declared that he loved London for its fogs, which enabled him to paint the much-desired *enveloppe* of atmosphere more readily, even, than on the Seine in early morning. He returned to London for painting campaigns in 1900 and 1901 – when he began his series of spectacular views of the Houses of Parliament seen from the opposite bank of the Thames, rivalling the painter Turner in his pyrotechnic sunsets. Returning to Giverny, Monet continued to refine the paintings until the time of their exhibition – in 1904 – when 37 paintings were shown, of which 18 were purchased by Durand-Ruel. It was Monet's greatest ever commercial success; but already he was at work on the series of paintings that were, in a sense, to culminate his career, the *Waterlilies* for which he is surely best remembered.

1 The seminal work on Monet's strategies of painting in series is Paul Hayes Tucker's 1989 catalogue *Monet in the '90s: the series paintings*, to which the author is most indebted. For the reactions of Degas, Pissarro and Renoir, see Tucker 1989, p 39
2 See W 1219, 1230 and 1221
3 Paul Focher and Octave Maus, cited in Tucker 1989, p 55 and note 34
4 Gustave Geffroy, 1891, quoted in Stuckey 1985, p 162
5 Octave Mirbeau, quoted in Stuckey 1995, p 222
6 Geffroy, quoted in Tucker 1989, p 145
7 Monet to Alice Monet, 29 Mar 1893, quoted in Kendall 1989, p 178
8 Tucker 1989, p 176
9 Tucker 1989, p 219
10 See Tucker 1989, pp 232–35, and Fronia E Wissman in Shackelford, Wissman et al 2002, pp 223–24
11 For chronological details, see Stuckey 1995, pp 232–37

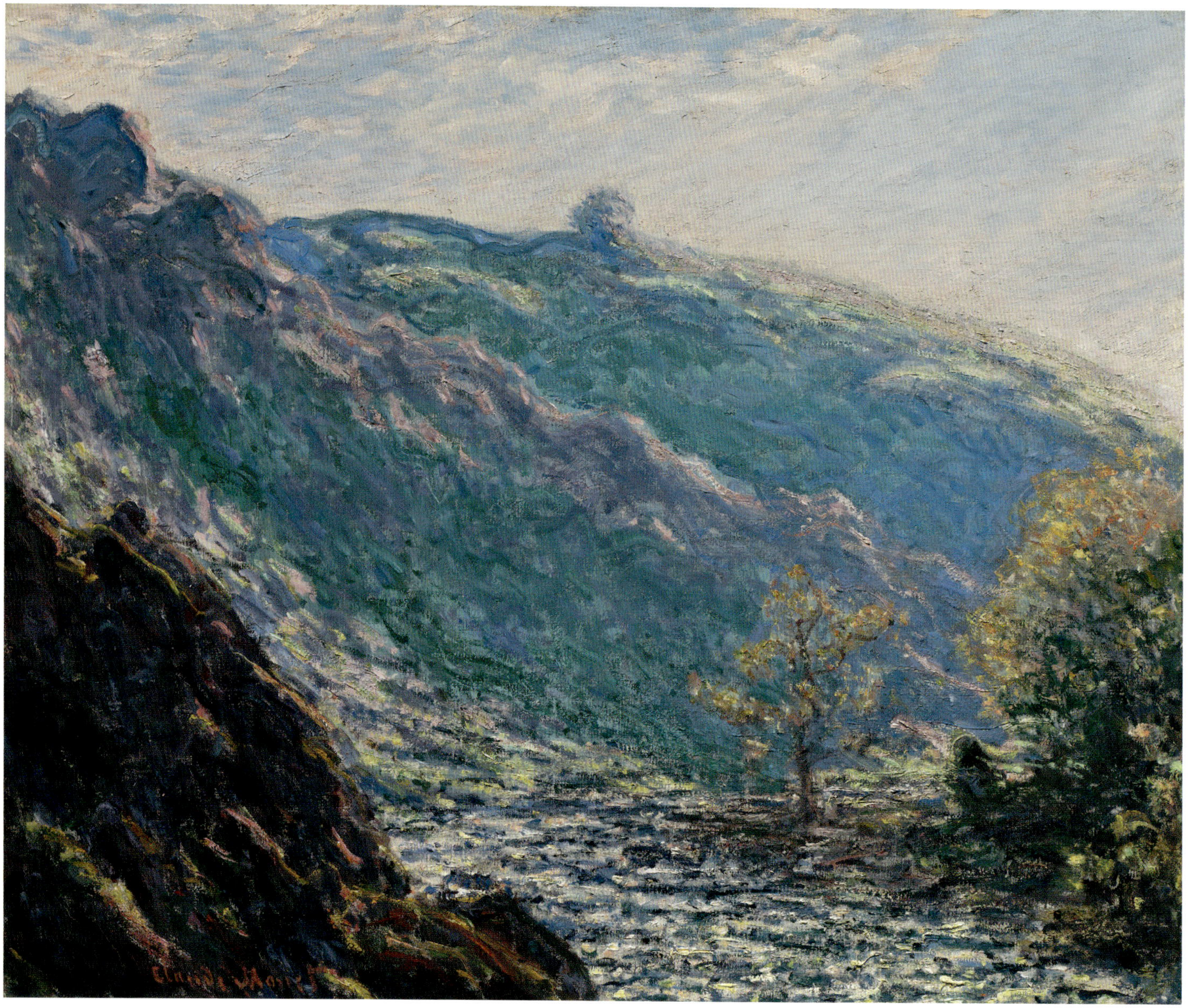

44

Claude Monet
Ravine of the Petite Creuse 1889

oil on canvas, 76.2 x 92.7 cm
Private collection, courtesy
Museum of Fine Arts, Boston

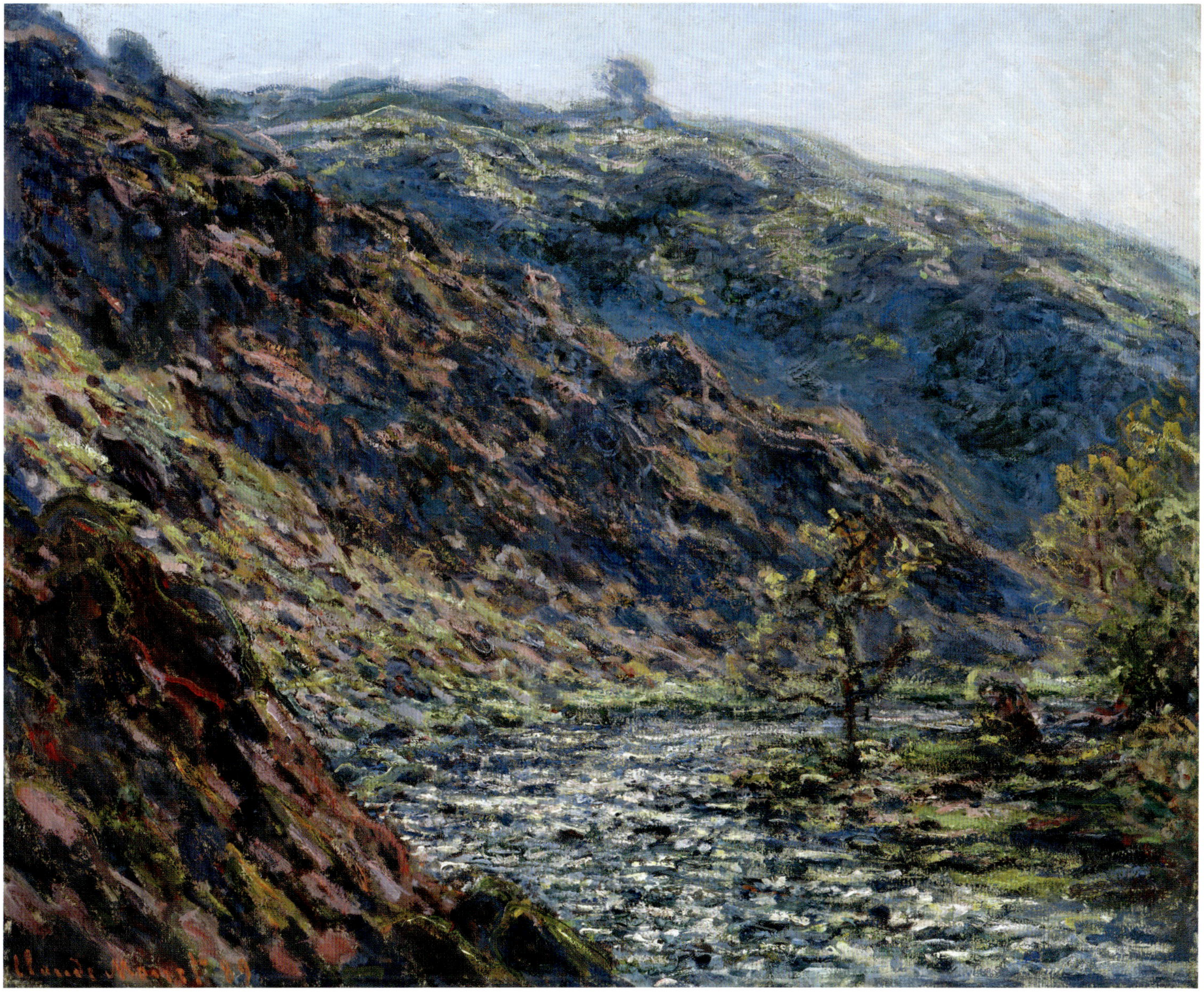

45

Claude Monet

Valley of the Petite Creuse 1889

oil on canvas, 65.4 x 81.3 cm
Museum of Fine Arts, Boston,
bequest of David P Kimball in memory
of his wife Clara Bertram Kimball
23.541

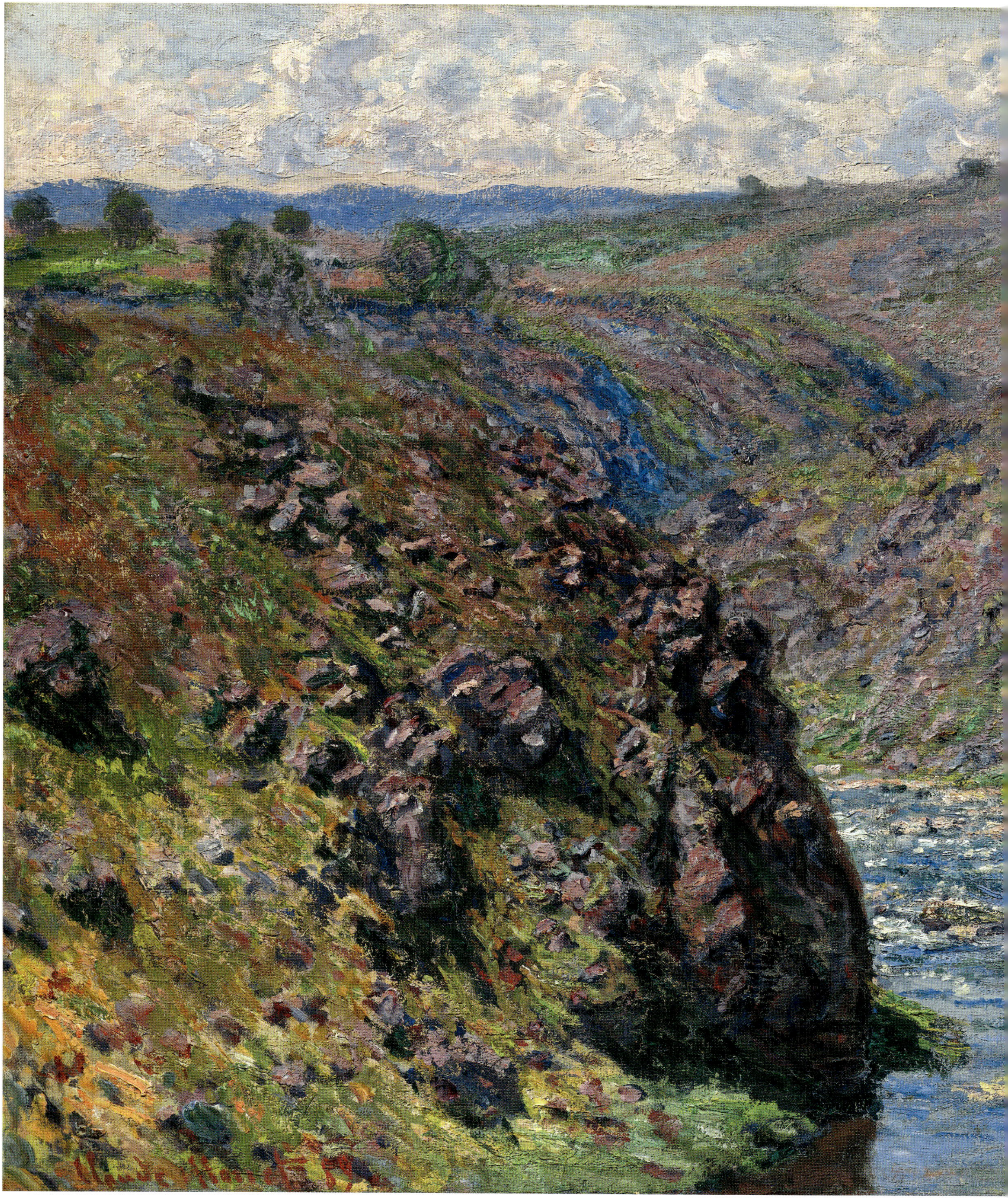

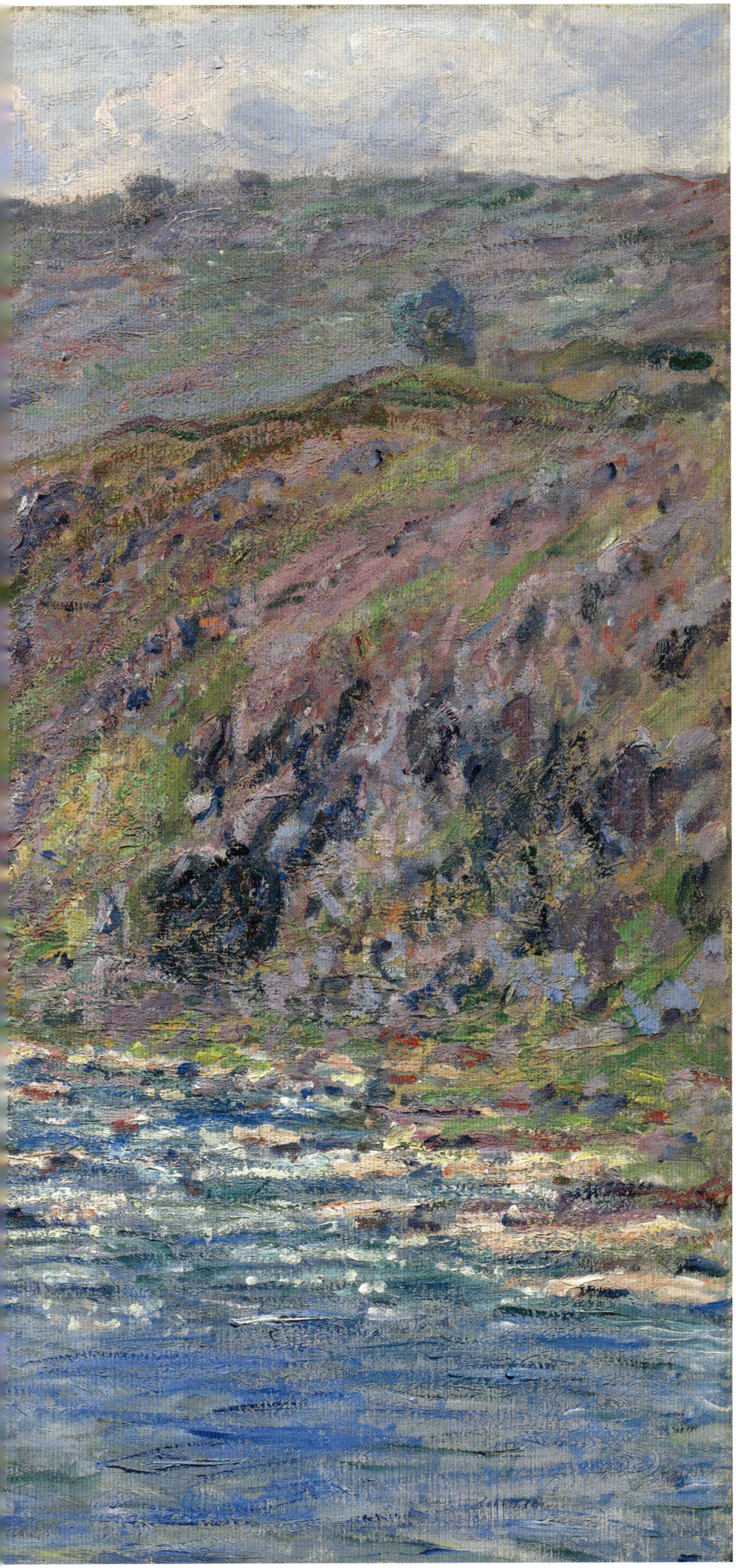

46

Claude Monet
Valley of the Creuse (sunlight effect) 1889
oil on canvas, 65.1 x 92.4 cm
Museum of Fine Arts, Boston,
Juliana Cheney Edwards Collection
25.107

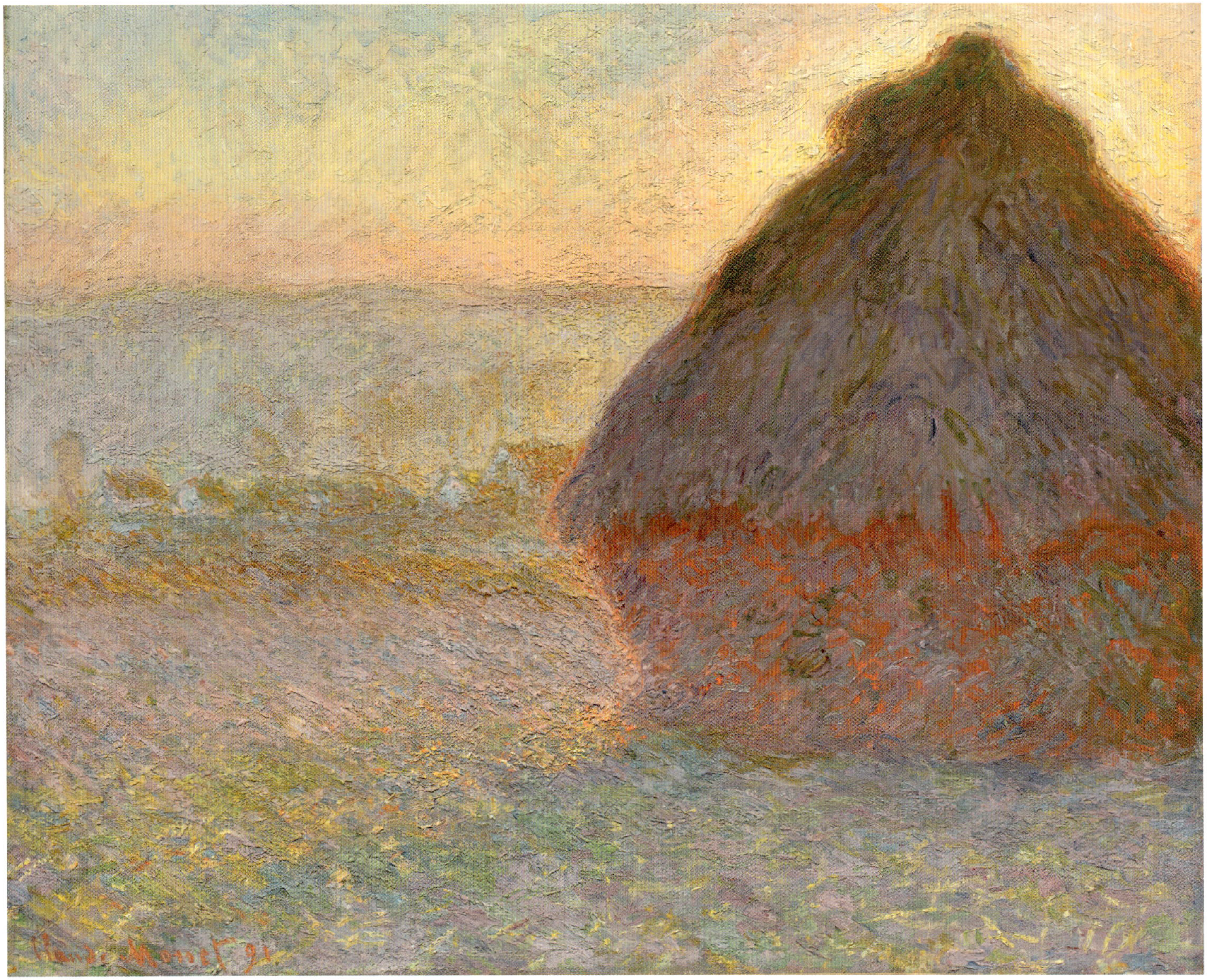

47

Claude Monet
Grainstack/Haystack (sunset) 1891

oil on canvas, 73.3 x 92.7 cm
Museum of Fine Arts, Boston,
Juliana Cheney Edwards Collection
25.112

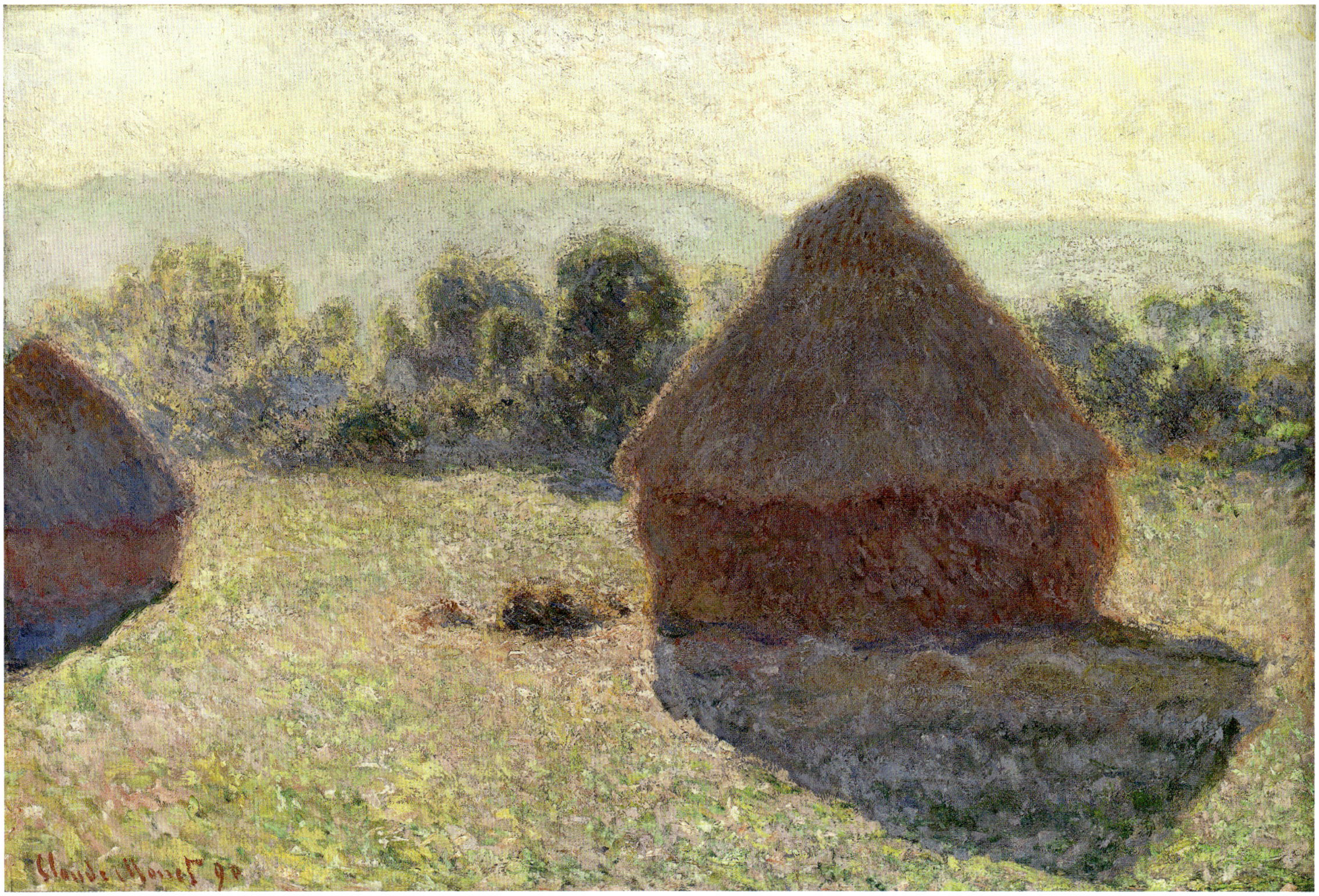

48

Claude Monet

Haystacks, midday 1890

oil on canvas, 65.6 x 100.6 cm
National Gallery of Australia,
purchased 1979
79.16

49

Claude Monet

Rouen Cathedral façade and Tour d'Albane (morning effect) 1894

oil on canvas, 106.1 x 73.9 cm
Museum of Fine Arts, Boston,
Tompkins Collection –
Arthur Golden Tompkins Fund
24.6

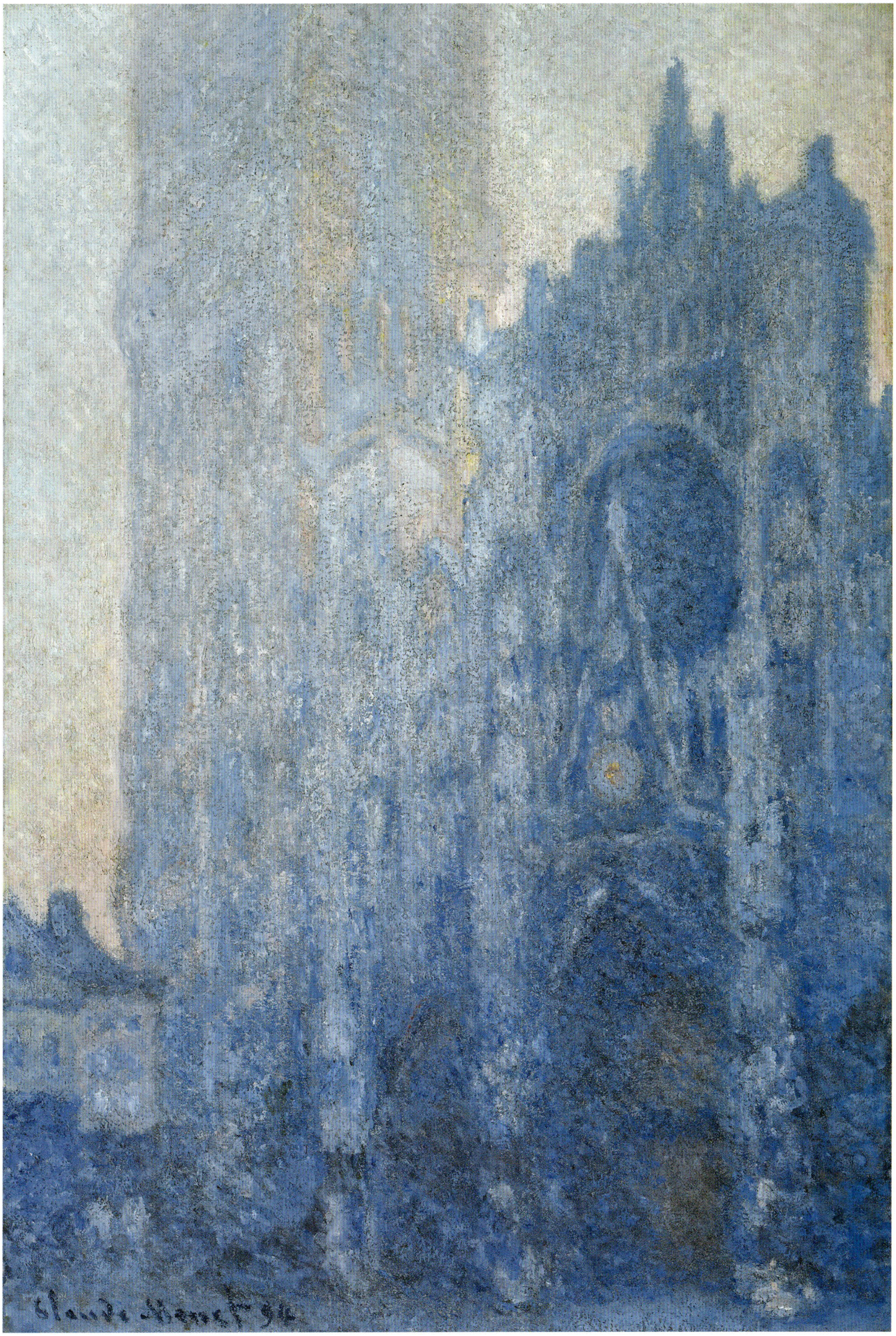

50

Claude Monet

Morning on the Seine, near Giverny 1897

oil on canvas, 81.3 x 92.7 cm
Museum of Fine Arts, Boston,
gift of Mrs W Scott Fitz
11.1261

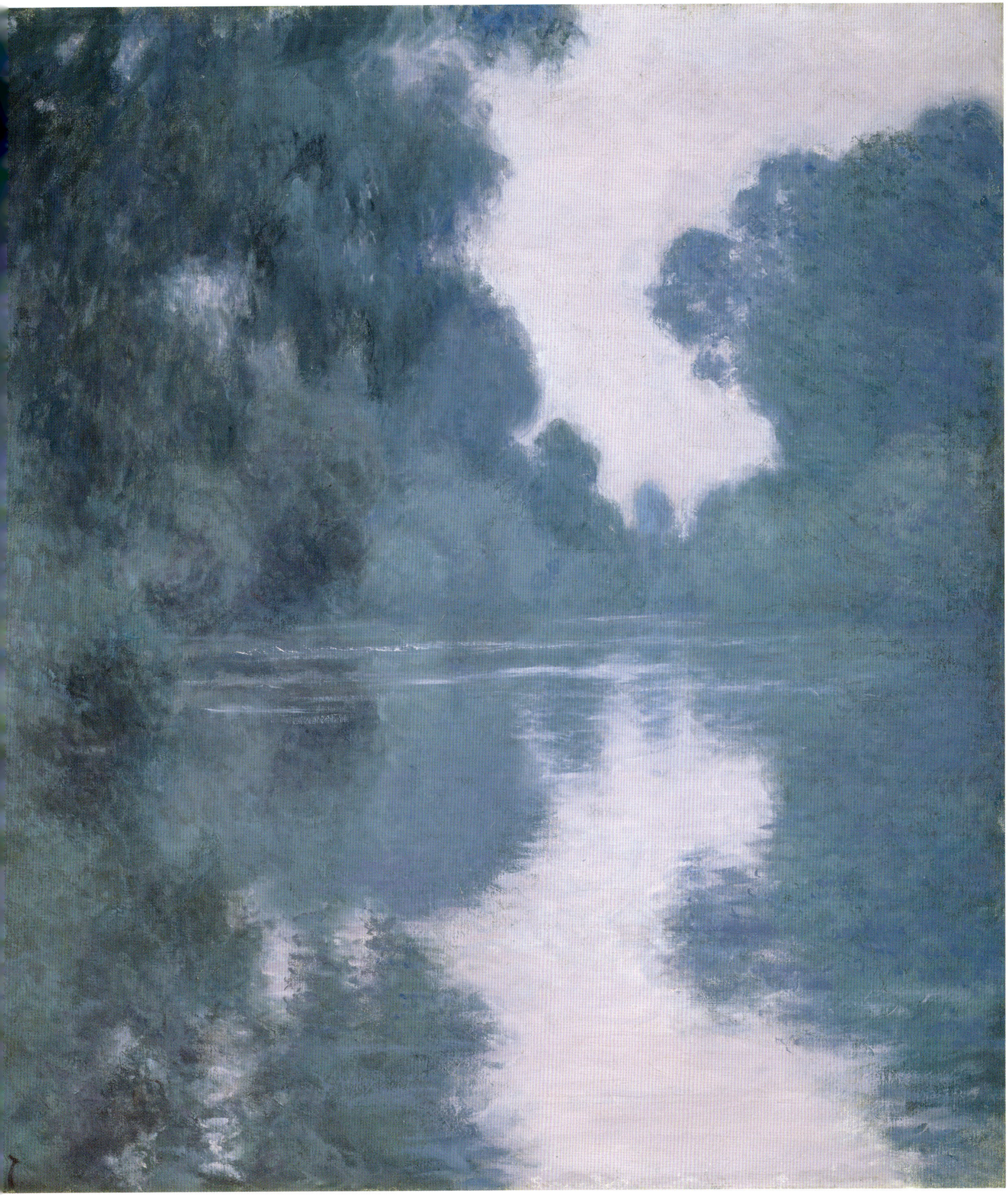

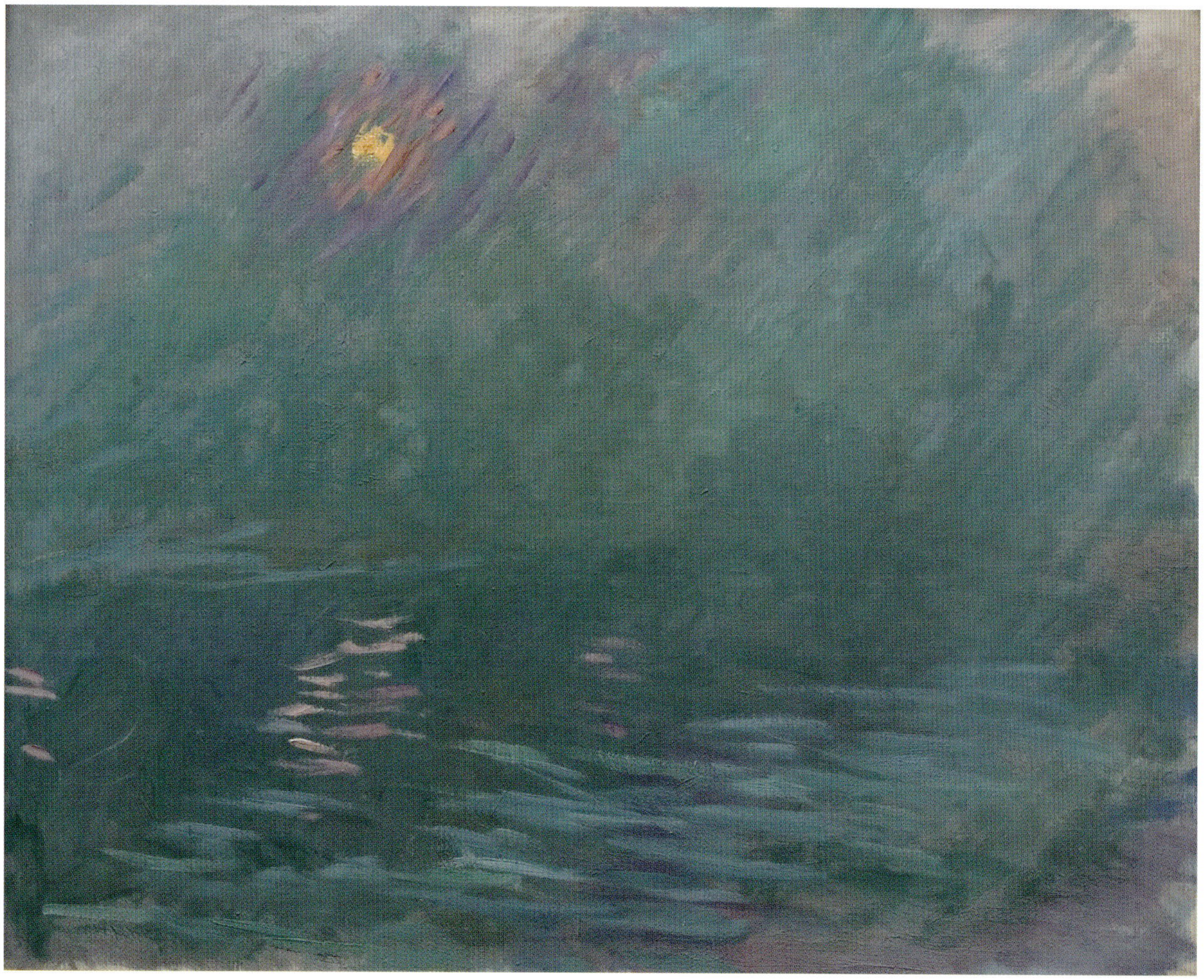

51

Claude Monet

Waterloo Bridge 1899–1901

oil on canvas, 64.7 x 81 cm

Kerry Stokes Collection, Perth

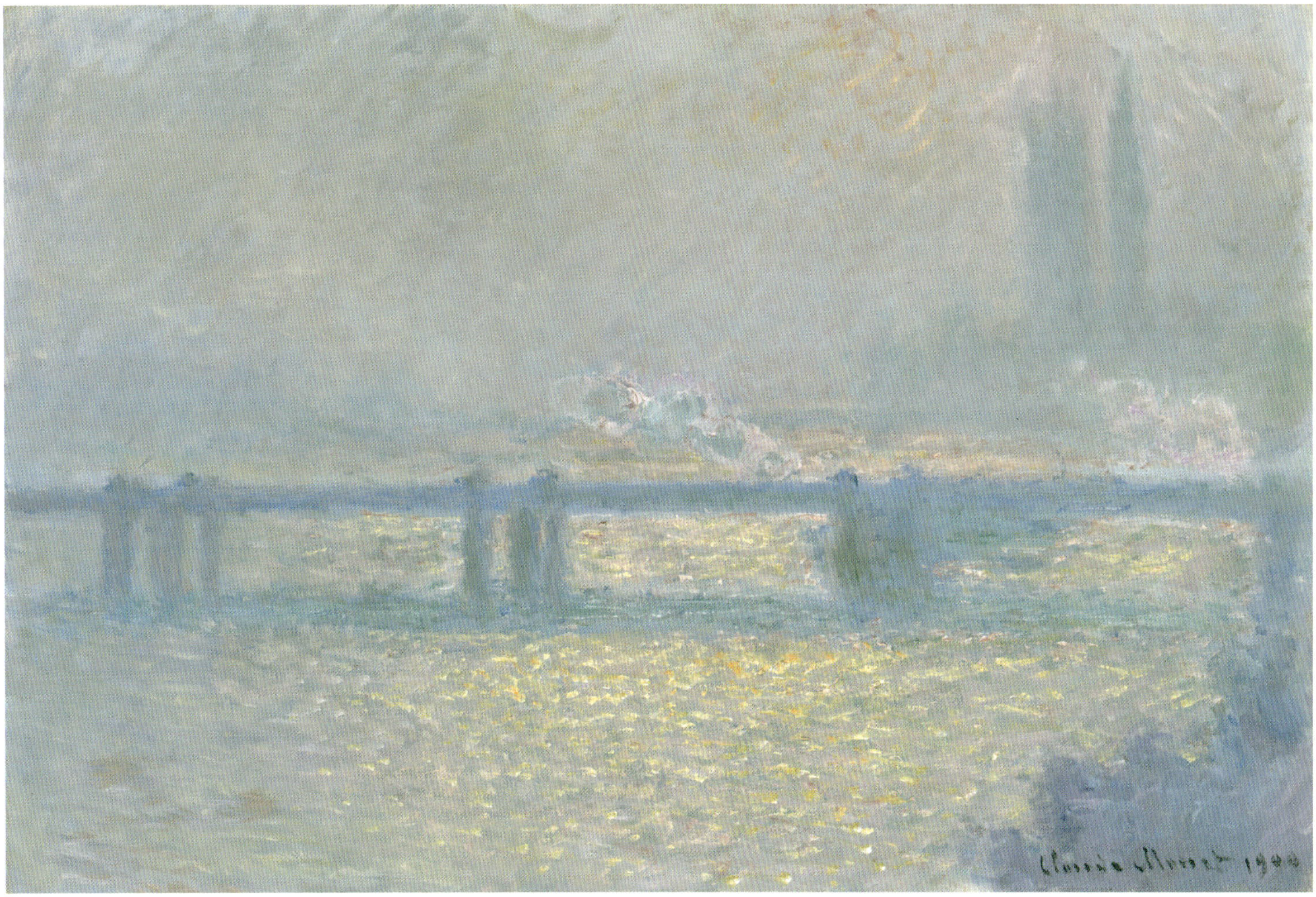

52

Claude Monet

Charing Cross Bridge (overcast day) 1900

oil on canvas, 60.6 x 91.5 cm
Museum of Fine Arts, Boston,
given by Janet Hubbard Stevens
in memory of her mother, Janet Watson Hubbard
1978.465

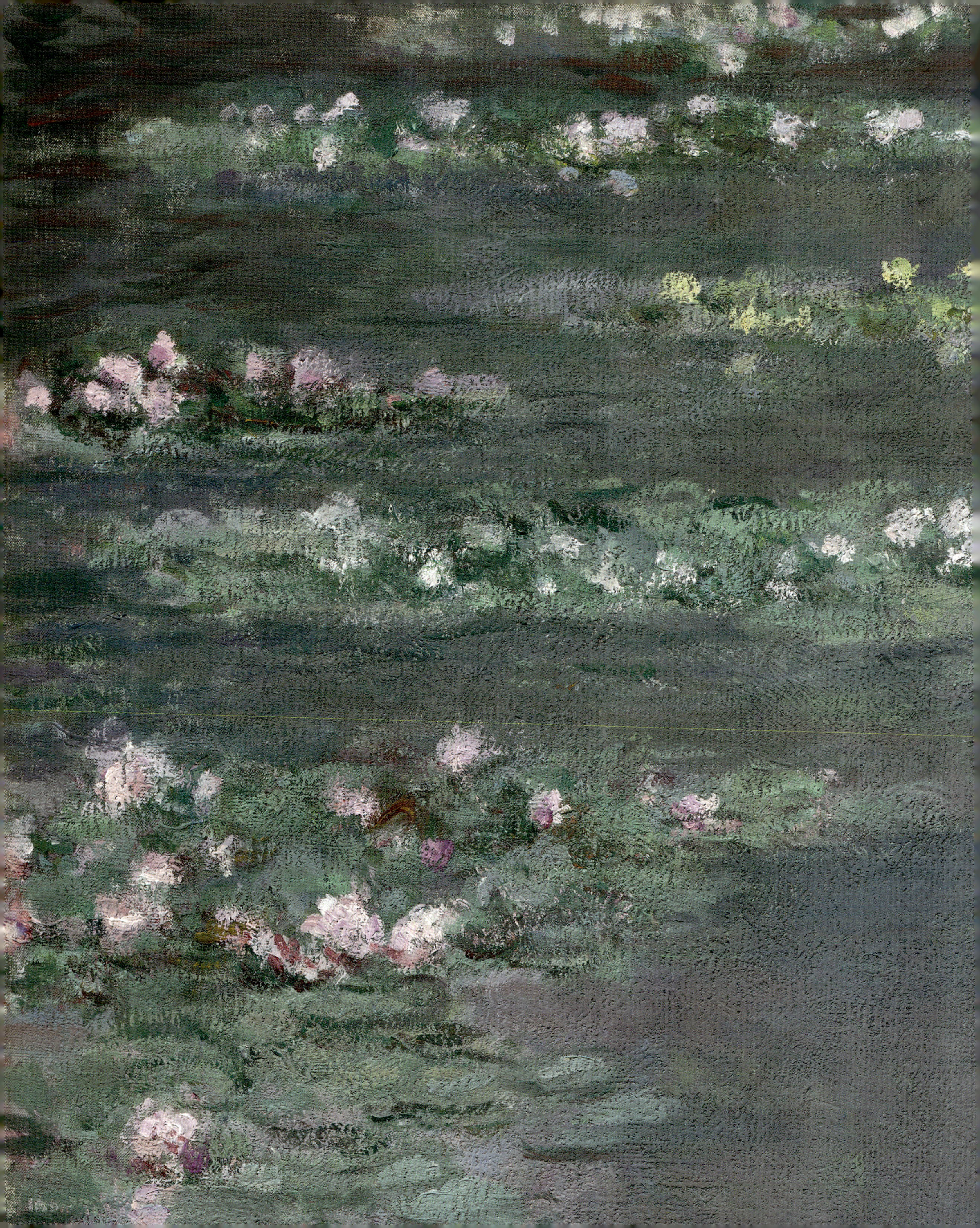

MONET AND IMPRESSIONISM AFTER 1900

In November 1900, Monet celebrated his 60th birthday. He was, by any reckoning, an extraordinarily successful artist. In the past year, he had undertaken two major new series of paintings – views of his Giverny water garden and its Japanese bridge on the one hand (see cat 43) and a vast series of paintings of the Thames, his *Londons*, on the other (cats 51 and 52). His fame had reached every country in the Western world – and was rising in the Pacific as well, through the influence of travellers to Paris. He was visited and courted by dealers and collectors, and as a result every year made more and more money from the sale of his paintings. He was equally sought after by journalists, who wrote about him again and again with fulsome praise. The Duc de Trévise, invited to Giverny on Monet's birthday, imagined him before they met as 'a sensitive dreamer, an intimate of what is fugitive, delicate like no other, a lyric poet, sometimes elated sometimes downcast; [and] on the other hand, a man whose immense and orderly output suggest uncommon vigour and calm good sense, and leads one to expect a simple, cogent and level-headed conversationalist'.[1]

Although at the height of his fame – and perhaps also of his powers as an artist – Monet could not help but be aware of his own mortality. The previous year, his old friend Alfred Sisley, born only a year before Monet, had died, having never achieved Monet's great critical or financial success. 'A week ago poor Sisley called for me to go and see him,' Monet wrote to Gustave Geffroy at the end of January 1899, 'and it was then that I saw he wanted to say goodbye. Poor old friend, poor dear children!' he exclaimed. 'For the time being,' he wrote after Sisley's funeral, 'I'm going to see about holding a sale for the children's benefit; that's the most urgent thing, then a good exhibition of Sisley's best work should be arranged.'[2] Boudin, Monet's first real teacher, had died in 1898.

Of the artists who had banded together in 1874 to organise the first Impressionist exhibition – and with whom Monet had maintained contact – only four others remained in 1900: Cézanne, Degas, Pissarro and Renoir. Through the 1890s, in spite of his frequent travels, Monet had kept in touch with these artists – for good or ill, as it turns out.

Cézanne, the recluse from Aix-en-Provence, came to stay in Giverny for three weeks in November 1894 and is known to have shared one of Monet's renowned meals with – amazingly – the prim Miss Mary Cassatt. At the time, Monet wrote to Geffroy – whom Cézanne would later paint – that the Provençal artist was 'so odd, so afraid to see a new face that I'm afraid he'll give us a miss, despite his keen wish to make your acquaintance. How sad that such a man hasn't had more support in his life! He's a true artist and has come to doubt himself overmuch. He needs encouragement, and he was thus very touched by your article'.[3] Cézanne, in his turn, would later say that '[Monet] is a great lord who treats himself to the grainstacks that he likes. If he likes a little field, he buys it'.[4]

Cézanne's important retrospective exhibition at the Galerie Ambroise Vollard, Paris, took place just a year after his visit to Giverny; the hermit was now exposed, and suddenly celebrated. Monet's admiration for Cézanne's art knew few bounds, and he collected works by the master from all periods of his career. 'In all humility,' the Duc de Trévise wrote of his conversation with Monet in 1920, 'I confessed to him that although Cézanne's research often interested me, its results often baffled me. "A great master, believe me!" Monet replied. "Cézanne! I have 14 Cézannes in my bedroom!"'[5]

Although Monet owned other portraits by Cézanne, he did not take advantage of the opportunity to buy the artist's *Self-portrait with a beret* (about 1898–99, cat 54) when it was with Vollard after Cézanne's death in 1905. Perhaps he thought that 14 paintings by his friend were enough: the much younger artist Maurice Denis recorded in his journal in 1906 that it was said Madame Monet hid her husband's Cézannes from him when she sensed that he was discouraged with his own work.[6]

Claude Monet *Waterlilies* 1905 (detail), cat 53

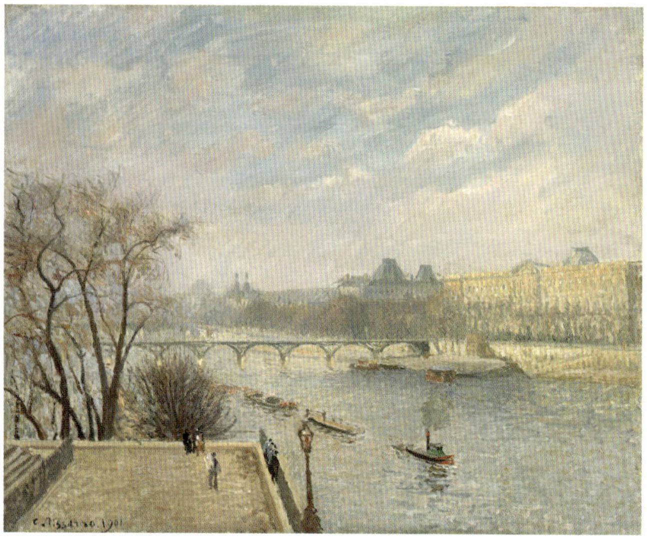

fig 27
Camille Pissarro
The Louvre, winter sunlight, morning 1901
oil on canvas, 73.7 x 92 cm
Scott M Black Collection

As Monet turned to painting views of the Thames in London, Camille Pissarro had become involved with painting views of Paris, though in a manner that – in comparison with Monet's most evanescent, Turner-like effects (cats 51 and 52) – could be called conservative, hearkening back to the Impressionism of the 1870s. But the dozens of such works he produced, including *The Louvre, winter sunlight, morning* (1901, fig 27), were ravishingly beautiful in their treatment of light falling on Parisian landmarks – in this case the eastern end of the Louvre and the Pont des Arts, both places that Monet and Renoir, rather than Pissarro, had painted in the 1860s and 1870s. Pissarro, who then had been Cézanne's companion in the country towns of Auvers and Pontoise, to the north of Paris, and from the 1880s a fairly near neighbour to Monet at Eragny, north of Giverny, died in mid November 1903. Monet was among the mourners at his funeral two days later.[7]

With Degas, Monet had maintained a polite, if sometimes cold, relationship since the 1880s. Never soulmates, they had shared an early friendship with Manet. But when, in 1898, Cézanne's long-estranged childhood friend Emile Zola published in *L'Aurore*, the newspaper founded by Monet's friend Georges Clémenceau, his article *J'accuse* in defence of Captain Alfred Dreyfus, a Jewish officer wrongly convicted of spying for Germany, Zola found a staunch supporter in Monet. Degas, on the contrary, defended what he felt to be the honour of France and its army. (It must be said that Renoir was equally reactionary in his views, though his friendship with Monet seems to have been less affected by 'the affair'. Paul Tucker has proposed that the Dreyfus debacle may have provoked Monet to abandon the French landscape to which he had for so long paid tribute, first to go to England in 1899 (see cat 52) and upon his return to take refuge in his own garden (see cat 53).)[8]

Monet was not without admiration for Degas's achievement, however. He had acquired in 1887, as partial payment for his sale of two paintings of Belle-Ile to the Galerie Boussod & Valadon, a superb pastel by Degas of a bather, probably in a brothel, drying herself by lamplight, which visitors to his collection said he hung in his bedroom.[9] Yet Degas was never, it appears, interested in purchasing a work by Monet, and was often caustically witty when they met. Degas said to Monet, after seeing his exhibition of *Waterlilies* in 1909, 'I remained for only a second at your exhibition. Your pictures gave me vertigo'.[10]

Degas must all the same have recognised that Monet's art was evolving, like his own, from its starting point in the 1870s into a 20th-century idiom. Degas's *After the bath* (cat 55) and *Dancers in the rehearsal room* (cat 56) probably date to the first few years of the century. Like so many of Monet's paintings of the same years, they engage, with new vigour and with new formal means, ideas that had long been dear to him. Here, in charcoal on tracing paper, Degas boldly sketches a bather drying her leg or dancers at work or in repose; in the latter work he sets his figures in a space that he had first invented in the 1870s, a fictive space in the Paris Opera – much as in *The waterlily pond* of 1900 (cat 43) Monet had returned to ideas that he had first explored in river views of the 1860s and 1870s. And Monet, clearly, was aware of their long history: after Degas's funeral, in the midst of the bombardment of Paris, Monet wrote to Degas's brother René of his 'great admiration for the talent of your brother Edgar Degas' and of their 'youthful friendship […] and our common struggle'.[11]

With Renoir, Monet remained a close ally as the two men aged – though Renoir became truly feeble long before Monet lost his strength. Monet and Renoir had remained in contact through the years even if they did not often meet. In 1895, in connection with the bequest by their friend the painter Gustave Caillebotte to the Musée du Luxembourg, they were together several times (and undoubtedly reminisced about their beginnings, as they looked over the paintings that their richer friend Caillebotte had collected). With Renoir, Degas and the poet Stéphane Mallarmé, Monet was in charge of the installation of the retrospective exhibition of the art of Berthe Morisot in March 1896.[12]

In 1900 Monet bought his most important painting by Renoir – his friend's superb *Mosque (Arabian festival)*.[13] Other interactions are documented in the years after 1900, including a visit by Renoir to Giverny in 1911. We do not know whether Monet was aware of Renoir's decision to take up sculpture – a medium entirely alien to Monet, in spite of his close friendship with Auguste Rodin. When Renoir became incapacitated by arthritis, he engaged the assistance of Richard Guino, a sculptor, to help him achieve works in three dimensions (as Vollard had suggested). Their first major composition was *Small Venus victorious* (cat 57), first cast in bronze about 1913. The standing goddess – a classic nude in the Renoir mould – holds out the apple of victory, standing proud on a plinth adorned with mythological scenes. The idea is completely alien to Monet's aesthetic of the years around 1910–15, but it accords perfectly with the classical equilibrium that Renoir sought from the mid 1880s until the end of his life. Degas, by contrast, made sculpture in private, sharing his experiments only with a few artist friends, including Renoir (see cat 58).

Renoir continued to paint up until just before his death, in 1919, at Cagnes-sur-Mer on the Mediterranean coast. Monet wrote to Félix Fénéon of his sorrow at Renoir's passing, saying that the critic might 'imagine how painful the loss of Renoir has been to me: with him goes a part of my own life. All I've been able to do these last three days has been to go back over our early years of struggle and hope [...] It's hard to be alone, although no doubt it won't be for long as I'm feeling my age increasingly as each day goes by, despite what people say'.[14]

These words were written in 1919, seven years before Monet's own death. And yet at that moment he was engaged on his most ambitious work, the creation of a great cycle of paintings of his water garden that he envisioned not only as a gift to France but as a kind of apogee of his own artistic vision. Massive views of the pond surface, measuring some two metres square, were stacked in the studio, and even larger paintings had been planned or were in process. The paintings that Monet had begun in 1899–1900 of the surface of the pond seen beneath the Japanese footbridge may have been the inspiration for the series, but it is the great canvases of 1903–08, including *Waterlilies* of 1905 (cat 53), that were the decisive catalyst in the creation of the cycle in the years after 1915.

Waterlilies marks the moment in 1905 when Monet eliminated altogether any reference to the bank of his pond, focusing his attention on the surface of the water itself. Large floating clusters of foliage and flowers in tones of pink, white and yellow intersect the shadowy vertical reflections of the trees on the opposite shore and the glowing sky between them. In a canvas painted two years later (fig 28), Monet maintained a similar point of view and compositional structure but responded to a different time of day and changing conditions of light. The trees cast into shade in the 1905 canvas are here bathed in gentle light, and the sky, which was rosy pink, mauve and lavender in the earlier composition, is here shot through with strokes of blue, from deep cornflower to palest turquoise.

Critics saw Monet's *Waterlilies* – which were exhibited at Durand-Ruel in May 1909 with the subtitle 'Series of water landscapes' – as a phenomenal achievement. The canvases represented a revolutionary departure from the conventions of landscape painting as it had been practised since the Renaissance, because the fundamental relationship of earth to sky – based on the principle of the horizon as the location of a perspectival vanishing point – had been abandoned. In his review of the exhibition, the critic Roger Marx proclaimed:

> No more earth, no more sky, no limits now [...] the dormant and fertile waters completely cover the field of the canvas; light overflows, cheerfully plays upon a surface covered with verdigris leaves [...] Here the painter deliberately broke away from the teachings of Western tradition by not seeking pyramidal lines

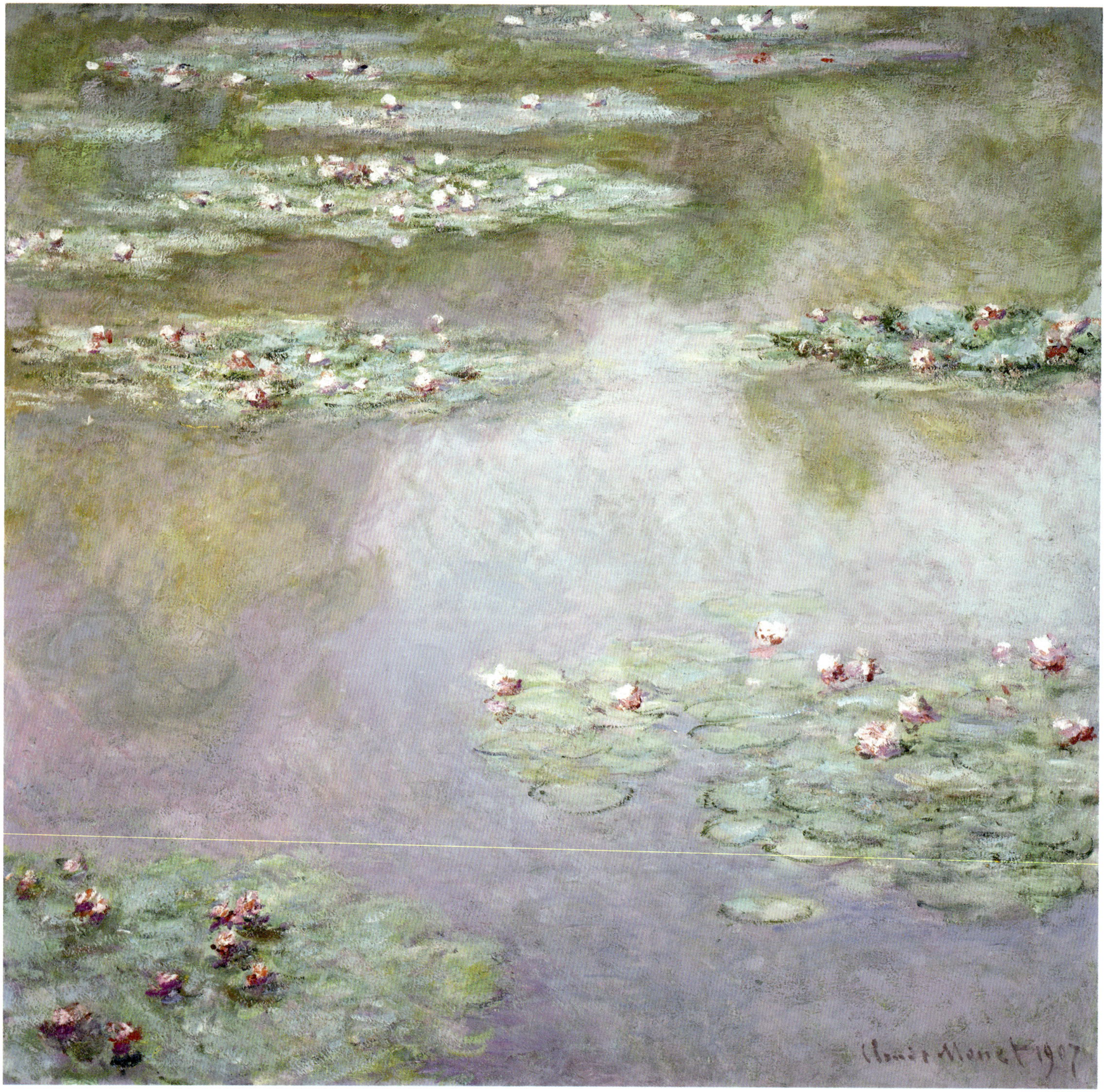
Claude Monet 1907

fig 28
Claude Monet
Waterlilies 1907
oil on canvas, 96.8 x 93.4 cm
Museum of Fine Arts, Boston,
bequest of Alexander Cochrane
19.170

fig 29
The exhibition of Monet's *Waterlilies*
at the Musee de l'Orangerie in Paris, 1930
Private collection, Roger-Viollet, Paris
/ The Bridgeman Art Library

This early photograph shows, in situ, Monet's last great cycle of *Waterlily* paintings, often referred to as the *grandes décorations*. The paintings were installed to Monet's specifications in this oval room at the Musée de l'Orangerie in 1927, where they remain to this day.

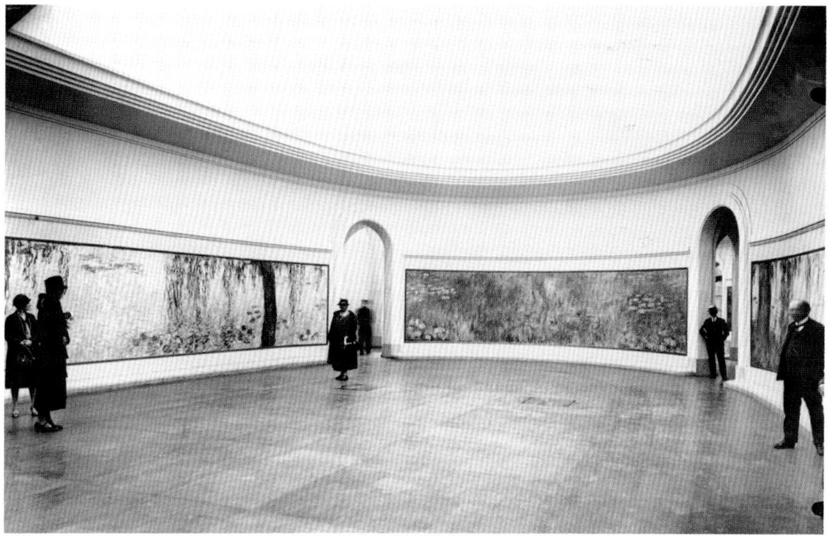

> or a single point of focus. The nature of what is fixed, immutable, appears to him to contradict the very essence of fluidity; he wants attention diffused and scattered everywhere.[15]

Marx's critical description of Monet's *Waterlilies* might be interpreted as an attempt to place the painter at the vanguard of abstraction. According to the critic, Monet stated that 'the indeterminate and the vague are modes of expression that have a reason for existing and have their own characteristics'; they might constitute, in effect, an aesthetic system in which 'sensations become lasting'. But, teetering at the brink of acknowledging his fluid veils of paint as the raison d'être of his art – of espousing, that is, the principle of 'art for art's sake' – Monet pulled back, asserting his dependence on the observation of the world around him. 'The richness I achieve comes from nature, the source of my inspiration [...] I aspire to no other destiny than to work and live in harmony with her laws.'[16]

Throughout his career, nonetheless, Monet was intensely aware of the ability of painting both to honour nature, her beauties and her laws and to manipulate human emotion and intellect on a purely aesthetic level. His late work – not only the *Waterlilies* exhibited here but also the great cycle of decorations executed for the French state in the aftermath of the First World War – is rooted in his direct observation of his garden at Giverny. It is also a profound meditation on the affective power of colour and form as a plastic means of retaining the sensation – vague or intense – remembered from that encounter. 'Beauty in art consists of truth', Camille Corot had said, 'imbued with the impression we received from the contemplation of nature ... We must never forget to envelop reality in the atmosphere it first had when it burst upon our view. Whatever the site, whatever the object, the artist must submit to his first impression'.[17]

1 The Duc de Trévise, in an article published in 1927, quoted in Stuckey 1985, p 319
2 Monet to Geffroy, 29 Jan and 3 Feb 1899, quoted in Kendall 1989, p 185
3 Monet to Geffroy, 23 Nov 1894, quoted in Kendall 1989, p 180
4 Cézanne, quoted in Stuckey 1995, p 226
5 The Duc de Trévise, recording a 1920 conversation with Monet, in an article published in 1927; quoted in Stuckey 1985, p 338
6 Stuckey 1995, p 238
7 Stuckey 1995, p 237
8 Tucker 1995, p 169
9 See Jean Sutherland Boggs et al, *Degas*, exh cat, Metropolitan Museum of Art, New York and National Gallery of Canada, Ottawa 1988, p 308 and Stuckey 1995, p 214. The pastel over monotype is now in the collection of the Norton Simon Museum, Pasadena, California
10 Degas, quoted in Boggs et al 1988, p 31
11 Monet to René Degas, 21 Oct 1917, quoted in Kendall 1989, p 251
12 Stuckey 1995, p 229
13 Stuckey 1995, p 232. The painting is in the Musée d'Orsay, Paris
14 Monet to Félix Fénéon, probably mid-December 1919, quoted in Kendall 1989, p 253
15 Roger Marx, quoted in Stuckey 1985, p 265. See also Tucker et al 1998, pp 37–50
16 Monet, as reported by Roger Marx, quoted in Stuckey 1985, p 266. This discussion is indebted to Paul Tucker in Tucker et al 1998, p 50
17 Corot, quoted in Michael Clarke, *Corot and the art of landscape*, British Museum Press, London and Cross River Press, New York 1991, p 109 and note 10

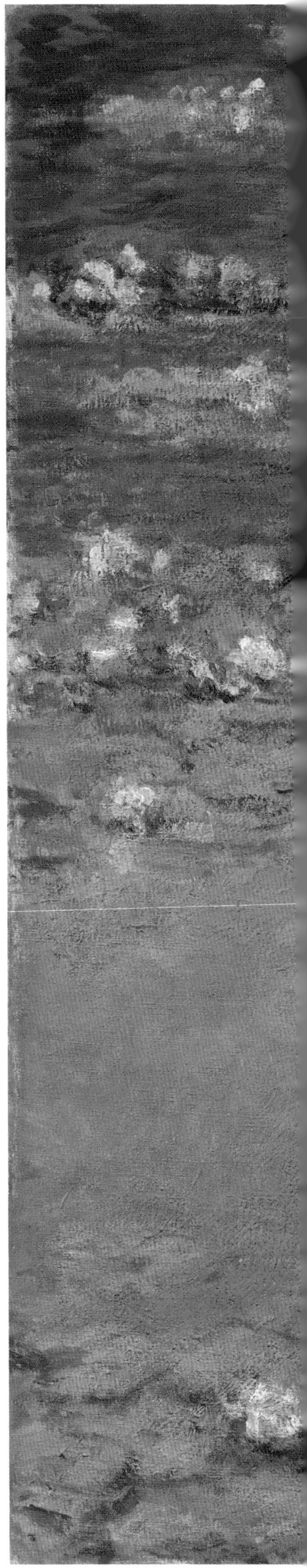

53

Claude Monet
Waterlilies 1905

oil on canvas, 89.5 x 100.3 cm
Museum of Fine Arts, Boston,
gift of Edward Jackson Holmes
39.804

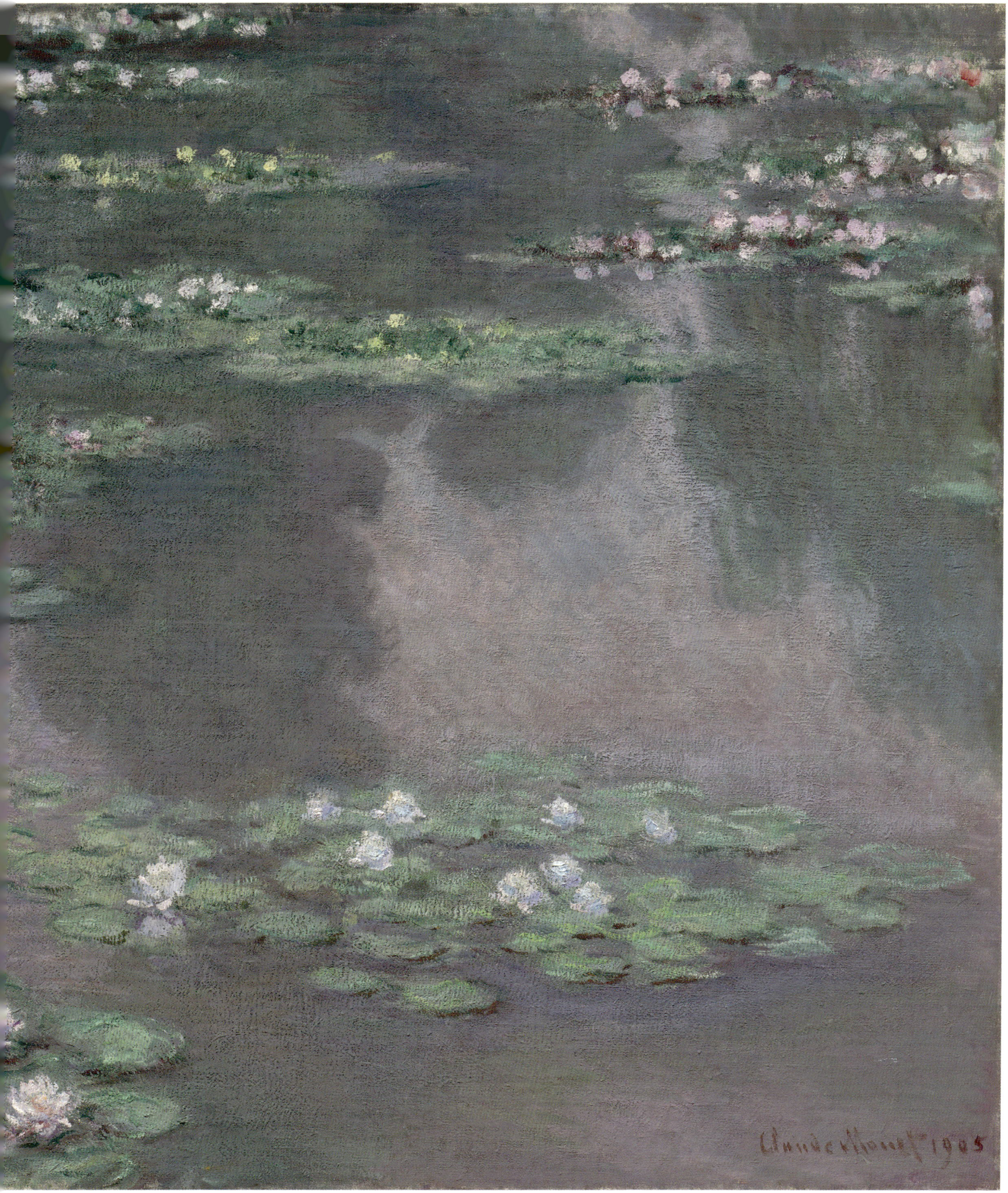

54

Paul Cézanne
Self-portrait with a beret c1898–99

oil on canvas, 64.1 x 53.3 cm
Museum of Fine Arts, Boston,
Charles H Bayley Picture and Painting Fund
and partial gift of Elizabeth Paine Metcalf
1972.950

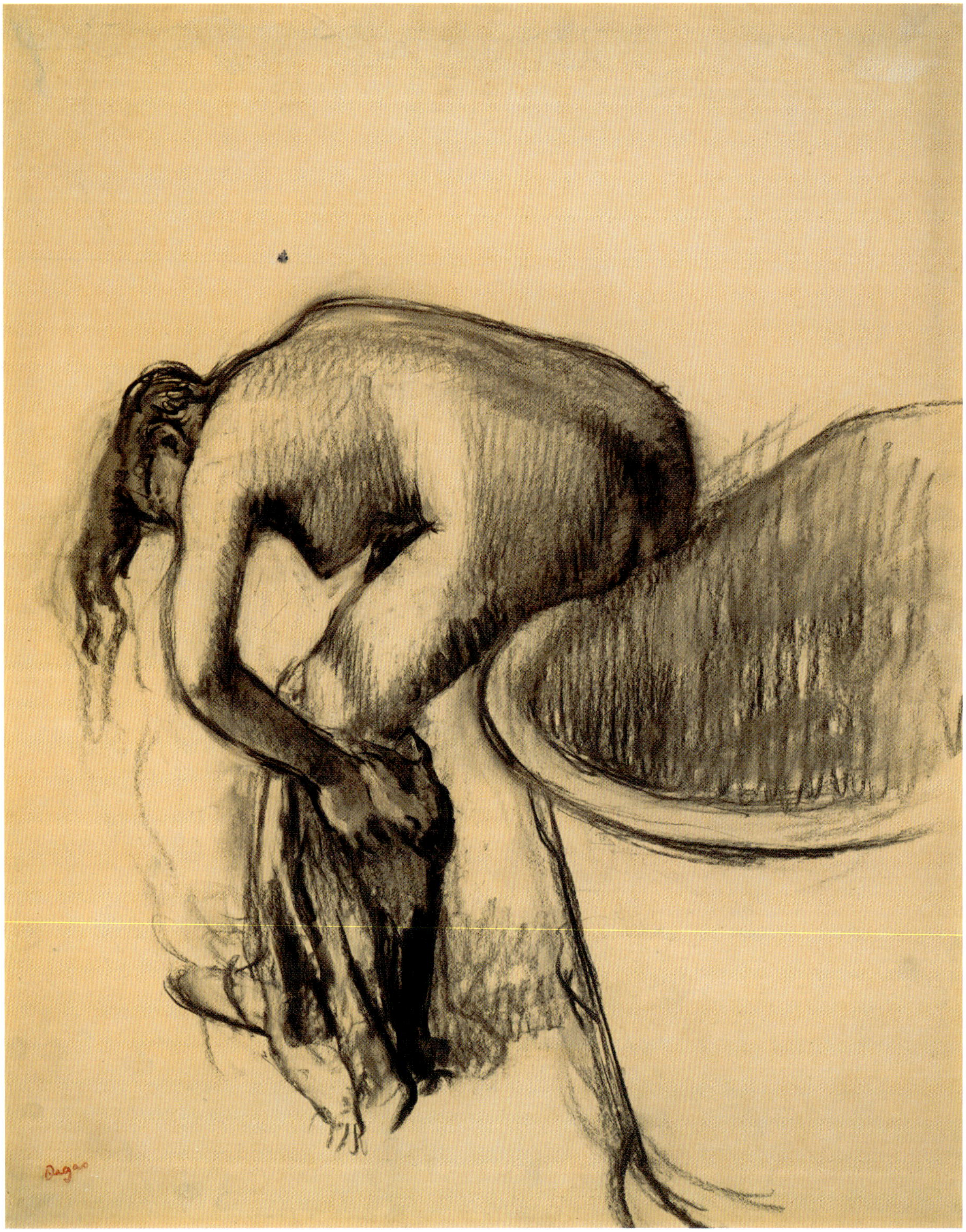

55

Edgar Degas
After the bath c1900

charcoal, 73.7 x 59.8 cm
Art Gallery of New South Wales,
Margaret Hannah Olley Trust 1994
222.1994

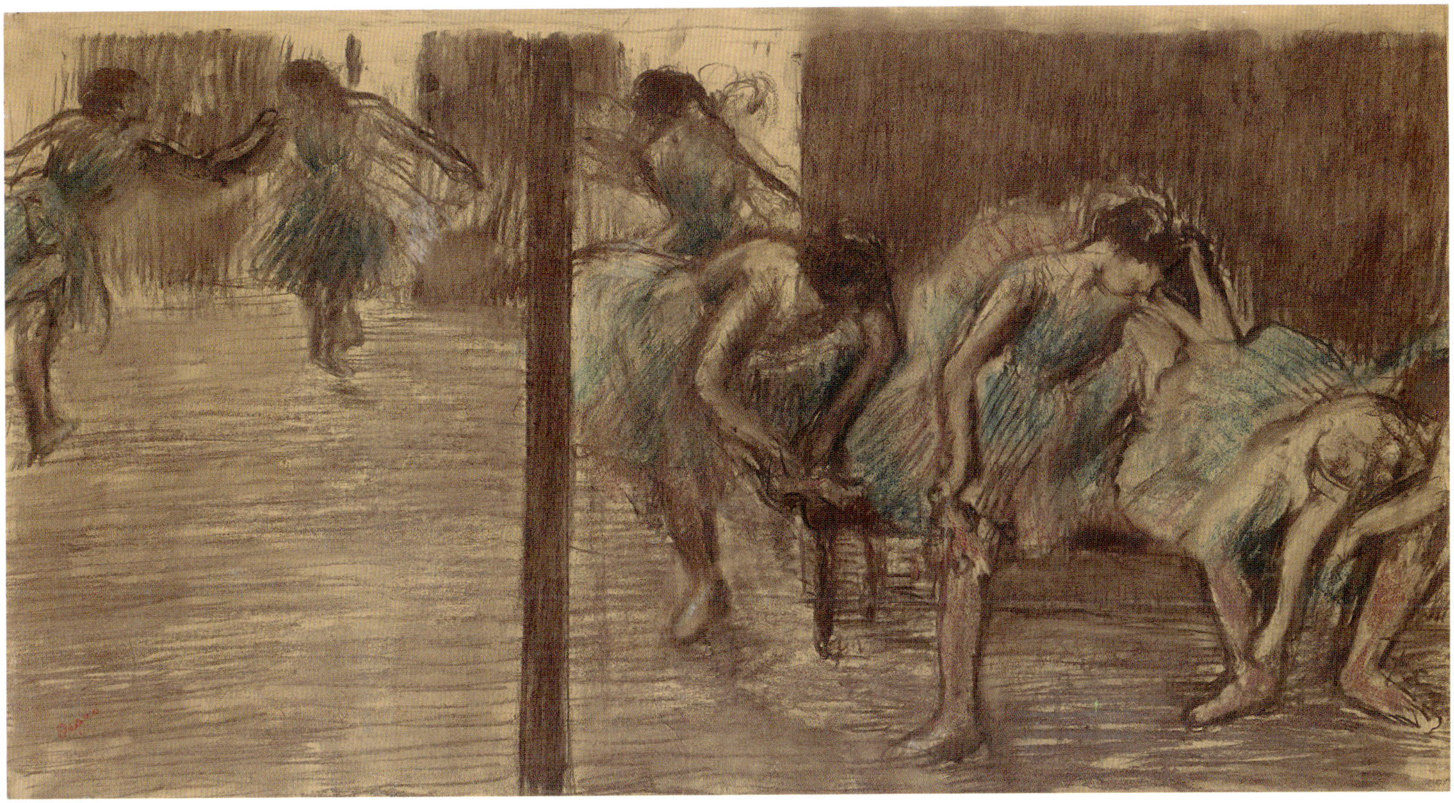

56

Edgar Degas

Dancers in the rehearsal room 1900–05

charcoal with pastel on paper,
mounted on cardboard, 45.4 x 85.1 cm
Museum of Fine Arts, Boston,
gift of Arthur Wiesenberger
54.1557

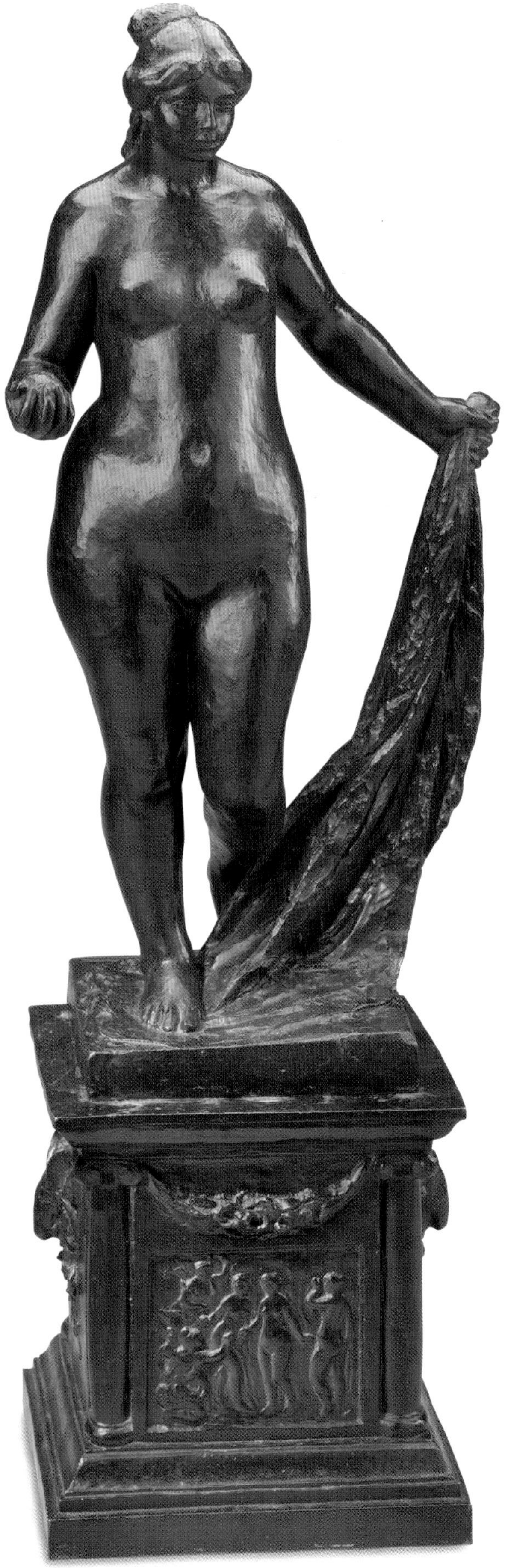

57
Pierre-Auguste Renoir
Cast by Valsuani
Small Venus victorious 1913
bronze, 85.1 x 22.9 x 22.9 cm
Museum of Fine Arts, Boston,
William Francis Warden Fund
56.259

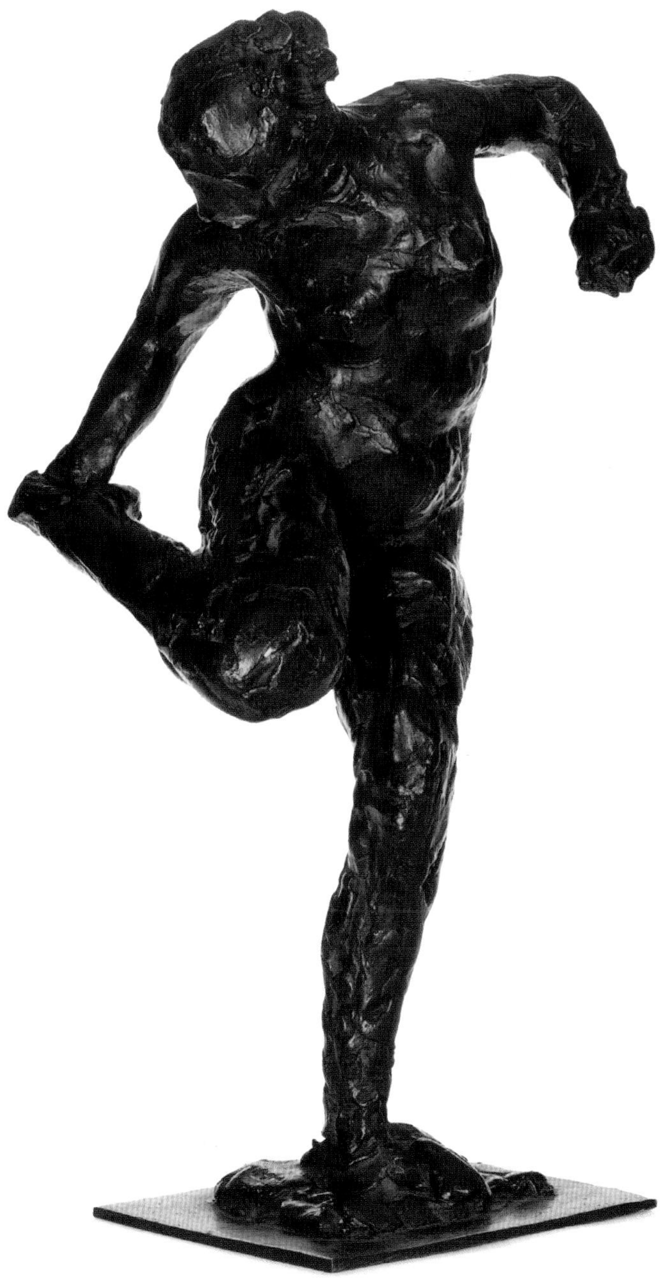

58
Edgar Degas
Dancer looking at the sole of her right foot
1900–10, cast 1919–21
bronze, cire perdu (lost wax), 48 cm height
Art Gallery of New South Wales,
bequest of Paul Haefliger 1982
60.1983

I'm not a great painter, neither am I a great poet. I only know that I do what I can to convey my experience before nature, and most often, to succeed in conveying what I feel, I totally forget the most elementary rules of painting – if they exist that is.

Claude Monet in a letter to Gustave Geffroy, 7 June 1912

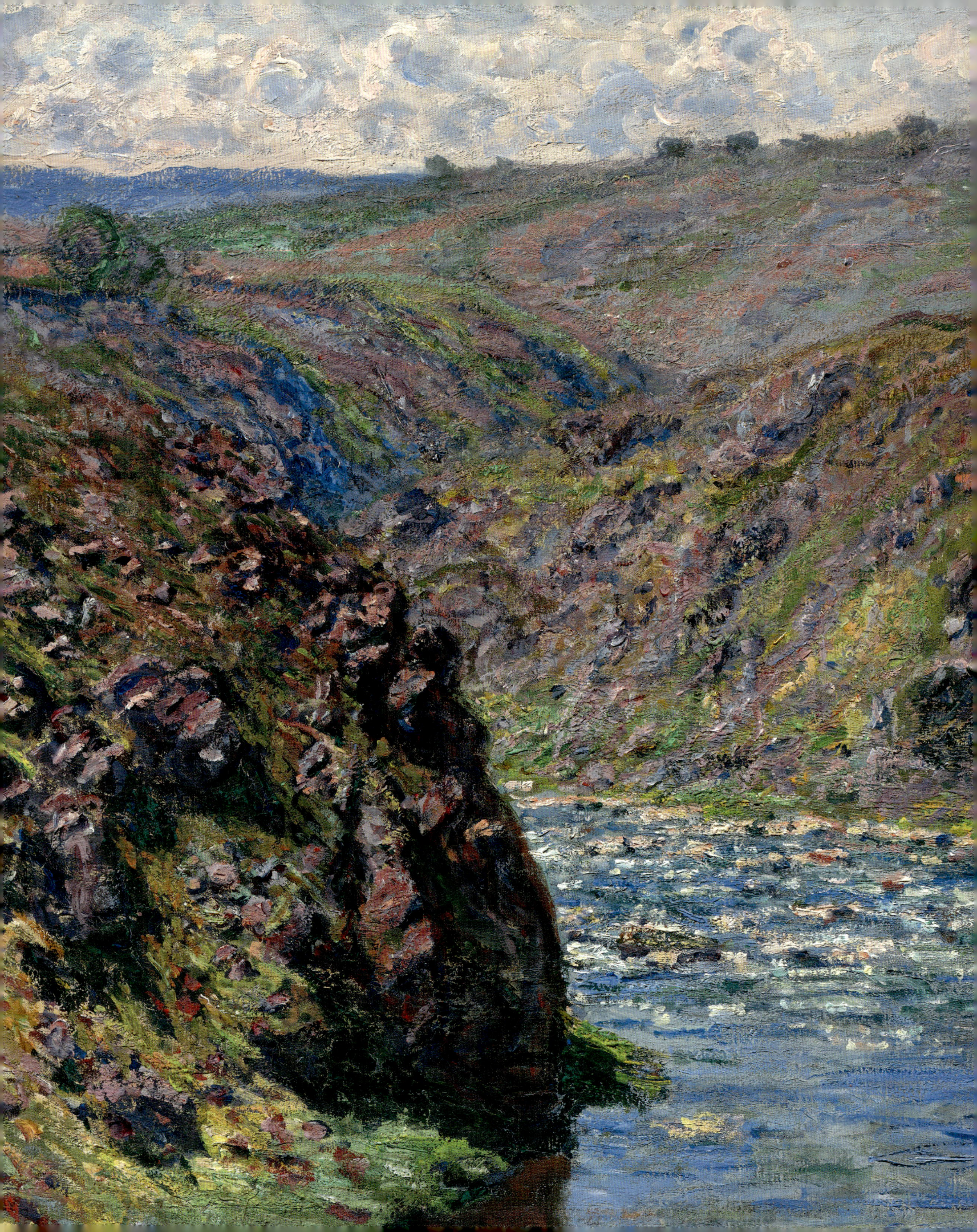

MONET'S TECHNIQUE

George T M Shackelford

To speak of Monet's technique may be foolhardy – perhaps we should speak of Monet's *techniques*, for his manner of working changed radically from the beginning of his career to its end, and even within a short period of time he could employ markedly different methods from canvas to canvas. Whether painting in bold patches, sometimes even employing a palette knife, or in thin, transparent washes and glazes, Monet seems to have suited his methods to the particular motif before him. Even within a closely knit group of canvases devoted to similar motifs from a single campaign of painting – from his *Venice* series of 1908, for example – some canvases are highly worked and texturally complex, while others have been left much more loosely finished. Both kinds of surface could please him, and he was happy to sign, date and sell paintings without insisting that they all conform to a uniform technical execution.

Some general observations can be made on the evolution of Monet's technique over the six decades of his career as a painter, illustrated by examples in *Monet and the Impressionists* or in the collections of the Museum of Fine Arts, Boston. And two paintings in particular, *Flower beds at Vétheuil*, from 1881 (cat 31), and *Valley of the Creuse (sunlight effect)* (cat 46), painted about eight years later, can serve as significant examples of how Monet's technique might vary from painting to painting.

Two great scholars of Monet's art, Robert L Herbert and John House, have devoted careful study to the ways in which he prepared a canvas, began to create an image upon it, elaborated that image, and then refined its exhibition surface. Both have cautioned that each painting by Monet must tell its own story. Although some generalisations can be made (and will be), it would be wrong to assume that Monet approached each canvas the same way.

To begin with the beginning, there is the canvas itself. House notes that, contrary to statements that the artist made late in life, most of the ground layers – that is, the priming of gesso, sometimes covered with a thin layer of paint – used by Monet in the 1870s until the 1890s were not pure white, but were almost always subtly toned.[1] This toning was most often warm in colour, a beige or pale buff, but depending on the motif in question could occasionally be a cooler grey shade.

The critic Théodore Duret referred to this ground layer as 'a clean canvas', and he observed Monet 'briskly start to cover it with slabs of colour which correspond to the coloured patches shown him by the natural scene. Often during the first session he can only make an *ébauche*'. The *ébauche*, or preliminary layer of thin paint, was a holdover from academic practice – painters in oil on canvas since the Renaissance have often laid in such a layer to guide their subsequent development of the composition, and Monet would have learned this technique in his brief academic career or through watching other plein-air painters at work. 'The next day, returning to the same spot,' Duret wrote, 'he adds to the first sketch, and the details are brought out, the contours sharpened'. The critic Gustave Geffroy said that Monet 'hurriedly [...] covers his canvas with the dominant values, studies their gradations, contrasts them, harmonises them'.[2] As House explains it, however: 'Monet had no fully consistent policy over what to include in his first session of work on a canvas. All that he needed from it was a framework of sorts, of forms and colours, which he could enliven and elaborate in subsequent sessions of work.'[3]

Some paintings by Monet, all the same, seem to have been painted in one sitting – left, that is, as a particularly refined *ébauche*. A good example is the MFA's *Ships in a harbour* (fig 13, see p 56), which was painted on one of Monet's pale grey grounds, suitable for the overcast day that he was depicting. The foreground water is, as one writer has noted, 'aquiver and alive' with movement, as Monet's brush drags strokes of dark blue and grey across the pale ground, then fills in the interstices with thin patches of paler blue and grey to suggest the reflected sky.[4] Here, then, is an *ébauche* that is a finished work in itself – as if Monet realised that to touch it

Claude Monet *Valley of the Creuse (sunlight effect)* 1889 (detail), cat 46

Detail of Monet's *Flower beds at Vétheuil* (cat 31), showing the complexity of Monet's colouristic invention and variegated brushwork

again would be to ruin its sense of truth to nature. Was *Rue de la Bavole, Honfleur* (cat 13) such a quickly painted picture – a *pochade*, as he might have said? It has a strong sense of immediacy, and we know that Monet 'refined' it later into a more carefully finished canvas; the first version has the quickly painted quality of Boudin's *Fashionable figures on the beach* (cat 10) or even Manet's *Basket of fruit* (cat 14).

Much more the norm, however, was Monet's practice of elaborating the surface of such a painting (or, according to the scanty evidence left us, even less-finished works) by the addition of further layers of brushwork – as an artist like Jongkind would do in his *Harbour scene in Holland* (cat 12). Careful looking at the complicated effects of brushwork in such paintings as *Camille Monet and a child in the artist's garden at Argenteuil* (cat 20) or *Boulevard Saint-Denis, Argenteuil, in winter* (cat 36), both painted in 1875, will demonstrate to the viewer how a painting, in the course of several sessions of work, could be given a rich sensation of texture – although thinly layered in the case of the image of woman and child, or more thickly worked with impasto in the snow scene.

Robert Herbert describes what he feels to be Monet's essential working method from the 1870s onward:

> It is possible to summarise the leading features of Monet's technique [...], as long as it is not thought of as an unvarying recipe. Monet varied his techniques constantly, but the heart of his method was as follows: First he defined the major parts of the composition in a rather thin scumbling of colour which was often allowed to show through here and there to help form the colour of a given area. Next came a complicated series of strokes, with drying time between applications. Some of these were texture strokes, usually in a light hue (because light colours are more easily covered over), and often involving more than one application. These were allowed to dry, over time reckoned in days rather than hours. Their direction and their texture retained the vital quality of spontaneity and expression even though some of them were hidden in other colours. The surface colours were applied in very thin coatings which did not disturb the existing texture of 'spontaneity'. They were not put on all at one time, but in several sessions. Some were deliberately mixed on the canvas while still wet, but most of them were applied over dry surfaces, one at a time.[5]

As the careful observer will see, this is often Monet's practice, particularly in works of the 1880s. Still, even in the 1880s, there are paintings that seem to have been painted in one sitting, without so many returns to a canvas before it reached perfection. A good example is *Flower beds at Vétheuil* (cat 31 and opposite), a view of the Seine at sunset over the flowers growing in Monet's riverside garden. A detail of the flower cluster at upper left shows how quickly the paint was brushed on to the bare canvas, brusquely outlining the shapes of leaves and blossoms. The patch of blue that indicates the colour of the hillside on the opposite bank seems almost an afterthought, inserted to maintain continuity of scale and distance.

At the lower left, the most densely worked area of the canvas, Monet seems to have laid down a pattern of dark green and blue green strokes to suggest the leaves of the flowering plants. On top of these strokes, before they were dry, he applied further strokes of bright colour. Red marks stand for the petals of roses or geraniums, surely; but are we to interpret the blue and yellow strokes as shadows and reflections on the leaves or as further flower varieties? No matter how complex the interplay of the colours, there is always ground showing through, tiny patches of near white that contribute a further element of sparkle to the riot of colour.

Finally, there is one almost disconcerting detail, which only reveals itself after long study of the painting: at almost the exact centre of the canvas, Monet emphasised the sense of movement that was his overall goal in the composition. Over the quickly brushed leaves

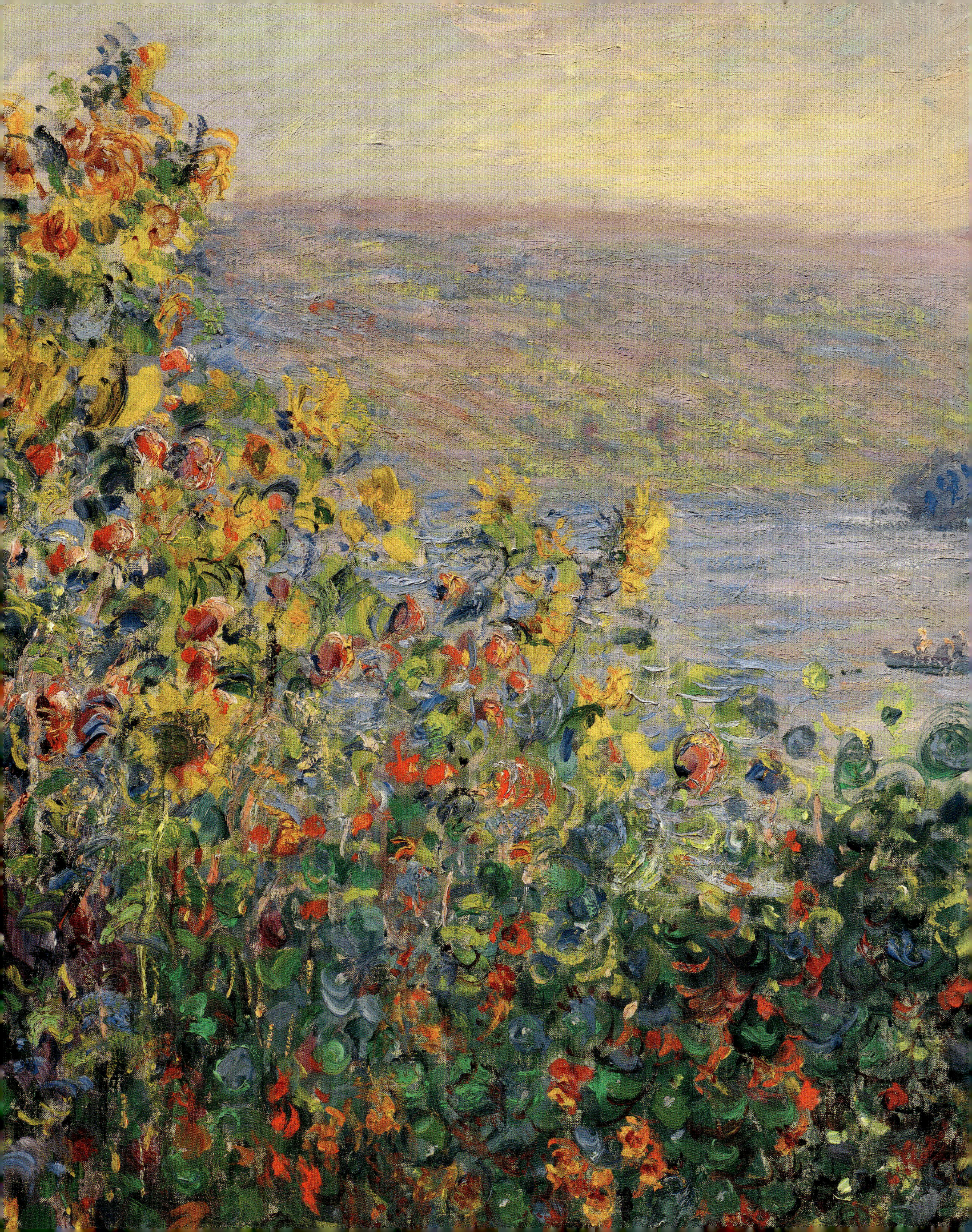

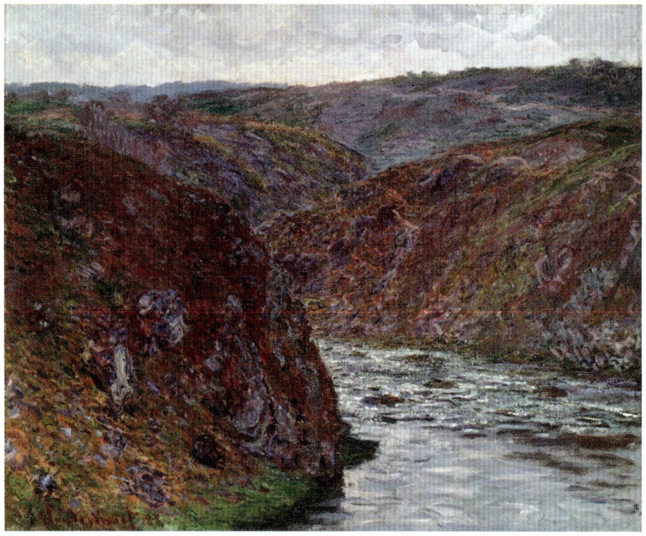

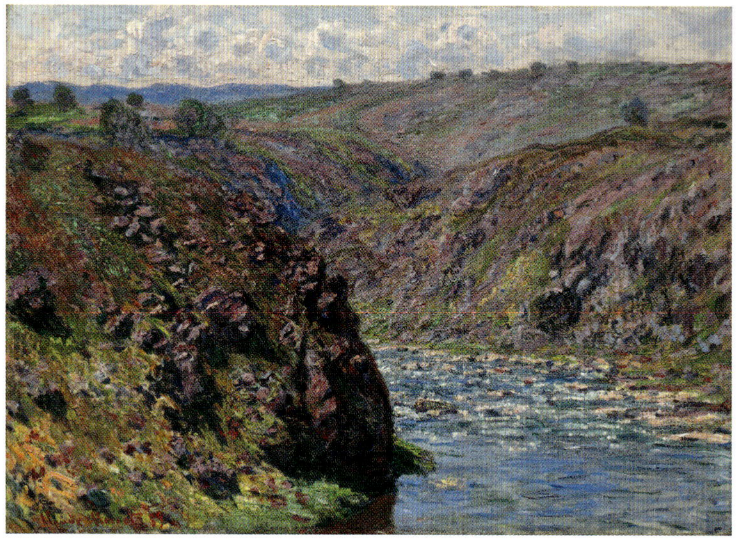

and petals of a branch of sunflowers, he suddenly applied slender but nonetheless perceptible tiny ribbons of blue paint – the same strokes that he had used to suggest the ripples in the water on the Seine. He seems to want to tell us that we are seeing two things at once – flowers and river – as they both move in the afternoon breeze.

Eight years later, painting in the Creuse Valley, Monet created an enormously varied body of canvases. One of the most complex is *Valley of the Creuse (sunlight effect)* (cat 46). In its composition it is almost identical to *Valley of the Creuse (grey day)* (fig 30), but it is far more brightly coloured. It is a perfect example, in fact, of the worked and reworked kind of canvas that Monet was to produce again and again, but not without exception, from the later 1880s until the end of his life. Numerous details point to the many changes that Monet undertook in the course of finishing the composition. Across the upper contour of the hills at the horizon, for instance, a strong stroke made with a brush nearly an inch wide left a swath of texture that has now been almost completely obliterated by other colours – as if Monet decided at some point to reduce the amount of sky visible above the gorge; most clearly, at the centre of the composition, where the water emerges from between the cliffs, endless numbers of strokes have been altered or coloured over with thin washes of paint. A comparison of two photographs of this part of the painting (opposite) – one taken in raking light to heighten the texture of the paint – will give an idea of the complexity of Monet's layering of brushstrokes and the thin layers of enhancing colour that are applied on top of them.

In the case of *Valley of the Creuse (sunlight effect)*, it may well be possible that the numerous changes that occurred over the course of the execution of the painting were due to elements beyond Monet's control – that is, due to elements that Monet chose to respect, for all his awareness that a painting would only be finished after he returned it to Giverny for a final examination and 'perfection'. 'With this damnable weather,' he wrote to Alice in April 1889, 'which is too sinister for words, progress is slow and the sight of my paintings terrifies me, they're so dark: what's more, several are skyless. A few have some sunlight in them but they were started so long ago that I'm very much afraid that when the sun finally re-emerges I shall find my effects considerably altered. Apart from this, the Creuse is bound to rise with all the rain we're having now and it will change colour, so I live in a state of continual suspense.'[6]

This letter to his companion and future wife, Alice, might well explain the eccentricities that we find in *Valley of the Creuse (sunlight effect)*. Complaining that some of his canvases are skyless, Monet contrives to make sure that, however high his horizon line, the sky will read clearly, with sunstruck clouds. He was forced to revise the water line at lower left centre, perhaps in response to the changing level of the Creuse itself. And above all, Monet seems at the very end of his campaign on this painting to have inserted a massive number of patches of pink, lavender and mauve, perhaps to compensate, as he predicted, for the considerable alteration in his effects once the sun reemerged.

While *Valley of the Creuse (sunlight effect)* reveals to the careful viewer the extent of Monet's revisions – his editing, rethinking, refining and final reworking – the artist undertook, in the 1890s and in the works after 1900, a perhaps more deliberate campaign to incorporate the physical effects of such revisions into canvases from their very beginnings. Herbert has argued that in such paintings as the *Cathedrals* series, Monet established a pattern of 'texture strokes' that were from the outset meant to create a surface upon which the painter could elaborate more intricate patterns of colour. That there are pure *ébauches* for the *Cathedrals* series suggests that Monet's procedure was not radically different from the one he had followed in the 1880s. But it is true that with the *Cathedrals* (see cat 49), Monet delighted in working on an unusually textured surface – built up of layers of paint, having almost nothing to do with the weave of the canvas itself – and that, in later years, he would return to this method.

opposite:

fig 30
Claude Monet
Valley of the Creuse (grey day) 1889
oil on canvas, 65.5 x 81.2 cm
Museum of Fine Arts, Boston,
Denman Waldo Ross collection
06.115

cat 46
Claude Monet
Valley of the Creuse (sunlight effect)

right:
Details of Monet's *Valley of the Creuse (sunlight effect)* (cat 46) in normal light (left) and raking light (right)

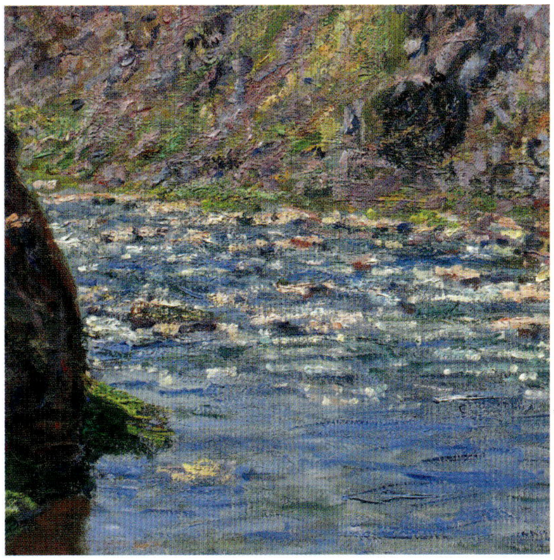

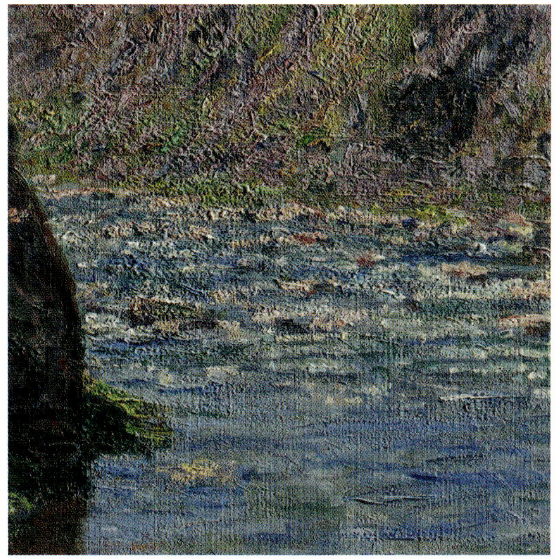

Indeed, when it came time to consider exhibiting the *Waterlilies*, many viewers noticed the degree to which at least some of the paintings had been belaboured. 'All those who saw the pictures in February and March [1908] considered them "overworked", that is, they showed too plainly how long they had stood on the easel', wrote one critic. 'One of Monsieur Monet's friends even went so far as to say that there were four or five different pictures on each canvas. Monsieur Monet admitted this himself, and stated how dissatisfied he was with his work.'[7] Be this as it may, the paintings were a resounding success; and Herbert succinctly analyses the visual and emotional effect of the surface of *Waterlilies* (cat 53), an extensively worked and reworked canvas, when he writes that

> Monet's corrugated textures are one of the most remarkable of his arbitrary devices, not at all 'spontaneous' but seemingly so. For the *Waterlilies* they have a special function. Their valleys are shaded by the ridges, and from a medium distance, the observer is aware of both surface and depth. This is translated by our mind, which has registered the image of water, as the surface of water and its underlying depths. The impasto ridges, like fine parallel ripples of water, are the slightly agitated surface of the pond; the dark interstices are the uncertainly seen depths.[8]

We must come to Monet's canvases with open eyes – looking at them closely, studying their effects with care. Effects that seem simple and offhand at first may be enormously complicated and the result of great effort on the painter's part. His technique – or once again, better yet, techniques – are revealed only through careful study, but that study will be endlessly rewarding.

1 See House, 1986, p 63
2 Théodore Duret and Gustave Geffroy, quoted in House 1986, p 69
3 House 1986, p 68
4 Fronia E Wissman in Shackelford, Wissman et al 2002, p 150
5 Robert L Herbert, 'Method and meaning in Monet', *Art in America* 67, no 5, Sept 1979, p 102
6 Monet to Alice Hoschedé, 4 Apr 1889, quoted in Kendall 1989, p 130
7 Anonymous writer, *The Standard*, 1908, quoted in House 1986, p 106
8 Herbert 1979, pp 100–01

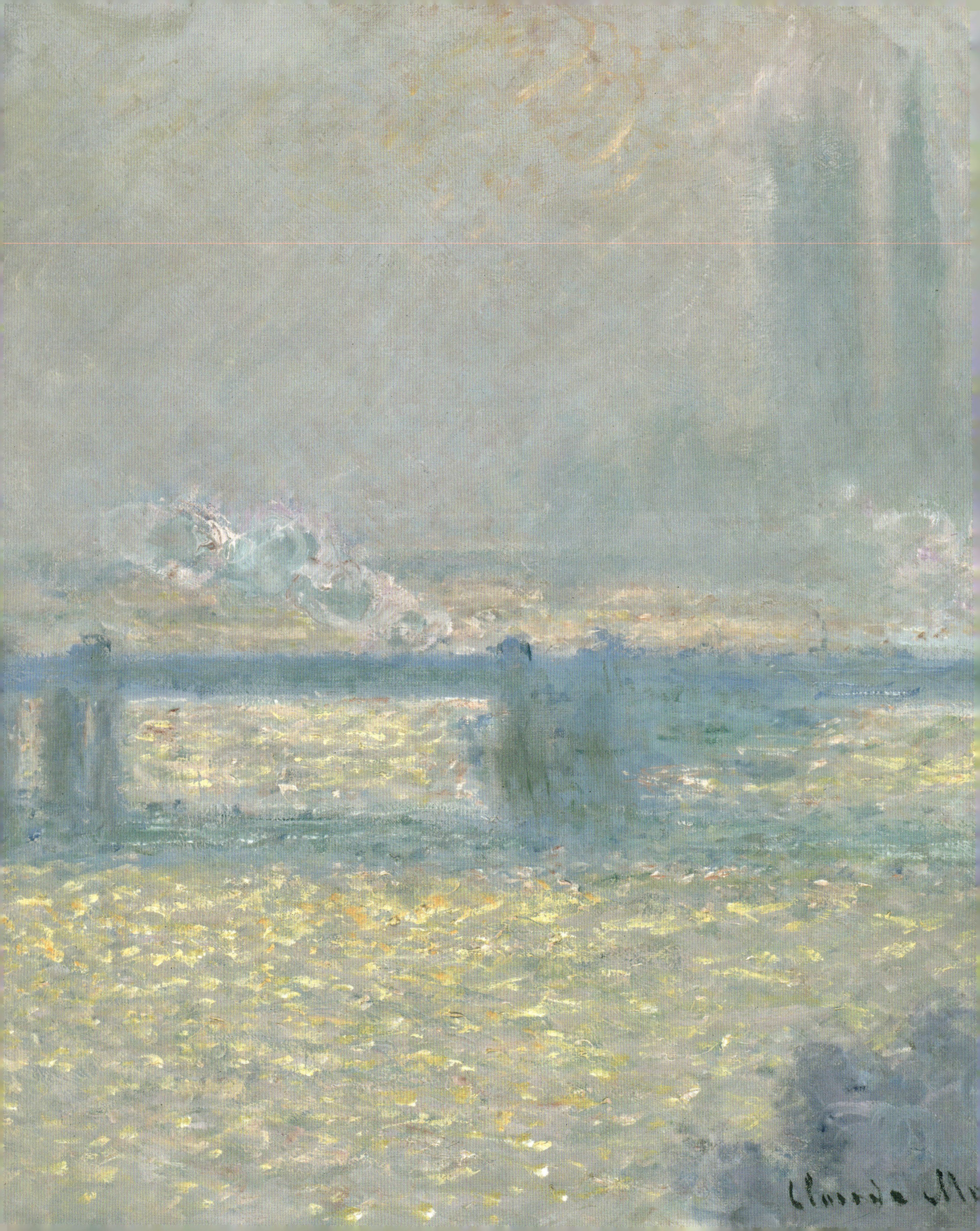

MONET'S IMPRESSIONS OF THE INDUSTRIAL ENVIRONMENT

Jonathan Mane-Wheoki

Among the paintings that convey the impact of the industrial revolution in France on modern landscape art, Claude Monet's marine painting *Impression: sunrise* 1872 (fig 2, p 23) is of particular significance. This was the painting which, when it was shown in Paris at the first exhibition of the Société des Artistes Peintres, Sculpteurs, Graveurs, etc in 1874, gave Impressionism its name.

Although Monet had painted the scene from the window of his harbourside lodgings in Le Havre on the estuary of the river Seine, he himself stated that it could not pass as a view of the port.[1] The painting records instead his instantaneous subjective response to the prevailing atmospheric conditions momentarily observed on a calm winter's morning, dashed down in an act of focused concentration, in broad washes of oil paint and summary brush-strokes on canvas. Transfixed by the effect of the rising sun, Monet rendered it in paint as a vivid chrome orange orb, blazing through a vaporous pall of what is usually described as fog or mist[2] suspended over the tranquil harbour basin. He delineated local features – port buildings and cranes, warehouses, factories and ships at anchor – as murky silhouettes, all reflected on the rippling water.

But it is not just fog or mist we see. The atmosphere is sullied by coal smoke produced by steam-driven machines and cranes, and pouring from the towering chimneys of factories alongside the harbour basin, and from the funnels of paddle steamers, ferries and packets and the smokestacks of the locomotives operated by Chemins de Fer de l'Ouest that terminated at the busy railway station nearby. These created the atmospheric pollution – the smog – that hangs over the locale Monet painted in *Impression: sunrise*. The 'impression' captures a moment in a dynamic, shifting scene at the great commercial port into which the industrial revolution had transformed Le Havre. It reminds us that modernism in 19th-century French painting, in the materials and practice of painting as well as content, was very much a product of the era.

The industrial revolution occurred much later in France than it had in Britain. Of the continental countries bordering France, Belgium was the first to be industrialised, producing coal, establishing industries and developing a railway network. South of the border, the coalfields of Nord-Pas-du-Calais in northern France provided fuel for iron and steel smelting and steam-powered machines. While Calais, Boulogne and Dieppe remained important ports for cargo and passengers travelling between England and France, it was Le Havre (in the Seine-Maritime department) at the mouth of the Seine on the English Channel that was to become one of the most thriving French seaports, ranking second only to the Mediterranean port of Marseille. Though 'somewhat longer than' the other links between England and France (Dover and Calais, Folkestone and Boulogne, Newhaven and Dieppe), Southampton to Le Havre was 'the great commercial thoroughfare between the two countries'.[3] Vast tonnages of raw materials and goods were imported into France through Le Havre, and coal and manufactures exported. Le Havre was also an important seaport for transatlantic passenger and cargo traffic. Regular steam communication with New York through Le Havre brought tens of thousands of visitors from the east coast of North America to France, most of them heading for Paris, but artists were also drawn by the mystique of Fontainebleau and Brittany. If American collections are particularly rich in modern French painting, it is because many of the visitors returned to North America with choice examples of the Barbizon school, Impressionism and Post-Impressionism. Le Havre was also an important point of departure for European emigrants – the 'tired', the 'poor', the 'huddled masses yearning to be free'[4] – setting out for the New World.

John Murray's 1854 edition of *A handbook for travellers* in France describes Le Havre as 'the port of the Seine and of Paris'.[5] (Napoleon is said to have commented that 'Paris, Rouen, and Havre formed only one city of which the Seine was the highway'.[6]) Murray noted that 'the use of steam is very general on the great rivers of France,

Claude Monet *Charing Cross Bridge (overcast day)* 1900 (detail), cat 32

but for purposes of travelling steamers are now nearly superseded by railways'.[7] The railway was to constitute a more efficient, economical and faster alternative highway.[8]

The building of the French railway system began after 1842, with Paris as the hub of the network, although railway routes terminated at a range of railway stations located somewhat inconveniently distant from each other in the capital. The Paris to Rouen line was opened in 1843. Transport from Le Havre was still by river or road. An American traveller recorded on 20 April 1844 that he had 'ascended the Seine to Rouen in the steamer *La Normandie* ...'[9]. Steamboats from Le Havre to Rouen completed the journey in eight to nine hours, necessitating a stopover on arrival for passengers en route to Paris. On 22 April 1844 the American then 'left Rouen and went to Paris by railroad'. The 137-kilometre trip took two-and-a-half hours by express train and five hours by the slow train. Passengers arrived at the terminus located in the Rue Amsterdam.[10] When the Monet family relocated from Paris in 1845, it would have been possible for them to travel by rail to Rouen and there transfer to a river steamer for Le Havre (see map p 167). Monet *père* had no doubt been drawn to Le Havre by the business opportunities that had opened up with the development of the port. The Rouen to Le Havre railway line opened in 1847. Murray predicted that the opening of the railway would probably put a stop to the steamers.[11] The 95-kilometre journey by rail took two-and-a-half to three hours. The train from Le Havre to Rouen arrived on the right hand bank of the Seine. Passengers for Paris then had to 'join company' with the train from Dieppe[12] which arrived on left bank of the river.[13]

Christopher Lloyd has observed that trains and steamers 'imposed [...] upon the Seine' during the mid 19th century gave 'a totally different character to the river that was of special significance for Impressionism – namely, trains and steamers'.[14] In fact coal-fired steamers had begun to appear in the work of an earlier generation of marine painters, from direct observation, as a mode of transport that was replacing sailing ships, not only on the rivers but in the harbours and on the coasts. Coastal ferries that brought fashionable young day-trippers to promenade on the beaches of Normandy, the first region of France to be promoted as a tourist destination, were depicted by Honfleur-born Eugène Boudin in such paintings as *Jetty and wharf at Trouville*, 1863[15] (see also his *Fashionable figures on the beach*, cat 10). In 1864, the painter Frédéric Bazille wrote to his parents that 'the steamboat took us down the Seine [...] to Honfleur'.[16] The Impressionists painted trains, steamers, bridges, factories, engineering works and other structures of burgeoning industrialism because they were there, because they were among the phenomena and facts of modern life, documenting the changing appearance of the environment, the march of progress.

Monet travelled a great deal. Rail transport had become such a normal part of life in France that he and his biographers scarcely mention his mode of travel. Few references to the railways occur in his published correspondence. 'Tomorrow, I am going to put a box on the express train containing three pictures', he wrote to Bazille in October 1864[17] and in April 1888 he advised his partner Alice Hoschedé that he would shortly be returning from Cap d'Antibes to Paris where he would 'catch the 1 o'clock train to Vernon'.[18] He must have undertaken local and regional train trips from a fairly young age but his first trip to Paris seems to have occurred in May 1859 when he visited the Salon.[19]

In a letter to his mentor Boudin (whom he had met in 1857), Monet mentions paintings by Camille Corot, Constant Troyon and Charles-François Daubigny, plein-air artists who were associated with the Barbizon school of naturalist landscape painting. The hamlet of Barbizon is located ten kilometres west of Fontainebleau[20] and around 55 kilometres from Paris. In the 1830s it would have been quite a business getting there as the railway had not yet been constructed. In July 1844 an American traveller records: 'Went to Fontainebleau, to Corbeil by railroad and thence by diligence.'[21] In 1848 Jean-François Millet, a native of Normandy, went from Paris to Barbizon and settled there for 27 years – most of the rest of his life.

Although the painters of the Barbizon school must have made good use of train travel when the line was extended to Fontainebleau, none appears to have allowed the railway to intrude into the tranquillity and timelessness of his rural landscape compositions.

The Paris to Lyon line passed through Fontainebleau, making the journey just an hour from Paris. The extension of the railway to the departmental capital of Mélun in 1849 brought hordes of visitors to the forest.[22] Nine kilometres from Barbizon, Mélun was the nearest railway stop.[23] In 1854 Murray reported that Fontainebleau had become 'the constant resort of French artists in the summer'.[24] Monet visited Fontainebleau, staying at the village of Chailly-en-Bière near Barbizon, in the summer of 1863.[25] He was back there, amongst 'a quite pleasant little group of artists', as he reported to Bazille, in 1865,[26] painting out in the open from direct observation.

Painting *en plein air sur le motif* was a practice that the industrial revolution had made feasible. The application of the principles of modern science, technology, industry and commerce to the business of painting allowed artists to forsake indoor studios and observe reality under natural conditions. The standardisation of units, prefabrication and mass production applied to the equipment and materials of painting not only reduced costs but made for greater portability and convenience. Pre-stretched canvases in standard sizes (ranging from 15.5 x 20.5 cm to 120 x 190 cm) primed with white gesso and ready for painting came on the market in the early 19th century. The longer landscape format was introduced in the early 1830s. The collapsible zinc paint tube was invented in 1841 and filled with paint of a more buttery consistency than the paints laboriously prepared through the grinding of pigment and binding with medium that formed part of traditional studio practice. The discovery of pigments such as chromium (in 1797) and cadmium sulphide (in 1817), the invention of artificial ultramarine (in 1824), the development of viridian (in 1838) and the advent of the first coal-tar dye in 1856, vastly expanded the range of colours available to artists, while not providing guarantees of greater colour-fastness and permanency. Nineteenth-century researches in the science of optics encouraged the Impressionists to lay out pure colours on their portable palettes in an approximation to the colours of the solar spectrum.

Unencumbered by the traditional paraphernalia of the academic artist's studio and the significant cost of maintaining it; equipped with a portable paint box into which were packed tubes of paint and a folding palette, a portable collapsible easel (as depicted in Renoir's *Monet painting in his garden* 1873[27]) and perhaps a sun umbrella; and with the wider mobility that train travel afforded, the painter who wished to commune directly with nature could do so with far greater convenience, efficiency and economy than was previously possible. Having arrived at a destination, such a painter could choose a site within easy walking distance of, or a short ride from, the railway station, unpack the portable equipment, set up a studio in the open air and get on with it. In a similar fashion, artists were able to utilise small boats as floating studios, as did Daubigny.[28] Monet owned 'a broad-bottomed boat fitted up with grooves to hold a number of canvases'.[29] Always an early riser, he would make his way at dawn to the boat anchored midstream with the assistance of a peasant who carried his canvases.[30]

There is something of the production line in Monet's painting methods, especially in his series. One observer recorded that 'he has 14 paintings all begun at the same time, a whole set of studies of one and the same subject, whose appearance may be altered by the time of day, the sun and the clouds'.[31] In London 'when he was at work on his Thames series', he was said to have 'installed all his easels in a succession of hotel rooms vacated of furniture, and worked on a hundred canvases at a time. A few strokes comprised a quarter of an hour's work on a riverscape, whose effect recorded nine o'clock in the morning. Then he moved on to the next effect and so on.'[32] But this was consistent with Monet's belief that 'no painter could paint for more than one half hour on any outdoor effect and keep the picture true to nature'.[33]

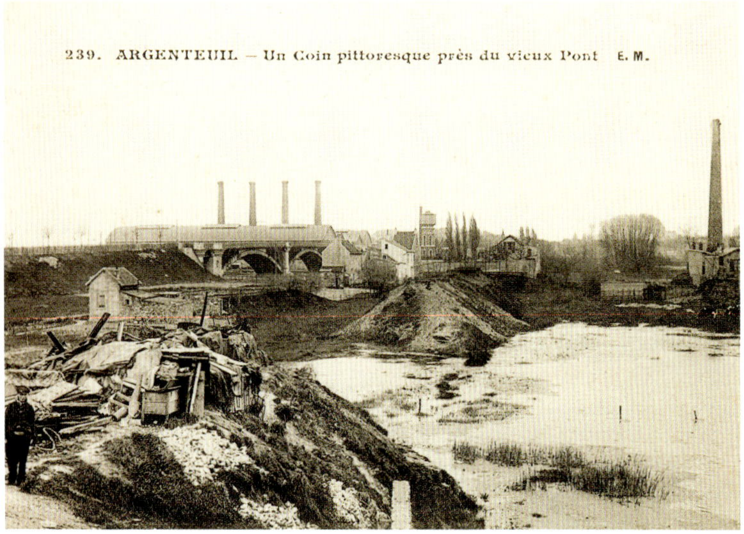

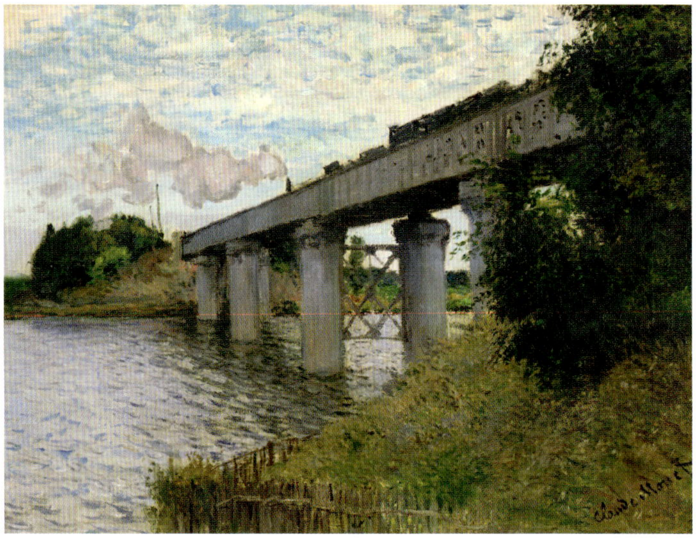

The leisure and recreation activities that provided many of the naturalist and Impressionist painters with modern urban life subject matter reflected a massive social transformation wrought by the industrial revolution in France. All spheres of society were affected by the distinction increasingly drawn between work and leisure (although change came more slowly for the class of agricultural labourers living in rural areas painted by Millet). Economic prosperity translated into disposable income that enabled greater numbers of young adults – especially fashion-conscious Parisians – to pursue, outside their work hours, a variety of hedonistic interests in an entirely secular lifestyle. The railways opened up the countryside to day trippers and picnickers. La Grenouillère, for example, a favourite bathing spot on the Seine painted in 1869 by Monet and Renoir, was only a 17-kilometre, 20-minute train ride from the Gare Saint-Lazare. The same line could deliver promenaders on weekend excursions to the stations or ferries that would land them on the beaches of Normandy, to Trouville (the 'bathing-place'[34]), Honfleur and Sainte-Adresse. In addition to river and sea bathing and swimming, boating and yachting were popular, as was horse-racing (see Degas, cat 17).

The river Seine and the western railway are thoroughfares that lie along a narrow geographic corridor between Paris and the Normandy coast. Monet, who lived the greater part of his life in Normandy, first in Le Havre and later in Giverny, travelled this corridor frequently and made regular painting expeditions to the coast and painted susta ined series of views, captured in a variety of atmospheric and lighting effects, of haystacks at Giverny (see cats 32, 47 and 48) and the cathedral at Rouen (see cat 49). In 1870, Monet fled France rather than face conscription into the military to fight an unwinnable war waged against Prussia by an empire whose politics he did not support. He no doubt travelled by rail to the coast and then by cross-channel steamer to England, boarding the train to London where he settled for the duration of the Franco-Prussian war.

Industrial air pollution in London produced the atmospheric and lighting effects that captivated Monet, and during his period of self-imposed exile he painted views of the river Thames in which the materiality of nature and the built environment were visually diminished by the smoke-filled atmosphere, for example, in *The Thames below Westminster* and *The pool of London*, both painted in 1871.[35] While in London he would have studied Turner's and Claude's paintings of harbours, ships and ports in the National Gallery, several of which – for example, Turner's *Sun rising through vapour*; *Fishermen cleaning and selling fish*, first exhibited in 1807 – provide points of future reference for Monet's Impressionist paintings of Le Havre.[36]

Following the collapse of the Second Empire and the rise of the Third Republic, Monet returned to Paris in 1871, settling the following year in Argenteuil on the Seine, 12.3 kilometres from the centre of Paris. Argenteuil was then in the aftermath of the Franco-Prussian war – the rail and road bridges across the river had been destroyed and in his paintings Monet recorded the progress of their reconstruction as in *Argenteuil, the bridge under repair* 1872.[37] It was also something of a frontier town in which nature and industry converged, a buffer zone between the countryside and the suburbs. The extension of the railway from Paris, a 15-minute train journey from Argenteuil, attracted many new factories and businesses. By the late 19th century, local industries included tanneries, chemical plants, and one of the largest iron works in France (see fig 31).

Monet lived in Argenteuil from 1871 to 1878 and witnessed the encroachment of industry and the urban expansion of greater Paris. In 1876 he gave his address as 2 Boulevard Saint-Denis 'opposite the station, pink house with green shutters' (cat 36)[38]. With its goods yards, the railway was a site of constant activity and clamour. In all weathers and seasons Monet painted the movement of trains (*The railway bridge at Argenteuil*, fig 32), the local streetscape (see cat 15) and the steamboats that plied, and the trains that crossed over, the river – all close to home. He also lugged his painting equipment

fig 31
Postcard of Argenteuil c1900

fig 32
Claude Monet
The railway bridge at Argenteuil c1873–74
oil on canvas 55 x 72 cm
Musée d'Orsay, Paris
Photograph: Giraudon/The Bridgeman Art Library

fig 33
Claude Monet
Arrival of the Normandy train, Gare Saint-Lazare 1877
oil on canvas 59.6 x 80.2 cm
The Art Institute of Chicago, Mr and Mrs Martin A Ryerson Collection 1933.1158
Photograph © The Art Institute of Chicago

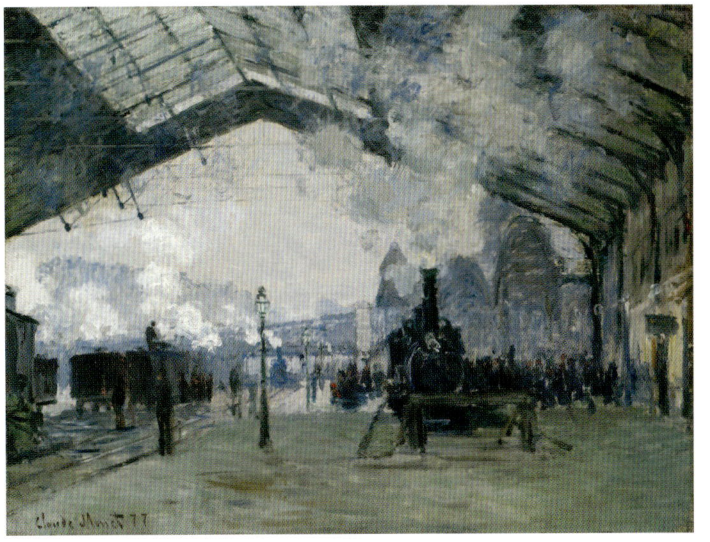

out into what in his paintings appears to be the open countryside to paint fields, wildflowers and trees, but at his back were the factory smokestacks and the constant sound of trains chugging across the landscape. In its subjects, as in its materials and techniques – in its science – Impressionism is a creature of the industrial revolution, even when it is not visibly referenced in a painting.

Virginia Spate has noted that 'in the 1870s Paris and Le Havre were the two poles of the east-west axis of the Seine valley which – with few exceptions – marked the limits of Monet's painting'.[39] From Argenteuil Monet continued to make regular trips to the Normandy coast, travelling by rail to the Gare Saint-Lazare and there transferring to a train bound for Le Havre. Two of the five paintings he showed in the first Impressionist exhibition were of harbour subjects painted in Le Havre: *Impression: sunrise* and *Fishing boats leaving the port* and coastal and port scenes were among the works he showed in the Impressionist exhibitions of 1876, 1877, 1879 and 1882. (He did not exhibit in the fifth exhibition in 1880, the sixth in 1881 or the eighth in 1886.) In paintings such as the *Great quay at Le Havre* 1872 and *Port of Le Havre*, also known as *View of the outer harbour at Le Havre* 1874,[40] Monet presented jostling scenes of steamboats, rigged sailing ships and traditional fishing boats on the harbour expressive of the continuity of commerce on the water.

The terminus in Paris for the Chemins de Fer de l'Ouest was the Gare Saint-Lazare, near the Pont de l'Europe (built in 1868). This was the first station to be opened in Paris and was rebuilt several times. The station and the bridge featured in paintings by Impressionist artists such as Edouard Manet and Gustave Caillebotte who lived in the vicinity. While Monet continued to live at Argenteuil, he rented a studio near the Gare Saint-Lazare in 1877 and embarked on a series of 11 compositions, eight of which he showed in the third Impressionist exhibition in April that year, including *Arrival of the Normandy train* (fig 33) and *Le Pont de l'Europe (Gare Saint-Lazare)*.[41]

Monet settled in Vétheuil some distance downriver from Argenteuil in 1878. From Vétheuil he continued to make the customary painting trips to the Normandy coast. In March 1881 he was at Fécamp; the following February at Dieppe and Pourville; and a year later at Etretat (see cat 23).

In April 1883 Monet moved from Vétheuil, with his future second wife, Alice, and their blended family of eight children, to Giverny on the banks of the river Epte (which flowed into the Seine). This was situated 75 kilometres from Paris, and 60 kilometres from Rouen. Here he created an oasis of calm and beauty with water gardens which became justly famous from the ravishing and radiant series of paintings of the waterlily pond and the Japanese bridge that traversed it and which he continued to produce even when, from 1908, his sight began to fail. The local environment provided him with an ever-changing resource of landscape subject matter. In 1885 he returned to a motif that he had first painted in 1865, the haystack, and in 1890 and 1891 foregrounded the motif in a series of impressions painted at different times of the day, across the seasons, and in a variety of atmospheres. The *Mornings* series (see cat 50) demonstrates Monet's delight in the enveloping and shifting effects of fog in the natural environment, remote from the sites of industry.

Giverny is the southern gateway to Normandy from Paris and not part of the Ile-de-France, to which it is often related. Monet's nearest mainline railway station, a short distance by horse-drawn vehicle, and later by car, was Vernon, on the opposite side of the river Seine from Giverny. From Vernon he would set out on a succession of painting expeditions. He travelled to the Mediterranean coast – in 1884 to Cap Martin, near Menton (see cat 25), and in 1888 to Cap d'Antibes. He notified his partner Alice Hoschedé (whom he was to marry in 1892) of his impending arrival from Cap d'Antibes, via Paris, at the Menton railway station.[42] In spring and early summer 1889 he was painting in the Creuse Valley in Limousin, central France. Monet made several

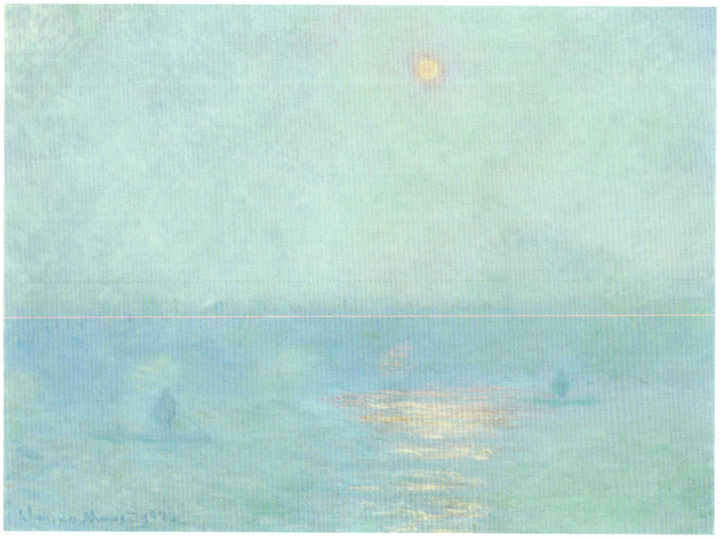

fig 34
Claude Monet
Waterloo Bridge: the sun in a fog 1903
oil on canvas 73.7 x 100.3 cm
National Gallery of Canada, Ottawa

trips to Rouen, which lay halfway between Giverny and Le Havre on the river Seine, between 1892 and 1894 to produce a series of works depicting the crusty façade of the cathedral viewed in all weathers, across the seasons and in various atmospheric and lighting conditions (see cat 49). These were as close to the effect of a sequence of time-lapse photographs as Monet's processes and the matière of painting would allow. When Paul Cézanne described him as 'an eye – but my God what an eye', he was describing a finely tuned organ of sight that was the highly sensitised biological counterpart to the mechanical eye of a camera (a product of the science of optics and the industrial era).

Monet visited London from September to October 1899, and again from late winter to early spring in 1900 and 1901, and painted the views from his window in the Savoy Hotel, looking downriver to Waterloo Bridge and upriver to Charing Cross Bridge and the Houses of Parliament (see cat 52).[43] He was astonished by the dramatic and brilliant, constantly shifting lighting and atmospheric effects, especially when the winter sun struggled to penetrate the dense blanket of smog that enveloped the city. London, capital of the earliest and most highly industrialised nation in the world, was experiencing the extremes of air pollution as coal smoke from steamboats and trains, factories and other industrial buildings, and domestic fireplaces, and gasworks and power stations (Deptford Power Station had opened in 1889 for the generation of electricity) poured into the atmosphere and thickened the winter fog along the river Thames to produce the notorious London 'pea-souper', at times obliterating the scene.[44] In a letter to his wife, dated 26 February 1900, he marvels at the completely yellow fog he had seen in the early hours of the morning[45] and in some paintings – *Waterloo Bridge: the sun in a fog* 1903 (fig 34), for example – the landmarks and buildings are rendered almost invisible by white-out conditions.

The great series of Houses of Parliament works painted mostly from the terrace of St Thomas's Hospital on the opposite bank of the Thames, close to Westminster Bridge, depicts Sir Charles Barry and Augustus Welby Pugin's iconic Gothic Revival masterpiece in silhouette against the setting sun and fading light, or looming out of the haze like 'an apparition'.[46] Monet's images of the dematerialised architectural complex situated between overcast skies and the glittering, visually scintillating, sunlight-reflecting river had been foreshadowed three decades earlier in *Impression: sunrise*.

Monet's long life – he died in 1926, aged 86 – spanned the industrial era, from the age of steam to the age of electricity and the internal combustion engine. Indeed he purchased a motor car in December 1900.[47] He was conversant with the writings of the French utopian socialist thinker Claude Henri de Rouvray (Henri de Saint-Simon) for whom science and industry were watchwords for a new social order.[48] Monet disavowed religion and his outlook – and his art – was very much of this world. Just as he had availed himself of the convenience of portable painting materials and equipment and steam-powered public transport, so he may be presumed to have invested in gas, electricity and many of the mod cons of the industrial era as they became available. He, like the art movement with which he is so closely associated, was a witness to the industrial revolution that created the modern era.

1 John Rewald, *The history of Impressionism*, 4th ed, Secker and Warburg, London, 1973, p 318

2 For example, the great Monet scholar John House states that the painting 'shows the port in mist' in *Monet*, Phaidon, London 1991 p 60

3 Edward Stanford, *Stanford's Paris guide*, London and Paris 1858, p 18

4 From *The new Colossus*, the sonnet composed by the New York poet Emma Lazarus in 1883 that appears on a bronze plaque affixed to the Statue of Liberty in New York in 1903

5 John Murray, *A handbook for travellers in France*, London 1854, p 62

6 Murray 1854, p 62

7 Murray 1854, p xxviii

8 'The arrival of the railway shortened journeys and made travel easier'. Jacques Lethève, *Daily life of French artists*, George Allen & Unwin, London 1972, p 94

9 From the 1844 diary of John Davies Mereweather, extracts of which are published online at www.mereweather.net/paris.htm

10 Murray 1854, p 30

11 Murray 1854, p 52

12 Murray 1854, p 26

13 *Stanford's Paris guide* 1858, pp 18, 26

14 Christopher Lloyd, 'Camille Pissarro and Rouen', in Christopher Lloyd ed, *Studies on Camille Pissarro*, Routledge & Kegan Paul, London and New York 1986, p 80

15 National Gallery of Art, Washington DC

16 Quoted in Lethève 1972, p 102

17 Kendall 1989, p 22

18 Kendall 1989, p 93

19 Kendall 1989, pp 28–29

20 Murray 1854, pp 344–47

21 Mereweather, 25 Jul 1844

22 Steven Adams, *The Barbizon school and the origins of Impressionism*, Phaidon, London 1994, p 8

23 Murray 1854, p 344

24 Murray 1854, p 347

25 Kendall 1989, p 29

26 Kendall 1989, p 31

27 Wadsworth Athenaeum, Hartford, Connecticut

28 Daubigny, The 'Botin' and steamboats from *Voyage en Bateau* 1862, etching. See Steven Adams, *The Barbizon school and the origins of Impressionism*. Phaidon, London 1994, p 192

29 Lilla Cabot Perry, see p 206 of this catalogue

30 Guillemot in *Revue illustrée*, Dec 1897 to Jun 1898, noted in Lethève 1972, p 105. See also Manet's *Monet painting in his floating studio* 1874, Bayerische Staatsgemäldesammlungen, Munich

31 Guillemot in *Revue illustrée*, Dec 1897 to Jun 1898, quoted in Lethève 1972

32 Louis Vauxcelles, trans Terence Maloon, see p 199 of this catalogue

33 Lilla Cabot Perry, p 207 of this catalogue

34 Murray 1854, p 70

35 National Gallery London and National Museum and Gallery Wales, respectively

36 See also Turner's *Moonlight; a study at Millbank* 1797 and *Le Havre: tour de François 1er* c1832 (both Tate London). Also Katharine Lochnan ed, *Turner, Whistler, Monet*, exh cat, Art Gallery of Ontario, Toronto 2004

37 Private collection, Marseille

38 In a letter to Victor Chocquet in Feb 1876, Kendall 1989, p 36

39 Virginia Spate, *Claude Monet: life and work*, Rizzoli, New York 1992, p 80

40 In the Hermitage Museum, St Petersburg and the Philadelphia Museum of Art, respectively

41 Musée Marmottan, Paris

42 Kendall 1989, p 93

43 See Sylvie Patin, 'The return of Whistler and Monet to the Thames', in Lochnan 2004, pp 179–83

44 See Jonathan Ribner, 'The poetics of pollution' in Lochnan 2004, especially pp 62–63

45 Kendall 1989, p 134

46 Patin in Lochnan 2004, p 198

47 Stuckey 1995, p 79

48 Karin Sagner-Düchting, *Monet*, Taschen, Cologne 1992, p 58

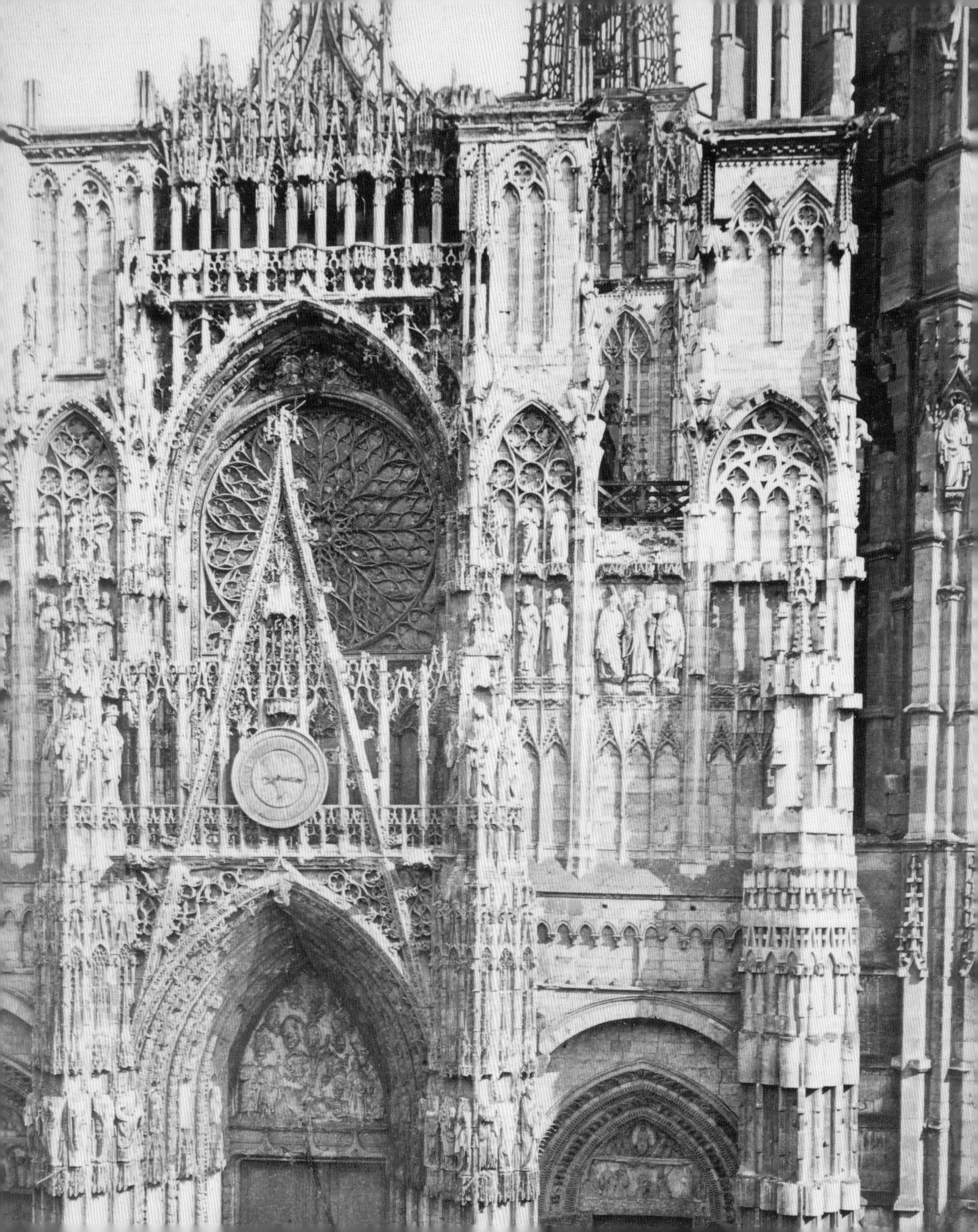

SEEING DOUBLE: PAINTERS AND PHOTOGRAPHERS

Claire Durand-Ruel Snollaerts

Painters and photographers are witnesses of their era, and their works can teach us a great deal about the history of landscape. Our world has been so much changed by human intervention since the 19th century that, without the landscape painters and photographers, we could easily forget how things appeared back then.

It is not often that the painter's way of seeing is directly compared to the photographer's. Composition is a reflection of personality, whether in painting or photography, but the principal difference between a photographer and a landscape painter is that the latter 'cheats' and can, at will, interpret the landscape by adding elements or removing them. In addition, the painter's touch, style of drawing and use of colour adds another dimension which is expressive of his or her personality.

Paintings and photographs can be destined for very different uses: a painter may hope that his or her works find a place on the walls of a collector, whereas a photographer whose picture is reproduced as a postcard may hope that this image will be chosen in preference to others that are in competition with it. Painters and photographers generally share the desire that their works please, intrigue and stir the person who sees them and, in consequence, may want to acquire them.

It is noteworthy that the great Impressionist masters, Monet, Sisley and Pissarro, always depended on and remained exceedingly faithful to nature, but also that – without ever working side by side – photographers and painters often chose to represent the same sites.

Notwithstanding this fact, the challenge of matching the paintings selected for this exhibition with vintage postcards and photographs has proven to be no easy task.

This compilation is based on the resources of various archival collections in Paris. Inevitably Monet is the best served of the participating artists, although two canvases by Sisley and one by Pissarro are also paired with contemporary photographs. The richest source of material was an immense collection of postcards compiled over many years by Alain Mothe, who has discovered photographic parallels, in thousands of examples, to the motifs chosen by 19th-century French painters. I am also indebted to the Wildenstein Institute Archives and to the Durand-Ruel Archives – both situated in Paris – for access to their rich documentation of the Impressionist era.

Photograph of Rouen Cathedral, 1890s, private collection

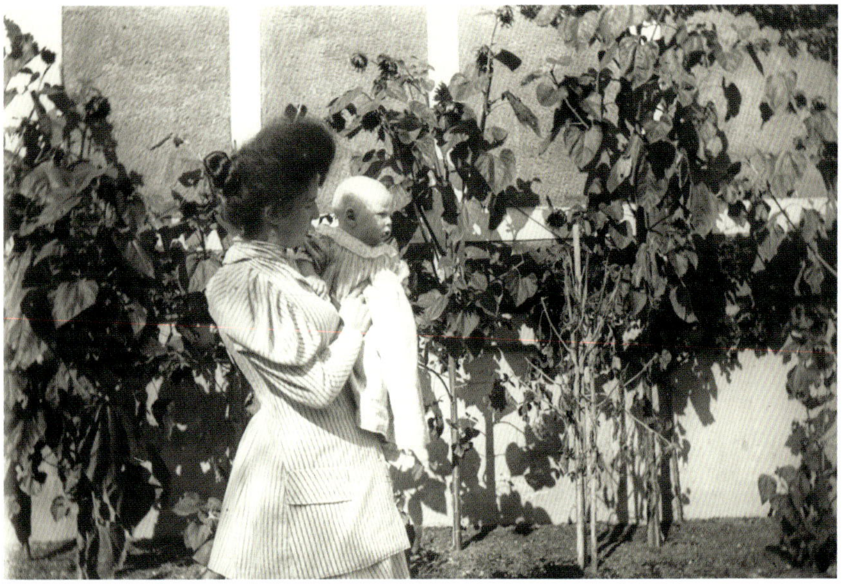

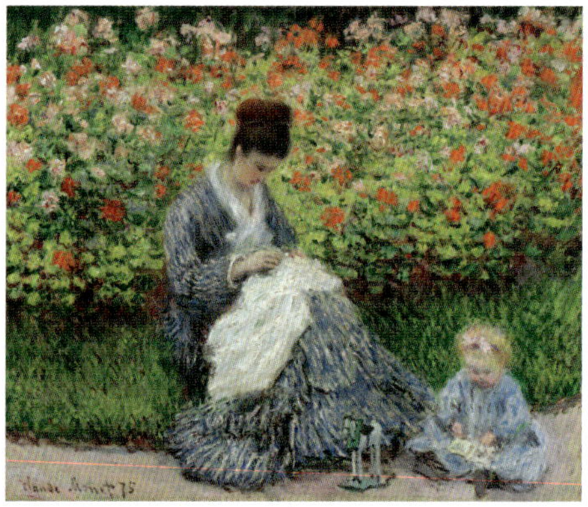

Camille Monet and a child in the artist's garden in Argenteuil (cat 20)

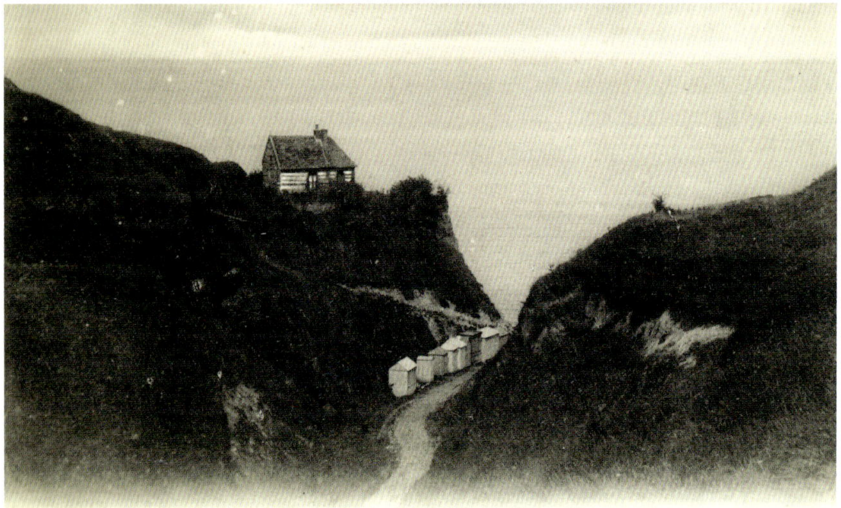

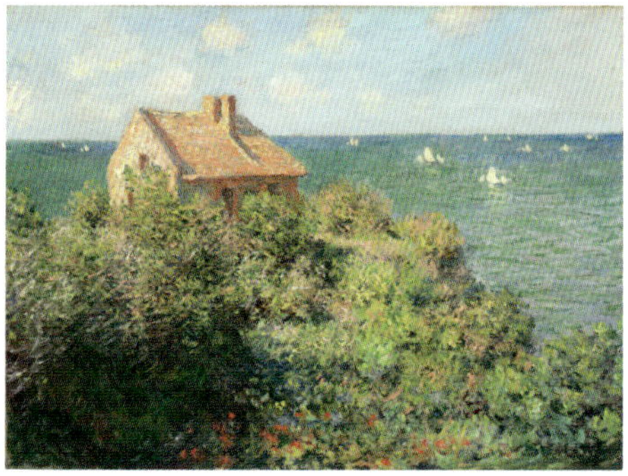

Fisherman's cottage on the cliffs at Varengeville (cat 24)

Camille Monet and a child in the artist's garden in Argenteuil (cat 20)
Claude Monet

Camille Monet, née Doncieux, was the first wife of Claude Monet. They had two sons together: Jean and Michel. On 5 September 1879 Camille died prematurely at the age of 32, when Michel was only a year old. When he became a widower, Monet entrusted his sons to the care of Alice Hoschedé, wife of the great textile merchant and art lover, Ernest Hoschedé. Monet married Alice after the latter's death, on 16 July 1892. Alice had six children by her first marriage: Suzanne, Germaine, Blanche, Marthe, Jacques and Jean-Pierre – all of them adopted by Monet. In the above photo taken in June 1893 at Giverny, the next generation of the Monet-Hoschedé family arrives on the scene: Jimmy is seen in the arms of his mother, Suzanne Hoschedé-Butler.

Photograph © Durand-Ruel Archives, Paris

Fisherman's cottage on the cliffs at Varengeville (cat 24)
Claude Monet

After the death of his wife Camille in 1879, Monet entered a period of both stylistic and personal transition. To distract himself from his grief, he painted prolifically, wandering everywhere along the stretch of Normandy coast between Pourville and Varengeville. This motif represents a fisherman's cottage, formerly a customs agent's house. Monet painted it from all angles at least 17 times. Contrary to the photographer, who stationed himself on a path of the gorge of the Petit Ailly, Monet took up his position on the heights overlooking the cottage. His mastery of the Impressionist technique is evident in the profusion of small touches of colour, the canvas bathed in sunlight. In other versions of the motif, Monet took exactly the same position as the photographer of this postcard.

Postcard: Alain Mothe Collection, Paris

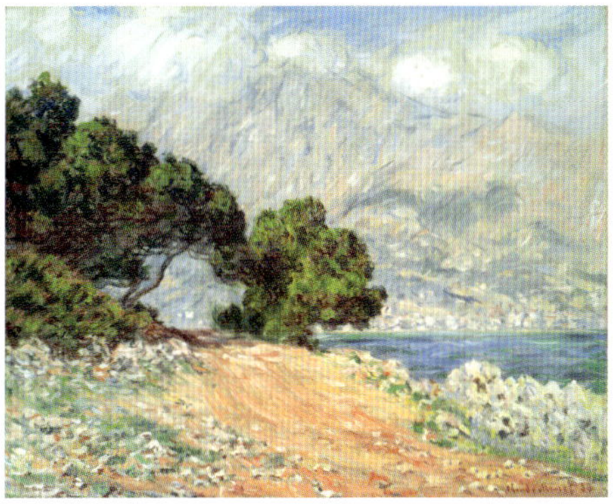

Cap Martin, near Menton (cat 25)

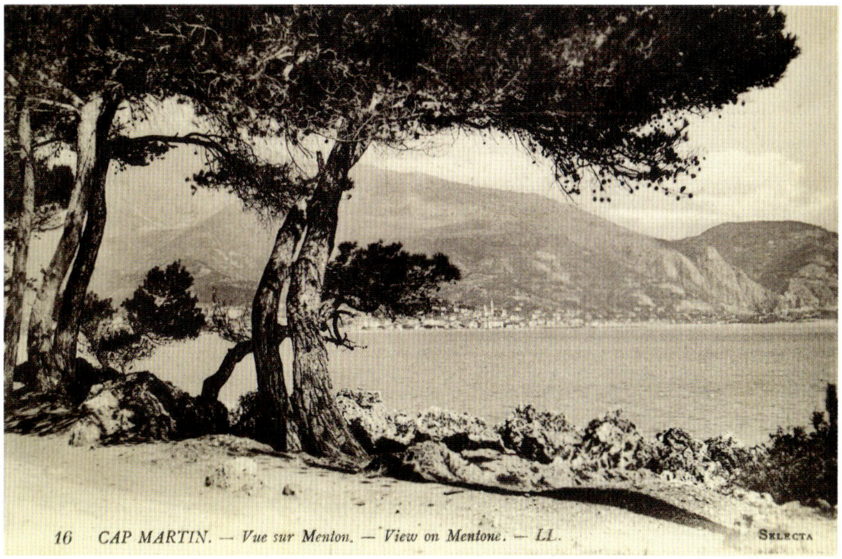

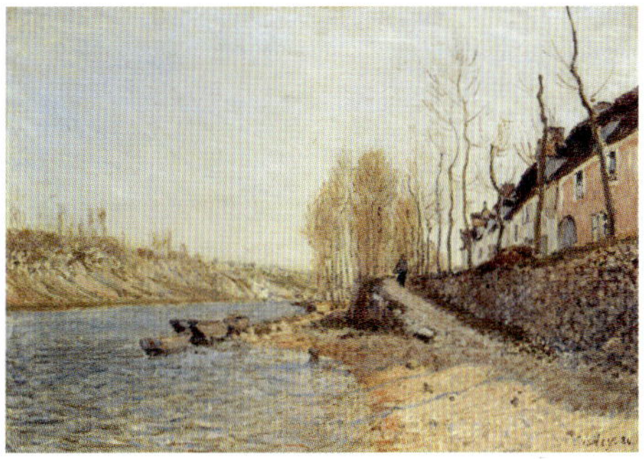

La Croix-Blanche at Saint-Mammès (cat 29)

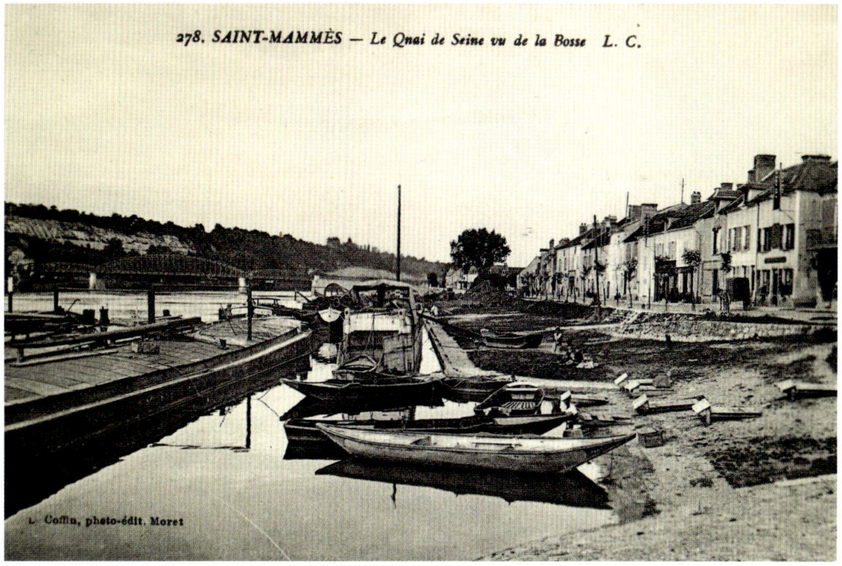

Cap Martin, near Menton (cat 25)
Claude Monet

Having settled in his new house in Giverny, Monet went to the Mediterranean coast at the end of December 1883 with his friend Renoir. There they discovered Bordighera, an Italian seaside resort east of Menton. Attracted by the pleasant climate and unique vegetation, Monet returned to the Riviera on his own a year later, arriving on 17 January 1884. In less than three months he painted some 40 canvases, two being views from Cap Martin, looking through the pines toward the village of Menton at the foot of the Franco-Italian Alps. The intense Mediterranean light compelled him to use new, very high-keyed tonalities – as he explained to his dealer, Paul Durand-Ruel: 'It will perhaps cause a bit of an outcry from the enemies of blue and pink, because it is just this sparkle, this enchanting light that I'm committed to render [...] Everything is pigeon-breast and brandy-flame; it's admirable, and every day the countryside is more beautiful; I'm delighted by this country' (11 March 1884). In both Monet's painting and the postcard above Menton is merely glimpsed through a natural frame made by the pine trees.

Postcard: Alain Mothe Collection, Paris

La Croix-Blanche at Saint-Mammès (cat 29)
Alfred Sisley

The art critic Gustave Geffroy wrote in 1923: 'Sisley found his region. It was on the fringes of the forest of Fontainebleau, a succession of small towns along the banks of the Seine and the Loing – Moret, Saint-Mammès ...' During the 15 years leading up to his death in 1894, Sisley painted many aspects of the waterfront of the village of Saint-Mammès (at the juncture of the Loing and Seine rivers) where the waterways were often animated by barges and other craft, as the photographer shows here.

Postcard: Alain Mothe Collection, Paris

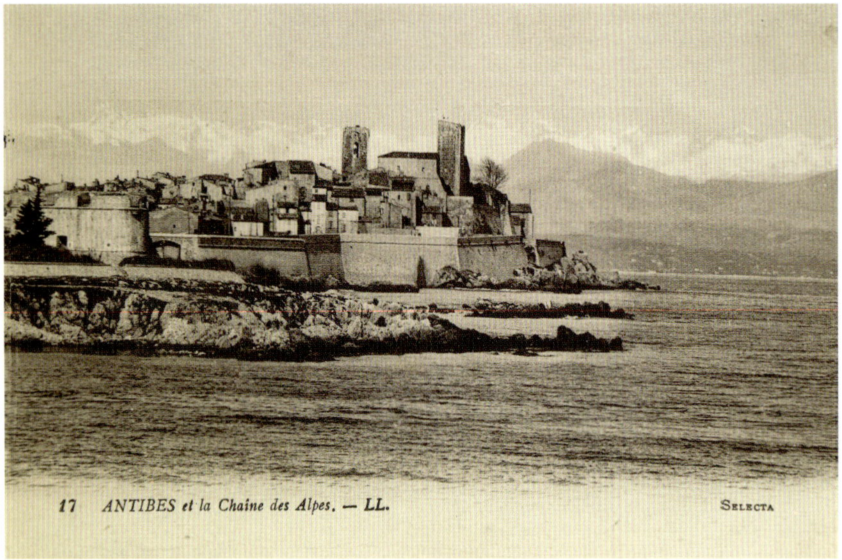

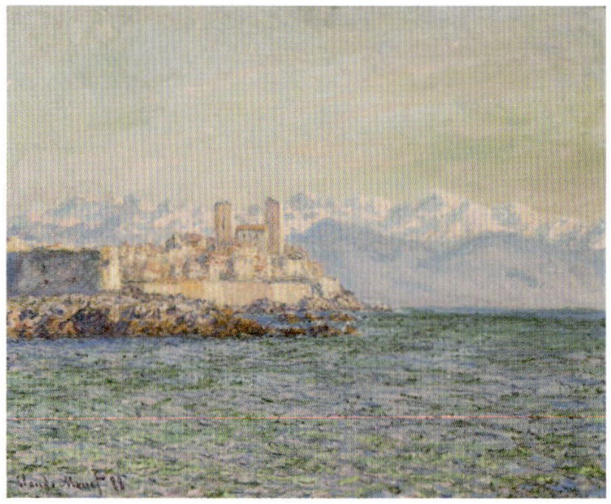

The fort of Antibes (cat 27)

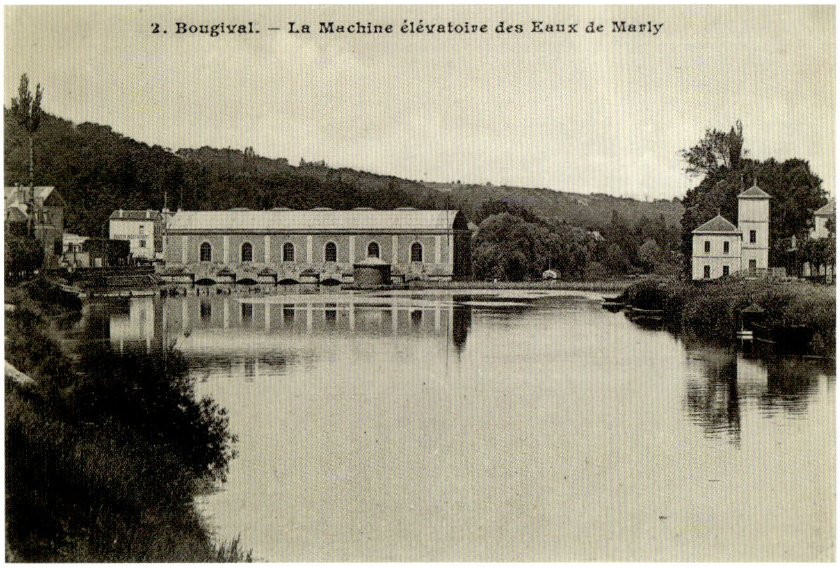

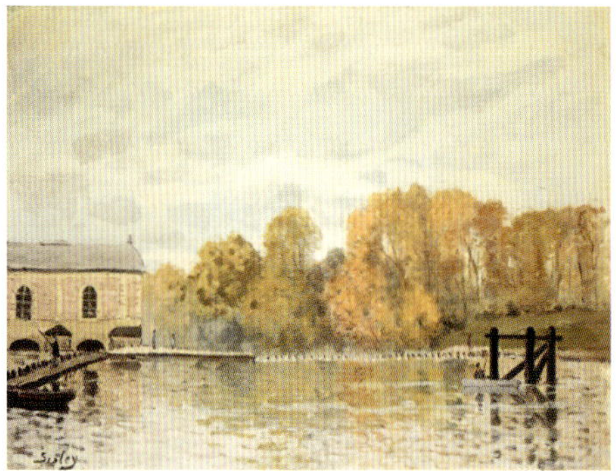

Waterworks at Marly (cat 22)

The fort of Antibes (cat 27)
Claude Monet

During the first six months of 1888 Monet settled in Antibes, in the south of France. His objective was to paint 'the town of Antibes, a small fortified town, gilded by the sun, set against beautiful blue and pink mountains and the chain of the Alps eternally covered with snow' (letter to Alice Hoschedé, 20 January 1888). The weather was superb, and Monet painted seven canvases of the same motif. He set out to represent the beautiful panorama by means of closely-ranked, small touches of pink, blue and white, working so conscientiously, 'that the merest touch which isn't right looks like a speck of dirt' (letter to Alice Hoschedé, 1 February 1888). Here Monet and this photographer chose exactly the same vantage point for their views of the fort of Antibes.

Postcard: Alain Mothe Collection, Paris

Waterworks at Marly (cat 22)
Alfred Sisley

The long building in the water, truncated in Sisley's picture, once housed an enormous, fantastic hydraulic machine known as 'The Machine of Marly'. It pumped water from the Seine to the ornamental ponds of the Châteaux of Marly and Versailles, conveyed there by the aqueduct of Louveciennes. The first machine was commissioned by Louis XIV in 1681, although it was replaced by several others. During the time that Sisley lived in the village of Marly-le-Roi, between 1874 and 1877, the machine of Napoleon III was in operation. There is no point these days looking for it during one's promenades along the Seine: it was demolished in 1967.

Postcard: Alain Mothe Collection, Paris

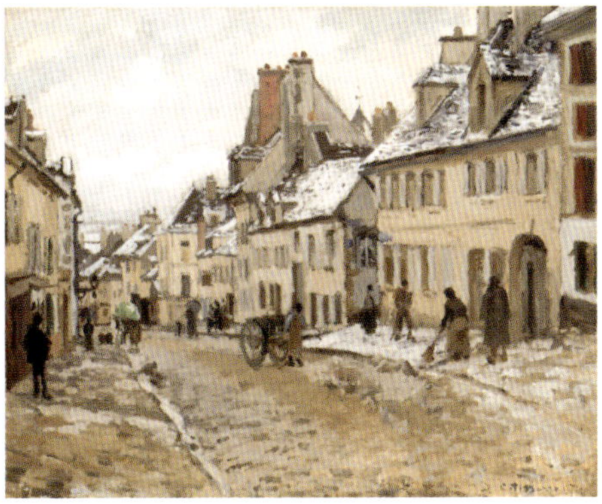

Pontoise, the road to Gisors in winter (cat 21)

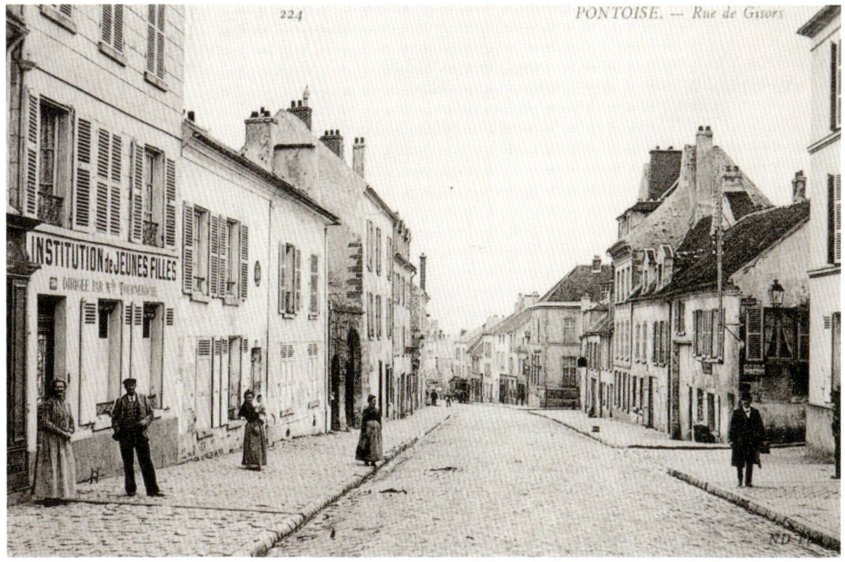

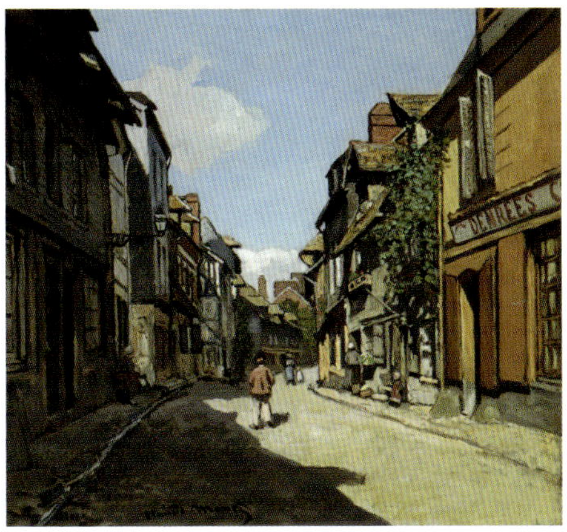

Rue de la Bavole, Honfleur (cat 13)

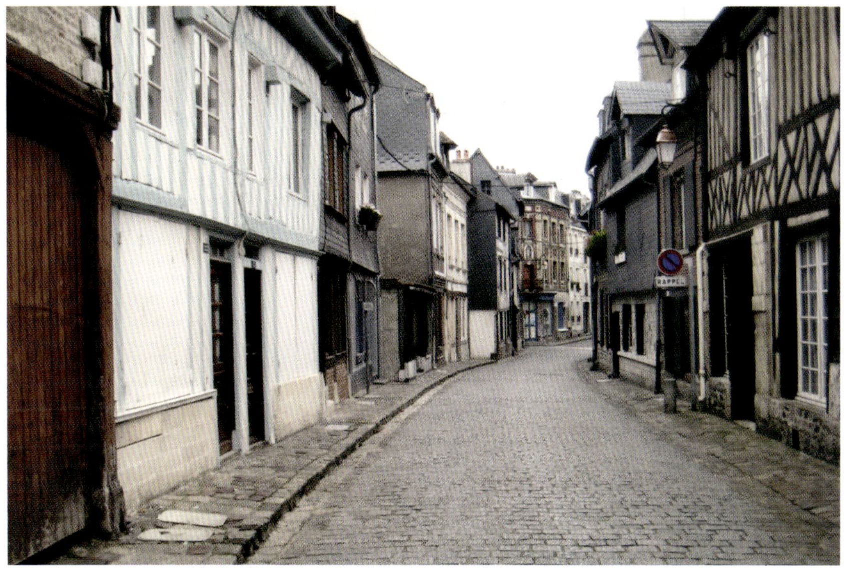

Pontoise, the road to Gisors in winter (cat 21)
Camille Pissarro

Pontoise is situated some 30 kilometres to the northwest of Paris. Camille Pissarro lived there for a dozen years, completing about 300 oil paintings of the town before he left in 1882. Instead of picturesque sites, he preferred ordinary street scenes – like this beautiful view of the Rue de Gisors after a snowfall. For the postcard illustrated above, the photographer planted his tripod right in the middle of the road. In Pissarro's painting we recognise all the buildings on the right in the photo. His representations were quite faithful to the motif, as were Monet's. The appearance of this street is little changed today.

Postcard: Alain Mothe Collection, Paris

Rue de la Bavole, Honfleur (cat 13)
Claude Monet

Monet spent the summer of 1864 in Honfleur (Normandy) in the company of his friend, the painter Frédéric Bazille. Honfleur is a delightful fishing port and was a flourishing artistic centre since the beginning of the 19th century. The town has preserved its picturesque little streets lined with old houses, which delight the tourists who flock there from all parts of the world every summer. Monet represented this street twice, making minor alterations to some of the pedestrians, but one of these versions must surely be a studio transcription of the other. This amateur photographer's picture reveals how faithfully Monet adhered to the architectural elements of the street.

Photograph: Alain Mothe Collection, Paris

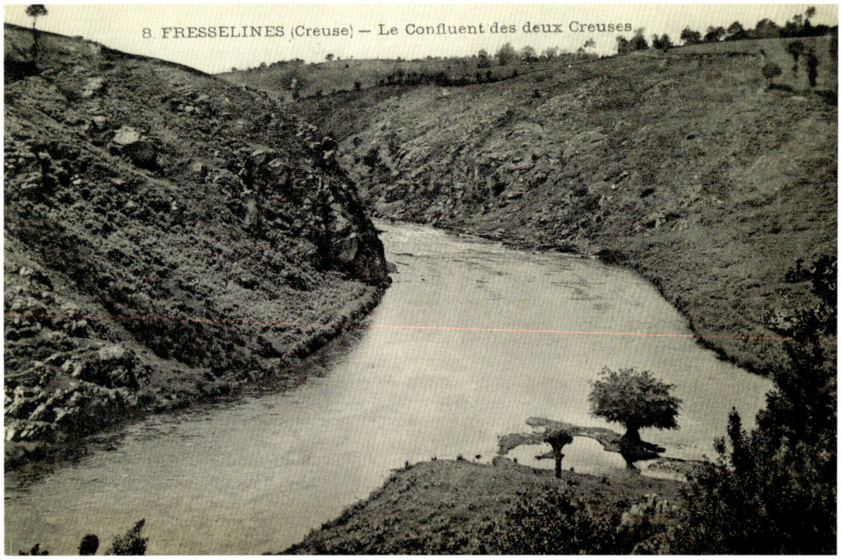

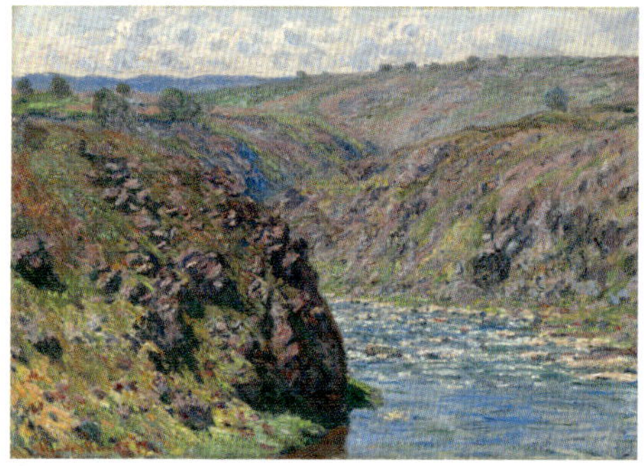

Valley of the Creuse (sunlight effect) (cat 26)

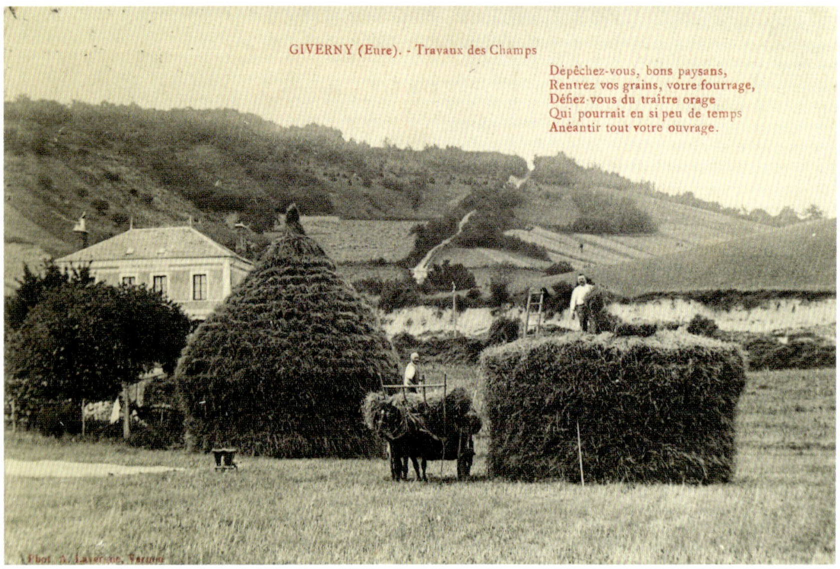

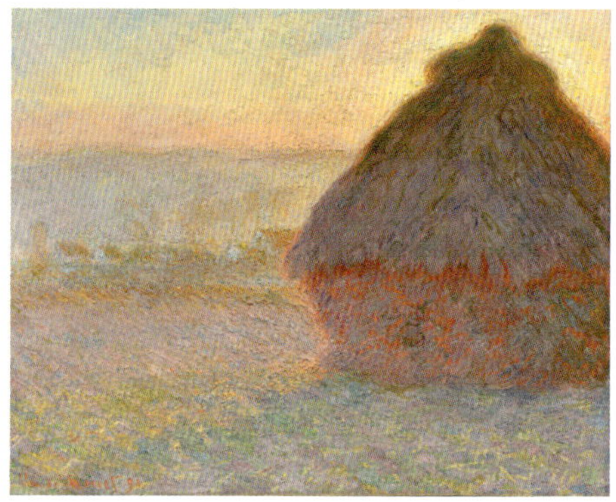

Grainstack/Haystack (sunset) (cat 47)

Valley of the Creuse (sunlight effect) (cat 46)
Claude Monet

The art critic Gustave Geffroy was responsible for Monet's discovery of the region of La Creuse, a department of France close to the Massif Central. Monet accompanied Geffroy during a visit to the home of the poet Maurice Rollinat in February 1889. Captivated by the place, Monet returned there on his own a month later. 'It is superb here, the wildness reminds me of Belle-Ile', he wrote. On his arrival he set up his easel in front of the large, austere rock, barren of life, at the base of which flows the river Creuse (as seen in the postcard above). He produced 10 canvases representing this single motif, all of them identical apart from the fact that the effects of light and the weather vary from one canvas to the next. For the first time, apparently, the idea of 'series' crystallises for Monet: 'I am terrified to see my canvases so sombre, several being without a sky. It's going to be a gloomy series' (letter to Alice Hoschedé, 4 April 1889). A photo on p 163 shows paintings of the Creuse hanging in Monet's second studio at Giverny, around 1900.

Postcard: Alain Mothe Collection, Paris

Grainstack/Haystack (sunset) (cat 47)
Claude Monet

'[Paul] Durand [-Ruel] doesn't respond to my canvases [...] It seems that he's selling a lot, but for the moment people only want Monets – apparently he can't paint enough of them. The worst thing is that they all want *Haystacks at sunset*!!!' These remarks by Camille Pissarro, written to his son Lucien on 3 April 1891, indicate Monet's newfound celebrity and Pissarro's anxiety about not attaining any comparable success. A month later Monet exhibited 15 recent paintings of haystacks at Durand-Ruel, prompting Pissarro to enthuse: 'No matter, he's truly a great artist! It goes without saying that it's a great success. It's so alluring, frankly, that it's not surprising; the canvases breathe contentment' (letter to Lucien Pissarro, 5 May 1891). The haystacks seen in Monet's paintings and in the postcard of Giverny are things of the past: the method of constructing them has completely changed. Manually-constructed haystacks – solid and well-balanced – were made by teams of skilled, experienced agricultural workers.

Postcard: Alain Mothe Collection, Paris

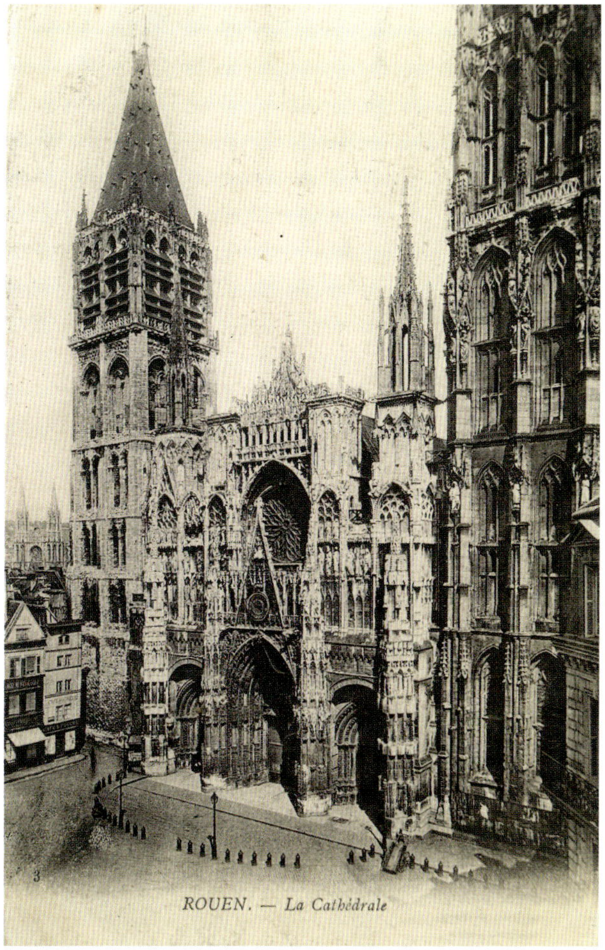

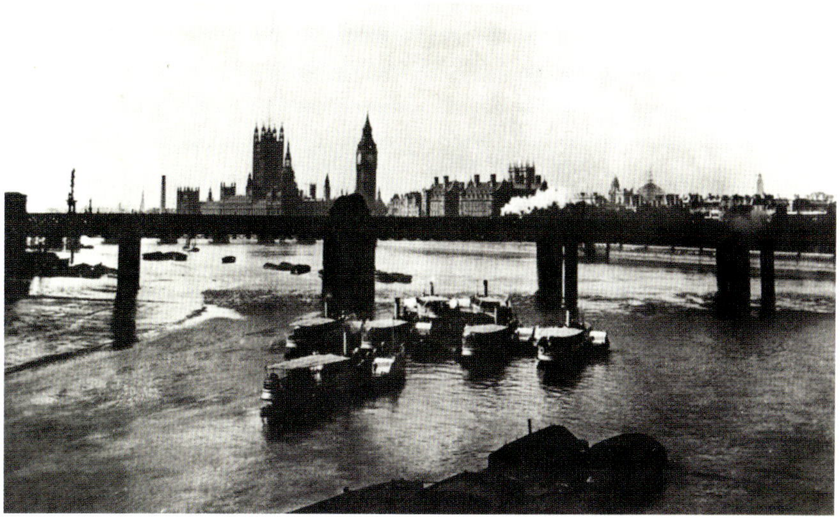

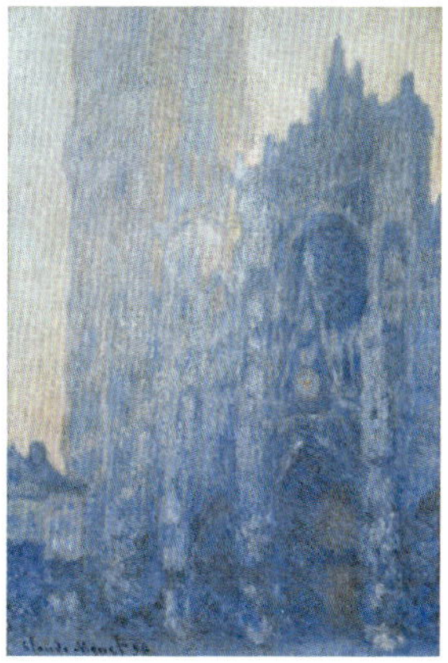

Charing Cross Bridge (overcast day) (cat 52)
left: *Rouen Cathedral façade and Tour d'Albane (morning effect)* (cat 49)

Rouen Cathedral façade and Tour d'Albane (morning effect) (cat 49)
Claude Monet

Variations of the same motif, seen at different times of day, became typical of Monet's painting. After the series of *La Creuse* in 1889, then the *Haystacks* and *Poplars* in 1890–91, Monet turned his hand to *Rouen Cathedral*, completing 30 versions during the course of two visits in 1892 and 1893. It was gruelling work: 'Every day I make additions, and latch onto something I haven't yet been able to see. It's terribly difficult, but it's moving ahead [...] I'm wrecked, worn out [...] I had a night filled with nightmares: the cathedral fell on top of me; it looked blue or pink or yellow' (letter to Alice Hoschedé, 3 April 1892). When Monet showed 20 of these works at the Durand-Ruel gallery in May 1895, Pissarro was dazzled by their technical ingenuity: 'It [the series] really has to be seen as a whole [...] I am bowled over by this extraordinary mastery [...] It is all willed and well thought-out, searching for the most elusive nuances of effects that I've never seen realised by any other artist' (letter to Lucien Pissarro, 26 May 1895).

Postcard: Alain Mothe Collection, Paris

Charing Cross Bridge (overcast day) (cat 52)
Claude Monet

Monet's first stay in London took place in 1871, but as the 19th century drew to a close he felt the need to go back to 'try to paint some effects of fog over the Thames' (letter to Théodore Duret, 25 October 1887). He chose three motifs: the Houses of Parliament, Charing Cross Bridge and Waterloo Bridge. Charing Cross Bridge is the motif of 35 canvases, but in this series the object is no longer important. Monet set out to recreate in colour, much like J M W Turner before him, the varied appearances of the fog over the water, enshrouding the buildings, sometimes resulting in an intense level of abstraction.

This photographic view of Charing Cross Bridge is strikingly distinct in comparison to Monet's painting. The lushness of the atmospheric effects created by Monet's brush cannot be matched in a black-and-white photograph.

Photograph © Wildenstein Institute Archives, Paris

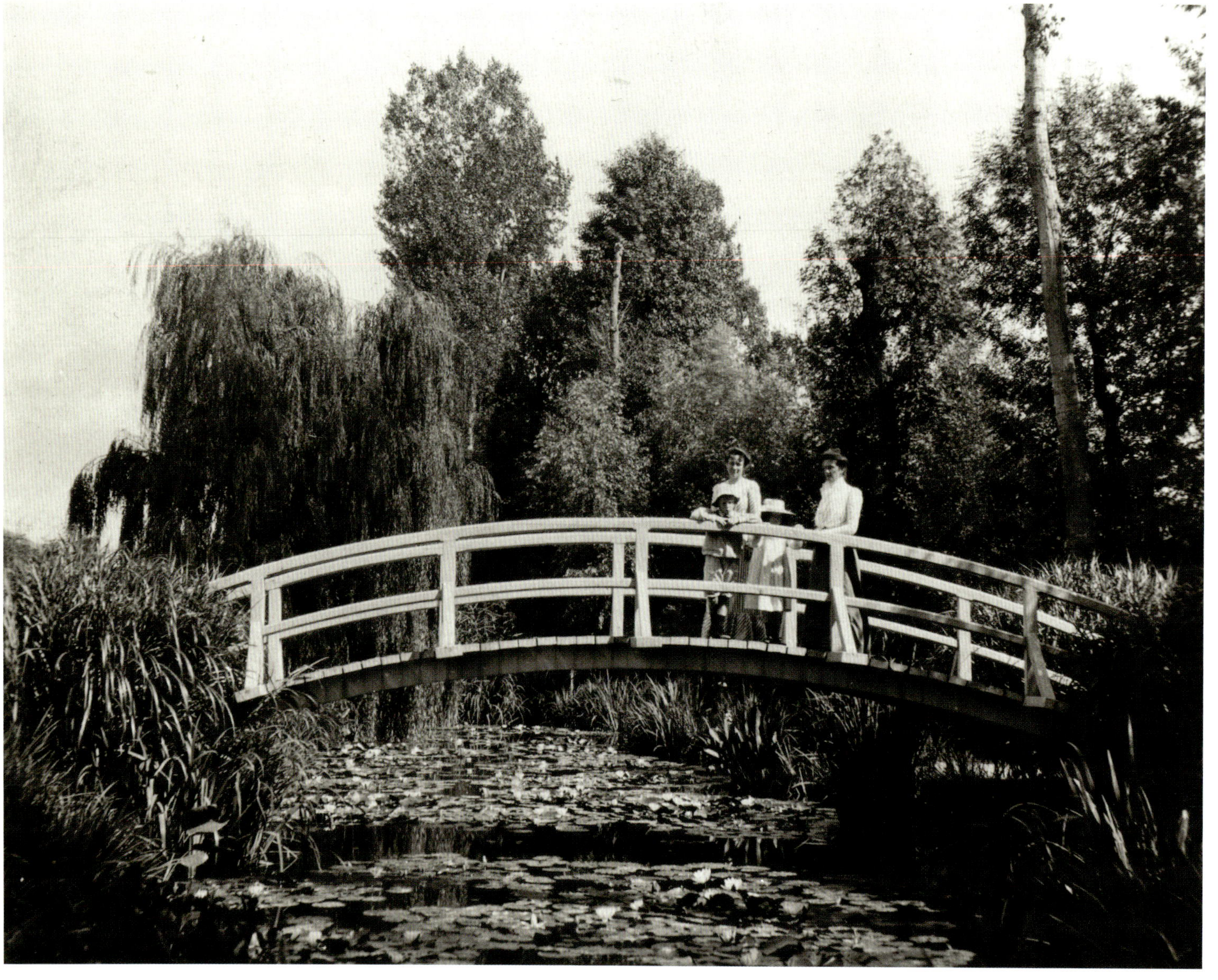

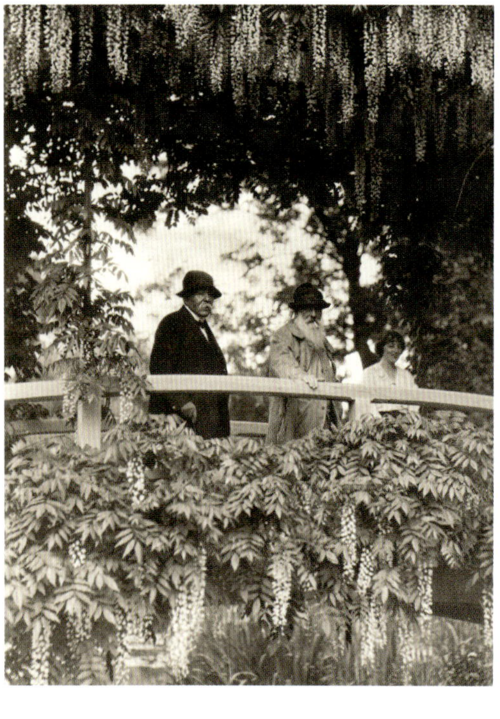

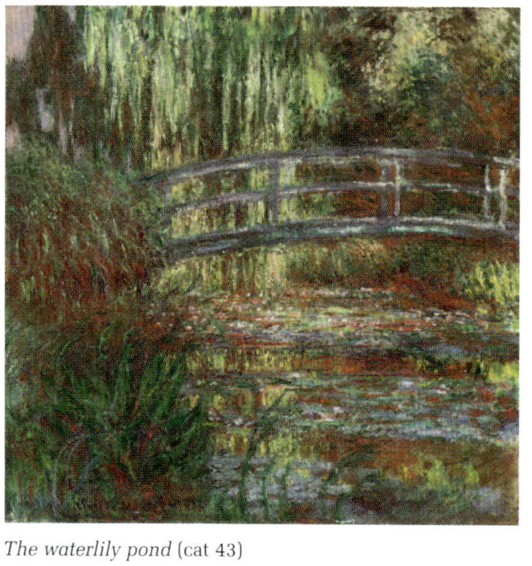

The waterlily pond (cat 43)

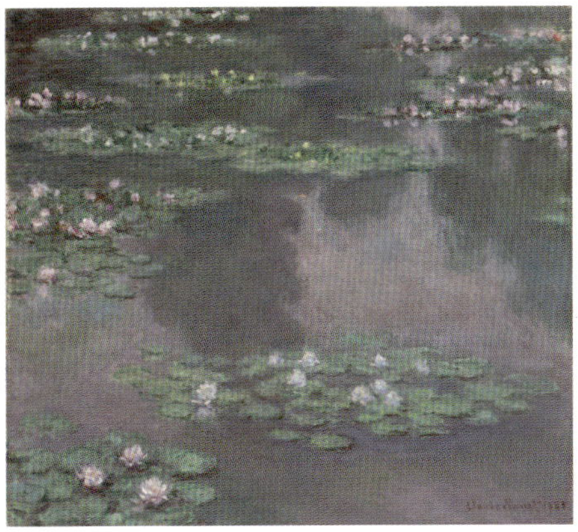

Waterlilies (cat 53)

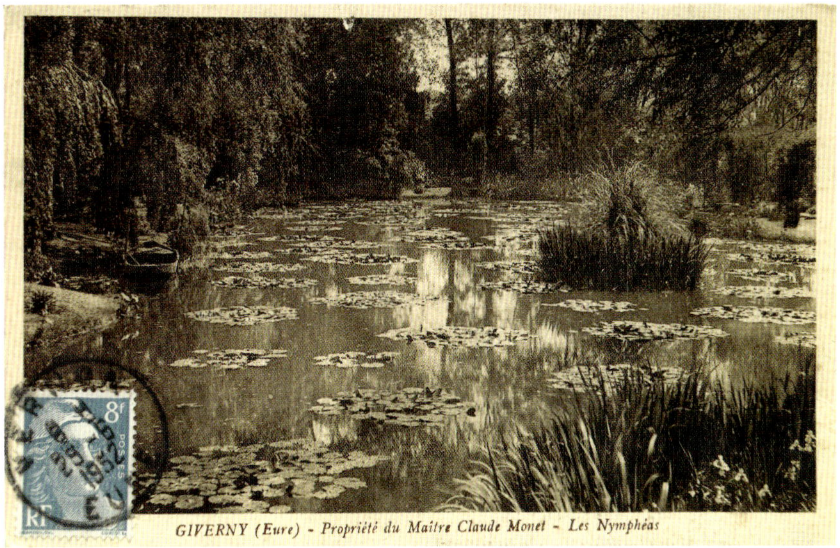

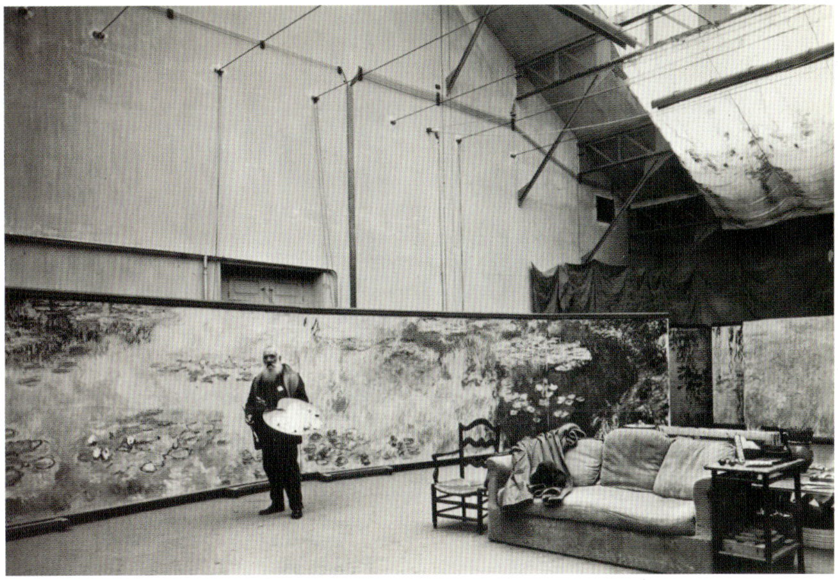

The waterlily pond (cat 43) (opposite)
Claude Monet

In 1890 Monet established a second garden (called the 'water garden') in Giverny, in which he installed a Japanese bridge. This bridge became the principal subject of a series he undertook between 1897 and 1899 (although he signed and dated the canvases in 1900). The series consists of large paintings nearly square in format. Here the bridge is suspended among the greenery with the bushes, trees and weeping willows reflected in a pond carpeted in pink, white and blue waterlilies. The zone of sky has been eliminated. Terrestrial and aquatic plants intermingle; luxuriant vegetation saturates the picture entirely. Many of Monet's visitors paused on the footbridge to be photographed mid-promenade. In the top photo, c1898, are Monet's stepdaughter Germaine Hoschedé (left) and Madame Joseph Durand-Ruel (right). Georges Clémenceau, doctor and politician, who twice served as prime minister of France (1907–10 and 1917–20), was one of Monet's closest friends towards the end of his life. They shared a passion for flowers, and Monet had no hesitation in writing to him: 'Just a word to let you know that the wisteria is about to come into bloom and will be splendid a few days from now, so your visit is obligatory' (16 May 1922). The photo below shows the Japanese bridge weighed down by wisteria. From left are Clémenceau, Monet and Lili Butler, the painter's granddaughter.

Waterlilies (cat 53)
Claude Monet

After 1904 Monet devoted his energies to a new series of *Waterlilies* which eventually numbered more than 50 works. In contrast to the preceding *Waterlily pond* series, the edges of the lake, the trees and the bridge have all disappeared: the waterlily itself has become the principal ornament, and the sheet of water acts like a mirror to the overhanging mass of foliage and the clouds. These canvases are explosions of colour, with emphatic brushwork and dense build-ups of paint. Encouraged by Clémenceau, Monet had a huge studio built (his third) in the garden at Giverny between 1914 and 1915. As shown in the photo above, daylight entered through the skylight, diffused through muslin awnings. It was here that Monet painted the cycle that crowned his *Waterlilies* series. The project commenced in 1916 and on 12 April 1922 Monet donated to the French state a set of eight panels to be installed in two oval rooms especially designed for them in the Musée de l'Orangerie (see fig 29). Recently renovated, these rooms now house Monet's paintings exactly as he intended, creating a haven of the utmost beauty.

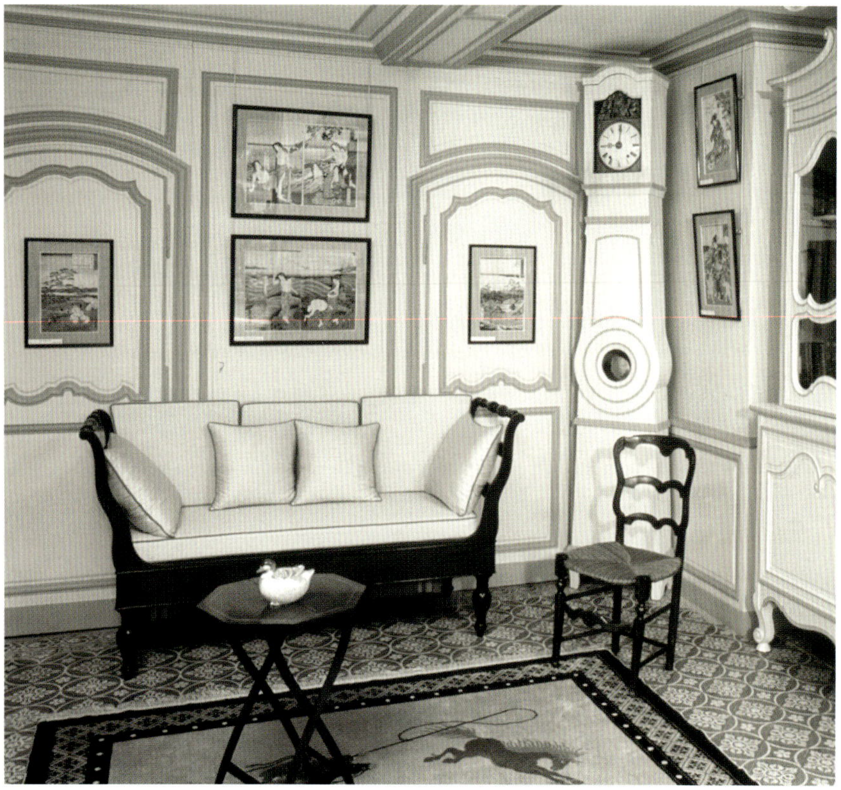

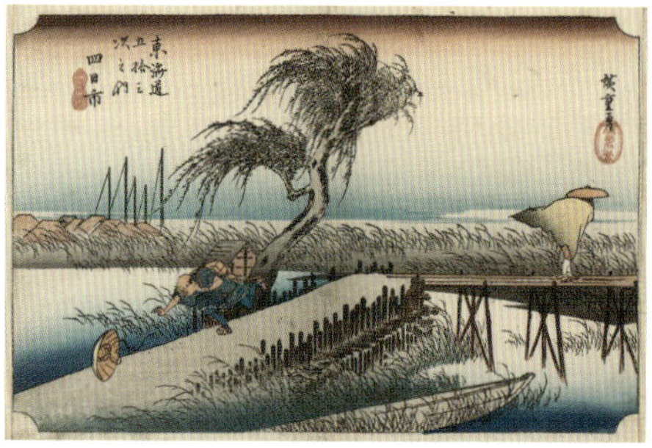

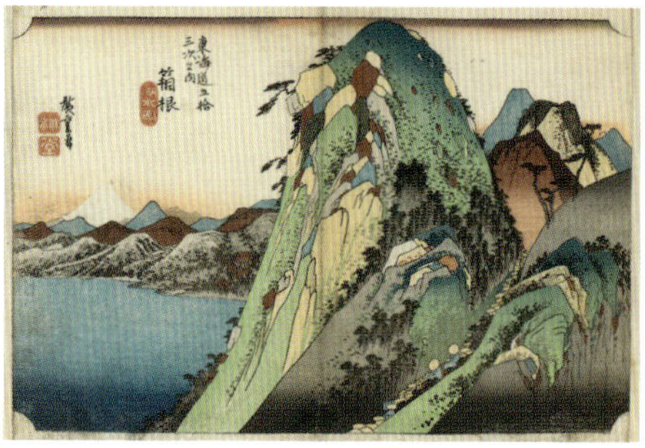

Yokkaichi: Mie River (cat 37)
Hakone: view of the lake (cat 40)
Utagawa Hiroshige I

Monet covered the walls of his house at Giverny with Japanese prints. He owned 231 of them. Among the artists who are best represented in his collection are Utamaro, specialising in the life of courtesans; Sharaku, whose work is centred on the kabuki theatre; and Hokusai and Hiroshige, both excellent landscapists. Many collectors and artists in France discovered Japanese art during the Universal Exhibition held in Paris in 1867, and subsequently there was an increasing number of Europeans and Americans who became passionately interested in it. There were shops in Paris which Monet frequented, specialising in the sale of Japanese prints. He was helped in his acquisitions by two Japanese specialists: the merchant Tadama Hayashi, living in Paris; and Kojiro Matsukata, an industrialist who was a great collector of the Impressionists. Monet's appreciation of images of this kind is easy to understand, for they illustrate the passage of time – a concept at the heart of all Monet's series – and they depict the everyday life of Japanese people. So it is no accident that Monet had a Japanese footbridge constructed in his garden, nor that he was smitten with an ambition to paint at all hours, in every kind of weather, under every condition of light. Monet's paintings became much sought after in Japan. He told the journalist Marcel Pays in 1921: 'Almost all my paintings go to America and Japan … I'm especially flattered that the Japanese understand me, since they are the masters who have felt and represented nature so profoundly' (*Excelsior*, 26 January 1921). The photographs above and opposite (top) show Monet's rooms at Giverny decorated with his elegant Japanese prints.

Photographs opposite: top © Wildenstein Institute Archives, Paris; bottom © Durand-Ruel Archives, Paris

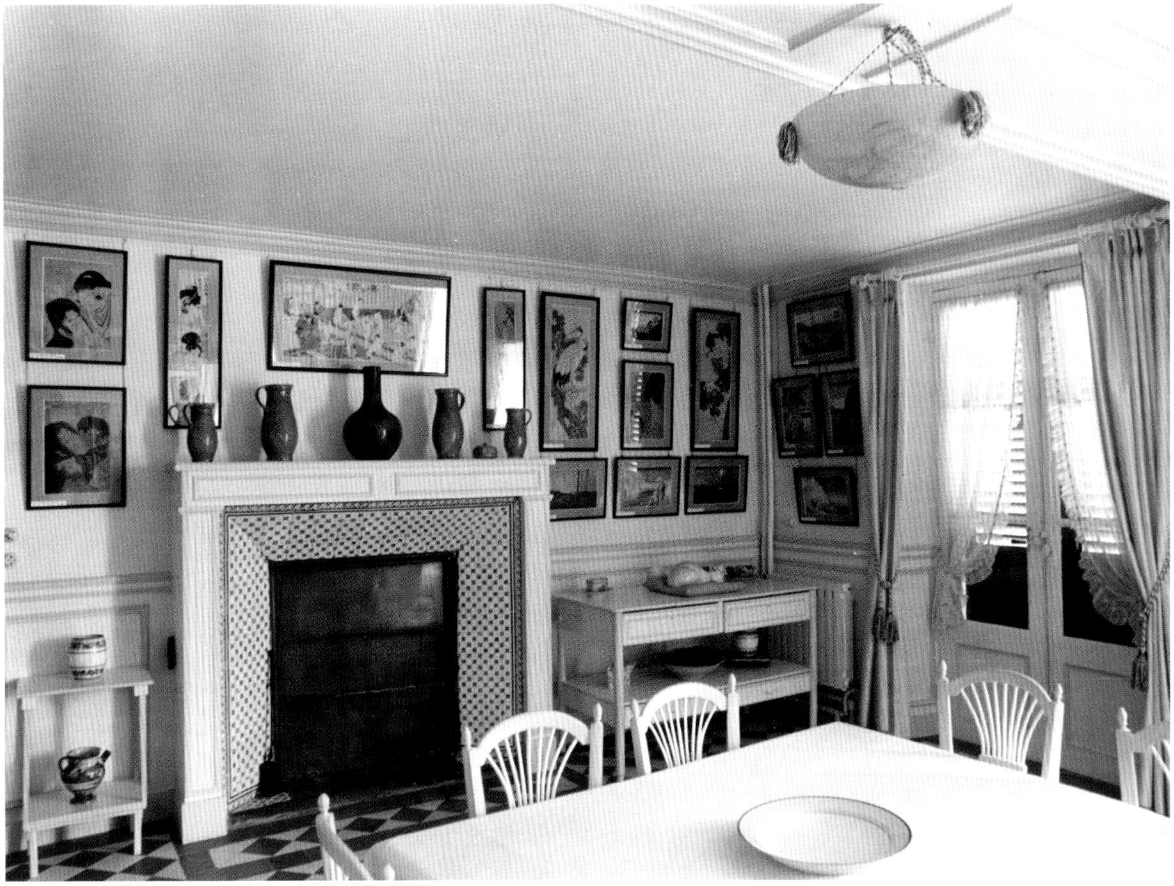

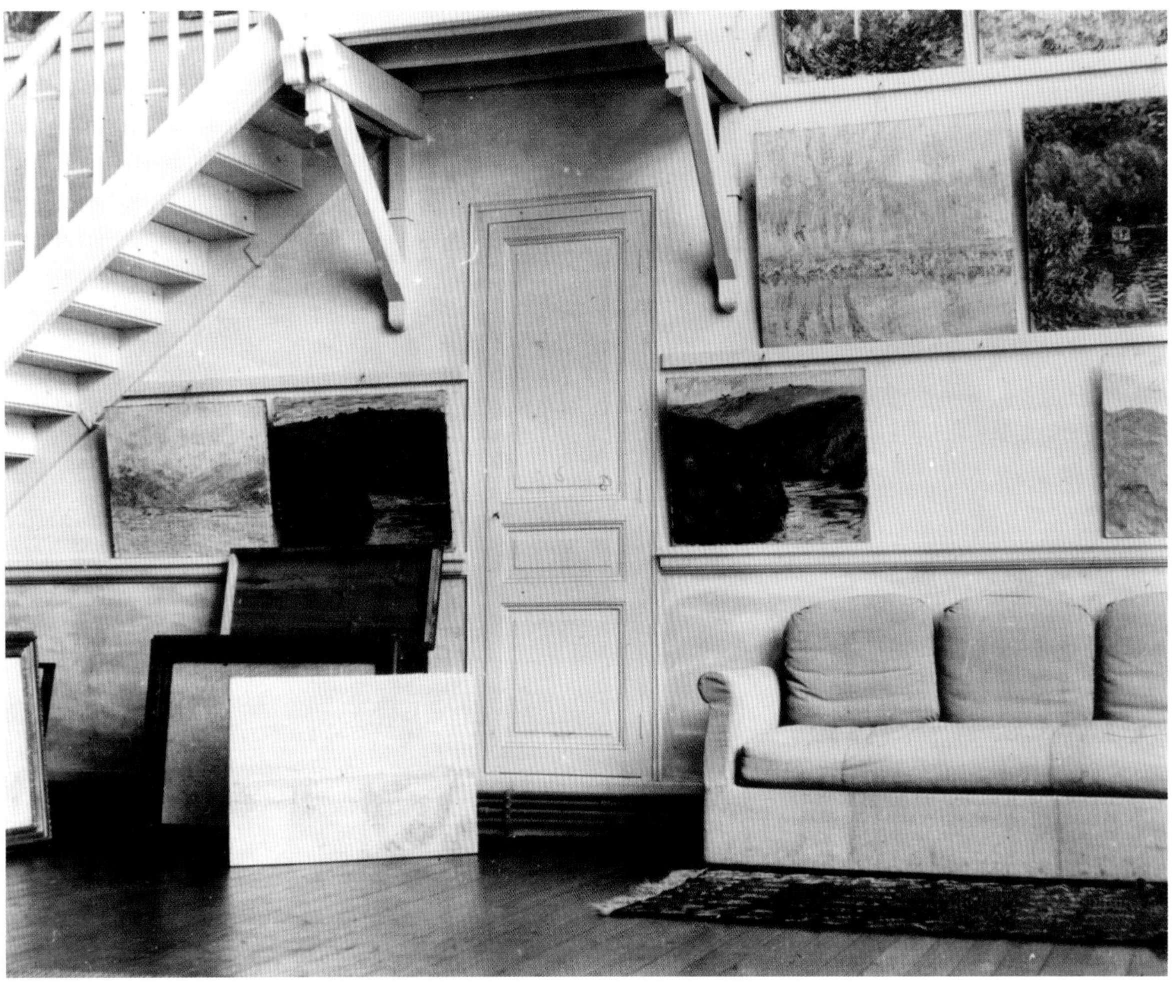

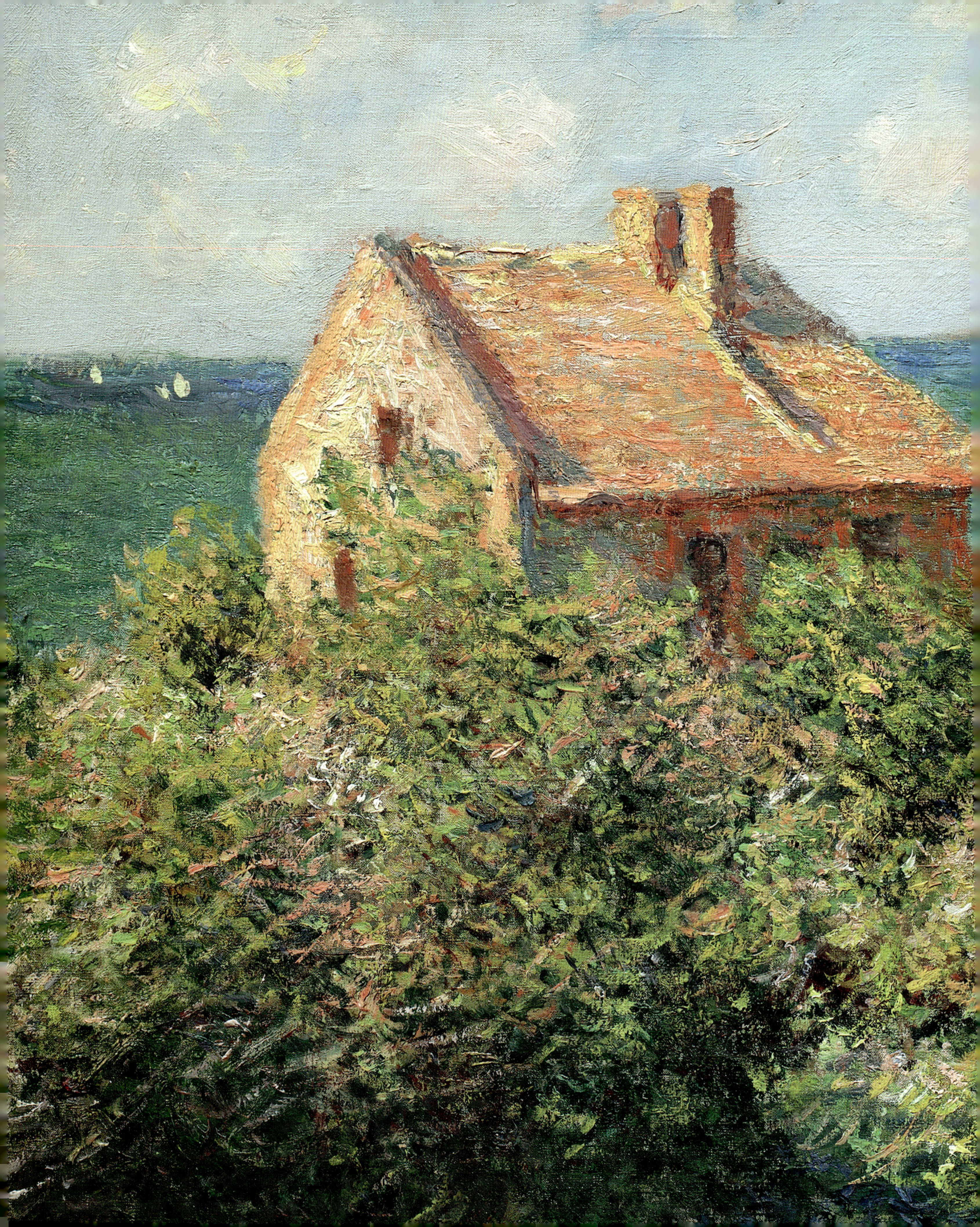

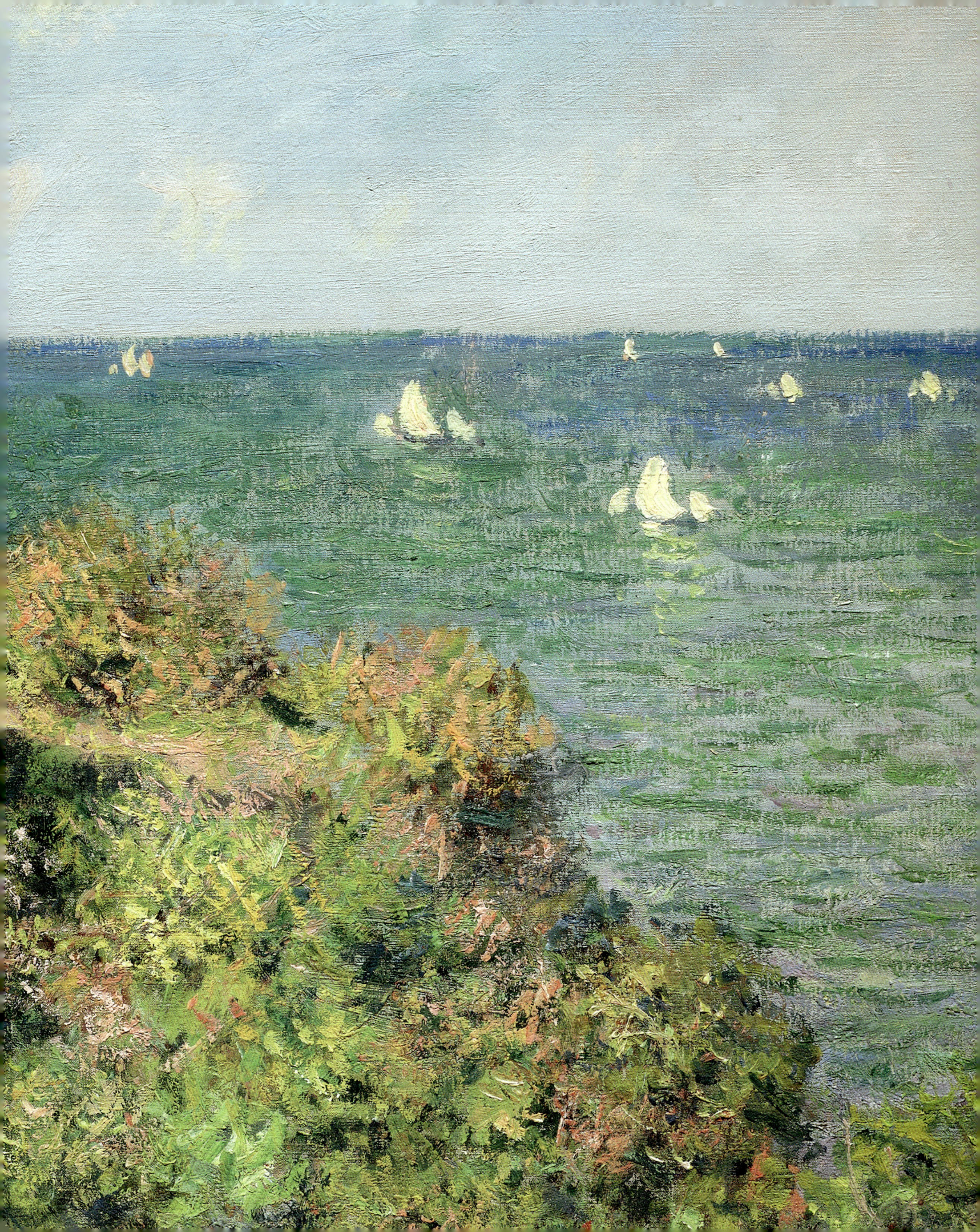

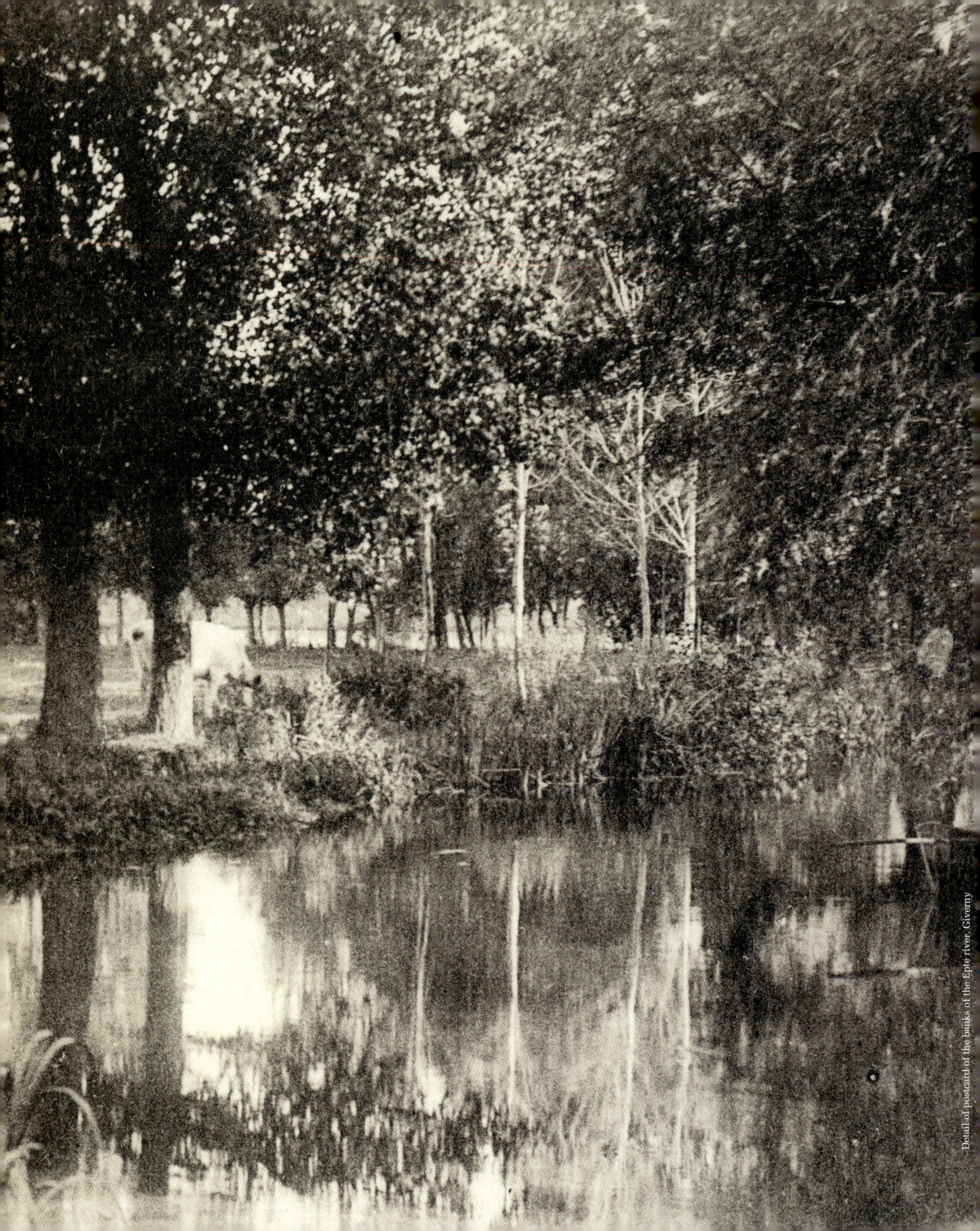

Detail of postcard of the banks of the Epte river, Giverny

IMPRESSIONIST FRANCE

Painting sites of Monet and the Impressionists

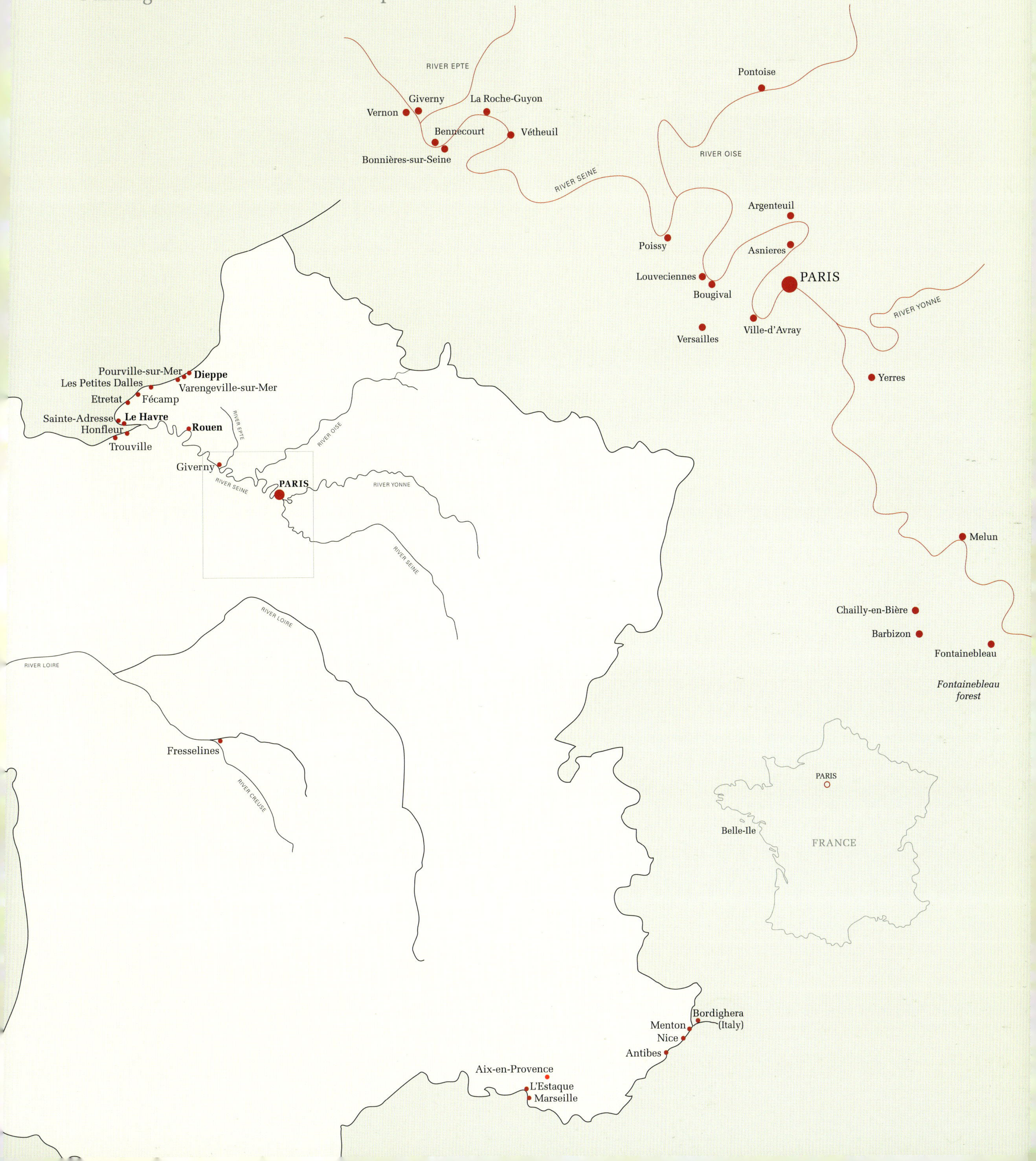

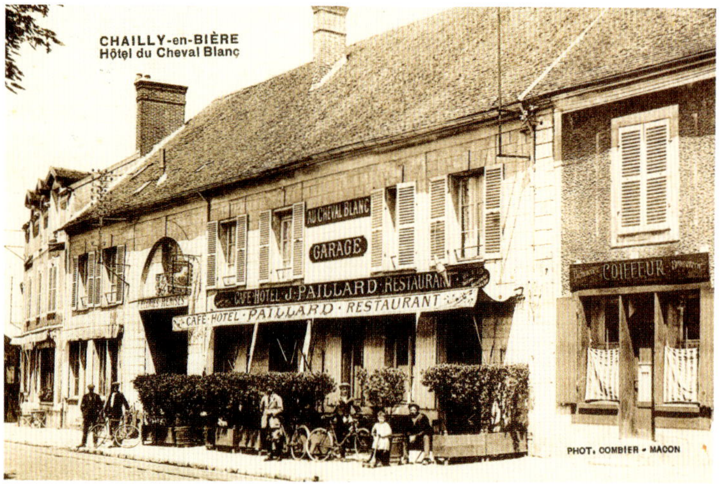

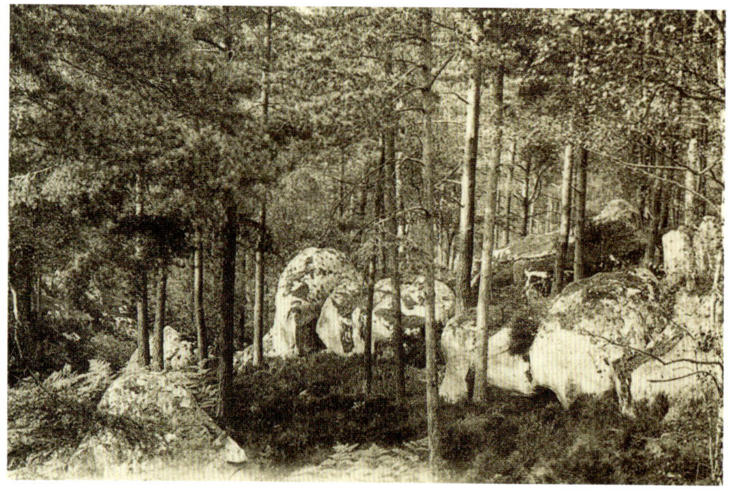

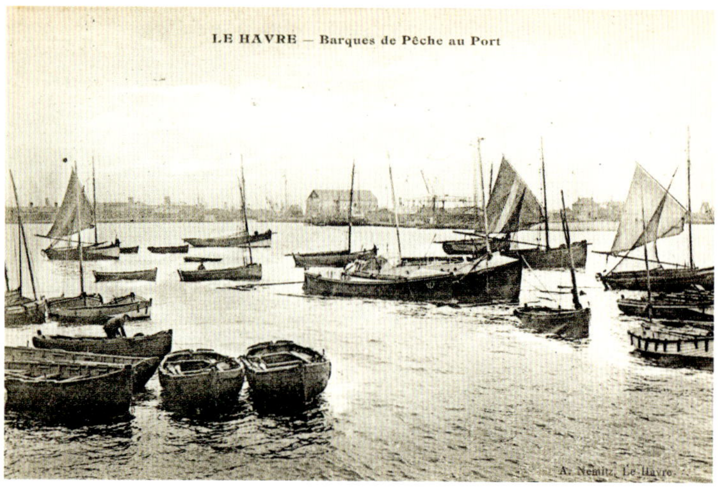

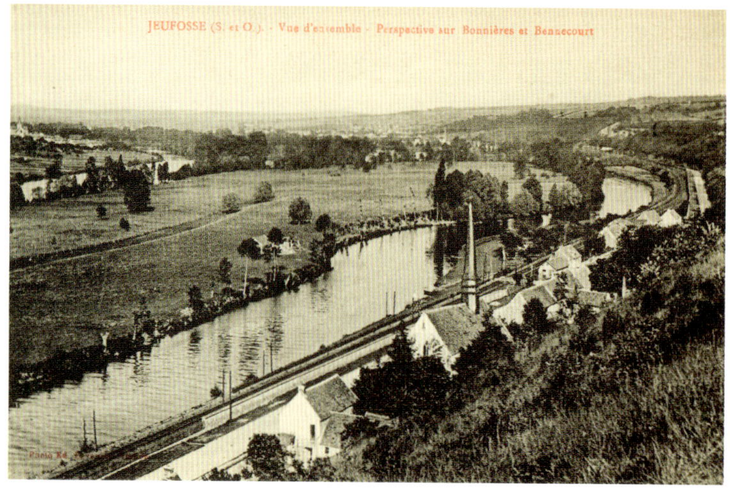

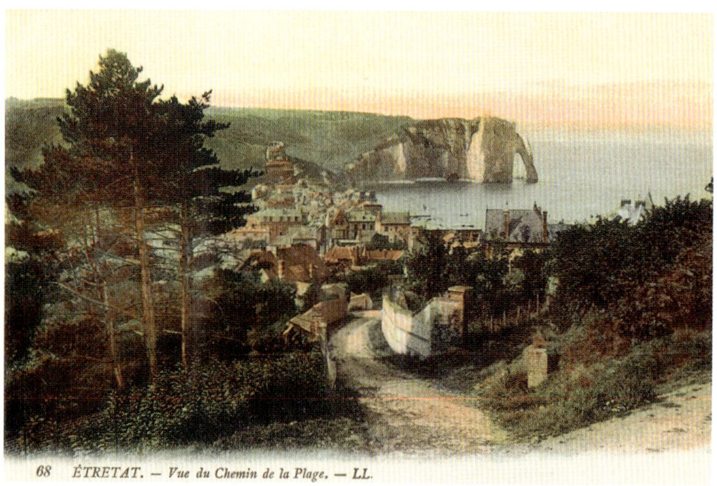

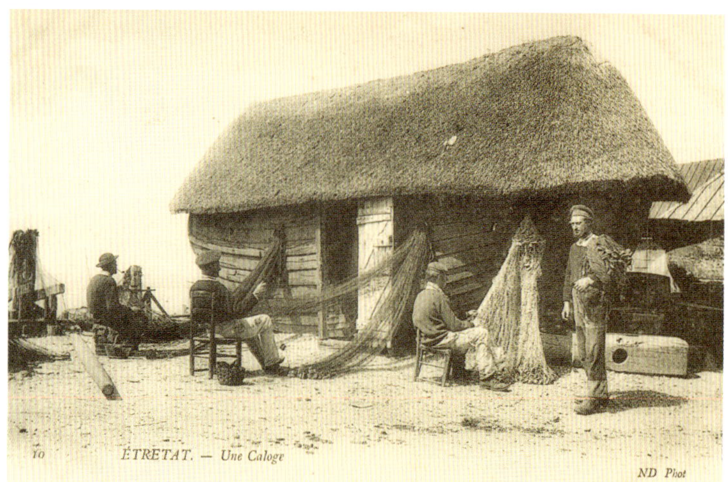

left from top:

The Hôtel du Cheval Blanc in Chailly, where Monet stayed in 1865

Fishing boats moored in the port of Le Havre

View of Etretat

right from top:

Barbizon forest

Bennecourt, where Monet painted in 1868

Fisherman's hut, Etretat

All postcards date from c1900

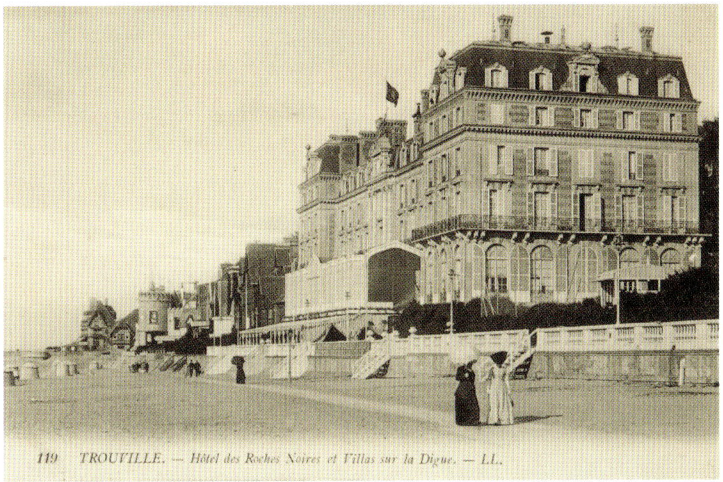

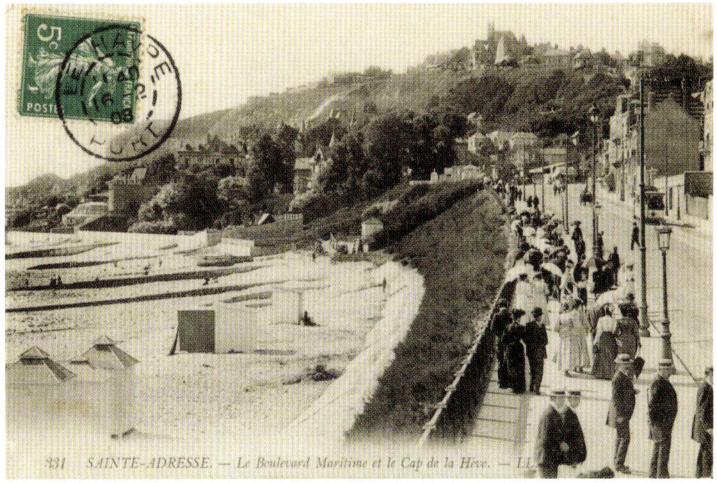

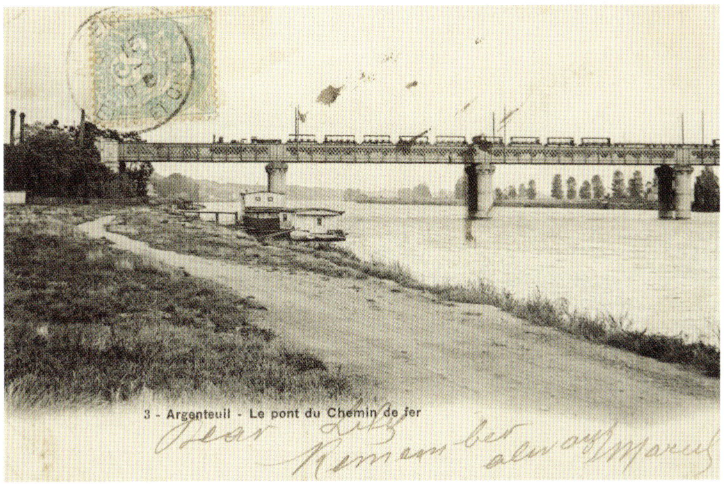

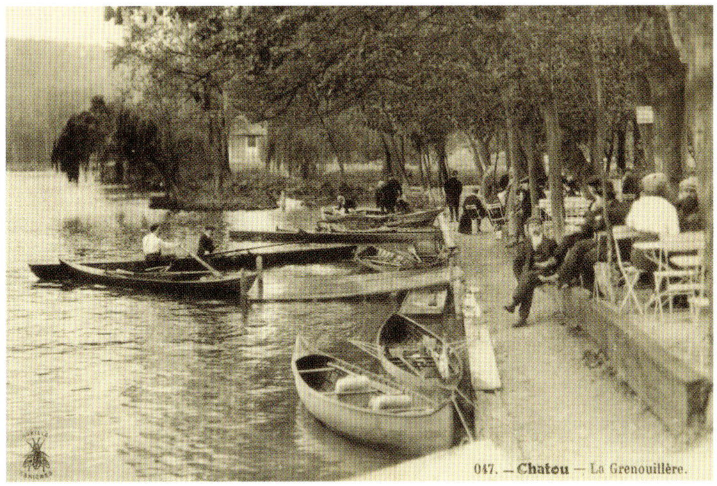

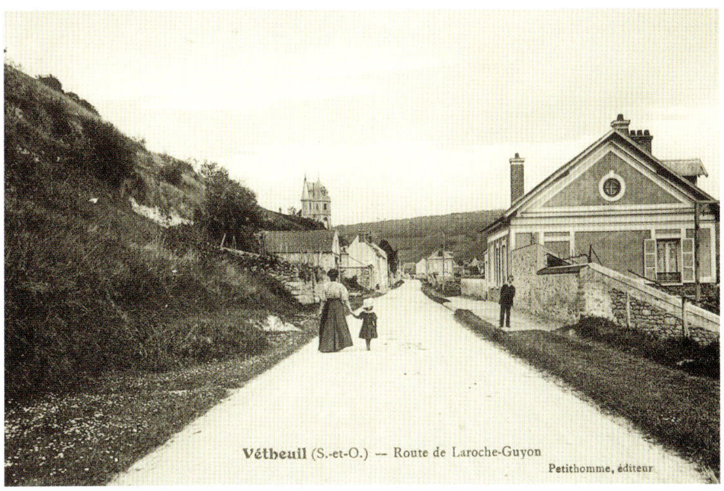

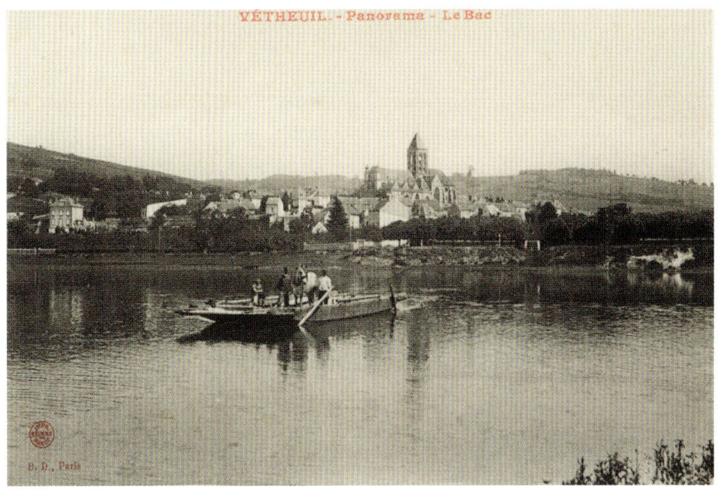

left from top:

The beachfront at Trouville

The railway bridge at Argenteuil

The road to La Roche-Guyon, Vétheuil

right from top:

The beach at Sainte-Adresse, where Monet painted in 1867

Waterside at La Grenouillère, where Monet and Renoir painted in 1869

View of Vétheuil

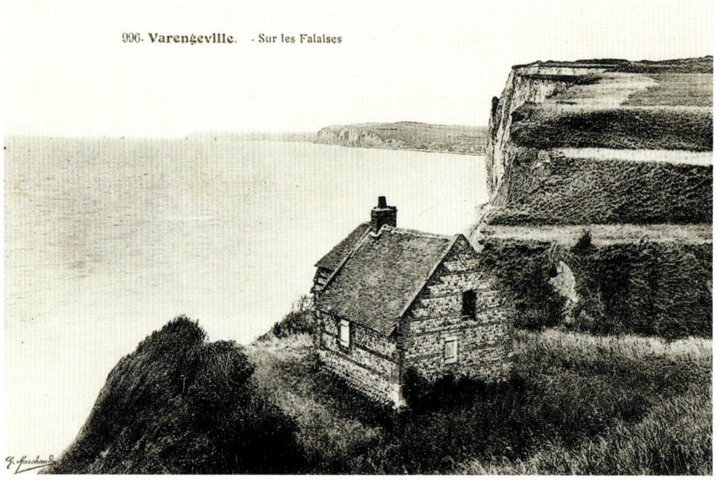

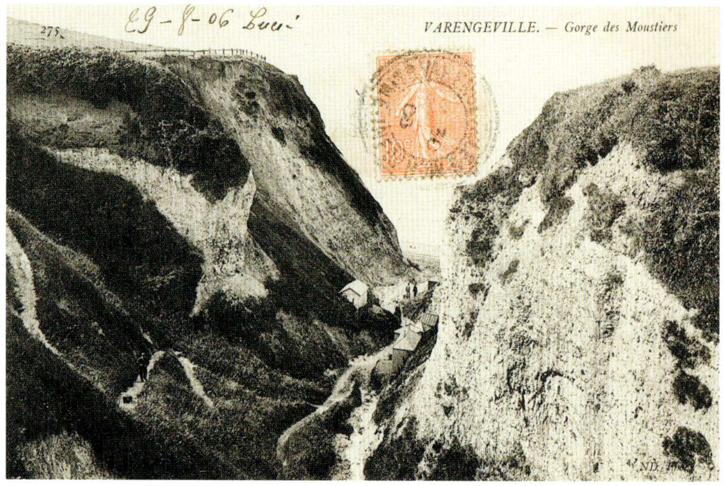

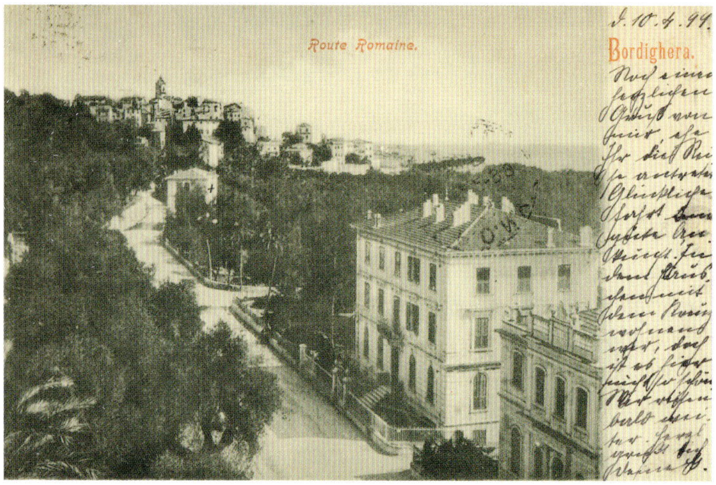

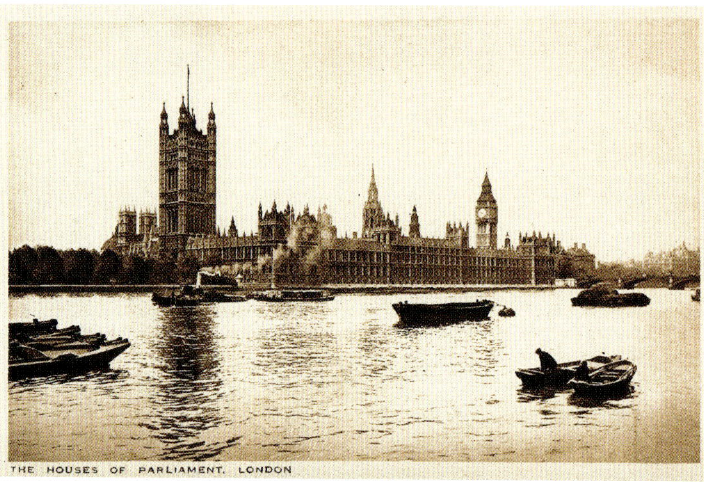

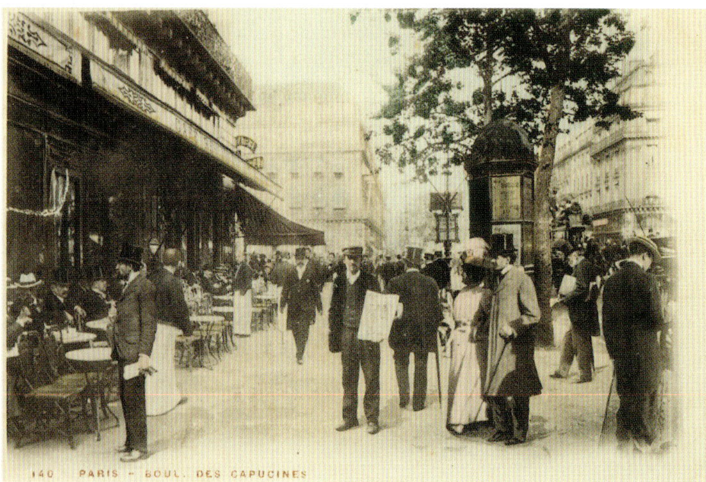

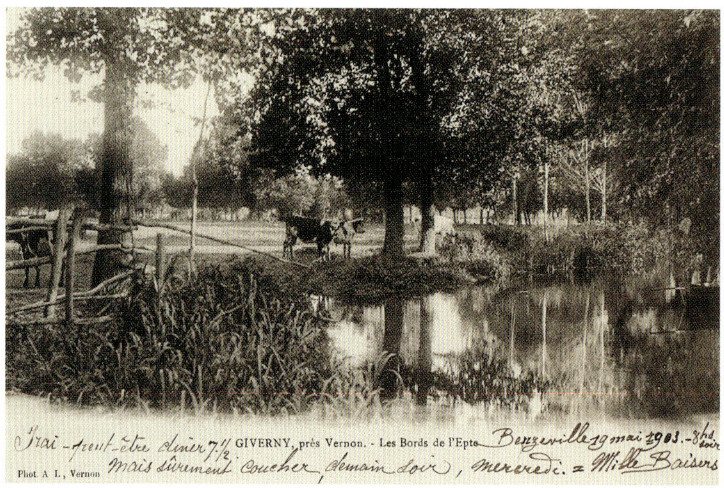

left from top:

Customs agent's cottage, Varengeville

The Roman road at Bordighera

The Boulevard des Capucines, Paris

right from top:

The Gorge des Moustiers, Varengeville

Houses of Parliament, London

A tributary of the river Epte, near Monet's house in Giverny

CHRONOLOGY

The life and work of Claude Monet

1840
Birth of Oscar-Claude Monet in Paris, 14 November.

c1845
Monet family moves to Le Havre.

c1856–58
First artistic successes selling caricatures in Le Havre. Meets the painter Eugène Boudin who becomes his mentor.

1858
Exhibits a landscape in the *Exposition municipale de la ville du Havre*.

1859–60
Visits Paris to see the Salon. Introduced to Constant Troyon and other Realist painters by the artist Amand Gautier. Frequents the Académie Suisse, where he most likely meets Camille Pissarro.

1860
Moves to Paris, living in Pigalle.

1861
Drafted for military service in Algeria.

1862
Given honourable discharge due to illness. Returns to Le Havre, where he meets Dutch painter Johan Barthold Jongkind.

1862–63
Returns to Paris and studies under Charles Gleyre, alongside Frédéric Bazille, Auguste Renoir and Alfred Sisley. Paints *Woodgatherers at the edge of the forest* (cat 2) around this time.

1864
Travels to Honfleur, site of *Rue de la Bavole, Honfleur* (cat 13) with Bazille, and later with Boudin and Jongkind.

1865
First submissions to the Salon – two seascapes – are accepted.

1866
Meets Edouard Manet. Spends time in Ville d'Avray (near Sèvres), where he works on the large-scale *Women in the garden* (Musée d'Orsay, Paris) and later in Honfleur.

1867
Returns to Paris and lives with Bazille at 20 rue Visconti. *Women in the garden* rejected by the Salon. Travels to Sainte-Adresse. His companion and future wife Camille Doncieux gives birth to their first child, Jean.

1868
One painting accepted and one rejected at the Salon. Suffering financial difficulties, he is helped by collectors in Le Havre, Monsieur and Madame Gaudibert. Awarded a silver medal at the *Exposition maritime internationale du Havre*. Lives mainly in Etretat.

1869
More submissions rejected at the Salon. Works alongside Renoir in Bougival.

1870
Marries Camille Doncieux. At the outbreak of the Franco-Prussian war they flee to England.

1871–72
Encounters Pissarro in London. Meets the art dealer Paul Durand-Ruel. Spends time in Zaandam, Holland. Eventually returns to France to settle in Argenteuil.

1872
Visits Rouen and Le Havre.

1874
First Impressionist exhibition. Exhibits his *Impression: sunrise* (fig 2), the painting that gives rise to the term 'Impressionism'. Around this time, paints *Snow at Argenteuil* (cat 15).

1875
Auction of paintings in Paris, alongside Morisot, Renoir and Sisley, obtaining very low prices. Paints *Camille Monet and a child in the artist's garden in Argenteuil* (cat 20), *Boulevard Saint-Denis, Argenteuil, in winter* (cat 36) and, around this time, *Meadow with poplars* (cat 16).

1876
Exhibits Argenteuil landscapes, amongst other works, in the second Impressionist exhibition. Paints decorations for the financier Ernest Hoschedé at Montgeron.

1877
Continues to live in Argenteuil, but works in Paris and exhibits in the third Impressionist exhibition.

1878
Moves to Paris early in the year, where second child Michel is born. Later the family move to Vétheuil, living with the Hoschedé family. Paints *Vétheuil* (cat 30).

1879
Exhibits 29 works in the fourth Impressionist exhibition. Camille Monet dies 5 September, leaving Monet living with Ernest and Alice Hoschedé and their children.

1880
Exhibits one landscape at the Salon, but refrains from participating in the fifth Impressionist group exhibition. First solo exhibition (18 works) at the offices of the magazine *La Vie Moderne*. Also submits works to the *Exposition de 1880 of the Société des amis des arts du Havre*. Visits his brother Léon in Normandy, where he paints the coastline in and around les Petites Dalles.

1881
Durand-Ruel begins to buy Monet's work regularly. Monet paints in Fécamp, Trouville (*Seacoast at Trouville*, cat 38) and Sainte-Adresse. Paints *Flower beds at Vétheuil* (cat 31). Moves with Alice Hoschedé from Vétheuil to Poissy.

1882
Lives in the hotel A la Renommée des Galettes, Pourville. Paints coastal scenes in the vicinity of Pourville and Dieppe, including *Fisherman's cottage on the cliffs at Varengeville* (cat 24). Shows 35 works in the seventh Impressionist group exhibition, organised by Durand-Ruel, including *Seacoast at Trouville* (cat 38), painted the year before. Renoir's *The Seine at Chatou* (1881, cat 28) also in this exhibition. Begins decorations for Durand-Ruel's Paris apartment.

1883
Spends time in Le Havre and Etretat, where he paints *Rough weather at Etretat* (cat 23). Solo exhibition at Durand-Ruel's gallery. Moves to Giverny, on the Seine, and begins painting the region. Travels to the Mediterranean coast with Renoir. They visit Cézanne in Aix-en-Provence.

1884
Travels to Bordighera and Menton where he paints *Cap Martin, near Menton* (cat 25), and later to Etretat.

1885
Participates in the *Exposition internationale* at the Georges Petit gallery to much acclaim. Absent from the eighth Impressionist exhibition. Paints *Meadow with haystacks near Giverny* (cat 32). In September, stays at the home of the singer Faure at Etretat with Alice Hoschedé and children. In October, the family return to Giverny, but Monet stays on in Etretat at the Hôtel Blanquet, spending time with the novelist Guy de Maupassant.

1886
Paints again at Etretat and later at Belle-Ile, off the coast of Brittany, where he paints *Port-Goulphar, Belle-Ile* (cat 41, signed 1887, presumably finished in the studio). Also paints *Meadow at Giverny* (cat 33). Meets the art critic Gustave Geffroy in Belle-Ile. Again participates in Petit's *Exposition internationale* as well as in the *Exposition des XX* in Brussels. Travels to Holland, painting landscapes with windmills and tulip fields.

1887
Participates in Petit's sixth *Exposition internationale*. Travels briefly to London at the invitation of Whistler. Paints mainly in Giverny (*Poplars at Giverny*, cat 34).

1888
Works at Antibes (*Cap d'Antibes, mistral*, cat 26, and *The fort of Antibes*, cat 27) and Juan-les-Pins, residing at the Château de la Pinède, a retreat for artists. Theo van Gogh, working for the dealers Boussod & Valadon, purchases and exhibits ten Antibes seascapes at their Paris gallery.

1889
Solo exhibition at Boussod & Valadon. Three of Monet's works included in the *Exposition centennale de l'art français*, along with Manet's *Olympia* 1863. Monet establishes a subscription to buy *Olympia* for the state. Lilla Cabot and Tom Perry visit Monet at Giverny. Paints landscapes of the Petite Creuse (cats 44, 45 and 46).

1890
Purchases house at Giverny, adding a new studio, and begins to work on the gardens. Works mainly on series of landscapes of Giverny, notably the *Haystacks* (cats 47, 48).

1891
Works on *Poplars* series in Giverny. Also paints *Grainstack/Haystack (sunset)* (cat 47). Fifteen canvases of *Haystacks* are exhibited at Durand-Ruel's gallery. Ernest Hoschedé dies in March.

1892
Spends time in Rouen, beginning a series of views of the cathedral. Marries Alice Hoschedé in July. Durand-Ruel exhibits 15 *Poplars* works.

1893
Continues working on *Rouen Cathedral* series. Attends the exhibition of Japanese prints (including those of Hiroshige) at Durand-Ruel's gallery. Acquires another piece of land at Giverny and begins work on the water garden, establishing the waterlily pond with its Japanese-style bridge.

1894
Cézanne visits Monet at Giverny. They are joined by Rodin, Geffroy and the statesman and supporter of the arts Georges Clémenceau on 28 November. Completes *Rouen Cathedral façade and Tour d'Albane (morning effect)* (cat 49).

1895
Spends time in Norway, painting the Christiania region. Exhibition at Durand-Ruel includes 20 of the *Rouen Cathedral* series.

1896–97
Works at Pourville and Varengeville on the Normandy coast. Also begins series of morning views of the Seine, such as *Morning on the Seine, near Giverny* (cat 50).

1898
Georges Petit exhibits Monet's recent work, including the *Mornings on the Seine* series.

1899
Travels to London, painting views of the Thames. Possibly begins *Charing Cross Bridge (overcast day)* (cat 52) and *Waterloo Bridge* (cat 51) at this time.

1900
Travels again to London, staying at the Savoy. In Giverny, paints *The waterlily pond* (cat 43). Durand-Ruel exhibits recent works, including a dozen *Waterlilies*.

1901
Durand-Ruel presents a similar exhibition of *Waterlilies* in New York. Monet again spends time painting in London. Enlarges waterlily pond at Giverny.

1902
Bernheim-Jeune gallery shows recent works by Pissarro and Monet, including six views of Vétheuil.

1903
Begins painting another series of *Waterlilies*.

1904
Durand-Ruel exhibits 37 of Monet's views of the Thames. Monet travels to Spain to see works by Velázquez.

1905
Visited by Louis Vauxcelles at Giverny. Paints *Waterlilies* (cat 53).

1908
Travels with Alice to Venice, painting scenes of the Grand Canal.

1909
Exhibition of 48 waterlily paintings at Durand-Ruel.

1910
Waterlily pond further enlarged.

1911
Alice Monet dies 19 May.

1912
Twenty-nine views of Venice exhibited at Bernheim-Jeune. Monet is diagnosed with cataracts.

1914
Begins building a new studio, completed in 1916, in which he will work on the monumental *Waterlilies* cycle (Musée de l'Orangerie, Paris). Eldest son Jean dies.

1918
Announces intention to donate *Waterlilies* cycle to the State.

1922
The Orangerie in the Jardin des Tuileries announced as intended site for *Waterlilies* cycle.

1923
Undergoes three operations to his right eye. Continues to re-work *Waterlilies* despite limited sight and ailing health.

1924
Durand-Ruel exhibits *Waterlilies* in New York.

1926
In June, Edouard Vuillard and Ker-Xavier Roussel visit Monet at Giverny. On 5 December, Monet dies at Giverny, aged 86.

1927
Waterlilies cycle installed in the Orangerie, to Monet's specifications.

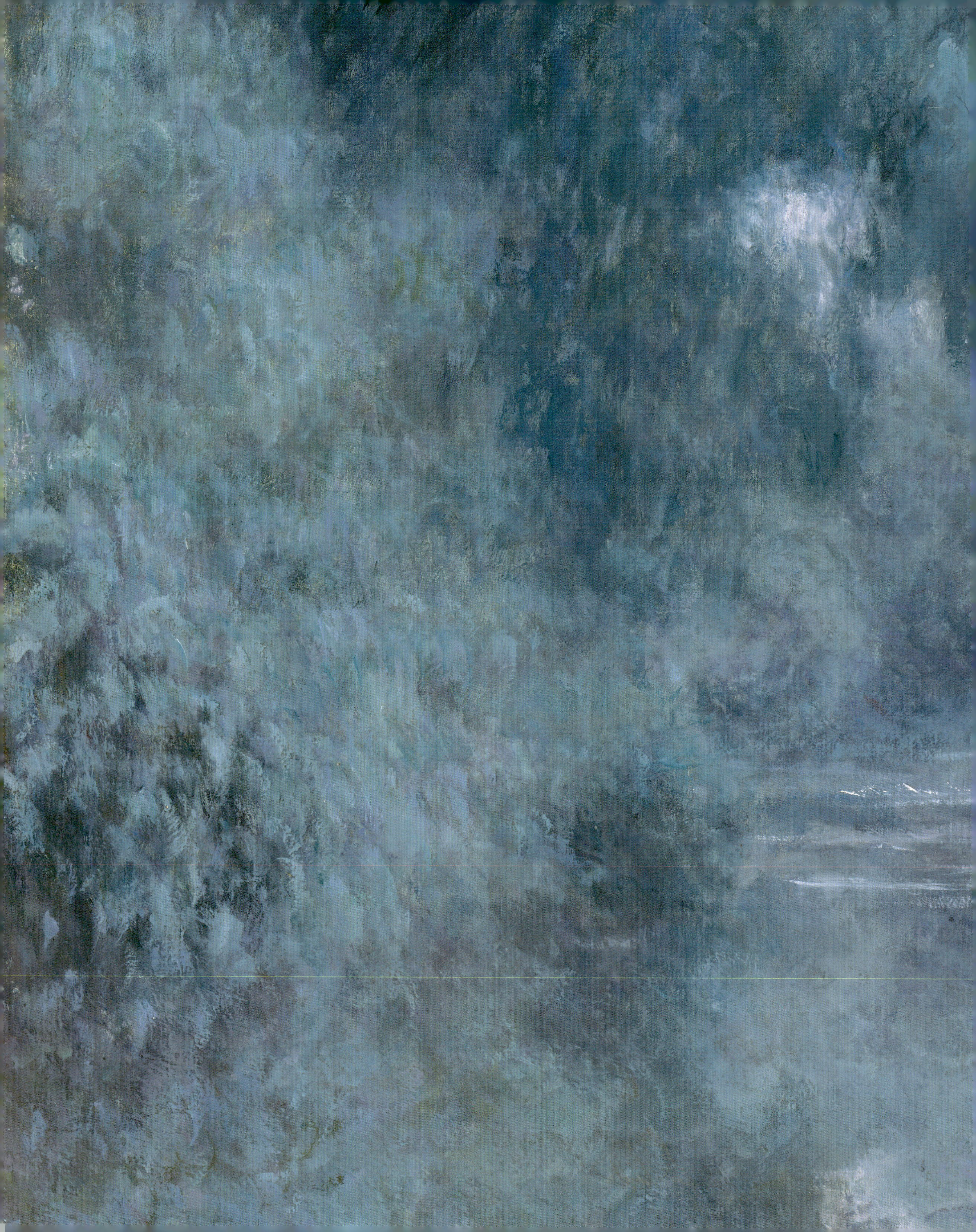

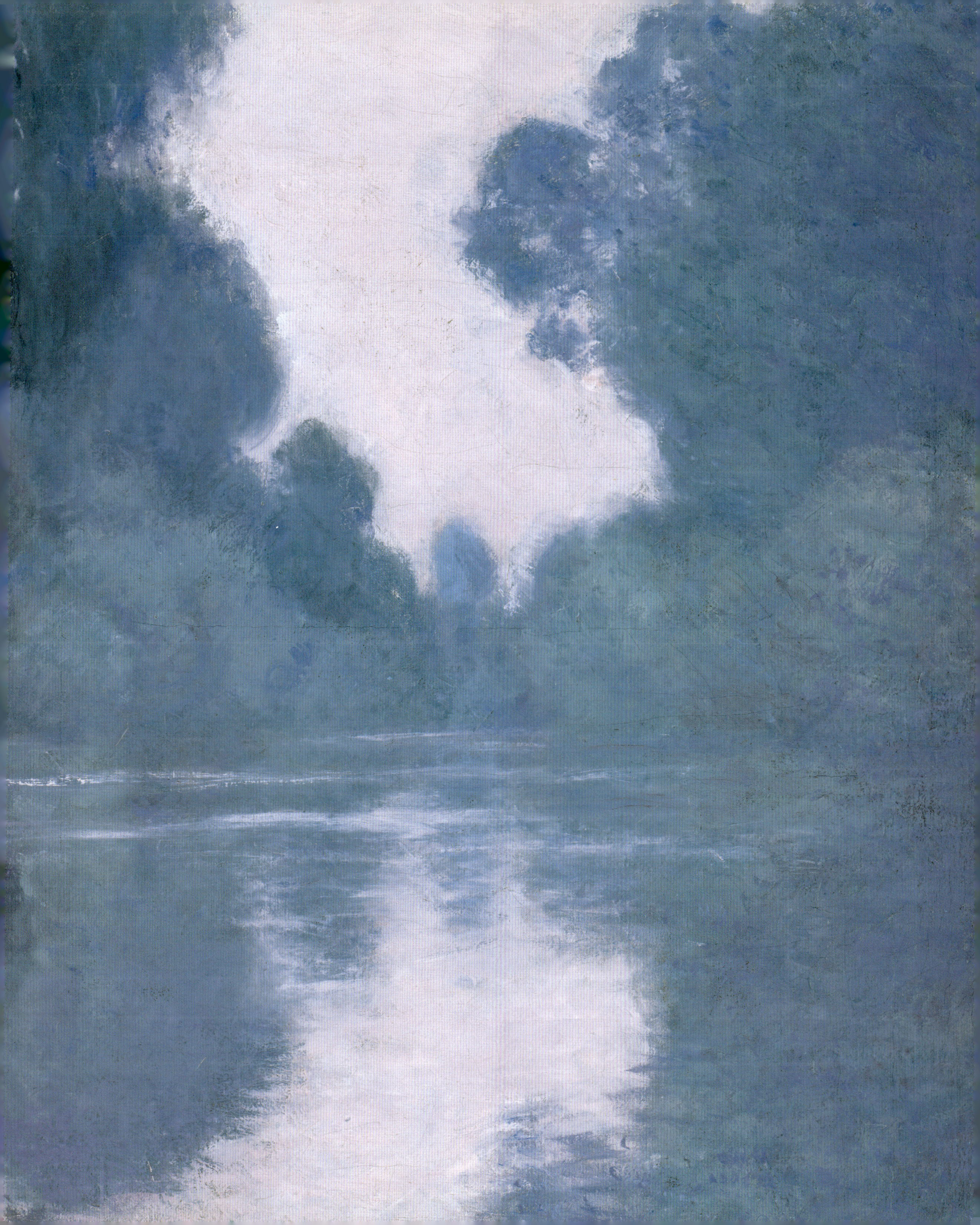

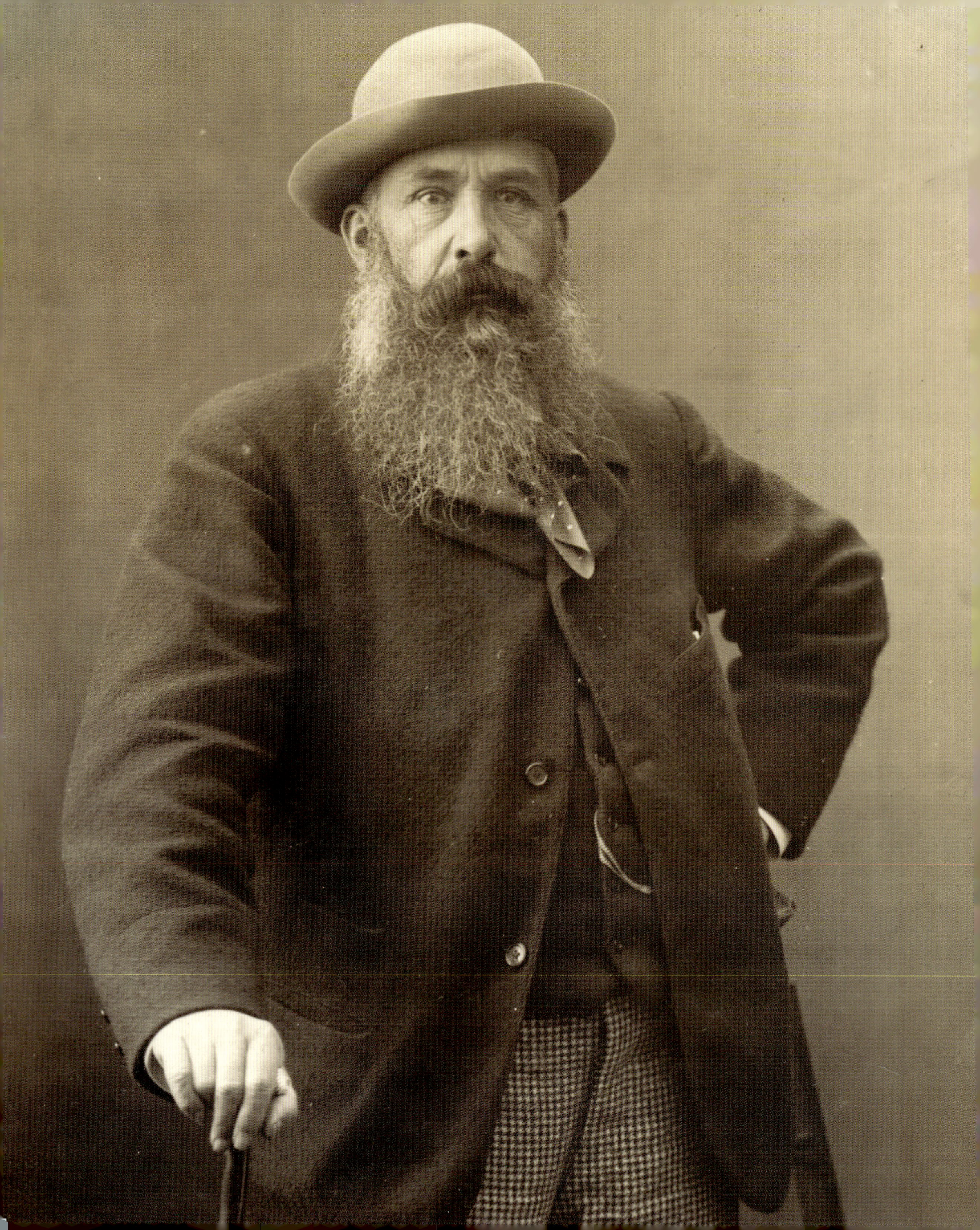

MONET'S POSTERITY

Terence Maloon

'It is the effect of sincerity to make works appear to be a protestation, when all the artist is thinking about is rendering his impression.'

Edouard Manet[1]

'If the only form of tradition, of handing down, consisted in following the ways of the immediate generation before us in a blind or timid adherence to its successes, "tradition" should be positively discouraged.'

T S Eliot[2]

Claude Monet was at the pinnacle of his success in 1909, when a visitor to his exhibition was overheard to exclaim that, compared to the magnificence of this exhibition, 'Salon paintings – all Salon paintings – are daubs, just daubs'.[3] Monet's moment in the sun had been a long time coming. Thirty-five years earlier he was a pariah in the Paris art world. Salon paintings then enjoyed all the privileges of official patronage, a near-monopoly of the art market, and immense popularity. It was in adverse comparison to *Salon paintings* that paintings by Monet and the Impressionists were once condemned as 'daubs, just daubs'. In the interim, however, a revolution in aesthetic judgement had occurred.

From the very beginning, Academic painters and Impressionists recognised their incompatibility: their works fought each other as soon as they were juxtaposed on a wall or put into the same room. On the level of appearance, this disagreement was technical and aesthetic – glaringly so. At a deeper level, there were important ethical and philosophical differences and, implicitly, political differences as well.

Academicians responded to the challenge of the Impressionists' paintings by excluding them from the Salon, or by including them with obvious bad grace, relegating them to the worst, most obscure positions in the hanging. That was the reason why Monet and a group of like-minded colleagues decided to show their work independently in 1874, bypassing the official exhibitions entirely. The art critic Philippe Burty, writing for an English magazine, explained why they had taken this decision:

> They feel that their style of painting, whether by simplicity of design, or by simplicity of tone, or by simplicity of composition, looks like a challenge or a caricature when placed side by side with works conceived under the pre-occupation of mannered design, artificial tones, or subjects intended to provoke laughter or emotion by the most vulgar artifices [...] They depend upon elements of interest strictly aesthetic, and not social or human – lightness of colouring, boldness of masses, blunt naturalness of impression.[4]

As is evident from the first section of this catalogue (pp 35–53), the Impressionists inherited many of their preoccupations from artists of a previous generation – from the landscapists of the 'School of 1830', the Barbizon painters, Corot, Boudin, Jongkind, Courbet and so on. Consider the remarks that Eugène Boudin jotted down in his sketchbooks between about 1854 and 1859, which seem to prophesy the Impressionists' achievements a decade or so later:

> Sometimes, during my melancholy walks, I gaze on this light that inundates the earth, that quivers on the water, that plays on clothing, and I grow faint to realise how much genius is needed to master so many difficulties, how limited is the power of man's mind to put all these things together in his brain. Then I feel that poetry is there [...] Sometimes I catch a glimpse of what must be expressed.
>
> Twenty times I have begun again in order to approach the delicacy, the charm of the light that plays everywhere. How fresh it is! It is soft, faded, rose-tinted. The objects are drowned. There are nothing but tones everywhere. The sea was superb; the sky

Claude Monet 1897, photo Paul Nadar © Durand Ruel Archives, Paris was soft, velvety. It then changed to yellow; it became warm; then the setting sun gave beautiful violet nuances to everything; the earth, the breakwaters also took on this hue.

Nature is so beautiful, so splendid; it is always in this that my secret torment lies when misery releases its grip a bit. It is a great blessing for us to see, to admire unceasingly, all these splendours of sky and earth, if it were only to admire them; but do not continually mix it with the torment of reproducing them [...][5]

It was Boudin who initiated the young Monet into plein-air painting and brought Monet to his life-changing realisation: 'Boudin was truly my first initiator, and at that moment my way opened and my fate was sealed; I would be a painter come what may.'[6] In fact, when we read Boudin's notes, we get the uncomfortable feeling that they may be more pertinent to Monet than to Boudin himself. Why so? Is it because Monet surpasses the achievement and outshines the talent of his precursor so completely and utterly?

Although the Impressionists and their precursors were 'painters of light', the disparity between their works is startling. One reason is that the Impressionists brought a 'new type of immediacy' to painting, Adrian Stokes noted in a landmark essay, yet he wondered how to explain this inter-generational quantum leap. As he put it: *why did the Impressionists produce such great paintings?*

Why could Monet record at Belle-Ile-en-Mer a flowing colour of the waves that colonies of painters, dedicated to this subject through several generations at seaside places, have been unable subsequently even on one occasion to approach?[7]

Why indeed. Whether they set out to do so deliberately or not, the Impressionists made the works of their precursors look polite and timid or turgid and dull – merely worthy and conventional. No wonder that so many of Monet's contemporaries refused to have their paintings hung anywhere near his.[8] Making one's peers look old-fashioned, uninteresting and obsolete is an acknowledged strategy of the avant-garde. Subsequent European avant-gardes all patterned themselves on the Impressionists, and on the Impressionists' negation of then-reigning artistic conventions. 'Destruction in art and re-creation must always proceed simultaneously', commented Adrian Stokes.

Four years before the death of Monet, T S Eliot wrote an essay about literary tradition in which he argued that a work of art not only influences works that lie ahead of it, but acts retroactively and seems to change the art that preceded it:

What happens when a new work of art is created is something that happens simultaneously to all the works of art which preceded it. The existing monuments form an ideal order among themselves, which is modified by the introduction of the new (the really new) work of art among them.[9]

Isn't this a perfect description of the way Monet's art affected his predecessors, and isn't this just the way that the avant-garde successors of the Impressionists put forward their claims in turn, finding ways of putting the Impressionists in the shade?

Monet and Fauvism

In 1905 the magazine *Mercure de France* conducted a poll of artists in Paris, asking them whether they thought contemporary art was in the doldrums. Nothing really new and challenging seemed to have happened in almost a decade: 'We are in the last days of *something*. Are we on the verge of *something*?' the art critic Charles Morice wondered in his preface.[10] Although the ascendancy of Impressionism was a fait accompli and its influence was widespread, its legacy had come to seem dubious – even though Monet, Renoir and Degas were still alive and Monet still had another 20 years of painting ahead of him. One of the questions the *Mercure* asked the artists was: 'Is Impressionism finished? Can it be renewed?'[11] Out of the 55 artists who replied, 15 were unequivocal: they thought Impressionism was dead. Nineteen responded affirmatively: Impressionism was a vital force that could be renewed and extended. Another six considered Impressionism's prospects favourably but made qualifications. Fifteen artists abstained from answering the question.

The artists who participated in the poll included Academicians; several former colleagues of Gauguin who were associated with the Pont-Aven school; and a group of ex-students of Gustave Moreau, some of whom would become involved in the first avant-garde manifestation of the 20th century: Fauvism. In the Salon d'Automne which opened in Paris a few months later, in September 1905, Fauvism (which did not yet have a name) was launched. The artists who were most closely identified with it (Matisse, Derain, Vlaminck, Camoin, Marquet, Van Dongen, Braque, Friesz, Dufy) all had important connections to Impressionism and to Monet in particular.

Henri Matisse's association with the Impressionists was the most complex of all. He had been taught the Impressionist technique by Monet's friend and acolyte John Peter Russell in Belle-Ile over the course of two visits there in 1896 and 1897. Around 1898 Matisse had met Camille Pissarro and subsequently sought his advice on several occasions. Between 1900 and 1903 Pissarro rented an apartment in the Place Dauphine on the Ile de la Cité, very close to where Matisse and other Fauves (Friesz, Marquet, Camoin) lived – they must have frequently passed each other in the street. Around 1903, Matisse was taken up by the Neo-Impressionist Paul Signac, who acted as his mentor. Much later, in 1917, Matisse and Albert Marquet went to Giverny to pay their respects to Monet, and in 1918 Matisse went to Cagnes to pay his respects to Renoir, both visits being apparently conceived as a symbolic gesture of apology or a declaration of truce, given the inter-generational warfare that the Fauves had waged against their elders.[12]

Georges Braque was born in Monet's former home town of Argenteuil and grew up in another town immortalised by Monet, Le Havre. The legend of the young Braque observing Monet at work at Le Havre is discounted these days, yet it was probably instigated by Braque himself – how he imagined himself entering the history of art.[13] Another Fauve painter, Maurice Vlaminck, declared: 'I owe the first great enthusiasms and the first revolutionary certitudes of my 20s to Monet.'[14] Vlaminck's best friend André Derain would have concurred. 'As for Claude Monet, I adore him in spite of everything, even because of his errors which are a lesson to me', wrote Derain in a letter to Vlaminck. 'In short, isn't he right to render the natural impression (which is only an impression and doesn't endure) by means of his fugitive, fleeting colour, thereby reinforcing the character of his painting?'[15]

The most telling sign of the Fauves' powerful affiliation to Impressionism was that they haunted the painting sites made famous by Monet, Pissarro and Renoir – Chatou and its vicinity, Le Havre, Honfleur, Varengeville, L'Estaque, the environs of the Pont-Neuf in Paris and the Thames embankment in London. Several Fauves made a point of preserving the characteristic palette of the Impressionists, restricted to the colours of the prism, dispensing with black, ochres and earth colours. They made an even more radical feature of the Impressionists' fragmentary brushstroke and the Impressionists' way of 'revealing the paint' and asserting the primacy of colour. Fauve painting, like Impressionist painting, didn't illustrate effects of light, but seemed to generate a light of its own. Key words in the Impressionists' theoretical vocabulary – 'instantaneity', 'sensation', 'rapports', etc – remained pertinent to Fauvism. The question of when a painting is complete (the question of aesthetic sufficiency), which was raised first by the Impressionists, was further pondered by the Fauve painters. However, any direct comparison between the two could prove devastating, because the Fauves had blasted away the tremulous iridescence, the dreamy atmospheres, the tender harmonies, the connotation of bourgeois interiors and luxurious living, the ubiquitous mauves and pinks, the alibi of 'naturalism'...

Monet and Cubism

In 1911, the poet and art critic Guillaume Apollinaire wrote a book review that quoted two of Eugène Delacroix's famous phrases: 'The enemy of all painting is grey!' and 'Banish all earth colours'.[16] These were phrases that had inspired and served to explain and defend the experiments of the Impressionists and Neo-Impressionists, yet they no longer held such authority in recent years, Apollinaire noted: 'The new painters paint in difficult grey tones and look for elegance in earth colours'. In other words, some of the younger artists who particularly interested him at the time had defected from the colouristic tradition of the 19th century and, in no uncertain terms, had marked their distance from Claude Monet. With his extraordinary perceptiveness of emerging talent and his joyous avant-gardism, Apollinaire became the spokesman and publicist for the rising generation, foremost among whom were Pablo Picasso and two ex-Fauves: Georges Braque and André Derain.

Apollinaire wrote the catalogue preface to Georges Braque's first exhibition held at Kahnweiler's gallery in 1908, which was the first public showing of Cubism. Since this was the first text ever published about Cubist painting, Apollinaire's preface is an archetype of how the vilification of Impressionism went hand in hand with the promotion of Cubism:

> Ignorance and frenzy, these are the characteristics of Impressionism. In saying ignorance I mean an absolute lack of culture in most cases [...] There is now a place for a nobler art – more measured, more orderly, more cultivated. The future will tell what role in this was played by magnificent examples such as Cézanne's, the solitary, unremitting labour of Picasso, the unexpected encounter of Matisse and Derain, preceded by that of Derain and Vlaminck.[17]

Apollinaire headlined his review of the Salon des Indépendants in 1910: 'The rout of Impressionism – young artists return to composition'.[18] Most of his articles and reviews appeared in newspapers, magazines and catalogues printed in very small editions, yet they circulated throughout Europe and fell into the hands of the people who mattered.

In spite of the rumblings of dissension and disparaging invective coming from the avant-garde, favourable and intelligent commentary on Monet's ongoing production continued to appear in the mainstream press, as did interviews with him and photo-spreads about his garden. The sale of his work also went from strength to strength. Generally the mainstream critics were mature, competent professionals who could write well and at length, who could describe convincingly what they were looking at and make reasoned judgments, but Apollinaire's art criticism was not like that at all. His articles tended to be extremely brief and written in a kind of semaphore. Most were little more than amalgams of publicity, gossip, unsubstantiated opinion and intellectual snobbery, yet as a talent scout and weathervane of artistic trends in the Paris of his time, he had no equal.

It soon became a convention for both avant-garde critics and reactionary fogeys to compare Monet unfavourably to his erstwhile Impressionist colleagues Cézanne and Renoir. Maurice Denis's famous article on Cézanne, published in 1907, provided an influential model of this strategy: 'First of all, we define Cézanne in reaction against modern painting, in reaction against Impressionism', Denis wrote in the preamble.[19] Another convention shared by avant-gardists and reactionaries alike was the strategy of holding up Monet's early paintings for praise in order to damn his recent ones – as Emile Bernard had done in his 'Refutation of Impressionism' published in the *Mercure de France* in 1911.[20]

Maurice Denis's 1907 essay on Cézanne was translated into English by Roger Fry for *The Burlington Magazine* in 1910. It served to endorse the concept of 'Post-Impressionism' that Fry was formulating for the two epoch-making exhibitions he organised at the Grafton Galleries in London in 1910 and 1912. In the catalogue introduction to the first Post-Impressionist exhibition, Fry attacked 'the receptive, passive attitude towards the appearances of things' which hindered the Impressionists from rendering the 'real significance' of things:

> Impressionism encouraged an artist to paint a tree as it appeared to him at the moment under particular circumstances. It insisted so much upon the importance of his rendering this exact impression that his work often completely failed to express a tree at all; as transferred to canvas it was just so much shimmer and colour. The 'treeness' of the tree was not rendered at all; all the emotion and association such as trees may be made to convey in poetry were omitted.[21]

He accused the Impressionists (from whom the mature Cézanne and the late Renoir were exempted) of forcing their contemporaries 'to accept pictures which lacked design and formal coordination to a degree which had never before been permitted. They, or rather some of them, reduced the artistic vision to a continuous patchwork or a mosaic of coloured patches without architectural framework or structural coherence'.[22] His definition of Post-Impressionism purported to be a critique and corrective of these abuses. According to Fry, Cézanne, Gauguin and Van Gogh were the originators of Post-Impressionism, with Matisse, Picasso and others pursuing the direction their elders had established. Their common goal was 'the re-establishment of purely aesthetic criteria in place of the criterion of conformity to appearance – the rediscovery of the principles of structural design and harmony'.[23]

In contrast to the moderation and lucidity of Roger Fry's writing, André Salmon was surely the most viciously contentious art critic of the time. 'We have killed the old criticism', he announced in the preface to a volume of his collected essays and reviews.[24] Salmon was a colourful bohemian, an acclaimed poet and loyal (one could say fanatical) partisan of Cubism, yet his writings on art and artists are terrible – like a one-dimensional, thuggish version of Apollinaire. Accordingly, Salmon's vilification of Impressionism knew no bounds: he recalled that, not so long ago, contemporary art was in mortal danger, threatened with 'dissolving into amorphousness'. Of course, it was 'Impressionism which confronted us with these perils'.[25] In contrast to the royal road of Cubism, the dangerous byways of contemporary art consisted of the continuance of Impressionism. Naming the principal villains, it was Bonnard and Vuillard who 'opened the abyss into which Matisse just missed jettisoning all of painting'.[26] Yet salvation was at hand: 'The Cubists saw the Post-Impressionists pushing painting into amorphousness, where art was only sustained by arbitrary and equivocal games of colour abandoned by all form', and they came up with a remedy which saved contemporary art from this atrocious fate.[27]

Where was Monet in all this? What did he think of the intrigue and agitation against him? Apparently he was quite oblivious and immune to it. He had faced a carping, hostile press throughout his professional life. Since the early 1900s he had more or less lost touch with contemporary art in Paris and become indifferent to its polemics: 'We spoke of modern painting, of which he was ignorant', René Gimpel noted in his diary in 1926. 'Of that which he was able to see, [Monet] said: "I don't understand it, but I don't say it's bad, because I remember those who didn't understand my works who used to say: it's bad."'[28]

However, there remained a solid showing of admiration for Monet from the ranks of the abstract painters, who began to emerge in increasing number from 1911 onwards. Evidently Monet was one of František Kupka's favourite artists;[29] Fernand Léger and Robert Delaunay both acknowledged that Impressionism had inspired their respective 'dialectics of liberation': 'Impressionism is the birth of Light in painting', wrote Delaunay,[30] who paid homage to 'the liberation of pictorial means through universal Impressionism'.[31] Another pioneer of abstraction, Wassily Kandinsky described the revelatory impact of one of Monet's *Haystack* paintings which he had seen in an exhibition in Moscow in 1896–97:[32]

> Suddenly, for the first time, I saw a picture. That it was a haystack, the catalogue informed me. I didn't recognise it. I found this non-recognition painful, and thought that the painter had no right to paint so indistinctly. I had a dull feeling that the object was lacking in this picture. And I noticed with surprise and confusion that the picture not only gripped me, but impressed itself ineradicably upon my memory, always hovering quite unexpectedly before my eyes, down to the last detail. It was all unclear to me, and I was not able to draw the simple conclusion from this experience. What was, however, quite clear to me was the unsuspected power of the palette, previously concealed from me, which exceeded all my dreams. Painting took on a fairy-tale power and splendour. And, albeit unconsciously, objects were discredited as an essential element within the picture.[33]

In hindsight it is easy to see that the refutation of Impressionism by the Cubists and their partisans was exaggerated for self-serving reasons. Picasso's and Braque's masterpieces of 1910–11 featured exquisite drifts of modulated brushstrokes and delectably congested surfaces which held the illusion of a concretised inner glow. These characteristics could not only be attributed to Cézanne's influence on Cubism, but also to Monet's and Pissarro's. Likewise, the façade-like compositions that became such a defining feature in Picasso's and Braque's classic Cubist paintings (and, a little later, the basis of Mondrian's proto-abstractions) obviously had antecedence in Monet's *Rouen Cathedral* series.

The Russian abstractionist Kasimir Malevich was less inclined than many of his contemporaries to deny and mystify his historical affiliations and sources. He repeatedly drew attention to Monet's significance for the artists of his generation: 'A work like *Rouen Cathedral* has a capital importance in the history of art. By dint of its action it obliges entire generations to change their attitude to pictorial works', he wrote.[34]

When the dust of their inter-generational battle had settled, even the Cubist hardliners came round to admitting their debt to Impressionism. Braque recognised that the breakdown of hierarchical distinctions in painting between figures and objects and the spaces around and between them was due to Impressionism's legacy to modern art:

> What is between the apple and the plate is also painted. And indeed, I think it is as difficult to paint the in-between as the thing. This in-between space seems to me to be just as important as that which they call the object. It is precisely the interrelations between the objects and between the object and the in-between that constitute the subject.[35]

And with the benefit of hindsight André Lhote, too, was able to perceive a unity in modern art that was not so evident to him before: 'In Impressionism, Cézannism or in Cubism between 1910 and 1914, it is not a matter of seeing the details of an ensemble *successively*, but of seizing them in a *simultaneous* way.'[36]

The death of Monet

Claude Monet died at the age of 86 on 5 December 1926. His obituaries noted the presence of eminent Parisians in his funeral cortege, including several artists: Pierre Bonnard and Edouard Vuillard were the best known, and Théodore Roussel, Alfred Veillé and Camille Pissarro's youngest son Paul-Emile among the lesser-known. Monet's obituaries show that the denigration of Impressionism had become general by this time:

> I know that during these last several years people are very much inclined to speak badly of Impressionism.[37]
>
> *Le Gaulois*, 8 Dec 1926

> [Impressionism is] a doctrine against which a generation reacts with good reason, a generation smitten with construction and volumes, which has no desire to revise the work of its elders.[38]
>
> *La Volonté*, 6 Dec 1926

> Impressionism perpetrated some fatal excesses. During a time when one only hears talk of architecture, discipline and construction, and when some regard giving pleasure as reprehensible, it is scarcely possible to do Monet justice. That his painting, based in sensual delectation as it is, suffers as a result is obvious. Although Monet, Pissarro, Sisley and Renoir exerted a strong influence and in some ways renewed our traditional vision, it is also true that their work led them away from composition and style.[39]
>
> *Le Figaro*, 6 Dec 1926

There was a commemorative issue of the magazine *L'Art Vivant* which came out a month later, in January 1927, with six articles devoted to Monet. One of them was a furious blast written by the socialite portrait painter, Jacques-Emile Blanche. Monet's paintings, Blanche claimed, were only collected by nouveaux riches; Monet 'invented mauve and many other outdated fashions'; the environs of Giverny translate into 'postcard niceties of a certain American taste'; Impressionism is constrained by its 'small vision'; Renoir and Cézanne 'were not Impressionists in this sense'. Blanche informed the readers of *L'Art Vivant* that he was preparing a longer text on the subject of Claude Monet, which duly came out the following month in the *Revue de Paris* – basically it was more of the same, but even more scathing.

One of the reasons for Blanche's detestation of Monet comes into focus when he refers to Monet's 'burial with no church bells, prayers or incense, a lugubrious end for the solitary unbeliever' – '*lugubre fin du solitaire incroyant*'.[40] Monet was an atheist. His 'civil' burial had been noted in several newspapers, [41] with the fullest report appearing in *Le Figaro*:

> No priest, not even a mortuary cloth and almost no flowers for the painter of flowers! On the bier someone had thrown an old cretonne cloth the colour of periwinkles, myosotis and hydrangeas.[42]

Such an unorthodox, unchristian burial would have appalled Jacques-Emile Blanche and other Catholic nationalists (with the painters Emile Bernard and Maurice Denis the most vocal among them) – united as they were in their anti-Impressionist mind-set, and tending to be especially harsh towards the 'unbeliever' Monet. Another thing that would surely have rankled them was that Monet had been a prominent Dreyfusard. He was among the first to rally to Emile Zola's support when, in a sensational newspaper article headlined '*J'accuse*' ('I accuse'), Zola challenged the trumped-up charges of treason laid against a French-Jewish military officer, Colonel Alfred Dreyfus.[43]

The ensuing scandal raged for nearly a decade and produced deep divisions in French society, even causing a government to fall. Two of the closest friends of Monet's old age, Georges Clémenceau and Octave Mirbeau, had been leading Dreyfusard activists[44] – whereas the Catholic nationalists, to a man, were fanatically anti-Dreyfusard and remained so even after Dreyfus's innocence was officially admitted in 1906. In fact, Maurice Denis glibly – shockingly – equated the supposed laxism and 'anti-classicism' of Impressionism with Dreyfusism (and with neurasthenia!) in an article about Cézanne published a year after Dreyfus' exoneration:

> Let us try to escape from prejudices engendered by Dreyfusism and neurasthenia: let us not succumb to the spirit of paradox, disorder and subtlety. The fact is that a work executed patiently is judged with contempt and people admire nothing better than sketches whose summary invention and rapid handling imply a sort of nihilism of art. It is a misplaced faith in the unfinished.[45]

Five months after Monet's death, the unveiling of his *Waterlilies* cycle, installed in two specially designed oval rooms in the Orangerie in the Tuileries gardens in Paris, was a much-anticipated event. The critical reception of these '*grandes décorations*' has been analysed in detail by Steven Z Levine and ably summarised by Sylvie Patin.[46] As both demonstrate, opinion was bitterly divided. Several critics hailed the Orangerie cycle as the summation of Monet's œuvre and

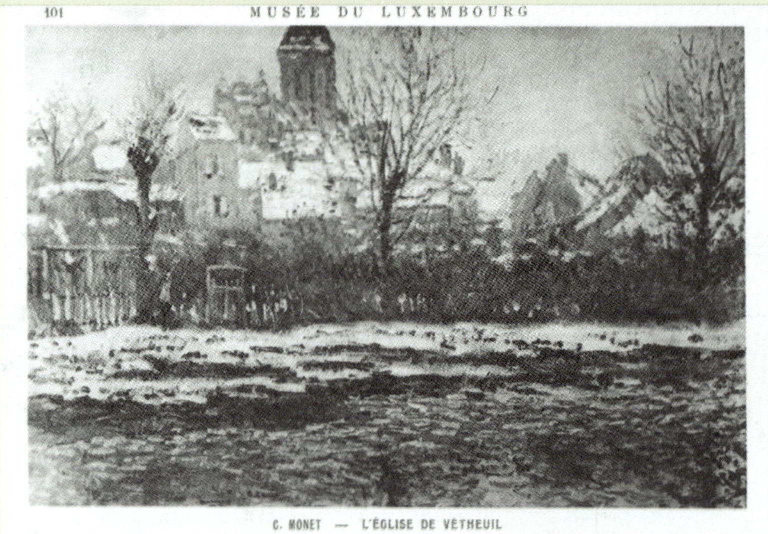

Early postcard of Monet's *Church at Vetheuil* 1879 from the Musée du Luxembourg (now Musée d'Orsay).
Private collection

This painting was one of the first by Monet to appear in a public collection. It was purchased directly from Monet in 1879 by the painter Gustave Caillebotte, who bequeathed it to the state in 1894. It formed part of a substantial intake of Impressionist paintings into the Musée du Luxembourg in 1896, which was in stark contrast to the exisiting collection of academically-oriented art (shown right) and gave rise to political and artistic controversy.

went into ecstasies about it – foremost among them, Louis Gillet:

> Astonishing painting without drawing and without edges, a canticle without words ... where art, unsupported by shapes, without vignette, without anecdote, without fable, without allegories, without a body or a face, is, solely by virtue of tones, simply an effusion, simply lyricism, where the heart tells, confides, sings its emotions.[47]

Intriguingly, Gillet's description presages similar accounts of the emotional chords struck by radically 'non-objective' paintings by Mark Rothko and Jackson Pollock several decades later. Yet not everybody was so susceptible to being moved, nor so ready to recognise the *Waterlilies* as a masterpiece, nor to acknowledge the uniqueness and originality of Monet's conception – for example, the Cubist painter André Lhote:

> For a painter, there is no light except that given by colour. That is all there is to see at the Orangerie, where the love of this phenomenon has led Claude Monet to formal suicide. The soul of the Ophelia of painting is dragged down ingloriously by a shroud of waterlilies.[48]

And Jacques-Emile Blanche returned to the attack, with a deadly punch-line saved for the end of his article: 'It seems that Claude Monet will need some luck if he is to remain well known.' While preparing to administer this coup de grâce, Blanche warmed up with a couple of unexpected jabs:

> These blotches, these spatters, these scratches inflicted on the canvas, over a surface of I don't know how many metres, join up with each other at a distance, without making any holes, in a perfect unity, yet they collide with each other when seen at close quarters. The execution seems prodigious. It is unanalysable and broadly synthetic – while Monet, confronting this lake of flowers, ceaselessly devotes himself to minutely dividing the colours of his palette in order to suggest a scientific, a mathematical palette. It is barely understandable: the act of painting the parts of this ensemble, one after another, without revisions, without touch-ups, without any sign of hesitation. Alas, a scene-painter in a theatre has the knack of producing something equivalent.[49]

We have the novel privilege of eavesdropping on a conversation about the Orangerie cycle that took place between Henri Matisse and his son-in-law Georges Duthuit, who was an art historian and critic. Their disagreement is a beautiful example of the obtuseness of people on opposite sides of a generation gap. Duthuit had just seen the Orangerie paintings for the first time and thought them 'limp'. Matisse protested: 'No, the colours are organised, yet it's true that a whole panel is covered just to bring out the value of a waterlily.' Aggravated by their difference of opinion, they recommenced their discussion the following day, as Duthuit recorded in his diary:

> Matisse said this painting isn't empty. There's one kind of painting that relies on the wall, resists the eye and organises the surface, and another kind that hollows out the surface and situates itself beyond the wall, but in spite of this isn't vacant – Monet was attached to that kind of painting.

Duthuit rejoined: 'All the same, it's rather floating.'

At which point Matisse stared him down: 'And Tintoretto? Isn't Tintoretto like that: floating?'[50]

Ought we to compare this chorus of destructive opinion, this systematic belittlement and trivialisation of Monet to pygmies trying to cut a giant down to size? To a war of 'sons' against 'fathers'? Was this simply the polarisation of the grand pendulum-swing of Hegelian dialectics – an interplay of thesis and antithesis – or was there a more moralistic and censorious dualism in operation, as in those medieval representations of the Virtues, each personified by a beautiful maiden in the act of trampling down another figure who represents the antithetical Vice? Or could we liken it to the work of enzymes breaking down food in order to make it digestible? In any event, the unity and meaning of Monet's œuvre was to all intents and purposes wrecked by a general refusal to see it whole:

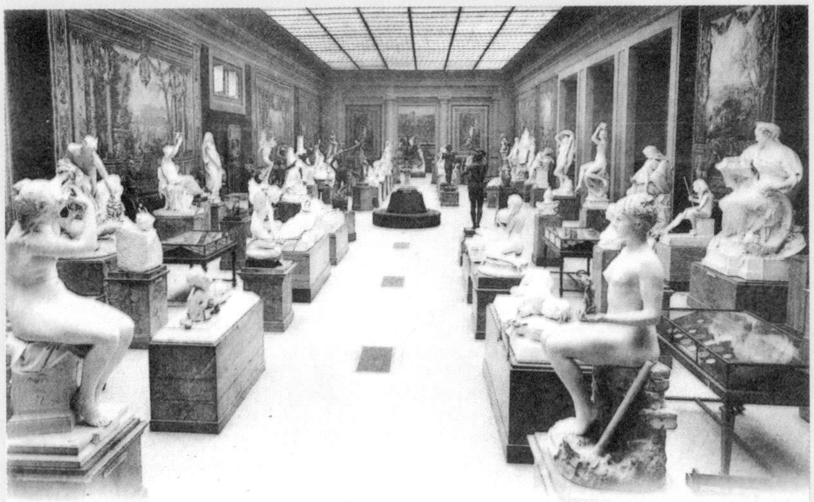
893 PARIS. – Le Musée du Luxembourg. – La Salle des Statues. – LL.

> It is regrettable that in his last manner Claude Monet deliberately sacrificed form to the light. During his long and peaceful old age the motifs he painted were merely iridescent panels, scattered bits of fairy gossamer. We prefer the surprising feats of virtuosity of his youth and maturity […] Alert to what was most changeable and unstable in the light, he began his famous 'series' around 1890. The object became, in a way, a passive mannequin which the light, like a couturier, wraps in its most beautiful, ephemeral robes.[51]

Robert Rey, the deputy curator of the Musée du Luxembourg, didn't like Monet's later series paintings much either:

> For me this period is no longer Impressionism, but its decline. It signals 'the formula'. Impressionism in its militant phase was the opposite of Impressionism in its triumphant phase: its characteristic was, precisely, a superb ignorance of formulas.
>
> When I see some of [Monet's] *Rouen Cathedrals* in the Camondo bequest in the Luxembourg Museum (a series which began in 1893), I am troubled. Will time preserve these works whose hastily applied colours blend in such dangerous mixtures? All this mud rendered precious, as if it contained dew and the powder of butterfly wings – won't it crack, strain and tarnish little by little, like a delicate but fragile cosmetic?
>
> Absence of doctrine erected into a doctrine is still a doctrine. And as soon as Claude Monet adopted it, his works were no longer so pure. Before, he made unforgettable pictures; after, he made superb Claude Monets.[52]

Even Monet's great friend and champion Georges Clémenceau was having second thoughts about Monet's series. He had written a long, laudatory article about the *Rouen Cathedral* series in 1895,[53] but had evidently changed his mind by 1929: 'I don't like everything that Monet does. He made mediocre things … his Rouen cathedrals … they're everything that you could wish, except it's not stone that he painted.'[54]

And so, during the years immediately following his death, Monet's reputation sank to an all-time low. When Clémenceau visited the Orangerie a year or two after the *Waterlily* rooms had been inaugurated, he was saddened to find the place wellnigh deserted: 'Yesterday I went to the Orangerie. There was absolutely nobody there. During the course of the day there came, I think, 46 men and women, of whom 44 were lovers in search of a secluded place.'[55] Twenty-three years later, in 1952, André Masson could still describe the Orangerie as 'a deserted place in the heart of the city'.[56]

The Monet revival

What were the first glimmers of the Monet revival? At first, that's all they were: glimmers. In 1945, an exhibition of 80 oil paintings and three drawings by Monet was held at Wildenstein's in New York, where it was reviewed by Clement Greenberg. He wrote:

> A reaction against what was called the 'formlessness' of Impressionist painting cast a pall for a time over the reputations of Claude Monet, Pissarro and Sisley. There now seems to be a reaction against that reaction. We have discovered more 'form' than had been supposed in their pictures.[57]

Who were the 'we' evoked by Greenberg? He had taken on a role of spokesman for a group of then completely unknown and marginal avant-garde artists in New York, including Jackson Pollock, Willem de Kooning, Mark Rothko, Clyfford Still, Philip Guston and Barnett Newman. From the early 1950s onwards, these painters would have a massive impact on art throughout the world – and they would also prove to be a fantastically effective catalyst in the Monet revival.

Among this group, Barnett Newman had begun expressing his enthusiasm for Impressionism and protesting against its denigration and underestimation as early as 1944.[58] Newman recalled first having studied landscapes by Monet and Pissarro at Kelekian's gallery in New York, and having been 'touched by their reality'.[59]

Thomas B Hess, the author of two monographic studies of Newman, was the charismatic editor of *Art News*, an influential, widely circulated art magazine that energetically promoted the New York school and played a leading role in the Monet revival during the 1950s.[60] In his first monograph on Newman, Hess explained how the re-estimation of Impressionism had initially occurred among a small coterie of artists and critics:

> Monet and Pissarro painted in front of nature, meticulously observing what they saw and noted it on the canvas in strokes of colour. Following the motif, they threw overboard all the appurtenances of Baroque and Classical manners – the composition developed among the lines of diagonals and ovals, the division of foreground and middle ground articulated by a *repoussoir* and similar, by then academic formulae […] Pissarro and Monet discovered that by articulating the surface with 'ugly' brush marks, the image was sucked flat to the plane and still offered the plays of depth and tension inherent in landscape painting. By breaking down the premeditated relationships between parts, they gave the image new life. But this became apparent to us only after Newman, Pollock, Still and the others had shown us to look for it; and they in turn appreciated the older masters only after they had been instructed by their own art.[61]

This account is borne out by the early critical commentary on the New York school, especially by Greenberg's articles, where the relevance of Monet is repeatedly emphasised in relation to painters such as Clyfford Still, Mark Rothko, Jackson Pollock and Barnett Newman. In an ambitious article conceived as a sort of manifesto for what Greenberg termed 'American-type' painting, Monet's name crops up in an unexpected context:

> Recently […] some of the late Monets began to assume a unity and power they had never had before. This expansion of sensibility has coincided with the emergence of Clyfford Still as one of the most important and original painters of our time […] As the Cubists resumed Cézanne, Still has resumed Monet – and Pissarro. His paintings were the first abstract pictures I ever saw that contained almost no allusion to Cubism.[62]

Evidence that a new spirit of curiosity and enthusiasm for Monet's late works had begun to pervade the art world is provided by a review, written in 1954 by Robert Rosenblum, of a new display of Impressionist paintings at the Brooklyn Museum:

> Some of these paintings surprise us because of their unexpected analogies to recent developments. Above all, there are three late Monets, surely the finest group in the show. Before these iridescent canvases one thinks inevitably of the pictorial explorations of a Rothko, a Pollock, a Guston. Like Monet, these new artists challenge traditional (here *Cubist*) conventions of formal structure, daring to make a cohesive work of art from unbounded colour areas, from the immediate excitement of the paint surface itself.

And the review concludes with an allusion to T S Eliot's famous statement from 'Tradition and the individual talent' – a statement that Greenberg might have had in mind and may have meant to imply in his otherwise questionable assertion that 'late Monets began to assume a unity and power they had *never* had before' (my emphasis). As Rosenblum put it:

> Who knows what additional dimensions these Impressionist paintings will gain during the future course of modern art? Once again one is reminded of the axiom that every new work of art changes the status of every old one.[63]

What was going on in Europe at this time? Here too, at first there were merely glimmers: an Impressionist exhibition was held at the Öffentliche Kunstsammlung in Basel in 1949; there was a donation by Emil Bührle of two spectacularly beautiful, large-scale, startlingly abstract *Waterlily* panels to the Kunsthaus in Zurich in 1952; and there were some new publications about modern art by Lionello

Venturi and Marcel Brion which urged a re-evaluation of Impressionism.[64] But the signal event in the Monet revival in Europe is usually taken to be the publication of an article by André Masson in the magazine *Verve* (republished pp 190–91).

Brief though it was, Masson's article was highly subversive in its effect, challenging the prevailing assumptions about Monet and proposing new ways of appreciating his art. One gauges its originality and impact from the number of writers who referred to it – Clement Greenberg, David Sylvester, Thomas B Hess, even *Time* magazine.

Although he was not a painter of the first rank, André Masson knew the world of art as thoroughly as anyone. His own painting had broadly based roots in Cubism, Surrealism and abstract painting, and his wide-ranging network of friends couldn't have been more different from the clannishness typical of artists' and writers' fraternities. Masson's cosmopolitan outlook helped him see, earlier than others, the signs of depleted energy, staleness and sterility in the aftermath of Cubism and Surrealism. While he lived as a refugee in the United States during the war, he did not spend much time in New York City. He lived in New Preston, Connecticut, although he did exhibit in New York galleries and was of course impressed by the vitality of the contemporary scene and the wealth and sophistication of the museums.

He shared the sense of contemporary art *in extremis* that spurred the Abstract Expressionists to their collective achievement. In fact, Masson was acquainted with several Americans – Arshile Gorky and Robert Motherwell among them – and had seen Jackson Pollock's early works at Peggy Guggenheim's gallery and much else besides.[65] After the war, Masson chose not to resettle in Paris. He went to live in Aix-en-Provence, from where he made visits to Henri Matisse in Vence, becoming a close friend of Matisse. All of these factors would have increased Masson's susceptibility to the 'revelation' of Monet.

In his paintings and drawings from the 1920s onwards Masson had made extensive use of what the Surrealists called 'pure psychic automatism'. That is to say, he was interested in generating images by involuntary and accidental means. He was excited to recognise something analogous in Monet's brushwork:

> Streaked or swept on in stripes, swirling or crazily entangled, this violence of the brush used to deter the scandalised crowds from 'seeing the landscape'. 'Step back from it', they would advise. Today you are recommended to do the opposite: come closer, let your eyes touch the proof of the wildest whirlwind that gives rise to the pictorial instinct.[66]

There were three Monet exhibitions mounted by museums in the United States in 1957 and these, according to the art historian Michael Leja, were the first of their kind in 30 years.[67] Also in 1957 a very large Monet exhibition (115 works) featured as part of the Edinburgh Festival. Organised by Douglas Cooper, it travelled to the Tate Gallery in London afterwards. Cooper observed in his catalogue introduction:

> Between 1930 and 1950 little was heard of the greatness of Monet, while his imaginative late works were decried [...] As a result, Monet passed slightly out of view and no attempt was made to see the whole of his work in retrospect. No stylistic analysis or evaluation of his aims and achievements was attempted, and even today Monet has been less studied than any of his friends and contemporaries with the exception of Sisley.
>
> Recently a new generation of historians, critics and, above all, artists has appeared on the scene. They have looked at Monet with fresh eyes, and during the last five or six years have focused attention on him in such a way that he has begun to regain some of the artistic stature he seemed to have lost. This time, however, Monet is presented to us as the begetter of the abstract movement in painting on the basis of the broad brushwork and polyphonic use of colour which occur in his late works.[68]

David Sylvester remembered a time in the early 1950s while he was teaching at the Slade School of Art in London, when 'Monet was [an] obsessive subject, since he was in the process of being rediscovered and revalued'.[69] Sylvester reviewed the 1957 Tate exhibition for the *New Statesman* and criticised the curator Douglas Cooper for not giving more prominence to Monet's late works. He wrote a second article about the exhibition which was published in the *New York Times*:

> The subject this year is Monet, the art world's most newly resurrected deity, the painter whose standing has risen more than that of any other as a result of post-war movements in taste – meaning post-war movements in art, since Monet's current high reputation is obviously a by-product of the growth of Abstract Expressionism and other current activities [...] It is of course, the late work that has won him this position, which is to say that his revival has been less of a rediscovery than a discovery, since much of the late work was never shown in his lifetime.
>
> What is it that makes us find Monet so peculiarly sympathetic? It's that he shares a certain basic attitude with us, namely, a desire for complete freedom from the constraints of art, a dislike of the 'well-composed' picture, of an order imposed by convention, of the ideal – in a word, of tradition. The freedom and spontaneity with which an experience is captured – this is what matters above all, especially above artistic beauty. We see him as a liberating force in our revolution against Cubist aesthetics, which dismissed his work as deliquescent and unorganised, and which we now in our turn reject as being sterile in their preoccupation with formal discipline.[70]

Like other budding art critics of his generation in England, Lawrence Alloway was drawn to late Monet and to American Abstract Expressionism simultaneously. He was especially impressed by the concept of 'field painting' that Clement Greenberg had defined in his essay '"American-Type" Painting'. Alloway understood that this was a philosophical concept. Intuitively he seems to have grasped what the notion of 'field' meant for Monet, whose artistic discipline can be seen as a striving to overcome dualism, to acknowledge the indivisibility of reality, and to reflect, enter into and identify with the wholeness of being. During an interview he gave in the 1980s, Alloway translated these insights into the phraseology of a 1960s art critic:

> The artists I was especially affected by, and who were the most unlike what I'd seen in Europe, were the so-called Field Painters. You know they'd been named in 1958 [sic] by Clement Greenberg in his article '"American-Type" Painting', and it seemed very fresh [...] One of the things about them that was very important to me, although this may not have been conscious to me at the time, is the field of the painting as a realm of potential meaning. When Greenberg coined the term 'Field Painting', he tended to talk about it in terms of Monet's tonal relations [...] There was the concept of the surface of the pictures as a whole rather than subdivided into small, median and large forms. I think I took that as a form of meaning in relation to the art, but also to the world-at-large. I saw the world as a continuum of changing relationships, whether like a field of pathways and nodes, like Jackson Pollock, or immersive plains of a single colour, like Barnett Newman. I sense the world like that [...] I believe in fields, not hierarchies.[71]

•

Claude Monet tolerated his critics, and never, so far as we know, tried to defend himself against them. He faced posterity with due modesty, as a realist and fatalist. We gather as much from the stoical letter he wrote to the Bernheim-Jeune brothers:

> As a painter I've done what I can, and to me that seems sufficient. I don't want to be compared to the great masters of the past, and my painting belongs to the critics. That is enough.[72]

1 Edouard Manet quoted by Georges Grappe, 'Claude Monet', *L'Art Vivant*, Paris, 1 Jan 1927, p 2

2 T S Eliot, 'Tradition and the individual talent', *The sacred wood: essays on poetry and criticism*, Methuen & Co, London 1920, p 43

3 Roger Marx, 'Les "Nymphéas" de M Claude Monet', *Gazette des Beaux-Arts*, Paris, Jun 1909, p 530; see p 200 of this catalogue

4 Philippe Burty, 'The Paris exhibitions: *Les Impressionnistes', The Academy*, London, 30 May 1874, p 616, reprinted in Ruth Berson ed, *The new painting: Impressionism 1874–1886*, 2 vols, Fine Arts Museums of San Francisco 1996, vol 1, p 10

5 Boudin quoted by William Seitz, *Claude Monet: seasons and moments*, exh cat, Museum of Modern Art, New York 1960, p 4

6 André Arnyvelde, 'Chez le peintre de la Lumière – *Je Sais Tout* interviewe Claude Monet', *Je Sais Tout*, Paris, 15 Jan 1914, p 32

7 Adrian Stokes, *Monet*, Faber and Faber, London 1958, p 5

8 On the reluctance of artists to exhibit their works near Monet's, see Louis Vauxcelles, 'Un après-midi chez Claude Monet', *L'Art et les Artistes*, Paris, Dec 1905, p 88. Also see pp 198–99 of this catalogue

9 Eliot 1920, p 44

10 Charles Morice in Philippe Dagen, *La Peinture en 1905: L'enquête sur les tendances actuelles des arts plastiques' de Charles Morice*, Archives des Arts Modernes, Paris 1986, p 47

11 Dagen 1986, p 50

12 Matisse went 'several times' to Giverny according to Hilary Spurling, *Matisse: the master*, Hamish Hamilton, London 2005, p 199. According to Joseph Baillio and Cora Michael, Monet bought a painting by Albert Marquet in 1917 and consequently invited Marquet and Matisse to Giverny. See Baillio et al, *Claude Monet (1840–1926): a tribute to Daniel Wildenstein and Katia Granoff*, Wildenstein and Company, New York 2007, p 177

13 This legend, recounted in a slightly garbled form, is laid to rest in Alex Danchev, *Georges Braque: a life*, Arcade Publishing, New York 2005, p 6

14 Maurice de Vlaminck quoted in 'Opinions', *L'Art Vivant*, Paris, 1 Jan 1927, p 23

15 Although Derain added: 'I am looking for something else, for the contrary, which is fixed, eternal, complex.' Undated letter (c1910?) in André Derain, *Lettres à Vlaminck*, Flammarion, Paris 1955, p 188

16 Guillaume Apollinaire, 'D'Eugène Delacroix au Néo-Impressionnisme', 1911, in *Chroniques d'art 1902–1918*, Gallimard, Paris 1960, pp 247–48

17 Guillaume Apollinaire, 'Georges Braque', 1908, in *Chroniques d'art 1902–1918*, Gallimard, Paris 1960, p 76

18 Apollinaire 1960, p 92

19 Maurice Denis, 'Cézanne', *L'Occident*, Paris, Sept 1907, reprinted in *Le Ciel et l'arcadie*, Hermann, Paris 1993, p 133

20 Émile Bernard, 'Réfutation de l'Impressionnisme', *Mercure de France*, Paris, 16 Nov 1911, reprinted in *Propos sur l'art*, 2 vols, Séguier, Paris 1994, vol 2, pp 252–65

21 Roger Fry, *Manet and the Post-Impressionists*, exh cat, Grafton Galleries, London 1910, reprinted in *A Roger Fry reader*, University of Chicago Press, Chicago 1996, p 82

22 Roger Fry, 'Art and life', 1917, in *Vision and design* Penguin Books, Harmondsworth 1961 (1920), p 18

23 Fry 1961, p 19

24 André Salmon, *L'Art vivant*, Les Éditions G Crès et Cie, Paris 1920, p 9

25 Salmon 1920, p 15

26 Salmon 1920, p 35

27 Salmon 1920, p 116

28 René Gimpel, *Diary of an art dealer*, translated from the French by John Rosenberg, Hodder and Staughton, London 1966, p 314

29 'Entretien entre Andrée Martinel-Kupka et Karl Flinker', in Suzanne Pagé and Jirí Kotalík eds, *František Kupka*, exh cat, Musée d'Art Moderne de la Ville de Paris, Paris 1990, p 353

30 Robert Delaunay, 'Light', 1920, reprinted in Arthur A Cohen ed, *The new art of color: the writings of Robert and Sonia Delaunay*, The Viking Press, New York 1978, p 81

31 From an undated work (perhaps from the early 1920s) by Robert Delaunay, reprinted in Cohen 1978, p 59

32 For the dating of Kandinsky's encounter with Monet's *Haystack* painting, see Michel Hoog, 'Note sur la postérité de Monet' in *Hommage à Claude Monet*, exh cat, Grand Palais, Paris 1980, p 359, footnote 9

33 Wassily Kandinsky, 'Reminiscences/three pictures', 1913, in Kenneth C Lindsay and Peter Vergo eds, *Complete writings on art*, Da Capo Press, New York 1994, p 363

34 K Malévitch, 'L'Esthétique', 1929, in *Les Arts de la représentation*, Editions L'Age d'Homme, Lausanne 1994, p 125. Malevich had also emphasised the significance of Monet's *Rouen Cathedral* paintings ten years earlier – see K Malévitch, 'Des nouveaux systèmes dans l'art', 1919, in *De Cézanne au Suprématisme*, Editions L'Age d'Homme, Lausanne 1974, pp 102–03

35 Georges Braque in G Charbonnier, *Le monologue du peintre*, Julliard, Paris 1959, p 10

36 André Lhote, 'L'art moderne', 1948, in *Les invariants plastiques*, Hermann, Paris 1967, p 152

37 Louis Gillet, 'Claude Monet', *Le Gaulois*, Paris, 8 Dec 1926

38 Louis Vauxcelles, 'Claude Monet est mort hier', *La Volonté*, 6 Dec 1926

39 Roger Dardanne, 'Un grand peintre, Claude Monet', *Le Figaro*, Paris, 6 Dec 1926

40 Jacques-Emile Blanche, 'Claude Monet,' *La Revue de Paris*, Paris, 1 Feb 1927, p 562. Blanche's campaign against Monet didn't end there. The latter article was reprinted in the collection of his writings, *Propos de peintre: de Gauguin à la Revue Nègre*, Emile-Paul Frères, Paris 1928, and there was another salvo in 'En me promenant aux Tuileries' in *L'Art Vivant*, Paris, 1 Sep 1927, pp 695–96

41 Marcel Sauvage, 'Le matin, à Giverny, les émouvantes et simples funérailles de Claude Monet', *L'Intransigeant*, Paris, 9 Dec 1926; *Journal de Vernon et de Ses Environs*, 11 Dec 1926; *Le Figaro*, Paris, 9 Dec 1926. *La Normandie*, 11 Dec 1926, reported euphemistically: 'No speeches were made at the cemetery.' On Monet's atheism, see the excellent essays by Adrian Lewis and Richard Kendall in Frances Fowle ed, *Monet and French landscape: Vétheuil and Normandy*, National Gallery of Scotland, Edinburgh 2006, pp 31–69 and 109–39

42 Henry Vidal, 'L'enterrement d'un peintre,' *Le Figaro*, Paris, 9 Dec 1926. Monet was buried in a family crypt marked by a white marble cross behind the apse of the church at Vernon, which already contained the remains of Ernest Hoschedé, Alice Hoschedé-Monet, Jean Monet and Suzanne and Marthe Hoschedé-Butler

43 Monet 'was one of the first to support Zola in the Dreyfus affair'; Théodore Duret, *Histoire des peintres*

impressionnistes, Floury, Paris 1906, p 104

44 Georges Clémenceau was in fact the editor of *L'Aurore*, the newspaper in which Zola's 'J'accuse' appeared on 13 Jan 1898

45 Maurice Denis, 'Cézanne', *L'Occident*, 1907, reprinted in *Le Ciel et l'arcadie*, Hermann, Paris 1993, pp 141–42

46 Steven Z Levine, *Monet and his critics*, Garland Publishing, New York and London 1976, pp 360–418; Sylvie Patin, *Regards sur les 'Nymphéas'*, Réunion des Musées Nationaux, Paris 2006

47 Louis Gillet, *Trois variations sur Claude Monet*, Plon, Paris 1927, quoted in Levine 1976, p 396

48 André Lhote, 'Monet et Picasso', 1932, in *Les Invariants plastiques*, Hermann, Paris 1967, pp 82–83

49 Blanche, Sept 1927, pp 695–96

50 Georges Duthuit, *Ecrits sur Matisse*, Ecole nationale supérieure des beaux-arts, Paris 1992, pp 282–83

51 Anonymous, 'Les deux Claude', *L'Echo de Paris*, Paris, 9 Dec 1926

52 Robert Rey, 'Claude Monet et l'impressionnisme', *L'Art Vivant*, Paris, 1 Jan 1927, p 14

53 Georges Clémenceau, 'Révolution des cathédrales', *La Justice*, Paris, 20 May 1895

54 Jean Martet, *M Clémenceau peint par lui-même*, Albin Michel, Paris 1929, p 48. On the following page he adds: 'His views of Venice are bad.'

55 Clémenceau quoted in Martet 1929, pp 89–90

56 André Masson, 'Monet le fondateur,' *Verve*, vol 7, nos 27–28, Paris 1952, p 68, reproduced this page

57 Clement Greenberg, 'Review of an exhibition of Claude Monet', *The Nation*, New York, 5 May 1945, reprinted in *The collected essays and criticism*, 4 vols, The University of Chicago Press, Chicago 1986–93, vol 2, p 20

58 On Newman's activism, see Michel Hoog, 'Note sur la postérité de Monet' in *Hommage à Claude Monet*, exh cat, Grand Palais, Paris 1980, p 351

59 According to the testimony of Thomas B Hess, *Barnett Newman*, Walker and Co, New York 1969, p 53. Dikran Kelekian, who died in 1951, had a gallery at 20 East 57th Street, where he showed modern art as well as antiquities. He was a friend of Mary Cassatt and had accumulated important holdings of Impressionist painting

60 See also Hess's own article on Monet: Thomas B Hess, 'Monet: Tithonus at Giverny', *Art News*, Oct 1956, p 42. The culmination of Greenberg's thoughts about Monet was published in an *Art News* annual, probably commissioned by Hess: Clement Greenberg, 'The later Monet', *Art News Annual*, New York 1957, reprinted in Greenberg 1986–93, vol 4, pp 3–11

61 Hess 1969, pp 53–54

62 Clement Greenberg, '"American-type" painting', *Partisan Review*, New York, Spring 1955, reprinted in Greenberg 1984–93, vol 3, p 228

63 Robert Rosenblum, 'Varieties of Impressionism', *Arts Digest*, New York, 1 Oct 1954, p 7. It is interesting to find these ideas in general circulation several months before they were set down in Greenberg's essay

64 On Venturi and Brion, see Douglas Cooper, *Monet*, exh cat, Edinburgh International Festival 1957, p 6

65 Masson's work had quite a strong influence on Pollock's early paintings, as he would have recognised

66 Masson 1952, p 68

67 Michael Leja, 'The Monet revival and New York School Abstraction', in Tucker et al 1998, p 98. One exhibition was shared by the museums of St Louis and Minneapolis, another was in Chicago and the third was held in Boston

68 Cooper 1957, pp 5–6

69 David Sylvester, 'Curriculum vitae' in *About modern art: critical essays 1948–2000*, Pimlico, London 2002, p 23

70 David Sylvester, 'Monet', 1957, in Sylvester 2002, pp 74–75

71 Lawrence Alloway, 'Field notes: an interview', in Michael Auping ed, *Abstract Expressionism: the critical developments*, exh cat, Buffalo Fine Arts Academy 1987, p 126

72 Claude Monet, Letter to G or J Bernheim-Jeune, 24 Nov 1918, in Wildenstein 1974–91, letter no 2290

André Masson

Monet the founder

Verve, vol 7, nos 27–28, 1952

André Masson (1896–1987) was part of the Surrealist group during the 1920s, yet his œuvre remains largely unclassifiable. His early work was influenced by Fauvism and Cubism, then he adopted the biomorphic abstraction of Surrealism. He moved to the United States during World War II and continued to extend the experimental Surrealist techniques of automatic drawing and painting. There he became loosely associated with – and exerted an influence on – Abstract Expressionist painters such as Arshile Gorky and Jackson Pollock, who shared his interest in a spontaneous, 'accidental' aesthetic.

The limpid eye, the Raphael of water, the master of Giverny ... He was venerated by his peers, then came the brutal obliteration of ancestors by a young generation champing at the bit, naturally impatient of 'other things'. There were oscillations of taste, a loss of popularity.

His place was and remains crucial, and it would not be lessened if we were to admit that, when all's said and done, it is futile to want to remake the history of art, even if an arbitrary change of values seems necessary to justify contemporary adventures and exploits.

Monet's work is one of the great turning points of painting, a commotion, the primacy of light (or, if you prefer, of colour-light). He spoke of the *flash*, the *flare*, the *flame* of Bordighera: 'Here everything is pigeon-breast and brandy-flame'. These few words sufficed to commend the place. Sun-loving, he saw luminosity everywhere, even in shadow, and there was nothing black in the festival he brought along with him, not even coal. His logic required it thus, his poetic also – and, though his luminist impulse affected all his companions, none followed him absolutely in this respect.

He was a painter of appearances (not a theologian), in tune with his vision of reality, of which he gave a lyrical, enthusiastic account. He accepted the flight of time, the ephemeral. He had a new way of seeing, feeling, loving nature. Perhaps he went too far in letting others say that he was satisfied with recording colour-sensations, 'letting the eye take its course'. The truth is that he knew better than anyone how to 'organise his sensations', how to choose a representative colour from the flood of infinite iridescence.

It must be emphasised: this atmospheric envelopment was recreated at the artist's initiative. He didn't abandon himself to a passivity of sight. Nature offered him a profusion of rapports which he simplified into a set of principal accords: here imagination exercised its rights.

There was no *a priori* form: based on the power of light, the exaltation of colour caused a negation of contours (or limits). The completed work found its balance through the fusion of elements.

Absence of formal limitation led to a fantastic inventiveness where *touch* was concerned. Touch distinguished the various aspects of the painting (the main body of it being atmosphere) – a touch of many accents: crisscrossed, ruffled, speckled. You have to see it in close-up – what a frenzy! Sometimes the touch has an unprecedented truculence, as in the *Cathedrals*.

In Monet's early work, his touch can be discreet and calm, attaining a serenely moving expression of luminous vibration, as in a masterpiece of that period, *Saint-Germain-l'Auxerrois*. In *Storm at Etretat* in the museum at Lyon, and in *Les galettes* he prefigures the manner of Van Gogh's *Sunflowers*, but without the graphic stylisation characteristic of the latter. Streaked or swept on in stripes, swirling or crazily entangled, this violence of the brush used to deter the scandalised crowds from 'seeing the landscape'. 'Step back from it', they would advise. Today you are recommended to do the opposite: come closer, let your eyes touch the proof of the wildest whirlwind that gives rise to the pictorial instinct.

A few synthetic lines, or *accents*, sometimes accompany coloured masses and 'particularise' them. There are certain pictures that Monet painted in Holland where he comes closest of all to Japanese prints. Broad surfaces, almost flat planes, already appear in some of the paintings of his youth that are indebted to Manet's frankness of manner, yet the surfaces in his paintings of Amsterdam are not conceived tonally – they are already pure colour. Monet's demon prevented him from succumbing to the puerile chromaticism of the imagery.

One can dream of Claude Monet applying himself to those great, clear, glimmering sheets of water that were the fiefdom of Veronese and Tiepolo, but we need dream no longer when we consider his supreme work, *The waterlilies*. Despite their monumental dimensions, these have none of the character of large-scale Venetian or Flemish decorative painting. Monet's mentality strikes me as that of a great easel painter who decides to give his field of vision greater scope in order to embrace the world. (A mirror of water suffices to identify the universe.) *Cosmic vision* I would like to have called it, had the term not gone awry and been applied to all and sundry in recent times. In a similar way to Monet, Michelangelo the creator of single, solitary figures had to bide his time before a chapel in the Vatican enabled him to take wing and show the full force of his powers. That is why I say in all seriousness that the Orangerie in the Tuileries gardens of Paris is the Sistine Chapel of Impressionism. A deserted place in the heart of the city, it bestows on the great work within it the blessing of inaccessibility. It is one of the summits of French genius.

Many months ago I wrote to Georges Besson[1] telling him how I wanted to see our young painters discover Claude Monet, and his rediscovery by the not-so-young painters would seem no less opportune. It would be an encouragement to make a fresh start, forcing destiny, in order to find divine sensation. *Divine*? – what I mean is: human in the extreme.

If we regain contact with the irreplaceable instant (with its ensuing sublimation), we should be able to extract ourselves from our various intellectual impasses. It will lead to the elaboration of new depths by means of a reinvented transparency.

We cannot 'go back' to Impressionism, yet we can, if we heed Monet's most precious counsel, *go forward*.

Translated from the French by Terence Maloon

1 Georges Besson (1882–1971), art critic for *Les Lettres françaises*, was a distinguished collector whose portrait was painted by Matisse in 1918. In 1963 he donated more than 300 works to the museum in Besançon.

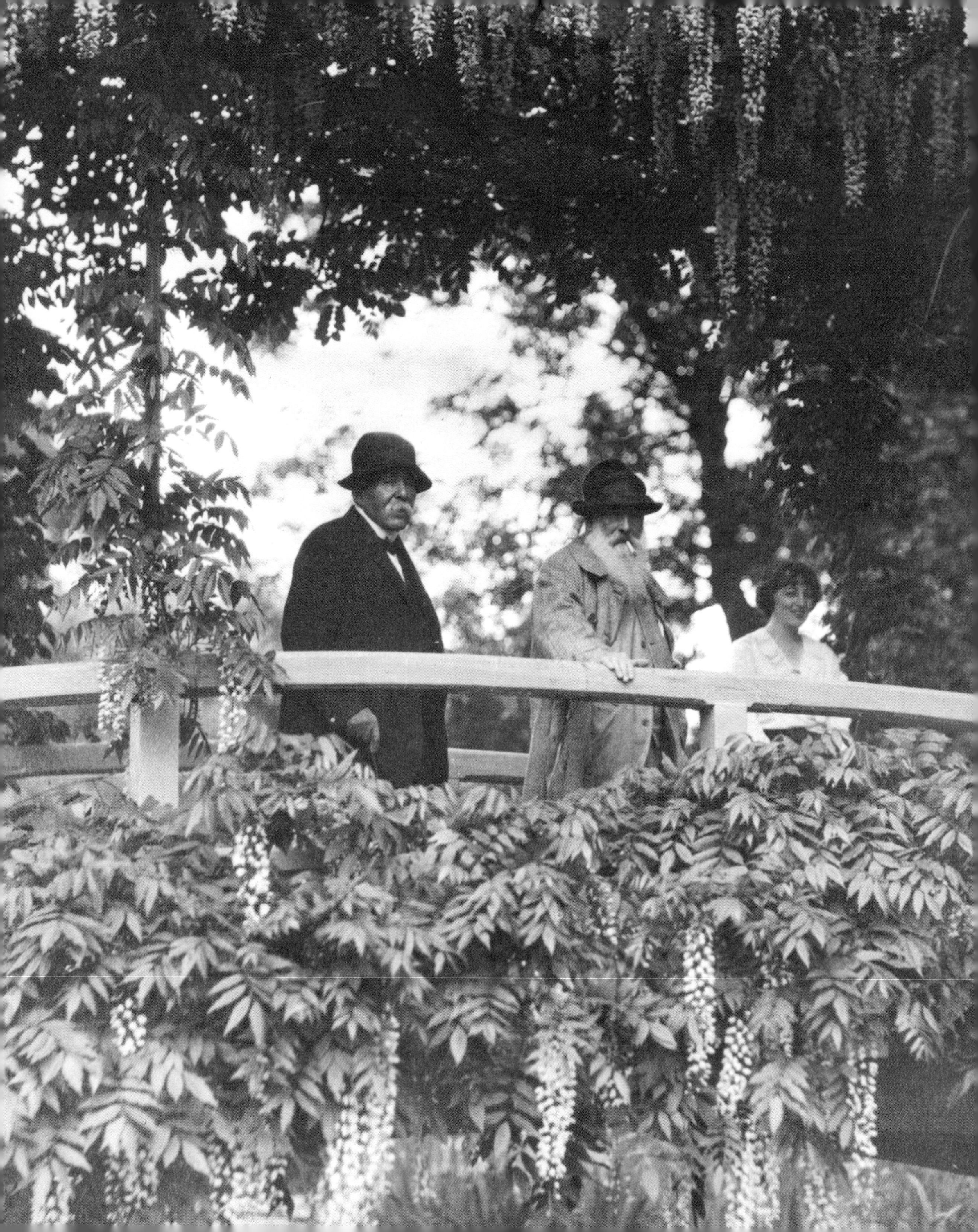

MEMORIES OF MONET

Claude Monet (centre) with Georges Clemenceau and Lili Butler on the Japanese bridge at Giverny

Meeting Monsieur Monet

An introduction to four eyewitness accounts

Terence Malooon

What was the colour of Monet's eyes? In the selection of articles that follows, two writers are in disagreement. Monet's eyes, according to Muriel Ciolkowska, were blue, whereas Louis Vauxcelles says they were steel grey. Other writers who knew Monet add to the uncertainty: René Gimpel refers to his 'small round chestnut-coloured eyes', Georges Lecomte says they were 'black, sharp and deep', whereas Emile Taboureux says they were 'limpid as spring water'.[1]

These descriptions occur in interviews, or in published accounts of writers' meetings with Claude Monet. Four such articles are reprinted here. We prize them for their stray remarks from Monet's conversation and for their vivid descriptions of his appearance and personality. In actuality, Monet granted dozens of interviews during his lifetime, and there were also dozens of eyewitness accounts of visits to his house and garden at Giverny, most of them appearing in print after 1900.[2] Naturally some of these articles are more substantial and interesting than others. The earliest interview with Monet took place in 1880, published in the smart Parisian journal *La Vie Moderne* by Emile Taboureux. At the time, interviews with artists were a novelty and Monet was still something of a pariah in the Paris art world. Taboureux informed his readers that his visit to Monet's home in Vétheuil was motivated by the desire 'to see at first hand one of those wild beasts of art known as Impressionists', although he professed to 'have no special or technical knowledge of painting'.[3]

It would seem that Monet used the occasion to build on the journalist's expectations of eccentricity and 'wildness'. He told Taboureux he didn't have a studio. Indeed, he said he had *never* had one. The great outdoors was his studio – there was little or no reason for an Impressionist to work indoors. When Monet took Taboureux inside his home, it was evident that he was extremely poor and had only the barest necessities. Taboureux described what he saw: 'the most elementary primitive objects' – a bed, a chest of drawers, a cupboard, a table, some books. In short, there was no sign of Monet having a female companion, nor any sign of family life within.

This does not square with what we know about Monet's circumstances at the time. Unbeknown to the journalist (or so it would appear), Monet's first wife had died a few months earlier, leaving him to care for two very young children. He was in desperate financial straits and profoundly depressed. Yet none of this was apparent to the readership of *La Vie Moderne*. Declining to conform to his interviewer's assumptions, refusing to bare his heart and pander to the idle curiosity of strangers, Monet deflected and redirected the journalist's inquiry to suit his own purposes. To those who knew him well, these stratagems seemed disingenuous and manipulative in the extreme: after the interview came out in *La Vie Moderne*, Degas accused him of 'frantic self advertising'.[4]

Was there really no woman, were there really no children at home when Taboureux came to call? Their absence from his account is extremely puzzling. Since October 1878, Claude and Camille Monet and their two children had shared a house in Vétheuil with Ernest and Alice Hoschedé and their six children. Why was there no sign of the co-occupants?

Let us try to situate this publication in what we know of the circumstances of Monet's life at the time. Ernest Hoschedé had been a wealthy textile manufacturer and avid collector of Monet's paintings until the time of his bankruptcy in June 1878, when Monet had invited him and his family to share a house in Vétheuil. Parlous times lay ahead for the Monet-Hoschedé clan: Camille Monet became gravely ill and by August 1879 was bedridden; the servants the Hoschedés had brought with them left their employ and sought legal action for unpaid wages; medical expenses for Camille drove Monet into ever increasing debt; Camille died in September 1879; unable to face his responsibilities, Ernest Hoschedé abandoned his family and ignored the pleas from Alice and Monet for him to return, leaving Alice exposed to gossip about her irregular situation with Monet; in January 1880 the newspaper *Le Gaulois* published a malicious article reporting that Claude Monet lived in Vétheuil with his 'wife' (meaning Alice), while his ruined former patron was consigned to 'spend his life in the studio of Monet, who clothes, lodges, feeds and … puts up with him'; in February the magazine *L'Artiste* reprinted the slanderous article; the letters of protest from Monet and Ernest Hoschedé to the editor of *Le Gaulois* were ignored.[5]

Those were the circumstances surrounding the Taboureux interview which took place in April 1880. The conspicuous sterility and solitariness of Monet's habitat, as described by Taboureux, was meant to scotch rumours. The statement that Monet didn't have a studio and had never had one was not altogether the self-publicising ruse and deliberate mystification that Daniel Wildenstein and others have taken it to be[6] – it was meant to shield Monet's private life from unwanted speculation and to defend the outraged dignity and damaged respectability of the Hoschedés.

But the questions remain: was there really no woman, were there really no children to be seen in Monet's house? Had Alice temporarily moved out? Was the scene deliberately staged for the journalist's benefit? Was the journalist in league with Monet in propagating disinformation? Had the journalist been briefed by his boss, Georges Charpentier, the editor and director of *La Vie Moderne* – which was not only a journal, but also a gallery where Claude Monet was about to hold an exhibition, and where, most likely, Ernest Hoschedé had spent a great deal of money in the past? Given the tangled interests and the conspiracy of silence, we may never get to the bottom of the mystery.

Unsurprisingly, Taboureux found Monet 'extremely wary'. He also found him 'intensely modest' and physically tough – the same characteristics noted by Vauxcelles 25 years later, and by Ciolkowska 40 years later. The hardiness journalists attributed to Monet was, in part, a metaphor for the psychological resilience he had built up over many decades of privation and struggle. He mistrusted idle curiosity and easy talk, and his unforthcoming responses to the journalist's questions returned the focus to his stocky, weatherbeaten physique – 'tough as an oak tree' according to Vauxcelles, 'the old oak tree of art' according to Georges Lecomte.

Lilla Cabot Perry knew Monet much better than did his other interlocutors. Her memoir reveals a much warmer, more vulnerable, candid and spontaneous character. Perry and her husband had been Monet's neighbours in Giverny intermittently between 1889 and 1909. Monet responded to her as an aspiring younger painter: he was attentive, empathetic, helpful – and, she was surprised to discover, he was disarmingly unsure of himself. She came to regard him as a friend, and concludes her memoir by surrounding him with hearts and flowers.

Perry gives a momentary glimpse of how close-knit the Monet-Hoschedé family was, but if we are seeking insights into aspects of Monet's character and ideas that are not revealed by interviews and memoirs, we have to turn to his voluminous correspondence – both the letters written by him, and letters written to him. Daily letters to Alice Hoschedé written during the many painting excursions that took him far from home, usually for weeks and months on end, testify to their intense closeness. It was to her that he confided his cares and anxieties, especially in relation to the adequacy and progress of his painting. He also had several close male friendships, and some of these lasted the better part of a lifetime.

That Monet was capable of being absolutely unlike an oak tree – that he could be humorous, playful and unselfconscious – we infer from the astonishing tone adopted by Georges Clémenceau in letters to Monet: frisky, teasing and so unguarded in expressions of affection and solicitude that you might think you were reading the correspondence of two gay boys, not the letters of an immensely distinguished, septuagenarian statesman – the former Prime Minister of France no less, nicknamed 'the Tiger' by his staff – to a fellow septuagenarian in failing health, who happened also to be the grand old man of French painting.

Autres temps, autres mœurs – different times, different manners. Very different, also, was Monet's dress sense: as Vauxcelles and Ciolkowska emphasise, Monet gave a good deal of thought to his clothes and dressed like nobody before or since. Readers may instinctively flinch and, so to speak, avert their eyes from the description of frills appearing at his wrist and neck (frills which took the place of a collar and cuffs), and the eye-catchingly expensive fabrics, the smart boots and jaunty hats that so fascinated journalists.

Before dictation machines and tape recorders were invented and before arts journalists had learnt to take shorthand, so-called interviews could be hit-and-miss affairs. How much of what was reported was really Monet's conversation? It is easy to believe the phrases that Perry and Vauxcelles impute to Monet are authentic, whereas the middle section of Roger Marx's article is obviously a fiction. Here we encounter a 'Monet' who conveys his thoughts through an eloquent, erudite oracle who is patently Roger Marx himself. Yet, while the voice rings false, it gives an extraordinarily impressive and gripping account of attitudes and ideas which have surely originated in Monet's conversations with the author.

Writing their articles in the afterglow of the Symbolist movement, when the prose-poem was de rigueur even for art criticism, even for journalism, Marx and Vauxcelles stake their respective claims as *littérateurs.* Yet Marx's text could not be further from the kind of pretentious, 'poetic' art-writing where a lack of expertise and uncertainty of judgement are concealed behind a smokescreen of wordiness. The energy of his thought, the exquisite accuracy of his descriptions, his passionate belief in Monet's art and the clairvoyance of his judgement cause his words to leap off the page a full century after they were written down.

In contrast, Louis Vauxcelles quickly drops the 'literary' pose and gets down to the practical business of guiding his readers through Monet's world. He has done his homework with exemplary thoroughness: he recognises the paintings on the walls and correctly identifies the periods or series they belong to. In addition, he brings a good deal of background knowledge to the interview, which enables him to provoke Monet into some interesting disclosures. Far from being untouched by his decades of struggle and penury, Monet harbours many grudges, and Vauxcelles knows exactly where the sore points lie and how to raise the great man's hackles.

Once again, Monet proves a far from innocent interviewee. By pretending this is a private conversation where everything he says is confidential, he peppers his talk with scurrilous anecdotes and drops remarks that will sting their targets – the art dealer Paul Durand-Ruel and the painters Gustave Loiseau and Jean-Charles Cazin are among his chosen victims. Yet, on the positive side, every interview and every conducted tour of Giverny had a kind of sacramental function, ending with Monet re-affirming his love and solidarity with the painters of his generation: Manet, Pissarro, Morisot, Degas, Renoir, Sisley and, most emphatically and insistently of all, Paul Cézanne.

Monet's art collection at Giverny eventually numbered 14 paintings by Cézanne, and his expressions of admiration in front of them became a recurrent feature of the interviews and guided visits. 'Yes, Cézanne, he's the greatest of us all', he averred in the presence of the journalist Michel Georges-Michel, and Vauxcelles, Ciolkowska and Perry report him saying much the same thing.[7] Cézanne was still alive when the first of these testimonials began to appear in print, and one can only imagine what it meant to him to know that he was so sincerely and so publicly admired by Claude Monet.

1 In the 1886 self-portrait (W 1078) Monet's eyes are brown. Muriel Ciolkowska, 'Memories of Monet' in *The Canadian Forum*, Toronto, Mar 1927, p 177; Louis Vauxcelles, 'Un après-midi chez Claude Monet' in *L'Art et les Artistes*, Paris, Dec 1905, p 85; René Gimpel, 'At Giverny with Claude Monet' in *Art in America*, New York, Jun 1927, p 171; Georges Lecomte, 'Claude Monet ou le vieux chêne de Giverny' in *La Renaissance de l'art français*, Paris, Oct 1920, p 403; and Emile Taboureux, 'Claude Monet' in *La Vie Moderne*, Paris, 12 Jun 1880, p 380

2 Stuckey 1995, pp 271–72, lists 33 publications where Monet's conversations are quoted, although, strictly speaking, some of the articles and books cited wouldn't be regarded as interviews by today's criteria and this list is far from exhaustive

3 Taboureux 1880, p 382

4 Daniel Wildenstein, *Claude Monet – or the triumph of Impressionism*, Taschen, Cologne 1996, p 163

5 These events can be pieced together from the excellent chronology in Stuckey 1995, pp 204–05; and Wildenstein 1996, pp 136–54

6 Wildenstein 1996, p 162

7 Michel Georges-Michel, *Peintres et sculpteurs que j'ai connus, 1900–1942*, Brentano's, New York 1942, p 35; see also Gérôme Maësse, 'Cézanne – L'Opinion de Claude Monet', *Les Tendances Nouvelles*, Paris, no 26, Dec 1906, p 432; and Felix Borchardt: 'Besuch bei Claude Monet' in *Der Kunstwanderer*, Berlin, 2 Oct 1924, p 73

Louis Vauxcelles

An afternoon with Claude Monet

L'Art et les Artistes, Paris, December 1905 (extracts)

Louis Vauxcelles (1870–1943) is reknowned for having coined the term 'les Fauves' in 1905 in a review describing the works of Matisse and his colleagues, and for having suggested the word 'Cubism' in a review of an exhibition by Georges Braque in 1908. He was one of the most prolific and widely-read critics in France, and a staunch defender of anti-academic art, notwithstanding his famously damning judgements of Fauvism and Cubism. The following article was illustrated with the first photographs ever published of Monet's garden at Giverny. Possibly due to Monet's vagueness or selective memory, there are a few factual errors in the text which have been footnoted.

Claude Monet is by no means the peasant painter, simple and coarse, that people in Paris think he is. There is no comparison between his life and that of Jean-François Millet, sunk in ignominious misery on the outskirts of the Bas-Bréau in Barbizon, or that of Alfred Sisley vegetating in a hovel in the shadow of the church of Moret-sur-Loing. Monet had a difficult beginning – of struggle, insults from the crowd, privation; he remembers this time of unavoidable hardship and does not deny its importance. Since then, he has struggled like an embattled sailor at Belle-Ile, on the reefs of Port-Domois and Port-Goulphar, tirelessly analysing the mangled rocks, the cliffs dashed with foam and stuck with mosses and lichens, and the bastions of granite battered by the waves which arrive in droves. And with his infallible brush he has unrelentingly described the bouquets of trees, the black pines, pale silver olive trees and indigo skies of Antibes and Bordighera. Yet he has been well and truly settled over the past 20 years in the gracious region of the Vexin, where he knows every leaf, every field, every wood.

Although in his 60s, Claude Monet is robust and tough as an oak tree, his face tanned by ocean spray and sun, with salt-and-pepper hair, an open-necked shirt, and penetrating, steel-grey eyes that can see all the way through to the bottom of things. Physically he makes one think of Meissonier.[1] He has the exquisitely affable manner of a gentleman-farmer. When Felix Borchardt (the fine German Impressionist painter)[2] and I arrived at Giverny, we found Monet dressed in a suit of checked beige tweed, a pleated blue silk shirt, a tawny-coloured felt hat, reddish leather boots. For a few moments we were left to ourselves in the first studio, whose walls formed a resumé of Monet's artistic life. There were 30 or so canvases – sketches from the time he worked close to Manet, some from the *Haystack* series, and from the *Cathedral* and *Waterlily* series. Since it was already four o'clock in the afternoon and 'waterlilies close before five in summer', he led the way to the second garden. As is well known, Claude Monet bought an orchard across the road from his property and flooded part of it to create a river, sowing a profusion of waterlilies across the surface [...] Monet places his easel near to a green, hump-backed footbridge. There are willow trees and aspens with delicate foliage. Most conspicuously, there are hundreds of flowers along the banks of the little river: gladioli, irises, rhododendrons, very rare brown-specked lilies. All of this forms a setting more pretty than grandiose, a very oriental dream.

When we entered the spacious, high-ceilinged second studio, Borchardt and I were transfixed – speechless, dazzled. Oh, the light is so much better than in the dungeons of Durand-Ruel's gallery! The *Cliffs* of Dieppe and Etretat, the tulip fields of The Hague, the fields of Vétheuil, sea and sky surrounded us; phantom churches merged into fog. Finally, there was the second series of waterlilies seen at all hours of the day, in lilac dawn, dusted in golden-brown midday, and in the violet shadows of dusk. The freshness of tone, the subtlety and elusiveness of the impression are inimitable.

Prominently hanging at eye-level was a large canvas of young women wearing crinolines, sheltering from the sun under miniscule sunshades with ivory handles, flecks of light streaming over their dresses and faces. Painted in the open air, this was Monet's first picture to be rejected by the Salon – notably by Jules Breton, an influential member of the Salon jury at the time, who, by eliminating this bold, innovative work, saved 'great art'.

There was also a library with a few well-chosen books and photographs of friends: Stéphane Mallarmé, with the face of a doleful dreamer; the sweet, care-worn face of Gustave Geffroy; and Mirbeau, with a harsh line on his forehead that looked like a sabre cut.[3]

We took our places on an immense divan [...] and, through the cigarette smoke, Claude Monet reminisced and smilingly, casually, wittily and modestly talked of his life.

He hates Paris, where you can't walk a hundred yards without being accosted by importuners, boors, pretentious ignoramuses and snobs. Sometimes eight or ten months will go by before he sets foot on the boulevards. He knows nothing of the coteries, the salons, or the French Institute. He prefers his garden and his work – not that he detests the big city. A few years ago he lived peacefully, alone and unremarked in London while he was working on his *Thames* series.

Claude Monet recalls that his very earliest works did not go unappreciated: he even succeeded in the Salon! But suddenly he was seized by the urge to paint figures and objects in the open air, and, from that time on, he was lost to 'serious people'. In the catalogue of the Salon of 1868 one finds the last trace of a submission, *A boat leaving the docks of Le Havre*.[4] Had he not insisted on following the path he had chosen, he would have achieved worldly success, commissions, medals. Encouraged by his comrades who were rebels in Gleyre's studio (Bazille, Renoir), he conceded nothing. Manet, whom Claude Monet greatly admired, was acutely jealous of him, yet Monet would go beer-drinking at the Café de Bade to listen to Manet's conversation with Baudelaire. Daubigny was one of the first to understand his work, and even stood down from a Salon jury because Monet and his friends had been rejected. His defenders among the critics were few: Burty, Duranty, Castagnary, Théodore Duret.

'Was Daubigny the only one to support the newly-fledged Impressionist? What did the real masters of the time say?' I asked him.

'Well, I remember we exhibited, Renoir and I, in a small shop. My picture was in the window. One day Daumier, a revered master, came by when I was there. He stopped, peered in, and asked the shopkeeper: "Who compels you to show such horrors to the passers-by?" I went home heartbroken that night. On the other hand, Diaz was enthusiastic about the same landscape. He shook my hand and predicted a great future, but I would have preferred the praise coming from Daumier and the criticism from Diaz.'

'And what about Corot, who welcomed the first efforts of Pissarro?'

'Corot said one evening to Guillemet: "My little Antonin, you've done well to have escaped from that crowd" ... When we were selling our canvases for 40 francs apiece, I barely knew the one sincere, disinterested collector of the time: Mr Choquet', said Monet. In a few words he proceeded to sketch a portrait of Chocquet – inquisitive, enlightened and, although without a personal fortune, someone who knew how to acquire the best works of Van Gogh, Cézanne and Pissarro, a true friend of painters and painting.[5] 'Of all the people I've encountered, only Chocquet and Georges de Bellio were art-lovers rather than speculators.'

Claude Monet at the height of his fame has no illusions. 'Do those who now support us understand us any better than those who used to insult us? If we removed the signatures from our paintings, who among the snobs would buy our "masterpieces"? In addition, they exaggerate our merits. Above all, there are some young people at the Salon des Indépendants who, instead of experimenting as we did 30 years ago, make the mistake of studying our handiwork, our technique too closely rather than trying to establish their own, so they lose all hope of personality. They ape us and they know it. Once, at Durand-Ruel's, I came in and saw a gentleman duck out of sight: it was Monsieur Loiseau ...'

I mentioned the Gauguin exhibition which was held not long ago at Vollard's gallery.

'Gauguin,' Claude Monet replied, 'I don't understand him. I see his debts to Puvis de Chavannes, Cézanne, the Japanese, but I can hardly see his own contribution. I never took him seriously anyway, and one wouldn't dare mention his name in Cézanne's presence! I remember Cézanne shouting in his Southern accent: "That Gauguin, I'll wring his neck."'

[...] Other names: Vuillard.

'Vuillard has a very good eye, and Maurice Denis has a lovely talent – and he's bright as well.' But Monet feels on shaky ground and prefers to dwell on old memories. He changes the subject back to heroic times in the past.

'Disgusted with the Salons and their juries, we formed a small group and exhibited with an art dealer. Manet preferred to fight it out in the Salon, on the enemy's turf – just like Zola, who wanted to break down the doors of the Academy. Manet treated us as if we were cowards, and when he obtained a modicum of success with *Le bon bock*, because of that painting's subject, he was still angry with Berthe Morisot, Renoir and me, repeating: "Why didn't you stick with me? Now I'm on top of things, don't you see?"'

'My first success came from an exhibition at Georges Petit's. Since Monsieur Durand-Ruel hadn't sent us a penny from America, I finally accepted an offer from Georges Petit – one needs to make a living.[6] I showed in the International Exhibition where the members politely asked me not to hang my canvases too close to theirs. Cazin was the only one who graciously tolerated my proximity, but at seven o'clock the next morning he came to remove his landscapes and rehang them six metres away … The critics solemnly pronounced that I had become tamer; only Geffroy defended us intelligently, but his paper, *Le Voltaire*, wasn't widely read. Then I exhibited with Rodin. Scenting success, Georges Petit said, before the opening, "I think we'll be in the *Figaro* … and what do you think of this: Albert Wolff asked me to pass on to you and Rodin an invitation to lunch? He's expecting you the day after tomorrow." I turned him down flat.'

And Rodin?

'I don't remember.' Claude Monet then held forth on Cézanne, whom he admires extremely and considers to be the master-painter of today: 'Would you like to see the Cézannes in my collection?'[7] We accepted the offer with pleasure and followed the master upstairs. In his bedroom, over the bed, was one of the most voluptuously beautiful Renoirs; there was a velvety portrait of a young woman by Manet; *The negro* by Cézanne, a stunning masterpiece worthy of Delacroix, depicting a bare-torsoed black man wearing blue trousers. There was a landscape by Pissarro pulsating with light; interiors by Berthe Morisot; a woman in a bathtub by Degas; *Apples* and *L'Estaque* by Cézanne; a snow-covered forest by Cézanne. Then there were two portraits of Claude Monet – one by Renoir, from the same period as Fantin-Latour's group portrait,[8] the other a very interesting work by Sevrac, showing a very young Claude Monet with curly hair overhanging a high forehead. But the noblest picture had a window frame around it and was wide open: it was the slopes of Giverny in the golden glow of sunset.

We then returned downstairs, through the living rooms hung with Japanese prints of chimeras and dragons, to the well-lit, cheerful dining room, Whistlerian in its arrangement, with bright yellow sideboards, table and chairs. We re-entered the studio and Monet spoke of his method of painting. In London, when he was at work on his *Thames* series, he installed all his easels in a succession of hotel rooms vacated of furniture, and worked on a hundred canvases at a time. A few strokes comprised a quarter of an hour's work on a riverscape, whose effect recorded nine o'clock in the morning. Then he moved on to the next effect, and so on.

Claude Monet repaints the same painting many times, never with the slightest trace of fatigue – we had before our eyes the dazzling *Waterlilies*. There are some pictures we could assume were hastily painted in an afternoon, but Monet spent several years on them. He paints in fits and starts, impulsively. While he is thus engaged, no-one has the right to disturb him – friends, visitors, buyers, no-one – but afterwards he might not touch a brush for eight days.

Claude Monet, with the lordly bearing that never deserts him, accompanied us to the gate. He took leave of us to go and instruct the gardener who was in a boat, weeding out unwanted shoots between the waterlilies. On the road home Felix Borchardt and I compared our impressions:

'This is a great man who is also happy.'

'And wise.'

Translated by Terence Maloon

1 Jean-Louis-Ernest Meissonier (1815–91) was a hugely successful Academic artist, renowned also for his physical fitness.

2 Much later, Felix Borchardt published his own account of their visit to Giverny: 'Besuch bei Claude Monet' in *Der Kunstwanderer*, Berlin, 2 Oct 1924, pp 72–74

3 Stéphane Mallarmé (1842–98) was the foremost Symbolist poet in France and a devoted friend of the Impressionists; Gustave Geffroy (1855–1926) was an art critic and man of letters, author of a classic study of Monet published in 1922; Octave Mirbeau (1848–1917) was a radical journalist, art critic, novelist, playwright, and close friend of Monet's

4 Monet's last submission to the Salon was in 1880, when his painting was accepted, although it was so badly hung that its placement was assumed to be a calculated insult

5 Victor Chocquet (1821–91) was one of the earliest collectors of Renoir and Cézanne, but Vauxcelles was mistaken about Van Goghs in his collection: there were none. In the sale of Chocquet's collection held after his death there were 32 Cézannes, 11 Renoirs, 11 Monets and only one Pissarro

6 Monet would later make amends for his bad-natured remarks about Durand-Ruel: 'From that moment (1871), Durand-Ruel supported us all. And it was an heroic adventure. And it is worthy of a study in its own right to describe the role the great dealer played in the history of Impressionism.' Monet quoted in André Arnyvelde, 'Chez le peintre de la lumière – *Je Sais Tout* interviewe Claude Monet', *Je Sais Tout*, Paris, 15 Jan 1914, p 34

7 Cézanne was still far from being generally admired and accepted in the year preceding his death. The editors of *L'Art et les Artistes* saw fit to add a disclaimer in a footnote to the sentence in Vauxcelles' text where Monet had praised Cézanne: 'The review *L'Art et les Artistes* is open to all sincere opinions; it is free of any bias, and aesthetic judgements found in its pages pertain only to those who pronounce them.'

8 Fantin-Latour's group portrait of Monet and his friends, *Un atelier aux Batignolles* 1870, is now in the Musée d'Orsay in Paris

Roger Marx

The waterlilies by Monsieur Claude Monet

Gazette des Beaux-Arts, Paris, June 1909, pp 523–31 (extracts)

Roger Marx (1859–1913) was art critic for the Parisian journal Le Voltaire *between 1883 and 1889, and rose to became an important arts administrator. He was one of the organisers of the Centennial Exhibition of Painting held in Paris in 1900, where Monet was shown in the company of Delacroix, Ingres and Corot – the first official recognition of him as a great French painter. Marx was one of the most brilliant art critics of his era: one example of his prescience is his catalogue essay for Matisse's first exhibition at Vollard's gallery in 1904. The following article was written in response to an exhibition held at the Durand-Ruel gallery in Paris between 6 May and 5 June 1909. There had already been an exhibition in 1900 of an earlier phase of Monet's* Waterlilies *series.*

[…] The initial reaction to these 48 works is bewildered surprise. Most viewers' objections will have nothing to do with painting, but with their own problems relating to the subject, the number of variations, and the apparently fragmentary character of the paintings. These works assert authority, independence, and supremacy of the Self – and this can pique our vanity and humble our pride.

Monsieur Claude Monet aims only to satisfy himself. He goes to great lengths – he takes pleasure – in distinguishing the sensations experienced during the course of a day while contemplating the same site. This is the aim of his art, which is apparently completely self-centred […] He assesses the worth of a theme according to how it arouses abundant and precious sensations […]

Monsieur Claude Monet now breaks his last ties to the Barbizon school. He renews his art by following his own vision and methods. His predilection for a particular site determines the parallelisms and contrasts in his series of paintings, influencing the stages of the cycle he will follow ... *A waterlily pond* was the generic theme of the series Monsieur Monet exhibited in 1900, and the ensemble he exhibits now is a logical continuation of it. Let us try to divide up the series, not according to date – as the catalogue arbitrarily does – but according to conceptions and themes that he returns to.

One painting is a link between the present and the past. Its background recalls the landscapes of 1900: the same tall trees with outstretched branches, the luxuriant, tufted vegetation, the hump-backed little bridge covered with lichens and moss … but this is an isolated, possibly accidental reminder.

Moving away from it, a new intention becomes evident. Monsieur Monet intends to do away with the earthly décor that blocked out the horizon and hemmed in his previous compositions. He shifts his viewpoint so that the embankment recedes and soon disappears. Barely perceptible at the summit of the earliest pictures is a narrow strip of land, edging with its green the dark bowl of water streaked with iridescent glimmers emitted by floating clusters of waterlilies ... no more earth, no more sky, no more limits.

Unchecked, the dormant, fertile water floods the field of the painting. The light stretches out and sparkles on the surface strewn with grey-green foliage, from which the waterlilies lift their corollas of white, pink, yellow and blue, avid for sun and air. Here the painter has deliberately broken with the teachings of the Western tradition: he does not look for lines to form a pyramid, nor does he try to focus the gaze on a single point. Everything that is fixed and unchanging seems to him to contradict the principle of fluidity. He wants the viewer's attention diffused and spread everywhere. He feels free to modify his archipelago of small gardens at whim, placing them to the right, to the left, to the top or bottom of the canvas.

Under a light veil of silvery mist, through an incense of soft vapours, 'indecision and precision are conjoined'.[1] Certainty becomes conjecture, and the mind opens to a world of illusion and to the infinity of dreams, drawn by the enigma of the mystery.

– What idealistic demon torments you, the artist protests, and why do you accuse me of being a visionary? Do you really think my feelings of exaltation and ecstasy – feelings that are the outcome and expression of my love of nature – lead to a 'beyond', to a fairy-land? You shouldn't assume I have devious, abstruse aims – the truth is far simpler.

– My only virtue is my submission to instinct. It's only because I rediscovered those secret, intuitive powers, and because I let myself be guided by them, that I became capable of identifying with creation and being absorbed into it. My art is an act of faith, love and humility. Yes, of humility.

– People who like to hold forth about my painting conclude that 'I've arrived at the last degree of abstraction and the alliance of the imagination with the real'.[2] I would prefer it if they recognised the complete abandon with

which I give myself. I've brushed these canvases like the monks of old used to illuminate their missals. They owe everything to a collaboration with solitude and silence, to a state of attention that is rapt, exclusive and virtually hypnotised.

– People don't like it that I have adopted a single motif and that I've undertaken to represent it in all circumstances, at all hours, in the variety of its successive attractions. But sparing oneself the effort of accommodation, which any encounter with a new theme inevitably entails, can bring about a gain in concentration – so much the better to seize the atmosphere and light in their fugitive, ever-changing play, which is the very life of painting. Does the subject really matter? An instant, an aspect of nature contains all of nature […]

– Perhaps originality in my case could be explained by the receptivity of an unusually sensitive organism and the effectiveness of the stenography that projects the impression received by the retina onto the canvas, as if onto a screen. If you absolutely insist on affiliating me to others, let it be to the old Japanese. The rareness of their taste always appealed to me, and I like the implications of their aesthetic, which evokes a presence by a shadow, an ensemble by a fragment. You can also put me in the company of our French 18th-century painters – I've always felt a kinship of sensibility and technique with them.

– Yet it would be so much more intelligent not to separate me from my epoch, since I belong to it with every fibre of my being. How much more informative for future generations to know that the disciple of Courbet and Jongkind was the contemporary of Stéphane Mallarmé and Claude Debussy![3] I agree with both of the latter – and with Baudelaire – that there are points of contact between the arts; there are harmonies and concerts of colour that suffice in their own right and succeed in touching us, like a musical phrase or a chord touches us to our very depths, unassisted by any precise, explicit idea. Vagueness and indeterminacy are means of expression that have their own raison d'être and properties: they prolong sensation; they constitute a symbol of continuity.

– I was tempted for a moment by the idea of extending the theme of the waterlilies to the decoration of a living room, developing it over the length of the walls, making a unity of all the surfaces. It would have had the illusion of an endless whole, of a wave with no horizon and no shore. For the inhabitants of the house, it would establish a sanctuary of peaceful meditation in the midst of a flowered aquarium, soothing nerves that are frayed by work – like the effect of still water.

– You smile. I can tell that the name of Des Esseintes[4] is on the tip of your tongue. Isn't it a shame, though, to deny that strength might express delicacy, to assume that refinement is incompatible with robust health? No, Des Esseintes isn't my prototype. I'm more like Monsieur Maurice Barrès's Philippe,[5] who 'methodically cultivates spontaneous emotions'. I've had a half-century of practice, and soon I'll be turning 69 – but, far from being diminished, my faculties are sharpened by age. Age holds no fears for me so long as the outside world can still arouse my curiosity and my hand remains a quick, faithful interpreter of my perception.

The guests at La Faustin's[6] dinner table declared that the French language 'used to be capable of only clumsy approximations, but is now cultivated by the most sensitive people – by people who want to communicate indescribable sensations …' That is what is happening in painting now, and Monsieur Claude Monet is not the kind of man to be satisfied with the 'approximations' of his precursors. He differs from them through his hyperaesthesia and the contradictions of his temperament. Passionate and cold at once, he surveys his impulses and submits them to reason. He is obstinate and lyrical, brutal and subtle. His art pulsates with feverish enthusiasm yet radiates serenity. The temper tantrums he directs at his work do not prevent him from pursuing the most attenuated, tender nuances. In some paintings the medium, so lovingly handled, takes on the porous appearance of matte sandstone which the viewer wants to caress. For as long as humankind has existed, for as long as people have painted, no-one has painted better – and never like this.

I had spent a long time in the gallery, looking and making notes in the catalogue, when an artist with a foreign accent came up to me: 'You are writing about this exhibition, sir. You should say that we are all ignoramuses and that beside these works, Salon paintings – all Salon paintings – are daubs, just daubs.' He went away throwing his arms in the air.

Isn't this the proof of admirable knowledge? Hasn't this great mastery produced a conception of landscape that is in tune with the modern spirit, as well as being utterly distinctive of the artist? The painters of yesteryear set themselves the task of isolating the eternal from the transitory. They differentiated the parts of their paintings – the bodies and the substances – aiming to give the most exact rendition of volumes and planes. Artists were encouraged to work in this way by philosophical doctrines and by their own leisurely analysis and painstaking craftsmanship. Haste of living, haste of production were unknown in that becalmed era of dulled nerves.

Monsieur Monet belongs to a completely different time: a time in the grip of vertiginous speed. Because artists today are subject to brief, violent impressions, they need to develop a greater alertness to the world and to themselves. It is no longer a question of fixing the things that abide, but of seizing what is passing. The concrete reality of things is not so interesting as the temporary links between things, the interdependent rapports. Until recently artists prided themselves on representing a palpable reality, yet there is a delicate interrelatedness that comprises and surrounds reality and seems to elude any kind of detailed transcription – however, this is just what Monsieur Claude Monet aspires to do, and where he excels [...]

Translated from the French by Terence Maloon

1 *'L'indécis au précis se joint'* – a quotation from the poem *L'Art poétique* by Paul Verlaine

2 This was a phrase of Théodore Duret's: *'Monet est parvenu ainsi au dernier degré d'abstraction et d'imagination allié au réel'*, in *Histoire des peintres impressionnistes*, Floury, Paris 1906, p 94

3 Stéphane Mallarmé (1842–98) was the foremost Symbolist poet and a great friend and admirer of the Impressionists – of Claude Monet particularly He is reported to have told Berthe Morisot: *'Je suis heureux de vivre à la même époque que Monet'* ('I am happy to be living in the same time as Monet') – quoted in Steven Z Levine, *Monet and his critics*, Garland Publishing, New York 1976, p 89. Claude Debussy (1862–1918) was the foremost contemporary composer in France; his brilliant orchestral effects are often compared to Impressionism

4 Des Esseintes is the protagonist of J-K Huysman's 'decadent' novel *À rebours* (*Against nature*, 1884)

5 Philippe is the protagonist of Maurice Barrès's novel *Sous l'œil des Barbares* (1888), the first of a trilogy which promotes an ideology of individualism, *'Le culte du moi'*

6 *La Faustin* – a reference to Edmond de Goncourt's play of the same name (1882), whose central character, Juliette Faustin, is a *grande dame* of the theatre. The allusion has a probably unintentional irony: many criticisms of Monet's early paintings objected to them as 'approximations', as not fully realised works – see Levine 1976 p 34

Muriel Ciolkowska
Memories of Monet

The Canadian Forum, March 1927, pp 177–80 (extracts)

Muriel Ciolkowska sometimes varied the spelling of her surname to 'Ciolowska' or 'Giolkowska'. She was a novelist and contributor to the 'little magazines' of the 1910s and '20s such as The Egoist *and* The Little Review. *She also wrote a book on Rodin published in 1912. Her visit to Monet took place in July 1922 and she published her first account of it ,'Monet – his garden, his world', in 1923 under the name of 'Muriel Giolkowska'.*[1] *Her obituary of Monet four years later includes, along with her reminiscences of this visit, some astute observations about Monet's art.*

On 5 December last, by the death of Claude Monet at the age of 86, a great landmark in the history of modern art disappeared from the world [...] The story of the life of Monet is, in the main, the story of the Impressionist school as a whole. To say, as is often done, that he survived its action and influence is not quite correct. The Impressionist movement, in some form or another, is with us today, for (besides several direct heirs) many notable artists could not disclaim blood ties with it if they would – for instance, Matisse [...]

The opposition which the Impressionists had to contend with is too well-known to be recalled. Suffice it to say here that Monet, a retiring man by taste, not a battler like Manet or Whistler, preferred to keep his pictures to himself until the public was ready to consider them without prejudice. Years after, his home in the little out-of-the-way village of Giverny in Normandy was not off the beaten track enough, the walls round his garden not too high, the gates not too well-barred to keep away the curious.

Within this garden he had sought almost complete seclusion but for the immediate society of his family and close friends, leaving it only on the rarest occasions. This garden, a very floral jungle, with Japanese-like touches in the design, was, with the refined pleasures of the table […] and […] besides his beloved painting, his favourite recreation […] Here he lived, almost secretly, for 20 years, literally buried in flowers.

When the privilege of meeting him was by his kind invitation granted to me, I was keenly aware that I was coming into the presence of a man of exceptional worth, one who had truly lived his long life without fear and without reproach – for never a word unfavourable has been spoken against Monet the man, whatever may have been said by the ignorant and partial against the Impressionist – one of those rare men who can present as calm a front in prosperity as in adversity – a far more difficult task, as Marcus Aurelius has well said […]

The independent equanimity of his mind, the stability of his character, were reflected in his physique. With his square, sturdy but not heavy frame, fine head, and long white beard, fresh complexion and blue eyes, he might have been taken for an old sailor as he glided towards us out of his flower-beds that summer afternoon. He was dressed in a spotless suit of pongee with neat little frills peeping out at his wrist and neck in lieu of a collar and cuffs. At this time he was well over 80. His eyes had already given him trouble yet he had just been painting in the garden. Also we had been asked to time our visit after the sun had begun to decline.

His candid look was accompanied by a soft voice and well-bred manner. His family did not allow him to over-exert himself in conversation, although Monet was never given to 'holding forth', which was more in Rodin's line. One of our party asked him what he thought of teachers and teaching in art and whether he had ever had any pupils. By his negative answer to the last question and the reasons he gave for it he replied to both: 'A good teacher', he said, 'implies a good painter – that is a "master". Now all a good painter can say to his pupils is, "Copy me", which is exactly what he should not say. Therefore a good painter cannot make a good teacher.' […]

The public galleries of America own some of Monet's most successful paintings, that is if one agrees that his best are his most ethereal, those of his most evolved phase. In this sense his progress was like that of Turner – increasingly immaterial. In his last years Turner concentrated on sunsets and sunrises; in his last Monet concentrated on water.

It is significant that Monet was pre-eminently a painter of water, as his earliest champion and most understanding commentator, the critic Theodore Duret, has pointed out. He was brought up on the seacoast; his first exercises were seascapes; he always elected to live near water and his fluid rendering of solid substances makes of him the mystic of the Impressionist group. In his early years he occasionally painted figures, but really never for their own sake as did Renoir, the theme, whatever it was, being in any case always but the pretext for the transcription of effects through tone. Monet was one of the first to revolt against the tyranny of the 'story' in pictorial art. To him the picture was the purpose of the subject, not the reverse.

His technique may for certain well-understood reasons be compared with that of the Orientals, if not actually in technique – the means disposed of being so different – at least in principle. It must not be forgotten that he loved the Japanese and that in his youth he must have caught some of the infection of the new enthusiasm for Oriental art as preached by the Goncourt brothers. Monet's art is Oriental in so far that it uses indirect means for the furtherance of its idea, in the relation also it implies between subject and object, especially in its aim to create simply a piece of beauty and to provoke a visual sensation of pleasure.

If Cézanne aimed at harmony through form, Monet aimed at melody through tone, and so from stage to stage, as his style acquired perfection and his eyes subtlety, it became more and more intangible, evading increasingly the matter-of-factness of definition through outline, and by means, I repeat, analogous to the Chinese artist's method of translating the form of a bird by painting its feathers, or of a sea-wave by numerous strokes building up a form within a form. In other words Monet's preoccupation was not with co-related form – as Cézanne's – but with vibrations within one form […]

1 Muriel Giolkowska, 'Monet – his garden, his world', *International Studio*, no 309, Feb 1923, pp 371–78

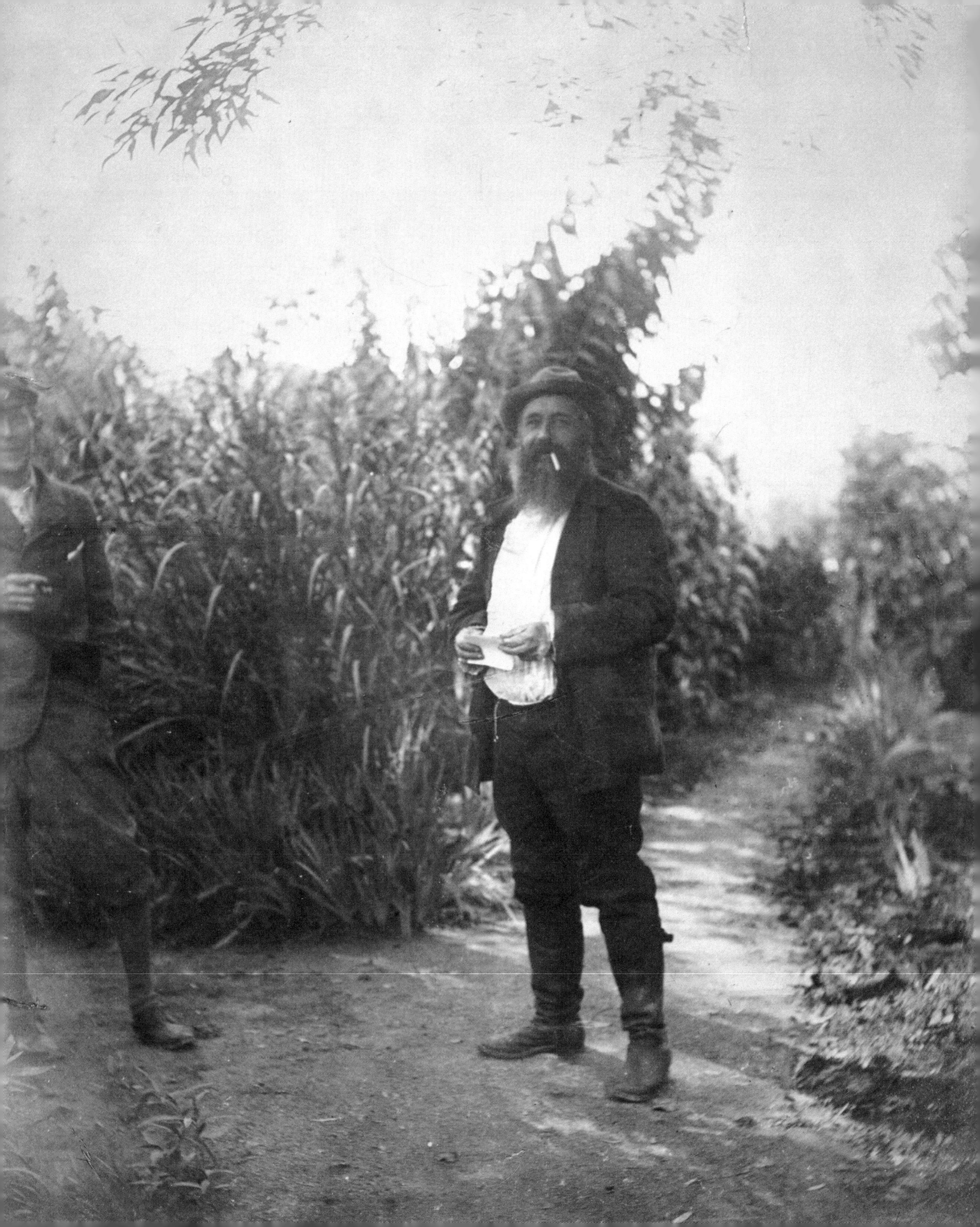

Lilla Cabot Perry

Reminiscences of Claude Monet from 1889 to 1909

The American Magazine of Art, vol 18, no 3, March 1927, pp 119–25

Lilla Cabot Perry (1848–1933) was a well-to-do American painter from Boston who studied in France with the history painter Tony Robert-Fleury and with Whistler's friend, Alfred Stevens. Increasingly attracted to plein-air painting, she became one of the earliest American Impressionists. Over ten summers, she and her husband were Monet's neighbours in Giverny and, as such, were forerunners of a sizeable colony of American artists who chose to live in proximity to Monet. Between 1893 and 1901 Perry lived in Tokyo where her husband held a teaching position.

Lilla Cabot Perry *Monet talking to Tom and me (Tom Perry and Lilla Cabot Perry)* 1890–95, photograph, gelatin silver print 50.9 x 41.2 cm. Museum of Fine Arts, Boston 1990.306

Monet is dead! How well I remember meeting him when we first went to Giverny in the summer of 1889! A talented young American sculptor told my husband and me that he had a letter of introduction to the painter, Claude Monet. He felt shy at going alone and implored us to go with him, which we were enchanted to do, having seen that very spring the great Monet-Rodin exhibition which had been a revelation to others besides myself. I had been greatly impressed by this (to me) new painter whose work had a clearness of vision and a fidelity to nature such as I had never seen before.

The man himself, with his rugged honesty, his disarming frankness, his warm and sensitive nature, was fully as impressive as his pictures, and from his first visit dates a friendship which led us to spend ten summers at Giverny. For some reasons, indeed, we had the house and garden next to his, and he would sometimes stroll in and smoke his after-luncheon cigarette in our garden before beginning on his afternoon work.

He was not then appreciated as he deserved to be, in fact that first summer I wrote to several friends and relatives in America to tell them that here was a very great artist only beginning to be known, whose pictures could be bought from his studio in Giverny for the sum of $500. I was a student in the Paris studios at that time and had shown at the Salon for the first time that spring, so it was natural that my judgment should have been distrusted. Only one person responded, and for him I bought a picture of Etretat. Monet said he had to do something to the sky before delivering it as the clouds did not quite suit him, and, characteristically, to do this he must needs go down to Etretat and wait for a day with as near as possible the same sky and atmosphere, so it was some little time before I could take possession of the picture. When I brought it home that autumn of 1889 (I think it was the first Monet ever seen in Boston), to my great astonishment hardly any one liked it, the one exception being John La Farge.[1]

This intense artistic conscientiousness was one of Monet's most marked traits. About 1906 I took a friend to his studio, she was much taken with a certain picture and tried hard to buy it, but he said he could not sell it until the series was finished as he did not feel sure it was up to his standard. A year or two later he dropped in one afternoon and casually mentioned that he had burnt up over 30 canvases that morning. I asked him whether Mrs Blank's picture was among those destroyed and he admitted that it was. 'I must look after my artistic reputation while I can,' he said. 'Once I am dead no one will destroy any of my paintings, no matter how poor they may be.'

His opinion of his own work was not, however, always calmly judicial. On one occasion, particularly disgusted at his own inadequacy, he decided to give up painting altogether. He was painting from his boat at the time, so overboard flew the forever-more useless paint box, palette, brushes and so forth into the peaceful waters of the little Epte. Needless to say, the night brought counsel and the following morning he arose, full of enthusiasm, but without any painting materials! It was, of course, a Sunday (such things always take place on Sundays), but a telegram to Paris sent a sympathetic colour man flying to his shop and a complete kit left by the next train for Normandy where a reconverted painter awaited its arrival with savage impatience.

There were two pictures on the walls of his studio which I particularly liked. They were of his stepdaughter in a white dress, a green veil floating in the breeze under a sunshade, on the brow of a hill against the sky. He told me that an eminent critic called them the Ascension and the Assumption! Seeing me looking at them one day with keen admiration, he took one down off the wall and showed me a tremendous crisscross rent right through the centre of the canvas, but so skilfully mended that nothing showed on the right side. I exclaimed with horror, and asked what on earth had happened with it. With a twinkle, he told me that one afternoon he had felt thoroughly dissatisfied with his efforts and had expressed his feelings by putting his foot through the canvas. As he happened to have on sabots, the result was painfully evident at the time.

Monet was a man of his own opinions, though he always let you have yours. Liked you the better for being outspoken about them. He used to tell me that my forte was 'plein-air', figures out-of-doors, and once in urging me to paint more boldly he said to me: 'Remember that every leaf on the tree is as important as the features of your model. I should like just for once to see you put her mouth under one eye instead of under her nose!'

'If I did that, no one would ever look at anything else in the picture!'

He laughed heartily and said: '*Vous avez peut-être raison, Madame*!' ['Perhaps you're right, Madame!']

In spite of his intense nature and at times rather severe aspect, he was inexpressibly kind to many a struggling young painter. He never took any pupils, but he would have made a most inspiring master if he had been willing to teach. I remember his once saying to me:

'When you go out to paint, try to forget what objects you have before you, a tree, a house, a field or whatever. Merely think, here is a little square of blue, here an oblong of pink, here a streak of yellow, and paint it just as it looks to you, the exact colour and shape, until it gives your own naïve impression of the scene before you.'

He said he wished he had been born blind and then had suddenly gained his sight so that he could have begun to paint in this way without knowing what the objects were that he saw before him.[2] He held that the first real look at the motif was likely to be the truest and most unprejudiced one, and said that the first painting should cover as much of the canvas as possible, no matter how roughly, so as to determine at the outset the tonality of the whole. As an illustration of this, he brought out a canvas which he had painted only once; it was covered with strokes about an inch apart and a quarter of an inch thick, out to the very edge of the canvas. Then he took out another on which he had painted twice, the strokes were nearer together and the subject began to emerge more clearly.

Monet's philosophy of painting was to paint what you really see, not what you think you ought to see; not the object isolated as in a test tube, but the object enveloped in sunlight and atmosphere, with the blue dome of Heaven reflected in the shadows.

He said that people reproached him for not finishing his pictures more, but that he carried them as far as he could and stopped only when he found he was no longer strengthening the picture. A few years later he painted his *Island in the Seine* series. They were painted from a boat, many of them before dawn, which gave them a certain Corot-like effect, Corot having been fond of painting at that hour. As he was showing them to me, I remarked on his having carried them further than many of his pictures, whereupon he referred to this conversation and said again that he always carried them as far as he could. This was an easier subject and simpler lighting than usual, he said, therefore he had been able to carry them further.

This series and the *Peupliers* [*Poplars*] series also were painted from a broad-bottomed boat fitted up with grooves to hold a number of canvases. He told me that in one of his *Peupliers* the effect lasted only seven minutes, or until the sunlight left a certain leaf, when he took out the next canvas and worked on that. He always insisted on the great importance of a painter noticing when the effect changed, so as to get a true impression of a certain aspect of nature and not a composite picture, as too many paintings were, and are. He admitted that it was difficult to stop in time because one got carried away, and then added:

'*J'ai cette force-là, c'est la seule force que j'ai!*' ['I have this strength, it's the only strength I have!'] And that from the greatest landscape painter in the world! I give his exact words, they show his beautiful modesty, as great as his genius.

One day he referred to the many criticisms of his work, comparing it to worsted work and so on, on account of his dragging the colour on to the canvas with the long flexible brushes he had made to order for his own use. He said he felt sure some of Rembrandt's pictures had been painted even more thickly and heavily than any of his, but that time with its levelling touch had smoothed them down. In illustrating this, he took out of one of the grooved boxes in which he kept his pictures a view of the Rouen Cathedral that had been kept in the box practically ever since it had been painted and put beside it one that had been hanging on the wall of his studio for some two or three years. The difference between the two was very marked, the one which had been exposed to the air and to the constant changes of temperature had so smoothed down in that short space of time that it had made the other one with all its rugosities look like one of those embossed maps of Switzerland that are such a delight to children.

He said he had never really seen these Rouen Cathedral pictures until he brought them back to his studio in Giverny as he had painted them from the window of a milliner's shop opposite the cathedral. Just as he got well started on the series the milliner complained bitterly that her clients did not care to try on their hats with a man about, and that he must go elsewhere to paint, since his presence interfered with her trade. Monet was not to be daunted, he persuaded her to let him build a little enclosure shutting him off from the shop, a small cell in which he could never get more than a yard away from his canvas.

I exclaimed at the difficulty of painting under such conditions, but he said that every young painter should train himself to sit near his canvas and learn how it would look at a distance, and that with time and practice this could be done.[3] Monet had already had experience of this sort in painting on 16 or more canvases one after the other for a few minutes at a time from his small boat on the Epte. Later on, in his water garden pictures he made he made good use of this same power. He had grooved boxes filled with canvases placed at various points in the garden where there was barely room for him to sit as he recorded the fleeting changes of the light on his waterlilies and arched bridges. He often said that no painter could paint more than one half hour on any outdoor effect and keep the picture true to nature, and remarked that in this respect he practised what he preached.

Once and once only I saw him paint indoors. I had come to his studio and, finding him at work, was for going away at once, but he insisted on my coming in and sitting on the studio sofa while he went on painting. He had posed his stepdaughter, a beautiful young girl in her teens, in a lilac muslin dress, sitting at a small table on which she rested one of her elbows. In a vase in front of her was one life-size sunflower. I was struck by the fact that this indoor picture was so much lower in key, so much darker than his outdoor figures or than most studio portraits and thought of this some years later when he paid the usual penalty of success by having many imitators.

One day as he came back from a visit to the Champ de Mars Salon I asked him how he liked the outbreak of pallid interiors painted in melted butter and spinach tones for which he was indirectly responsible. As he sat there with his hands upon his knees I shall never forget the impetuous gesture with which he clasped his hands to his head and growled despairingly: '*Madame, des fois j'ai envie de peindre noir!*' ['Madame, there are times I want to paint black!']

My husband and I were much interested in the reminiscences of his early struggles. He told us that his people were *dans le commerce* (in business) at Le Havre and when, a boy in his teens, he wished to become a painter, they opposed him vigorously in the approved traditional manner. He went through some very hard times. He painted portrait heads of sea captains in one sitting for five francs a head, and also made and sold caricatures.

Boudin saw one of these caricatures in a small shop, sought his acquaintance and invited him to go out painting with him. At first Monet did not appreciate this unsought privilege and went reluctantly, but, after watching Boudin at work and seeing how closely his landscapes resembled nature, he was only too glad to learn all he could from the older man. There are still some early Monets extant which plainly show Boudin's influence. Even after he had painted many landscapes that were purely in his own style, the young Monet had had the utmost difficulty in selling them at the modest price of fifty francs apiece.

Faure, the singer, who was by way of being a collector, bought a landscape about this time for, I believe, the sum of one hundred francs, but brought it back a few days later and asked for his money back. He said he liked the picture himself, but his friends laughed at him so much that he could not keep it on his walls. Monet said he then and there made up his mind never to sell that picture, and he never did, though often offered large sums for it by rich Americans and others. He told me he had '*la mort dans l'âme*' [he was 'sick at heart'] when the picture was brought back and that he would sell the last shirt off his back before he would sell it! When we left Giverny in 1909, it was still hanging on the walls of his studio, a charming view of the church at Vétheuil, seen across the Seine on a misty winter's day with cakes of ice floating in the water. It is called *Les glaçons*, and is a most exquisite and exact portrayal of nature. One can only wonder why Monsieur Faure's friends laughed at it, and laugh at them in return.

Monet was most appreciative of the work of his contemporaries, several of whom had been less successful than he in obtaining recognition during their lifetime. In his bedroom, a large room over the studio, he had quite a gallery of the work of such

Monet and Alice during a voyage to Venice, feeding pigeons in the Piazza San Marco, c1908
Wildenstein Institute Archives, Paris

Impressionists as Renoir, Camille Pissarro, a most expressive picture of peasant women done during his pointillist period, a charming hillside with old houses on it by Cézanne, about whom Monet had many interesting things to say.

There was also a delightful picture by Berthe Morisot, the one woman of his set I have heard him praise. And richly she deserved it! I met her only once, at Miss Cassatt's, she was a most beautiful white-haired old lady. She died shortly afterward and Monet and Pissarro worked like beavers hanging her posthumous exhibition at Durand-Ruel's. It was a wonderful exhibition, and I think that the picture Monet owned was bought at this show. Monet was a most devoted friend to dear Pissarro, whom no one could help loving, and after his death he acquired another of his pictures which was kept in the studio and praised to all visitors.

Monet was one of the early admirers of Japanese prints, many of which decorated his living room walls. The walls were painted a light yellow which showed up the prints' delicate tonality admirably, and also the blue china which was the only other decoration in the room. It was a charming room with long windows opening on the garden, windows left open at mealtimes to permit countless sparrows to come in and pick up a friendly crumb. He pointed out to me one little fellow that had lost a leg and had come for three years in succession.

This serious, intense man had a most beautiful tenderness and love for children, birds and flowers, and this warmth of nature showed in his wonderful, warm smile, a smile no friend of his can ever forget. His fondness for flowers amounted to a passion, and when he was not painting, much of his time was spent working in his garden.

One autumn we were in Giverny I remember there was much interest in a new greenhouse. The heating must have been on a new plan, for when the plants were all in place and the heater first lit, Monet decided he must watch it throughout the night, to be sure everything went smoothly. Once his mind was made up there was little hope of moving him, so Madame Monet speedily acquiesced and made her own plans for sharing his vigil. When the daughters heard of this there were loud outcries. What! Let their parents sit up all night with no one to look after them? Unheard-of neglect! It ended with the whole family spending the night with the gloxinias. Fortunately the heater was impeccably efficient so the adventure did not have to be repeated.

When I first knew Monet, and for some years later, he used a wheelbarrow to carry about his numerous canvases. Later on he had two beautiful motor cars to take him about, but that is not the measure of his achievement, nor is it to be measured by the fact that he lived to see the French government build proper housing under his directions for his latest pictures. His real success lies in his having opened the eyes not merely of France but of the whole world to the real aspect of nature and having led them along the path of beauty and truth and light.

1 John La Farge (1835–1910) was an American painter and stained-glass designer who had studied in France with Thomas Couture. He was married to Lilla Cabot Perry's sister-in-law

2 See Roger Fry, 'Henri-Matisse' (1935) in Christopher Reed ed, *A Roger Fry reader*, The University of Chicago Press, 1996, p 403: 'In Impressionism the eye, by an act of supreme renunciation, succeeds in purifying itself of all those inductions from the visual image which the whole business of life requires us to make before we leave our cradles. In Impressionism the artist deliberately recovers the long lost naïveté of the new born baby's.'

3 In notes for a talk that Lilla Cabot Perry gave to art students in the Museum of Fine Arts in Boston in Jan 1894, she emphasised that Monet 'can sit down with his nose to his canvas, and can see almost how his paintings are going to look' – quoted by Steven Z Levine, *Monet and his critics*, Garland Publishing, New York 1976, p 157. Similar stories had been told about J M W Turner: during varnishing days at the Royal Academy, Turner's colleagues were astonished to observe that he never stepped back to judge the effect of what he was painting – he instinctively knew what the effect at a distance would be

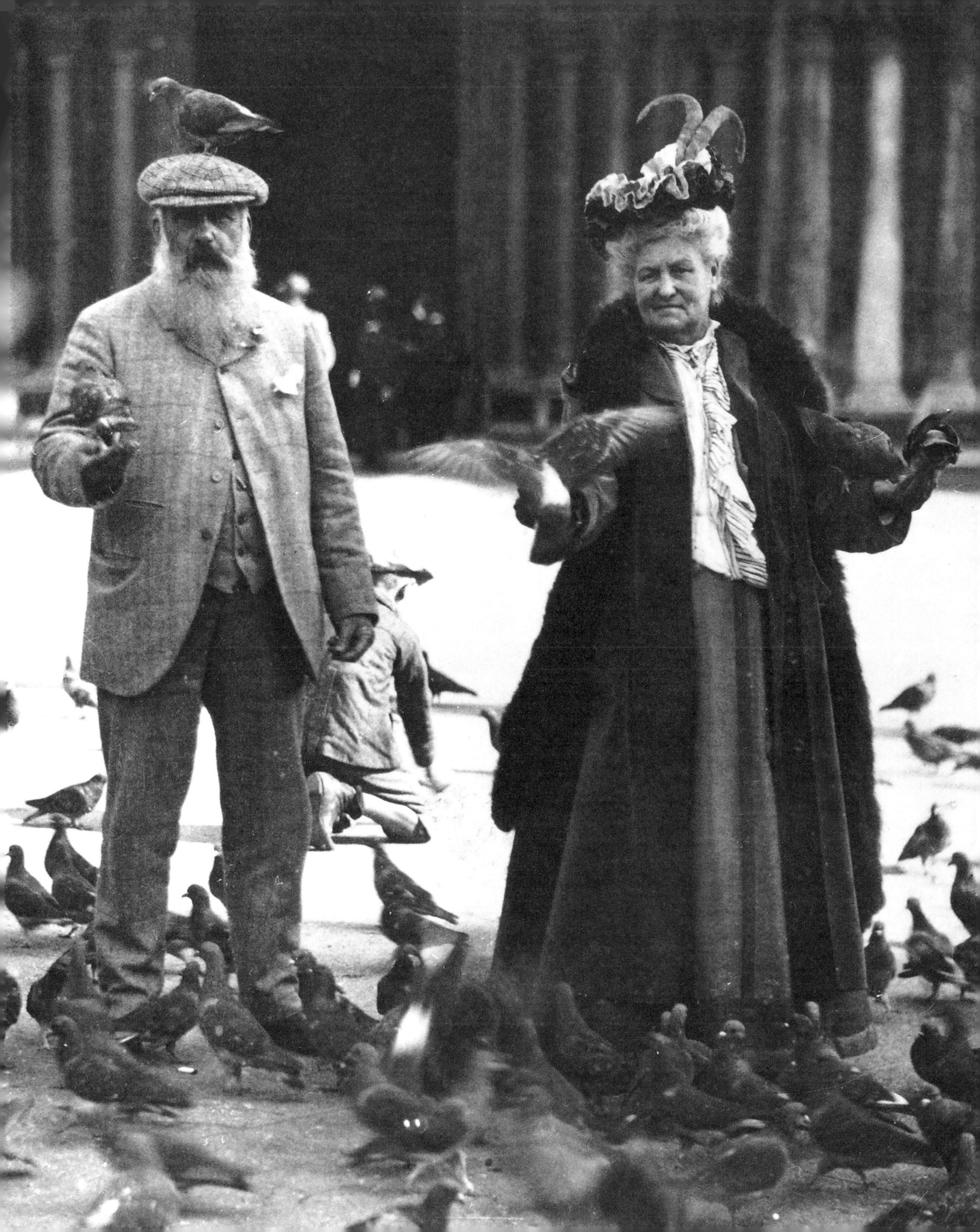

THE ARTISTS

Biographical notes

Claude Monet

born Paris 1840, died Giverny 1926

Monet's prodigious talent was first recognised by Eugène Boudin, whom he met in Le Havre in 1858. Boudin encouraged Monet to give up drawing caricatures and to paint out of doors, which he did in the company of both Boudin and Johan Barthold Jongkind. Monet's short tenure (1862–64) in the atelier of Charles Gleyre (1808–74) was decisive, for not only did Gleyre encourage his students to go their own way, but it was there that Monet met Frédéric Bazille (1841–70), Pierre-Auguste Renoir, and Alfred Sisley. After limited success at the Salon during the 1860s, Monet became a leader of a group that exhibited independently of the Salon. They became known as the Impressionists after the title of one of Monet's canvases. Monet chose to live not in Paris but in the suburbs ever farther from the art capital, drawing on his surroundings for motifs. For additional challenges he travelled to the coasts of France, as well as to Norway, London and Venice. He was a canny businessman, playing dealers against one another and carefully orchestrating his exhibitions and their attendant publicity. He moved to Giverny, 60 kilometres northwest of Paris, in 1883 and in 1890 bought property there. He worked on the grounds for decades, diverting streams and maintaining a water garden. The area around Giverny and his gardens provided the subjects for his series paintings of single motifs.

Eugène Boudin

born Honfleur 1824, died Deauville 1898

The son of a ship's captain, Boudin opened a framing and stationery shop with a partner in Le Havre in 1844. As was the custom before commercial art galleries were established, he exhibited in his window paintings by local artists. Constant Troyon and Jean-François Millet were two of these, and they convinced him to try painting himself. The local art society gave him a scholarship to study art in Paris. At its end, in 1854, he returned to the Normandy coast and painted directly from nature. He met the young painter Claude Monet in 1858 and convinced him, as he himself had been persuaded, to paint out of doors. In 1859 he became friends with Gustave Courbet and in 1862 with Johan Barthold Jongkind, whose fresh vision of marine painting made a significant impact on him. Boudin's works were accepted regularly at the Salon beginning in 1859, and he showed several works in the first Impressionist exhibition in 1874. His reputation was secure after 1871, and he began to travel, visiting Belgium, the Netherlands, the south of France and Venice. Despite his popular success and financial security (after 1883 the Parisian dealer Paul Durand-Ruel held exclusive rights to his output), Boudin received official honours only late in life – a third-class medal at the Salon of 1881, a gold medal at the 1889 Universal Exposition, and was made a Chevalier of the Legion of Honour in 1892.

Paul Cézanne

born Aix-en-Provence 1839, died Aix-en-Provence 1906

Cézanne studied law for three years in his native Aix; at the same time, however, he took lessons in the free city drawing school. When his father finally relented and allowed him to go to study art in Paris in the summer of 1861, he was unhappy there and returned home where he worked in his father's bank. Restless, he was back in Paris in 1862 and enrolled again at the Académie Suisse. He showed in the Salon des Refusés of 1863 and came to know Camille Pissarro, Claude Monet, Pierre-Auguste Renoir and others. After 1864 he would divide his time between Paris and Aix. Cézanne was able, thanks to his prosperous family, to devote himself singlemindedly to his art. Cézanne's early paintings are marked by romantic, violent and erotic themes and a deep regard for the old masters. Pissarro introduced Cézanne to painting out of doors and to a new way of applying paint. Although he showed with the independent artists in 1874 and 1877, his vision of structure and solidity was at odds with their sensuousness and spontaneity. He withdrew from them physically and artistically, living in Aix and no longer showing his work in the capital. Only in 1895 did Ambroise Vollard hold an exhibition of his work in Paris, an event that galvanised young artists. The 1905 exhibition of more than 30 of his canvases at the Salon d'Automne established Cézanne's status as a role model for 20th-century painters.

Camille Corot

born Paris 1796, died Paris 1875

After showing himself to be uninterested in business, Corot was given money by his parents to devote himself to painting. He studied in the ateliers of Jean-Victor Bertin (1767–1842) and Achille-Etna Michallon (1796–1822) and then, from 1825 to 1828, visited Italy. There he painted small studies out of doors, something he had already been doing in France. He had a successful Salon career, showing in every exhibition from 1827 to the posthumous presentation of his works at the Salon of 1875. Up to about 1850 he showed composed landscapes, often with subjects drawn from the Bible or classical mythology. After mid-century, however, he developed a softer style, with diaphanous foliage and indeterminate subject matter. This, often called his poetic or lyrical style, became extremely popular. Corot was an inveterate traveller, returning to Italy in 1834 and again in 1843, and visiting Switzerland, the Netherlands and England. He stayed in Paris during the winters, working in his studio, but during the summer months he crisscrossed northern France, staying with his many friends and painting out of doors. He was a close friend of Charles-François Daubigny and Jean-François Millet; Antoine Chintreuil and François-Louis Français considered themselves his pupils and he gave advice to Berthe Morisot (1841–95), Alfred Sisley and Camille Pissarro. Of an older generation, with a classical bent, Corot never entirely understood the Impressionists, although his commitment to painting his impressions of nature allied him to the younger painters.

Gustave Courbet

born Ornans, Franche-Comté 1819,
died La Tour de Peilz, Switzerland 1877

Courbet went to Paris in 1839, ostensibly to study law. He spent time at the Académie Suisse but should be considered self-taught, having spent much time in the Louvre learning from the old masters, particularly the Dutch, Venetian and Spanish schools. His submissions to the Salon in the early 1850s, such as *Burial at Ornans* (Musée d'Orsay, Paris), gave rise to controversy because of their use of everyday subject matter on a heroic scale. In 1855 he erected his Pavilion of Realism within the grounds of the Universal Exposition, a move that impressed younger artists for its independence from official sanction. In it he showed 40 paintings and two drawings and accompanied them with a Realist manifesto; these actions made him the chief proponent of Realist painting. After this time his art became less polemical, and he painted more nudes, portraits and landscapes. Critic Edmond About explained that Courbet 'affects not to choose, but to paint all that he meets, without preferring one thing before another ... His theory may be thus given: all objects are equal before painting' (*Nos artistes au Salon de 1857*). Courbet, like many other artists, painted on the Normandy coast, first going to Le Havre in 1859, where he met Eugène Boudin. Courbet's involvement with the Paris Commune and his alleged role in the destruction of the Vendôme Column led him to move to Switzerland in 1873.

Edgar Degas

born Paris 1834, died Paris 1917

Degas's father, a banker interested in music and art, did not object much when his son wanted to pursue a career in art instead of law. Degas first studied with Félix-Joseph Barrias (1841–1905) and then, more importantly, with Louis Lamothe (1822–69), a pupil of Jean-Auguste-Dominique Ingres (1780–1867). Ingres's supple draftsmanship and classical orientation were deciding factors in Degas's early development. From 1856 to 1859 Degas visited Italy, where he copied ancient and Renaissance works in Naples and Florence (in both cities he stayed with relatives) and in Rome. On his return to Paris he painted portraits and scenes from history and modern life and was accepted at the Salon from 1865 to 1870. Increasingly, however, he became a member of groups of independent-minded artists of a Realist or naturalist aesthetic, who gathered with Degas's friend Edouard Manet at the Café de la Nouvelle Athènes and the Café Guerbois. Degas exhibited with the group known as the Impressionists in all but one of their eight shows, sharing with them an interest in Japanese prints, subjects of modern life and innovation. Degas distinguished himself from almost all other progressive artists of the later 19th century by the combination of his devotion to the figure and his constant technical experimentation. His increasingly poor eyesight led him to work in bolder forms, as well as in the media of sculpture, poetry and photography.

Utagawa Hiroshige

born Edo 1797, died Edo 1858

Utagawa Hiroshige (also known as Andō Hiroshige) was born Andō Tokutarō, the eldest son of a samurai fire-fighting official in Edo (now Tokyo). In 1811 he entered the workshop of his most significant teacher, the ukiyo-e artist Utagawa Toyohiro (1773–1828), from whom he derived his artistic name. Hiroshige's career was concomitant with a new wave of interest in landscape prints, the genre he came to epitomise both in Japan and in the West, along with his near-contemporary Katsushika Hokusai (1760–1849). Hiroshige's first series to meet with high acclaim was *Famous views of the eastern capital* c1826, celebrated for its unusual colouring and distinctive views of his native Edo. He followed this with another landscape series in 1833–34: *Fifty-three stations of the Tōkaidō road*, composed of views of the Eastern Sea Road that linked Edo with the capital Kyoto. Several other landscape series followed, including *Famous places in the sixty-odd provinces [of Japan]* in 1853 and *One hundred famous views of Edo* 1856. Hiroshige employed the intricate *nishiki-e* (polychrome printing) technique, a complex process involving printing colours from separate blocks. His richly coloured, geometric compositions were highly influential amongst French artists from the 1870s onwards: his prints featured in Monet's collection and Vincent van Gogh (1853–90) famously made copies after two of Hiroshige's *One hundred famous views of Edo*.

Johan Barthold Jongkind

born Lattrop, Netherlands 1819, died Côte Saint-André, Isère 1891

Jongkind's first teacher was the foremost Dutch landscape painter of the time, Andreas Schelfhout (1787–1870), with whom he studied in The Hague. A government stipend allowed Jongkind in 1846 to go to Paris for further study under Eugène Isabey. Jongkind made watercolours and sketches in the outdoors, from which he composed his oil paintings in the studio. Early public success (acceptance at the Salon, a third-class medal in 1852, several purchases by the state, and support from the dealer Pierre Firmin-Martin) was cut short by the withdrawal of the Dutch stipend in 1853. Jongkind fell into debt, drank heavily, and was forced to return to the Netherlands in 1855. A sale of works by Jongkind's artist friends in 1860 realised enough money to allow him to return to Paris. Once back, he met Madame Joséphine Fesser-Borrhée. Her friendship and the support of her family literally gave Jongkind a new lease on life. He lived with them until his death (he died at their family home). They travelled frequently to the Normandy coast, where in 1862 he met the young Claude Monet. He also returned to the Netherlands and visited the south of France and the Dauphiné. Jongkind's art was a path-breaking combination of compositional structures taken from the land- and seascape traditions of 17th-century Dutch art and a careful study of specific light conditions and a free manner of painting.

Edouard Manet

born Paris 1832, died Paris 1883

Manet's father, a wealthy magistrate, first resisted his son's desire to paint. In 1850, Manet entered the atelier of Thomas Couture, where he spent six years, supplementing his training by studying the old masters and Velázquez. Manet's unconventional flatness, bright tones and contemporary subjects shocked a public accustomed to the smooth surfaces and classical motifs of Academic painting. The jury rejected his first Salon entry in 1859, but awarded him an honourable mention in 1861. In 1863, all of his entries were rejected and exhibited instead at the Salon des Refusés, including the notorious *Le Déjeuner sur l'herbe*. Manet frequently showed his work privately and earned success at later Salons and in private galleries. His *Olympia* was shown at the Salon in 1865, attracting moral outrage for its modern, frank and unidealised handling of the nude subject, despite support from critics such as Charles Baudelaire and Emile Zola. Though admired by younger artists, including Monet, Manet never exhibited with the Impressionists. In the 1870s, he introduced Impressionist colour and brush-work to his work. By the late 1870s his output diminished due to ill health, but he completed one last major work in 1882, *A bar at the Folies-Bergère*, which was hung in the Salon that same year. Manet was made a Chevalier of the Legion of Honour in 1881.

Jean-François Millet

born Gruchy near Cherbourg, Manche 1814, died Barbizon 1875

Millet took lessons in Cherbourg from the portrait painter Bon Dumouchel (1807–46) and the history painter Lucien-Théophile Langlois (1803–45). A municipal stipend from Cherbourg underwrote his study in Paris in the studio of Paul Delaroche (1797–1856) in 1837, but the stipend was withdrawn when Millet left that studio following his failure in the Prix de Rome competition. He spent the 1840s painting portraits and genre and pastoral scenes. In 1847 he met the collector Alfred Sensier, who became his most constant supporter and, later, biographer. Millet used money from a government commission to flee the cholera epidemic of 1849; he settled in Barbizon, a village in the forest of Fontainebleau. There he concentrated on the pastoral themes that brought him fame. In Barbizon he was closely associated with Théodore Rousseau, Constant Troyon and Narcisse Virgile Diaz de la Peña. Rousseau encouraged Millet to paint landscapes, which he did increasingly after 1863. His paintings sold well in the last decade of his life, and he received many public and private commissions. Although Parisians tended to assume he was uneducated, Millet's early schooling with two village priests inculcated a thorough knowledge of Latin literature and a love of reading.

Camille Pissarro

born Saint-Thomas, Danish West Indies 1830, died Paris 1903

Pissarro learned to draw when his parents sent him for schooling in Paris in 1841. After an unsettled period during which he first worked in his father's store and then went to Venezuela with the Danish painter Fritz Melbye (1826–96), Pissarro returned to Paris in 1855, in time to see the World's Fair. He enrolled in both the Ecole des Beaux-Arts and the less regimented Académie Suisse. Pissarro asked Camille Corot for advice, and aspects of the older painter's style can be seen in Pissarro's silvery palette and soft touch through the mid 1860s. After that time the more assertive style of Gustave Courbet is evident. After sporadic success at the Salon, Pissarro was eager to find alternative exhibition venues. He was the only artist to participate in all eight of the Impressionist group shows. Pissarro preferred living in the country to the city, and he settled in Pontoise as early as 1866, moving from there to increasingly rural locales. By all accounts a generous and kindly man, Pissarro counselled Paul Cézanne in the early 1870s and was himself influenced by the younger painters Georges Seurat (1859–91) and Paul Signac in the later 1880s. Although success came late to Pissarro, he continued to find challenging motifs. He also left an impressive body of prints, many of which are technically innovative.

Pierre-Auguste Renoir

born Limoges 1841, died Cagnes 1919

At age 13 Renoir was apprenticed to porcelain painters in Paris, where his family had moved in 1844. He worked for a manufacturer of window blinds and other decorative objects in 1858. In 1860 he received permission to copy paintings in the Louvre. In 1862 he entered the Ecole des Beaux-Arts and the studio of Charles Gleyre (1808–74), where he met the progressively minded painters Frédéric Bazille (1841–70), Alfred Sisley and Claude Monet. They painted together during the summers in the forest of Fontainebleau. Renoir showed in the Impressionist exhibitions of 1874, 1876, 1877 and 1882, but he became increasingly drawn to the classical tradition, and also submitted to the Salon regularly. His primary subject matter was the figure, and he also experimented with portraits, genre scenes and images of female bathers. In the early 1880s he travelled to Italy, North Africa and the south of France. Renaissance art and the light of the south prompted him to adopt a brighter, warmer palette, giving increased emphasis to line and structure. Increasingly crippled with arthritis, he wintered in the south of France. In 1907 he bought a property in Cagnes.

Théodore Rousseau

born Paris 1812, died Barbizon 1867

Rousseau received traditional training first from a cousin and then from Jean-Charles-Joseph Rémond (1795–1875) and Guillaume Guillon-Lethière (1760–1832). He was already painting in the forest of Fontainebleau in the late 1820s and travelled to the Auvergne, Normandy, Switzerland and the Jura. His work was first accepted at the Salon in 1831. Rousseau visited Barbizon in 1836, which was also the year that the Salon jury first rejected his submissions; he was again rejected in 1838, 1839 and 1840. He chose not to submit again, showing only in the unjuried Salon of 1849, when he won a first-class medal. By then his work had attracted the attention of the writers Charles Baudelaire and Georges Sand and, importantly, the critic Théophile Thoré. Rousseau divided his time between Barbizon, where Jean-François Millet was his closest friend, and Paris, where he kept a studio and where he could remain involved in the art world. Barbizon and its environs became his chief subject matter, and his compositions were influenced by 17th-century Dutch landscapes and Japanese prints. In 1866 the dealers Durand-Ruel and Brame bought his early sketches, which gave him sufficient money to live; he was appointed president of the jury for the Universal Exposition of 1867.

Alfred Sisley

born Paris 1839, died Moret-sur-Loing 1899

The son of British parents living in Paris, Sisley retained his British citizenship his whole life. He went to London in the late 1850s to prepare himself for a career in business, benefiting from the opportunity to visit museums where he studied the work of British painters, particularly John Constable (1776–1837). On his return to Paris his father was amenable to his studying art and he entered Charles Gleyre's (1808–74) studio in 1860 through an introduction from Frédéric Bazille (1841–70). There he met Claude Monet and Pierre-Auguste Renoir and with them painted in the countryside around Paris, especially the forest of Fontainebleau. He had limited success at the Salon in the late 1860s and participated in four of the seven Impressionist group shows. He moved often in the 1870s, but remained close to Paris. However in 1880 he settled in the area where the Loing river empties into the Seine, beyond Barbizon and Fontainebleau, where he remained until his death. The Franco-Prussian War ruined his father financially, and from 1871 on Sisley had to support himself, his mistress and their two sons by the sale of his paintings. Despite a coterie of collectors, the good services of Durand-Ruel and Georges Petit, and participation in major exhibitions, Sisley never achieved economic success.

Auguste Toulmouche

born Nantes 1829, died Paris 1890

Toulmouche was a successful genre painter who briefly mentored the young Monet. He exhibited his work at the Salon from 1848 onwards, receiving numerous accolades, including a silver medal at the Salon of 1861 and a bronze medal at the 1878 Universal Exposition. Married to a cousin of Monet's aunt Lecadre, Toulmouche accepted Monet into his atelier in 1862. In the same year he encouraged Monet to enter the studio of the Swiss history painter Charles Gleyre (1808–74), under whom he had also studied. Along with others of Gleyre's students, Toulmouche was briefly associated with the classicising *néo-grec* style, led by Jean-Léon Gérôme (1824–1904). Although he also produced portraits and landscapes, he is primarily known for his intimate interior scenes of domestic life. His paintings exhibit the polished, Academic style typical of Gleyre and his followers. In 1870 he was made a Chevalier of the Legion of Honour.

Constant Troyon

born Sèvres 1810, died Paris 1865

Troyon was one of many 19th-century painters who, like Pierre-Auguste Renoir, was trained as a porcelain decorator. Although he exhibited successfully at the Salon from 1833 with conventional landscape subjects, he was encouraged by Théodore Rousseau and Paul Huet, whom he met in 1843, to paint more directly. Since Troyon had already been painting out of doors, this advice was a validation. Crucial to Troyon's career was a trip to the Netherlands in 1847. In Amsterdam he saw the animal paintings of Albert Cuyp (1620–91) and Paulus Potter (1625–54), and began to add animals to his landscapes. These became very popular with the public not only in France but in England, the Netherlands, Germany and Austria as well. To meet the demand, Troyon hired assistants to fill in the backgrounds so that he could concentrate on the animals, be they cows, sheep or dogs. Troyon also painted pure landscapes and in his later years frequently visited the Normandy coast. There, freed from market demands, he painted in a more exploratory fashion, recording variations in light. He was the first of the artists associated with Barbizon and rural French subjects to be awarded the cross of the Legion of Honour, in 1849.

LIST OF WORKS

Monet's early years: sources of inspiration

1
Théodore Rousseau
Gathering wood in the forest of Fontainebleau c1850–60
oil on canvas, 54.6 x 65.4 cm
Museum of Fine Arts, Boston,
bequest of Mrs David P Kimball
23.99

2
Claude Monet
Woodgatherers at the edge of the forest c1863
oil on panel, 59.7 x 90.2 cm
Museum of Fine Arts, Boston,
bequest of Mrs David P Kimball
1974.325

3
Jean-Baptiste-Camille Corot
Morning near Beauvais c1855–65
oil on canvas, 35.9 x 41.6 cm
Museum of Fine Arts, Boston,
Julia Cheney Edwards Collection
39.668

4
Jean-Baptiste-Camille Corot
Twilight 1845–60
oil on canvas, 50.2 x 37.1 cm
Museum of Fine Arts, Boston,
bequest of Mrs Henry Lee Higginson
35.1163

5
Jean-François Millet
Washerwomen c1855
oil on canvas, 43.5 x 53.7 cm
Museum of Fine Arts, Boston,
gift of Mrs Martin Brimmer
06.2422

6
Jean-François Millet
Priory at Vauville, Normandy 1872–74
oil on canvas, 89.9 x 116.8 cm
Museum of Fine Arts, Boston,
gift of Quincy Adams Shaw through
Quincy Adams Shaw Jr and
Mrs Marian Shaw Haughton
17.1532

7
Constant Troyon
Field outside Paris 1845–51
oil on paperboard, 27 x 45.5 cm
Museum of Fine Arts, Boston,
Henry C and Martha B Angell
Collection
19.117

8
Gustave Courbet
Landscape with stag 1873
oil on canvas, 65.5 x 81.6 cm
Art Gallery of New South Wales,
purchased 1997
194.1997

9
Auguste Toulmouche
Reading lesson 1865
oil on canvas, 36.5 x 27.6 cm
Museum of Fine Arts, Boston,
gift of Francis A Foster
24.1

10
Eugène Louis Boudin
Fashionable figures on the beach 1865
oil on panel, 35.5 x 57.5 cm
Museum of Fine Arts, Boston,
gift of Mr and Mrs John A Wilson
1974.565

11
Eugène Louis Boudin
The beach 1864
oil on panel, 30.9 x 47.1 cm
Art Gallery of New South Wales,
purchased 1926
1123

12
Johan Barthold Jongkind
Harbour scene in Holland 1868
oil on canvas, 41.9 x 55.9 cm
Museum of Fine Arts, Boston,
gift of Count Cecil Pecci-Blunt
61.1242

13
Claude Monet
Rue de la Bavole, Honfleur c1864
oil on canvas, 55.9 x 61 cm
Museum of Fine Arts, Boston,
bequest of John T Spaulding
48.580

14
Edouard Manet
Basket of fruit c1864
oil on canvas, 37.8 x 44.4 cm
Museum of Fine Arts, Boston,
bequest of John T Spaulding
48.576

Monet and early Impressionism

15
Claude Monet
Snow at Argenteuil c1874
oil on canvas, 54.6 x 73.7 cm
Museum of Fine Arts, Boston,
bequest of Anna Perkins Rogers
21.1329

16
Claude Monet
Meadow with poplars c1875
oil on canvas, 54.6 x 65.4 cm
Museum of Fine Arts, Boston,
bequest of David P Kimball in memory
of his wife Clara Bertram Kimball
23.505

17
Edgar Degas
Racehorses at Longchamp 1871
(possibly reworked in 1874)
oil on canvas, 34 x 41.9 cm
Museum of Fine Arts, Boston,
S A Denio Collection – Sylvanus
Adams Denio Fund and general income
03.1034

18
Paul Cézanne
The pond c1877–79
oil on canvas, 47 x 56.2 cm
Museum of Fine Arts, Boston,
Tompkins Collection – Arthur
Gordon Tompkins Fund
48.244

19
Pierre-Auguste Renoir
Woman with a parasol and small child on a sunlit hillside c1874–76
oil on canvas, 47 x 56.2 cm
Museum of Fine Arts, Boston,
bequest of John T Spaulding
48.593

20
Claude Monet
Camille Monet and a child in the artist's garden in Argenteuil 1875
oil on canvas, 55.3 x 64.7 cm
Museum of Fine Arts, Boston,
anonymous gift in memory of
Mr and Mrs Edwin S Webster
1976.833

21
Camille Pissarro
Pontoise, the road to Gisors in winter 1873
oil on canvas, 59.7 x 73.7 cm
Museum of Fine Arts, Boston,
bequest of John T Spaulding
48.587

22
Alfred Sisley
Waterworks at Marly c1876
oil on canvas, 46.5 x 61.8 cm
Museum of Fine Arts, Boston,
gift of Miss Olive Simes
45.662

Monet and the triumph of Impressionism: the 1880s

23
Claude Monet
Rough weather at Etretat 1883
oil on canvas, 65 x 81 cm
National Gallery of Victoria,
Felton Bequest 1913
582-2

24
Claude Monet
Fisherman's cottage on the cliffs at Varengeville 1882
oil on canvas, 60.6 x 81.6 cm
Museum of Fine Arts, Boston,
bequest of Anna Perkins Rogers
21.1331

25
Claude Monet
Cap Martin, near Menton 1884
oil on canvas, 67.2 x 81.6 cm
Museum of Fine Arts, Boston,
Juliana Cheney Edwards Collection
25.128

26
Claude Monet
Cap d'Antibes, mistral 1888
oil on canvas, 66 x 81.3 cm
Museum of Fine Arts, Boston,
bequest of Dr Arthur Tracy Cabot
42.542

27
Claude Monet
The fort of Antibes 1888
oil on canvas, 65.4 x 81 cm
Museum of Fine Arts, Boston,
anonymous gift
1978.634

28
Pierre-Auguste Renoir
The Seine at Chatou 1881
oil on canvas, 73.3 x 92.4 cm
Museum of Fine Arts, Boston,
gift of Arthur Brewster Emmons
19.771

29
Alfred Sisley
La Croix-Blanche at Saint-Mammès 1884
oil on canvas, 65.4 x 92.4 cm
Museum of Fine Arts, Boston,
Juliana Cheney Edwards Collection
39.680

30
Claude Monet
Vétheuil 1878
oil on canvas, 60 x 81 cm
National Gallery of Victoria,
Felton Bequest 1937
406-4

31
Claude Monet
Flower beds at Vétheuil 1881
oil on canvas, 92.1 x 73.3 cm
Museum of Fine Arts, Boston,
John Pickering Lyman Collection,
gift of Miss Theodora Lyman
19.1313

32
Claude Monet
Meadow with haystacks near Giverny 1885
oil on canvas, 74 x 93.5 cm
Museum of Fine Arts, Boston,
bequest of Dr Arthur Tracy Cabot
42.541

33
Claude Monet
Meadow at Giverny 1886
oil on canvas, 92.1 x 81.6 cm
Museum of Fine Arts, Boston,
Julia Cheney Edwards Collection
39.670

34
Claude Monet
Poplars at Giverny 1887
oil on canvas, 74.3 x 91.4 cm
Private collection, courtesy
Museum of Fine Arts, Boston

Monet and Japanese art

35
Utagawa Hiroshige I
Publisher: Takenouchi Magohachi
Kanbara: night snow
second state, from the series *Fifty-three stations of the Tōkaidō road*, also known as the *First Tōkaidō* or *Great Tōkaidō*
Japan, Edo period, c1833–34
woodblock print; ink and colour on paper, approx 24.5 x 35 cm
Museum of Fine Arts, Boston,
William Sturgis Bigelow Collection
11.17295

36
Claude Monet
Boulevard Saint-Denis, Argenteuil, in winter 1875
oil on canvas, 60.9 x 81.6 cm
Museum of Fine Arts, Boston,
gift of Richard Saltonstall
1978.633

37
Utagawa Hiroshige I
Publisher: Takenouchi Magohachi
Yokkaichi: Mie River
from the series *Fifty-three stations of the Tōkaidō road*, also known as the *First Tōkaidō* or *Great Tōkaidō*
Japan, Edo period, c1833–34
woodblock print; ink and colour on paper, 24.5 x 35 cm
Museum of Fine Arts, Boston,
William Sturgis Bigelow Collection
11.30167

38
Claude Monet
Seacoast at Trouville 1881
oil on canvas, 60.7 x 81.3 cm
Museum of Fine Arts, Boston,
John Pickering Lyman Collection,
gift of Miss Theodora Lyman
19.1314

39
Utagawa Hiroshige I
Publisher: Koshimuraya Heisuke
Kai Province: Monkey Bridge
from the series *Famous places in the sixty-odd provinces [of Japan]*
Japan, Edo period, 1853
woodblock print, ink and colour on paper, 37 x 25.4 cm
Museum of Fine Arts, Boston,
William Sturgis Bigelow Collection
11.26224

Monet in his garden at Giverny 1923–24

40
Utagawa Hiroshige I
Publisher: Takenouchi Magohachi
Hakone: view of the lake
from the series *Fifty-three stations of the Tōkaidō road*, also known as the *First Tōkaidō* or *Great Tōkaidō*
Japan, Edo period, c1833–34
woodblock print; ink and colour on paper, 24.7 x 34.8 cm
Museum of Fine Arts, Boston, William Sturgis Bigelow Collection
11.26106

41
Claude Monet
Port-Goulphar, Belle-Ile 1887
oil on canvas, 81 x 65 cm
Art Gallery of New South Wales, purchased 1949
8356

42
Utagawa Hiroshige I
Publisher: Uoya Eikichi
Inside Kameido Tenjin shrine
from the series *One hundred famous views of Edo*
Japan, Edo period, 1856
woodblock print; ink and colour on paper, 35.6 x 24.2 cm
Museum of Fine Arts, Boston, gift of Dr G S Amsden
52.1423

43
Claude Monet
The waterlily pond 1900
oil on canvas, 90.2 x 92.7 cm
Museum of Fine Arts, Boston, given in memory of Governor Alvan T Fuller by the Fuller Foundation
61.959

Monet's series

44
Claude Monet
Ravine of the Petite Creuse 1889
oil on canvas, 76.2 x 92.7 cm
Private collection, courtesy Museum of Fine Arts, Boston

45
Claude Monet
Valley of the Petite Creuse 1889
oil on canvas, 65.4 x 81.3 cm
Museum of Fine Arts, Boston, bequest of David P Kimball in memory of his wife Clara Bertram Kimball
23.541

46
Claude Monet
Valley of the Creuse (sunlight effect) 1889
oil on canvas, 65.1 x 92.4 cm
Museum of Fine Arts, Boston, Juliana Cheney Edwards Collection
25.107

47
Claude Monet
Grainstack/Haystack (sunset) 1891
oil on canvas, 73.3 x 92.7 cm
Museum of Fine Arts, Boston, Juliana Cheney Edwards Collection
25.112

48
Claude Monet
Haystacks, midday 1890
oil on canvas, 65.6 x 100.6 cm
National Gallery of Australia, purchased 1979
79.16

49
Claude Monet
Rouen Cathedral façade and Tour d'Albane (morning effect)
1894
oil on canvas, 106.1 x 73.9 cm
Museum of Fine Arts, Boston, Tompkins Collection – Arthur Golden Tompkins Fund
24.6

50
Claude Monet
Morning on the Seine, near Giverny 1897
oil on canvas, 81.3 x 92.7 cm
Museum of Fine Arts, Boston, gift of Mrs W Scott Fitz
11.1261

51
Claude Monet
Waterloo Bridge 1899–1901
oil on canvas, 64.7 x 81 cm
Kerry Stokes Collection, Perth

52
Claude Monet
Charing Cross Bridge (overcast day) 1900
oil on canvas, 60.6 x 91.5 cm
Museum of Fine Arts, Boston, given by Janet Hubbard Stevens in memory of her mother, Janet Watson Hubbard
1978.465

Monet and Impressionism after 1900

53
Claude Monet
Waterlilies 1905
oil on canvas, 89.5 x 100.3 cm
Museum of Fine Arts, Boston, gift of Edward Jackson Holmes
39.804

54
Paul Cézanne
Self-portrait with a beret c1898–99
oil on canvas, 64.1 x 53.3 cm
Museum of Fine Arts, Boston, Charles H Bayley Picture and Painting Fund and partial gift of Elizabeth Paine Metcalf
1972.950

55
Edgar Degas
After the bath c1900
charcoal, 73.7 x 59.8 cm
Art Gallery of New South Wales, Margaret Hannah Olley Trust 1994
222.1994

56
Edgar Degas
Dancers in the rehearsal room
1900–05
charcoal with pastel on paper, mounted on cardboard, 45.4 x 85.1 cm
Museum of Fine Arts, Boston, gift of Arthur Wiesenberger
54.1557

57
Pierre-Auguste Renoir
Cast by Valsuani
Small Venus victorious 1913
bronze, 85.1 x 22.9 x 22.9 cm
Museum of Fine Arts, Boston, William Francis Warden Fund
56.259

58
Edgar Degas
Dancer looking at the sole of her right foot 1900–10, cast 1919–21
bronze, cire perdu (lost wax), 48 cm height
Art Gallery of New South Wales, bequest of Paul Haefliger 1982
60.1983

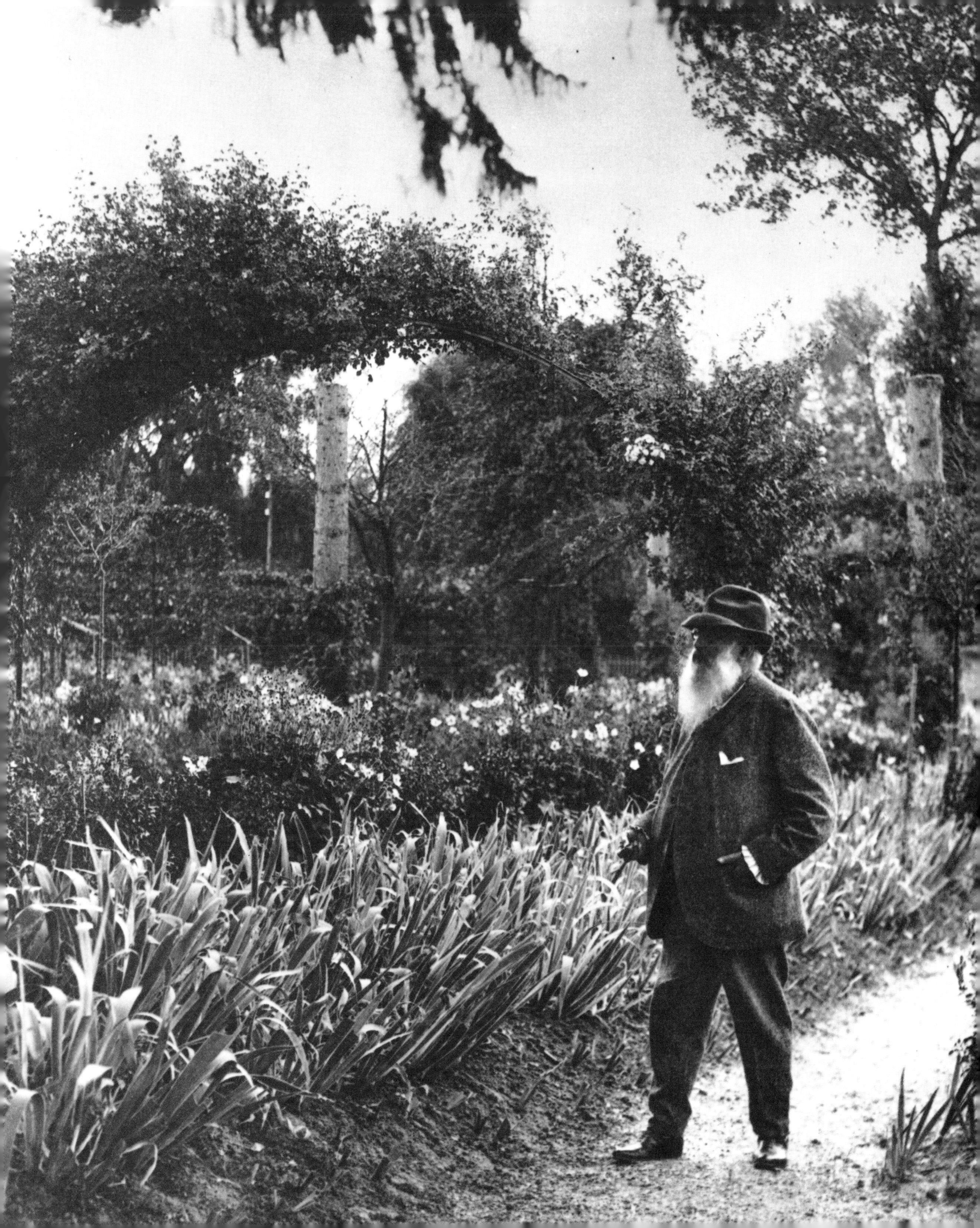

Selected references

Further readings

House, John. *Monet: nature into art*, Yale University Press, New Haven, Connecticut 1986

Kendall, Richard ed. *Monet by himself: paintings, drawings, pastels, letters*, trans Bridget Strevens Romer, Macdonald Orbis, London 1989

Rewald, John. *The history of Impressionism*, 4th rev ed, Museum of Modern Art, New York 1973

Spate, Virginia. *Claude Monet: life and work*, Thames and Hudson, London and Rizzoli International Publications, New York 1992

Stuckey, Charles F ed. *Monet: a retrospective*, H L Levin, New York 1985

Stuckey, Charles F. *Claude Monet, 1840–1926*, exh cat, Thames and Hudson, New York and Art Institute of Chicago, Chicago 1995

Tucker, Paul Hayes. *Claude Monet: life and art*, Yale University Press, New Haven 1995

Wildenstein, Daniel. *Monet: catalogue raisonné*, 4 vols, Taschen, Cologne 1996

Additional works cited

Aitken, Geneviève and Marianne Delafond. *La collection d'estampes japonaises de Claude Monet à Giverny*, Bibliothèque des arts, Lausanne 2003

Bailey, Colin B et al. *Renoir landscapes, 1865–1883*, exh cat, National Gallery, London and Yale University Press, New Haven 2007

Bareau, Juliet Wilson. *Manet, Monet, and the Gare Saint-Lazare*, exh cat, National Gallery of Art, Washington, DC and Yale University Press, New Haven, Connecticut 1998

Berson, Ruth ed. *The new painting: Impressionism, 1874–1886. Documentation*, 2 vols, The Fine Arts Museums of San Francisco, San Francisco 1996

Boggs, Jean Sutherland et al. *Degas*, exh cat, Metropolitan Museum of Art, New York and National Gallery of Canada, Ottawa 1988

Bourguignon, Katherine M ed. *Impressionist Giverny: a colony of artists, 1885–1915*, exh cat, Musée d'Art Americain, Giverny and Terra Foundation for American Art, University of Chicago Press, Chicago 2007

Clarke, Michael. *Corot and the art of landscape*, British Museum Press, London and Cross River Press, New York 1991

Raeburn, Michael ed. *Renoir*, exh cat, Hayward Gallery, Arts Council of Great Britain, London 1985

Herbert, Robert L. 'Method and meaning in Monet', *Art in America* 67, no 5, Sept 1979, pp 90–108

Hirshler, Erica E. *Impressionism abroad: Boston and French painting*, exh cat, Royal Academy of Arts, London and New York 2005

Kendall, Richard ed. *Degas by himself: drawings, prints, paintings, writings*, Macdonald Orbis, London 1987

Loyrette, Henri and Gary Tinterow. *Impressionnisme: les origines, 1859–1869*, exh cat, Réunion des musées nationaux, Paris 1994

Moffett, Charles S et al. *The new painting: Impressionism, 1874–1886*, exh cat, The Fine Arts Museums of San Francisco, San Francisco 1986

Pissarro, Camille. *Correspondance de Camille Pissarro*, ed Janine Bailly-Herzberg, 5 vols, Presses Universitaires de France, Paris 1980–91

Pissarro, Joachim. *Monet and the Mediterranean*, exh cat, Rizzoli, New York in association with Kimbell Art Museum, Fort Worth, Texas 1997

Rewald, John and Frances Weitzenhoffer eds. *Aspects of Monet: a symposium on the artist's life and times*, H N Abrams, New York 1984

Shackelford, George T M, Fronia E Wissman et al. *Impressions of light: the French landscape from Corot to Monet*, exh cat, MFA Publications, Boston 2002

Shone, Richard. *Sisley*, Phaidon, London and Harry N Abrams, New York 1992

Spate, Virginia, Gary Hickey and David Bromfield. *Monet and Japan*, exh cat, National Gallery of Australia, Canberra and University of Washington Press, Seattle 2001

Tinterow, Gary, Michael Pantazzi and Vincent Pomarède. *Corot*, exh cat, Metropolitan Museum of Art, New York 1996

Tucker, Paul Hayes. *Monet in the '90s: the series paintings*, exh cat, Museum of Fine Arts, Boston in association with Yale University Press, Boston 1989

Tucker, Paul Hayes et al. *Monet in the twentieth century*, exh cat, Museum of Fine Arts, Boston and Royal Academy of Arts, London 1998

Vollard, Ambroise. *Degas: an intimate portrait*, trans Randolph Weaver, George Allen and Unwin, London 1928

Wildenstein, Daniel. *Claude Monet: biographie et catalogue raisonné*, 5 vols, La bibliothèque des arts, Lausanne 1974–91

Baillio, Joseph et al. *Claude Monet (1840–1926): a tribute to Daniel Wildenstein and Katia Granoff*, exh cat, Wildenstein and Company, New York 2007

Index

Page numbers in bold refer to the main plates. Other illustrations are indicated by page numbers in italics.

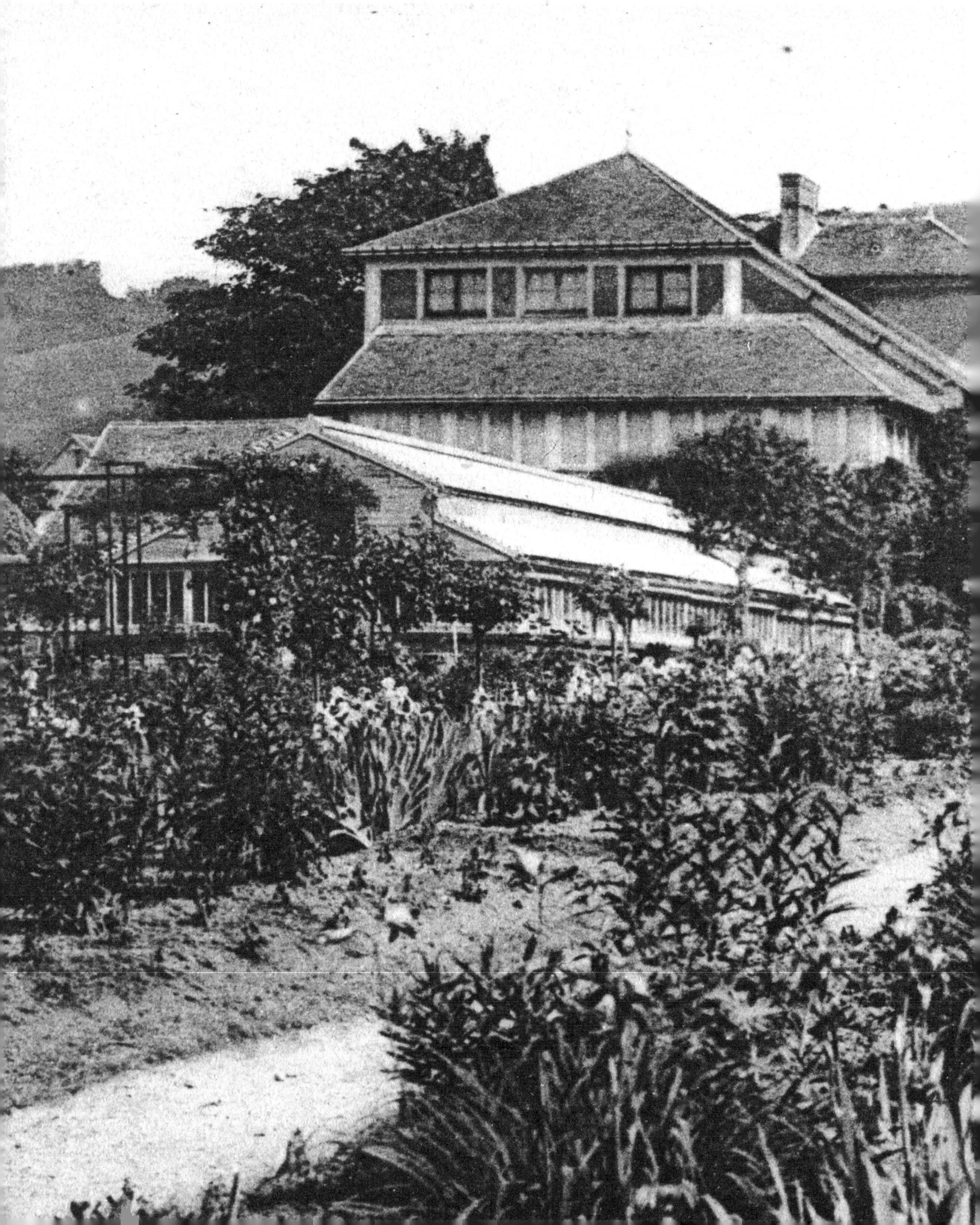

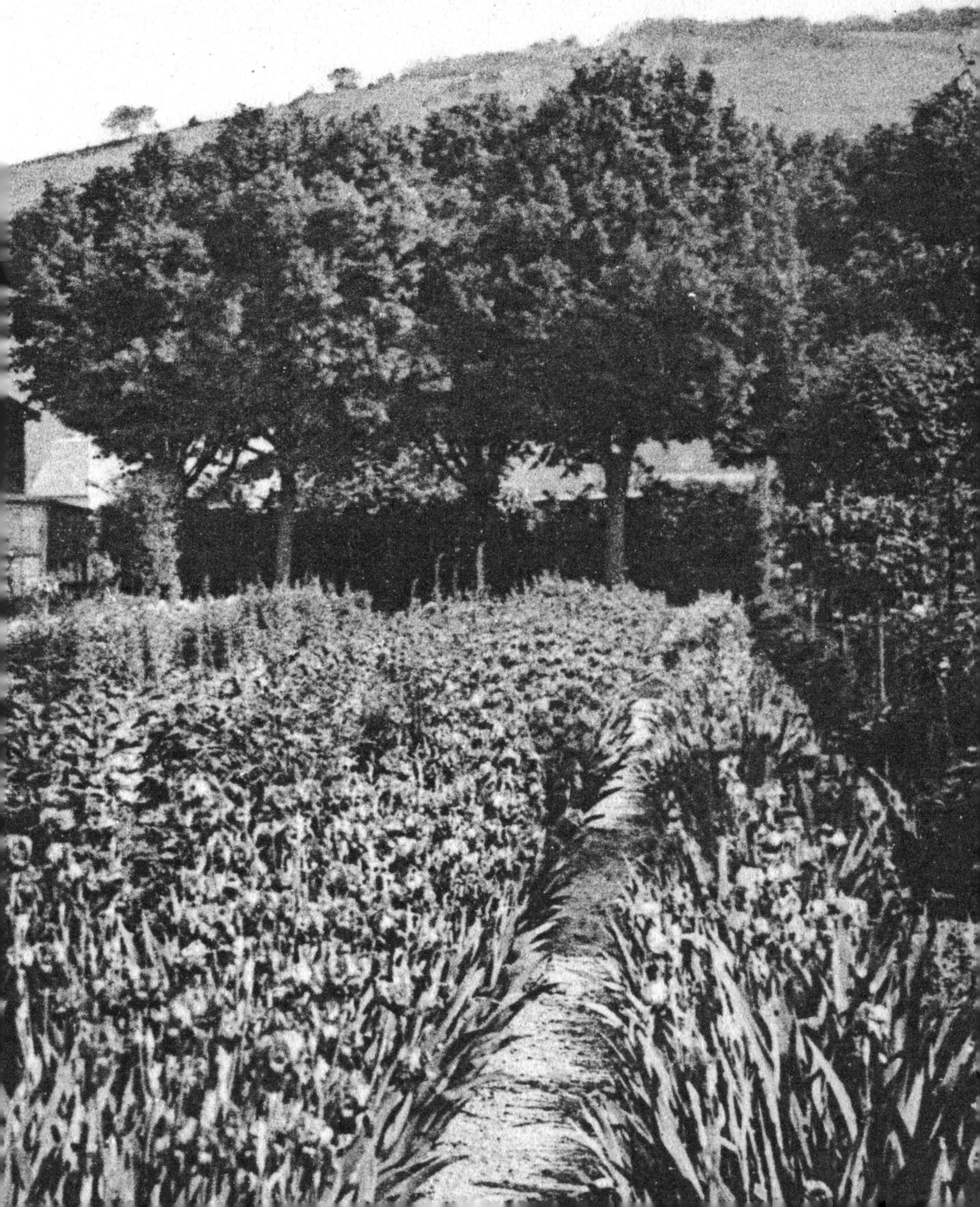

Contributors

George T M Shackelford is chair, art of Europe and Arthur K Solomon curator of modern art at the Museum of Fine Arts, Boston. He is a graduate of Dartmouth College and received his PhD from Yale University. He is the author of many publications on late 19th- and early 20th-century art. He has organised a series of exhibitions on Impressionist and Post-Impressionist painting, including *Degas: the dancers* (1984), *Monet in the 20th century* (1998), *Impressionist still life* (2002) and *Gauguin Tahiti* (2004).

Claire Durand-Ruel Snollaerts is a Paris-based art historian. A direct descendant of the art dealer Paul Durand-Ruel, she studied art history at the Sorbonne. Her major project for the past 13 years has been the monumental *Pissarro: critical catalogue of paintings* (2003, three volumes, Wildenstein). Her current research concerns Pissarro's work in pastels and gouache. She is also part of the Renoir committee at the Wildenstein Institute, Paris.

Jonathan Mane-Wheoki is director of art and collection services at the Museum of New Zealand Te Papa Tongarewa. He was educated at the University of Canterbury and the Courtauld Institute of Art, London. He has lectured and written on a variety of subjects, including early modern English and French art, Victorian architecture and Maori art. He is currently a governor of the Arts Foundation of New Zealand, deputy chair of the Council for the Humanities, and a member of the Council of the Royal Society of New Zealand. In 2008 the University of Canterbury awarded him an honorary doctorate of letters.

Terence Maloon is senior curator of special exhibitions at the Art Gallery of New South Wales. His recent exhibitions include *Camille Pissarro* (2004), *Picasso: the last decades* (2002), *Drawing the figure: Michelangelo to Matisse* (co-curated with Peter Raissis, 1999) and *Classic Cézanne* (1998). He has also curated monographic exhibitions of contemporary artists such as Tony Tuckson, Alan Mitelman and Virginia Coventry, and published and lectured widely on 19th- and 20th-century art.

Acknowledgements

A publication and exhibition of this size and scope is not possible without the assistance of many individuals and institutions. In addition to those acknowledged elsewhere in this catalogue, sincere thanks to the following for their contributions to the project:

Claudia Brueheim & Susan Freeman (Freeman Ryan Design); Wayne Chandler (NSW Treasury Managed Fund); Mike Griffin & Andrew Kemp (Global Specialised Services); Marguérite de Lastours; Maryanne Leigh (Acoustiguide); Graham Maslen (Spitting Image); Paul Murphy (Australian Book Connection); Jo Rudd; Judith White; New Zealand Government & Ministry of Culture and Heritage; and the Wildenstein Institute in Paris (in particular, Marie-Christine Maufus and Marie-Christine Decroocq)

Art Gallery of New South Wales

Craig Brush; Analiese Cairis; Jenni Carter; Victoria Collings; Charlotte Davy; Leith Brooke; Erica Drew; Anne Flanagan; Belinda Hanrahan; Robert Herbert; Cara Hickman; Brian Ladd; Jethro Lyne; Elizabeth McCarthy; Michelle Munro; Barbara Penson; Tristan Sharp; Jill Sykes; Kirsten Tilgals; Josephine Touma; Sheona White

Museum of Fine Arts, Boston

Sabrina Abron; Brett Angell; Danielle Berger; Elliot Bostwick Davis; Helen Connor; Joe Earle; Frank Egloff; Jacki Elgar; Katherine Getchell; Deanna M Griffin; Andrew Haines; Quintana Heathman; Erica Hirshler; Ales Hlousek; Abigail Hykin; Allison Jackson; Patricia Loiko; Adeline Lutts; Rhona MacBeth; Annette Manick; David Matthews; Patrick McMahon; John Robbe; Abraham Schroeder; Sarah Thompson; Sarah McGaughey Tremblay; Lydia Vagts; Siobhan Wheeler; John Woolf; Jean Woodward; Joan Wright; Kim Pashko

Museum of New Zealand Te Papa Tongarewa

Ginevera Millicent Ambrosia; Emily Bayley; Steve Brady; Anna Brookes; Katherine Campbell; Gisella Carr; Victoria Esson; Jeff Fox; Leimomi Gorsich; Liz Grant; Rachel Jefferies; Jane Keig; Rosemary Laurenson; Florence Liger; Glenn Lust; Clayton McGregor; Barry Mildenhall; Diana Minchall; Stephen Owen; Janet Purdey; Victoria Robson; Frances Samuel; Sir Ronald Scott; Celia Thompson; Hutch Wilco

Principal sponsor

Exhibition program sponsor

Support sponsor

Official airline

Published by
Art Gallery of NSW
Art Gallery Road, The Domain, Sydney 2000, Australia
www.artgallery.nsw.gov.au

in association with the exhibition
Monet and the Impressionists

Art Gallery of New South Wales
11 October 2008 – 26 January 2009

Museum of New Zealand Te Papa Tongarewa
14 February – 17 May 2009

Distribution:
Art Gallery of NSW
Art Gallery Road, The Domain, Sydney 2000 Australia
Yale University Press
32 Temple Street, New Haven, CT 06520, USA
Thames & Hudson
181A High Holborn, London WC1V 7QX, England

Cataloguing-in-publication data:
Monet, Claude, 1840–1926.
Monet and the Impressionists/George T.M. Shackelford with contributions by Jonathan Mane-Wheoki, Clare Durand-Ruel Snollaerts and Terence Maloon.

Includes bibliographic references and index.
ISBN
Softcover: 9781741740295
Hardcover: 9781741740301

1. Monet, Claude, 1840–1926--Exhibitions. 2. Impressionism (Art)--France--Exhibitions.
I. Shackelford, George T.M., 1955– II. Art Gallery of New South Wales. II. Museum of New Zealand Te Papa Tongarewa.

Curator: George T M Shackelford
Catalogue editor: Terence Maloon
Editorial assistance and coordination: Josephine Touma
Additional coordination: Charlotte Davy
Text editing: Judith White
Design: Analiese Cairis
Production: Cara Hickman
Prepress: Spitting Image, Sydney
Printing: Australian Book Connection

Details:
cover: Claude Monet *Waterlilies* 1905, cat 53
pp 2–3: *Monet in his studio at Giverny, with the grandes décorations*, Durand-Ruel Archives, Paris
pp 4–5: Claude Monet *Poplars at Giverny* 1887, cat 34
pp 10–11: Claude Monet *Snow at Argenteuil* c1874, cat 15
pp 12–13: Claude Monet *Meadow with haystacks near Giverny* 1885, cat 32
pp 164–65: Claude Monet *Fisherman's cottage on the cliffs at Varengeville* 1882, cat 24
pp 174–75: Claude Monet *Morning on the Seine, near Giverny* 1897, cat 50
pp 224–25: *Monet's home at Giverny*. Private collection
p 228: *Monet in his house at Giverny*. Private collection
Photograph: Roger-Viollet, Paris/The Bridgeman Art Library

The Art Gallery of NSW is a statutory body of the NSW state government

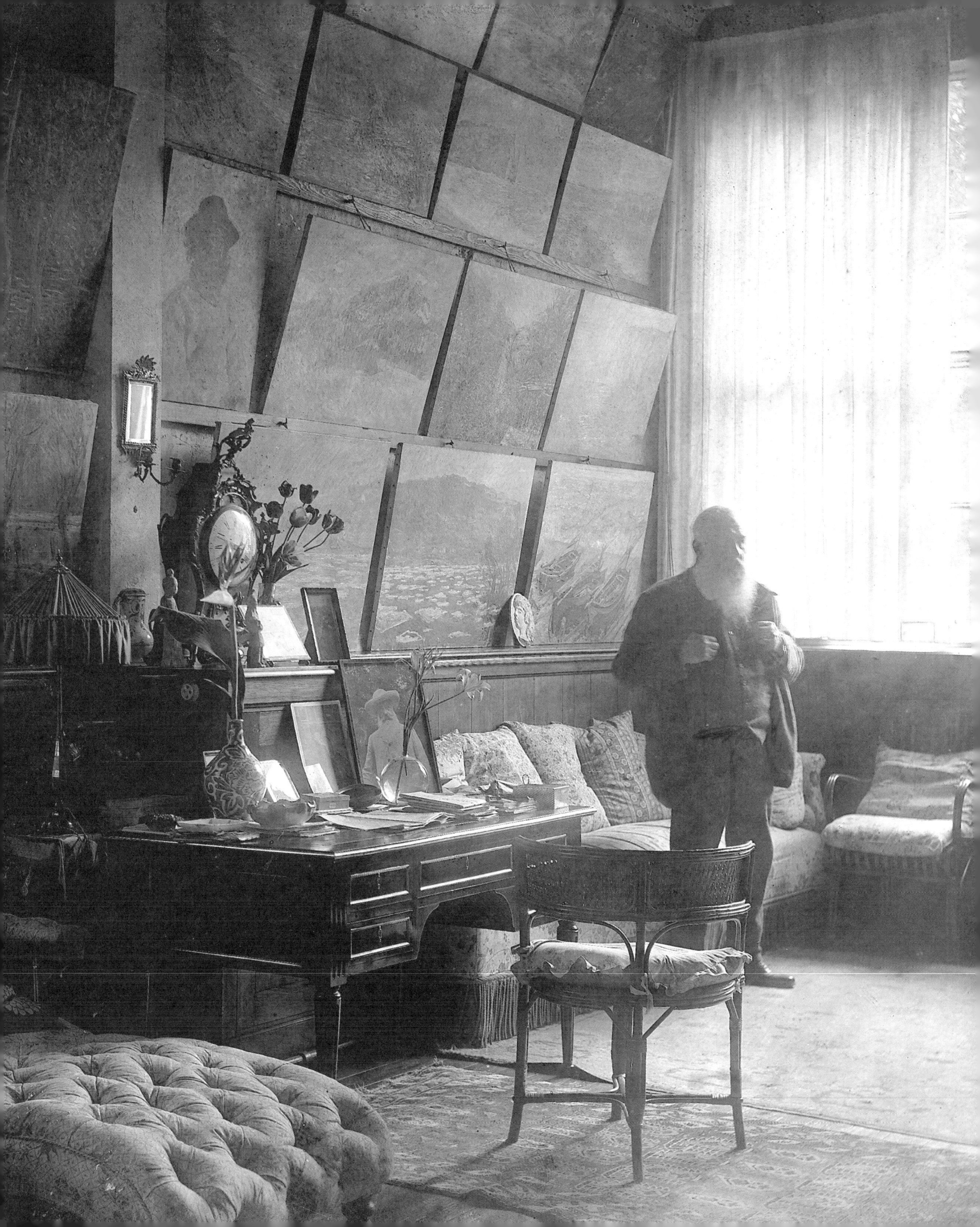